Benchmark Papers
in Geology

Series Editor: Rhodes W. Fairbridge
Columbia University

Benchmark Papers in Geology

RIVER MORPHOLOGY

Edited by
STANLEY A. SCHUMM
Colorado State University

GB
1203
S38

Dowden, Hutchinson & Ross, Inc.
Stroudsburg, Pennsylvania

Copyright © 1972 by **Dowden, Hutchinson & Ross, Inc.**
Library of Congress Catalog Card Number: 72-78310
ISBN: 0–87933–001–5 (Hardbound)
ISBN: 0–87933–139–9 (Paperbound)

74 75 76 5 4 3

Manufactured in the United States of America.

Exclusive distributor outside the United States and Canada:
JOHN WILEY & SONS, INC.

Acknowledgements and Permissions

ACKNOWLEDGEMENTS
Government Printing Office—U.S. GEOGRAPHICAL AND GEOLOGICAL SURVEY OF THE ROCKY MOUNTAIN REGION
"Land Sculpture, Chapter 5 in: Geology of the Henry Mountains"

Government Printing Office—U.S. GEOLOGICAL SURVEY PROFESSIONAL PAPERS
"The Hydraulic Geometry of Stream Channels and Some Physiographic Implications"
"Studies of Longitudinal Stream Profiles in Virginia and Maryland"
"River Channel Patterns: Braided, Meandering and Straight"

Government Printing Office—U.S. DEPARTMENT OF AGRICULTURE TECHNICAL BULLETIN
"Some Principles of Accelerated Stream and Valley Sedimentation"

Mississippi River Commission, Vicksburg—U.S. WATERWAYS EXPERIMENT STATION
"A Laboratory Study of the Meandering of Alluvial Rivers"

PERMISSIONS
The following papers have been reprinted with the permission of the authors, publishers, and the present copyright owners.

Yale University—THE AMERICAN JOURNAL OF SCIENCE
"Steps of Progress in the Interpretation of Landforms"
"On Denudation in the Pacific"
"Equilibrium Theory of Erosional Slopes Approached by Frequency Distribution Analysis"

American Society of Civil Engineers—TRANSACTIONS
"Stable Channels in Erodible Material"
"River-bed Scour During Floods"
"Mississippi River Valley Geology in Relation to River Regime"

American Society of Civil Engineers—PROCEEDINGS
"The Importance of Fluvial Morphology in Hydraulic Engineering"

Geological Society of America—BULLETIN
"Concept of the Graded River"

American Geophysical Union—TRANSACTIONS
"Rational Equation of River-bed Profile"
"On the Longitudinal Profile of the Graded River"

Society of Economic Paleontologists and Mineralogists—SPECIAL PUBLICATION
"Sedimentary Structures Generated by Flow in Alluvial Channels"

H. W. Shen—RIVER MECHANICS: VOLUME I
"Fluvial Geomorphology"

The University of Chicago Press—THE JOURNAL OF GEOLOGY
"Streams and Their Significance" by Douglas Johnson

Series Editor's Preface

The philosophy behind the "Benchmark Series" is one of collection, sifting and rediffusion. Scientific literature today is so vast, so dispersed and, in the case of old papers, so inaccessible for readers not in the immediate neighborhood of major libraries, that much valuable information has become ignored, by default. It has become just so difficult, or time consuming, to search out the key papers in any basic area of research that one can hardly blame a busy man for skimping on some of his "homework."

The "Benchmark Series" has been devised, therefore, to make a practical contribution to this critical problem. The geologist, perhaps even more than any other type of scientist, often suffers from twin difficulties—isolation from central library resources and an immensely diffused source of material. New colleges and industrial libraries simply cannot afford to purchase complete runs of all the world's earth science literature. Specialists simply cannot locate reprints or copies of all their principal reference materials. So it is that we are now making a concentrated effort to gather into single volumes the critical material needed to reconstruct the background to any and every major topic of our discipline.

We are interpreting "Geology" in its broadest sense: the fundamental science of the Planet Earth, its materials, its history and its dynamics. Because of training and experience in "earthy" materials, we also take in astrogeology, the corresponding aspect of the planetary sciences. Besides the classical core disciplines such as mineralogy, petrology, structure, geomorphology, paleontology, or stratigraphy, we embrace the newer fields of geophysics and geochemistry, applied also to oceanography, geochronology, and paleoecology. We recognize the work of the mining geologists, the petroleum geologists, the hydrologists, the engineering and environmental geologists. Each specialist needs his working library. We are endeavoring to make his task a little easier.

Each volume in the series contains an Introduction prepared by a specialist, the volume editor—and a "state-of-the-art" opening or a summary of the objects and content of the volume. The articles selected, usually some 30–50 reproduced either in their entirety or in significant extracts, attempt to scan the field from the key papers of the last century until fairly recent years. Where the original references may be in foreign languages, we have endeavored to locate or commission translations. Geologists, because of their global subject, are often acutely aware of the oneness of our world. Its literature, therefore, cannot be restricted to any one country and, whenever possible, an attempt has been made to scan the world literature.

To each article, or group of kindred items, some sort of "Highlight Commentary" is usually supplied by the volume editor. This should serve to bring that article into historical perspective and to emphasize its particular role in the growth of the field. References or citations, wherever possible, will be reproduced in their entirety; for by this means the observant reader can assess the background material available to that particular author, or, if he wishes, he too can double check the earlier sources.

A "benchmark," in surveyor's terminology, is an established point on the ground, recorded on our maps. It is usually anything that is a vantage point, from a modest hill to a mountain peak. From the historical viewpoint, these benchmarks are the bricks of our scientific edifice.

Rhodes W. Fairbridge

Contents

VI. CHANNEL PATTERNS

VII. BED FORM, SCOUR AND DEPOSITION

VIII. GEOLOGIC PERSPECTIVE

Author List

Introduction

The literature on rivers, their behavior, morphology and significance, is large, and in order to select a few papers of significance, some criteria were needed. The first, of course, was the requirement that the papers deal with the morphology of river channels. However, if one considers that the size, shape, and pattern of a river is the result of a multitude of upstream influences as well as the recent geologic history of the river basin, then it becomes obvious that to consider a river without regard to these variables is to adopt a superficial view of an exceedingly complex problem. Nevertheless, if we do not concern ourselves with the origin of the sediment and water that moves through a channel, the problem can be isolated, and a short reach of a river can be the subject of detailed investigation. This approach is frequently used with success in both geomorphic and engineering investigations, but it is always well to remember that the channel is a component of a bigger and more complex system, the drainage basin.

The papers selected for inclusion in this volume were chosen to provide not only an overview of the topic, but to make accessible some papers that are generally difficult to obtain (e.g., Gilbert, Friedkin). Two additional criteria were used in the selection. First, although old, a paper should be of more than historical interest. It is intended that the selections be appropriate for assignment as collateral reading in a course in geomorphology or potamology. For the most part, the papers are current in that they are frequently cited in the geologic and engineering literature. The reader who wishes to be informed concerning the historical development of the subject and of geomorphology in general should consult recent works on the history of geomorphology (Chorley, Dunn, and Beckinsale, 1964).

The third criterion for selection of papers was that both geologic and engineering literature should be included, and one-third of the papers selected are from the engineering literature. The past lack of communication between engineers and geologists on the important subject of rivers is to be regretted and to be corrected. Nevertheless, it is true that the description and classification of rivers by geomorpholog-

1

ists has not provided the engineer with useful information that can be applied to river control problems. On the other hand, the concern of the engineer with the relatively rapid response of a river to the influence of structures has caused him to lose sight of the fact that the river has a history and that the present morphology of a river may strongly reflect the recent geologic history of its drainage basin. The quantitative data of the engineer unquestionably can be brought to bear on studies of paleochannels and sedimentary deposits. In turn, the qualitative geomorphic understanding of long-term river response to past changes of climate, sea level and tectonics is required for the prediction of river response to modern man-induced alterations of hydrologic regimen. Increased cooperation is essential if the scientific investigation of river morphology and river mechanics is to progress in a rational and productive manner.

The papers selected are grouped into eight sections. These include the history of the subject and the possible directions in which it could have developed (Beginnings and Directions). These sections are followed by two that show the engineering and geomorphic approaches to stable channels and channel response (Regime Theory and Hydraulic Geometry; The Graded River and its Adjustment). Two sections on specific morphologic properties of streams follow (Longitudinal Profile and Gradient; Channel Patterns). The remaining two sections consider some aspects of open-channel hydraulics (Bedform, Scour and Deposition) and the value of the historical geologic approach to river studies (Geologic Perspective).

Many excellent papers have not been included and the editor's bias in selecting the papers is probably apparent. One may attribute the lack of foreign language papers to this bias, but, in fact, fluvial morphology is a subject which has developed primarily in English speaking countries. The significant British, Indian, and Pakistani contributions are summarized in Lane's paper on stable channels. References to other significant papers are made in the introductory paragraphs to each section, and additional references can be found in the works of Leopold, Wolman, and Miller (1964), Morisawa (1968), Chow (1959), Leliavsky (1955), Scheidegger (1970), Shen (1971), Schaffernak (1950), Sundborg (1956), and Inglis (1949).

Beginnings

I

If one were forced to select the writings having the most impact on man's interpretation, not only of rivers but of the entire landscape, he would be forced to choose several verses from chapters 6 and 7 of Genesis. It is impossible to overestimate the influence of the Biblical description of the Noachian Deluge on geomorphic thought. A hydrologic event of this magnitude, during the assumed relatively short history of the earth, left one with little option but to explain many erosional and depositional features as the results of this great flood.

This is clearly demonstrated by Gregory in his paper on the history of geomorphology, and excerpts from this paper were selected to provide a brief introduction to the subject of river morphology. The effectiveness of river erosion was a topic generating considerable controversy during the 19th century. Gregory was close enough to this controversy that his statements reflect his highly critical opinion of dogma. The paper appeared in a special centenary issue of the *American Journal of Science*, as one of twelve papers reviewing the progress of American science during the first 100 years of the Journal. The author, H. E. Gregory, was a general geologist in the best sense of the word and his reports for the U. S. Geological Survey on the geology and geomorphology of the Southwest not only are valuable scientific contributions, but, in addition, they are interesting reading (Gregory 1938, 1950, 1951).

The foundation of a science is its published literature. The men who publish determine the direction and character of a science. The personality and style of the writer are important, for correct ideas frequently have remained unaccepted because an error was espoused with vigor and conviction. Thus some truly landmark papers were published decades or even generations too soon and remain unappreciated to this day. On page 109 of Gregory's paper there is reference to the work of James Dana, and the second selection is a paper by Dana in which he clearly

3

describes the erosional formation of valleys by running water. This paper has more than historical interest, for it also illustrates how a significant contribution can be ignored because it was published 50 years too soon (1850). Finally it is a fine example of field work which demonstrates the necessity of an investigator seeing many and diverse examples of his subject in the field. Dana was geologist on the Wilkes Exploring Expedition during the years 1838–1842, and is better known as a mineralogist, but his description of Pacific Islands in various stages of erosion should be a classic of geomorphic literature. He further applied these observations to the valleys of the Blue Mountain of New South Wales, Australia, and he was highly critical of Darwin's earlier conclusion that these valleys had a marine origin (Gregory, p. 109: Dana, 1850). Inherent in Dana's description of the Pacific Islands is the concept of the erosional evolution of landscapes, which was developed by W. M. Davis about 50 years later.

Dana was the outstanding fluvialist of the mid 19th century and he was one of the world's outstanding geologists (Chorley *et al.*, 1964, p. 367; Merrill, 1906, p. 694; Gilman, 1899).

American Journal of Science, 1918, V. 46, p. 104-117; 127-131.
Copyright 1918 by Yale University

1

Steps of Progress
in the Interpretation of Land Forms

H. E. GREGORY

Art. III.—*A Century of Geology.—Steps of Progress in the Interpretation of Land Forms;* by Herbert E. Gregory.

The essence of physiography is the belief that land forms represent merely a stage in the orderly development of the earth's surface features; that the various dynamic agents perform their characteristic work throughout all geologic time. The formulation of principle and processes of earth sculpture was, therefore, impossible on the hypothesis of a ready-made earth whose features were substantially unchangeable, except when modified by catastrophic processes. In 1821, J. W. Wilson wrote in this Journal: "Is it not the best theory of the earth, that the Creator, in the beginning, at least at the general deluge, formed it with all its present grand characteristic features?"[1] If so, a search for causes is futile, and the study of the work performed by streams and glaciers and wind is unprofitable. The belief in the Deluge as the one great geological event in the history of the earth has brought it about that the speculations of Aristotle, Herodotus, Strabo, and Ovid, and the illustrious Arab, Avicenna (980-1037), unchecked by appeal to facts but also unopposed by priesthood or popular prejudice, are nearer to the truth than the intolerant controversial writings of the intellectual leaders whose touchstone was orthodoxy. A few thinkers of the 16th century revolted against the interminable repetition of error, and Peter Severinus (1571) advised his students: "Burn up your books . . . buy yourselves stout shoes, get away to the mountains, search the valleys, the deserts, the shores of the seas. . . . In this way and no other will you arrive at a knowledge of things." But the thorough-going "diluvialist" who believed that a million species of animals could occupy a 450-foot Ark, but not that pebbles weathered from rock or that rivers erode, had no use for his powers of observation.

Sporadic germs of a science of land forms scattered through the literature of the 17th and 18th centuries found an unfavorable environment and produced inconspicuous growths. Even their sponsors did little to

[1] Numbers refer to titles listed in the Bibliography at the end of this article.

cultivate them. Steno (1631-1687) mildly suggested that surface sculpturing, particularly on a small scale, is largely the work of running water, and Guettard (1715-1786), a truly great mind, grasped the fundamental principles of denudation and successfully entombed his views as well as his reputation in scores of books and volumes of cumbrous diffuse writing.

At the beginning of the 19th century a sufficient body of principles had been established to justify the recognition of an earth science, geology, and the 195 volumes of the Journal thus far published carry a large part of the material which has won approval for the new science and given prominence to American thought. From the pages in the Journal, the progress of geology may be illustrated by tracing the fluctuation in the development of fact and theory as relates to valleys and glacial features, the subjects to which this chapter is devoted.

THE INTERPRETATION OF VALLEYS.
The Pioneers.

Desmarest (1725-1815) might be styled the father of physiography. By concrete examples and sound induction he established (1774) the doctrine that the valleys of central France are formed by the streams which occupy them. He also made the first attempt to trace the history of a landscape through its successive stages on the basis of known causes. His methods and reasoning are practically identical with those of Dutton working in the ancient lavas of New Mexico; and Whitney's description of the Table Mountains of California might well have appeared in Desmarest's memoirs.[2] The teachings of Desmarest were strengthened and expanded by DeSaussure (1740-1799), the sponsor for the term, "Geology," (1779) who saw in the intimate relation of Alpine streams and valleys the evidence of erosion by running water (1786).

The work of these acknowledged leaders of geological thought attracted singularly little attention on the Continent, and Lamarck's volume on denudation (Hydrogéologie), which appeared in 1802, although an important contribution, sank out of sight. But the seed of the French school found fertile ground in Edinburgh, the center of the geological world during the first quarter of

7

the 19th century. Hutton's "Theory of the Earth, with Proofs and Illustrations," in which the guidance of DeSaussure and Desmarest is gratefully acknowledged, appeared in 1795. The original publication aroused only local interest, but when placed in attractive form by Playfair's "Illustrations of the Huttonian Theory" (1802), the problem of the origin and development of land forms assumed a commanding position in geological thought. Hutton was peculiarly fortunate in his environment. He had the support and assistance of a group of able scientific colleagues as well as the bitter opposition of Jameson and of the defenders of orthodoxy. His views were discussed in scientific publications and found their way to literary and theological journals. Hutton's conception of the processes of land sculpture—slow upheaving and slow degradation of mountains, differential weathering, and the carving of valleys by streams—has a very modern aspect. Playfair's book would scarcely be out of place in a 20th century class room. The following paragraphs are quoted from it:[3]

" . . . A river, of which the course is both serpentine and deeply excavated in the rock, is among the phenomena, by which the slow waste of the land, and also the cause of that waste, are most directly pointed out.

The structure of the vallies among mountains, shews clearly to what cause their existence is to be ascribed. Here we have first a large valley, communicating directly with the plain, and winding between high ridges of mountains, while the river in the bottom of it descends over a surface, remarkable, in such a scene, for its uniform declivity. Into this, open a multitude of transverse or secondary vallies, intersecting the ridges on either side of the former, each bringing a contribution to the main stream, proportioned to its magnitude; and, except where a cataract now and then intervenes, all having that nice adjustment in their levels, which is the more wonderful, the greater the irregularity of the surface. These secondary vallies have others of a smaller size opening into them; and, among mountains of the first order, where all is laid out on the greatest scale, these ramifications are continued to a fourth, and even a fifth, each diminishing in size as it increases in elevation, and as its supply of water is less. Through them all, this law is in general observed, that where a higher valley joins a lower one, of the two angles which it makes with the latter, that which is obtuse is always on the descending side; . . . what else but the water itself, working its way through obstacles of unequal

8

resistance, could have opened or kept up a communication between the inequalities of an irregular and alpine surface . . .

. . . The probability of such a constitution [arrangement of valleys] having arisen from another cause, is, to the probability of its having arisen from the running of water, in such a proportion as unity bears to a number infinitely great.

. . . With Dr. Hutton, we shall be disposed to consider those great chains of mountains, which traverse the surface of the globe, as cut out of masses vastly greater, and more lofty than any thing that now remains.

From this gradual change of lakes into rivers, it follows, that a lake is but a temporary and accidental condition of a river, which is every day approaching to its termination; and the truth of this is attested, not only by the lakes that have existed, but also by those that continue to exist.''

Steps Backward.

Even Hutton's clear reasoning, firmly buttressed by concrete examples, was insufficient to overcome the belief in ready-made or violently formed valleys and original corrugations and irregularities of mountain surface The pages of the Journal show that the principles laid down by Playfair were too far in advance of the times to secure general acceptance. In the first volume of the Journal, the gorge of the French Broad River is assigned by Kain to ''some dreadful commotion in nature which probably shook these mountains to their bases,''[4] and the gorge of the lower Connecticut is considered by Hitchcock (1824)[5] as a breach which drained a series of lakes ''not many centuries before the settlement of this country.'' The prevailing American and English view for the first quarter of the 19th century is expressed in the reviews in this Journal, where the well-known conclusions of Conybeare and Phillips that streams are incompetent to excavate valleys are quoted with approval and admiration is expressed for Buckland's famous ''Reliquiæ Diluvianæ,'' a 300-page quarto volume devoted to proof of a deluge. The professor at Yale, Silliman, and the professor at Oxford, Buckland, saw that an acceptance of Hutton's views involved a repudiation of the Biblical flood, and much space is devoted to combating these ''erroneous'' and ''unscientific'' views. For example, Buckland says:[6]

''. . . The general belief is, that existing streams, avalanches and lakes, bursting their barriers, are sufficient to account for all their phenomena, and not a few geologists, especially those of the Huttonian school, at whose head is Professor Playfair, have till recently been of this opinion. . . . But it is now very clear to almost every man, who impartially examines the facts in regard to existing vallies, that the causes now in action, mentioned above, are altogether inadequate to their production; nay, that such a supposition would involve a physical impossibility. We do not believe that one-thousandth part of our present vallies were excavated by the power of existing streams. . . . In very many cases of large rivers, it is found, that so far from having formed their own beds, they are actually in a gradual manner filling them up.

Again; how happens it that the source of a river is frequently below the head of a valley, if the river excavated that valley?

The most powerful argument, however, in our opinion, against the supposition we are combating, is the phenomena of transverse and longitudinal valleys; both of which could not possibly have been formed by existing streams.''

Phillips writes in 1829:[7] ''The excavation of valleys can be ascribed to no other cause than a great flood of water which overtopped the hills, whose summits those vallies descend.''

Faith in Noah's flood as the dominant agent of erosion rapidly lost ground through the teaching of Lyell after 1830, but the theory of systematic development of landscapes by rivers gained little. In fact, Scrope in 1830,[8] in showing that the entrenched meanders of the Moselle prove gradual progressive stream work was in advance of his English contemporary. Judged by contributions to the Journal, Lyell's teaching served to standardize American opinion of earth sculpture somewhat as follows: The ocean is the great valley maker, but rivers also make them; the position of valleys is determined by original or renewed surface inequalities or by faulting; exceptional occurrences—earthquakes, bursting of lakes, upheavals and depressions—have played an important part. Hayes (1839)[9] thought that the surface of New York was essentially an upraised sea-bottom modified by erosion of waves and ocean currents. Sedgwick (1838)[10] considered high-lying lake basins proof of valleys which were shaped under the sea. Many of the valleys in the Chilian Cordillera were thought by Darwin (1844) to have been the work of waves and tides, and water gaps are ascribed to currents ''bursting through the range at those points where the strata have been least inclined and the height consequently is less." Speaking of the magnificent stream-cut canyons of the Blue Mountains of New South Wales, gorges which lead to narrow exits through monoclines, Darwin says: "To attribute these hollows to alluvial action would be preposterous."[11]

The influence of structure in the formation of valleys is emphasized by many contributors to the Journal. Hildreth in 1836, in a valuable paper,[12] which is perhaps the first detailed topographic description of drainage in folded strata, expresses the opinion that the West Virginia ridges and valleys antedated the streams and that water gaps though cut by rivers involve pre-existing lakes. Geddes (1826)[13] denied that Niagara River cut its channel and speaks of valleys which "were valleys e'er moving spirit bade the waters flow." Conrad (1839)[14] discussed the structural control of the Mohawk, the Ohio, and the Mississippi, and Lieutenant Warren (1859)[15] concluded that the Niobrara must have originated in a fissure. According to Lesley (1862)[16] the course of the New River across the Great Valley and into the Appalachians "striking the escarpment in the face" is determined by the junction of anticlinal structures on the north with faulted monoclines toward the south; a conclusion in harmony with the views of Edward Hitchcock (1841)[17] that major valleys and mountain passes are structural in origin and that even subordinate folds and faults may determine minor features. "Is not this a beautiful example of prospective benevolence on the part of the Deity, thus, by means of a violent fracture of primary mountains, to provide for easy intercommunication through alpine regions, countless ages afterwards!" The extent of the wandering from the guidance of DeSaussure and Playfair after the lapse of 50 years is shown by students of Switzerland. Alpine valleys to Murchison (1851) were bays of an ancient sea; Schlaginweit (1852) found regional and local complicated crustal movements a satisfactory cause, and Forbes (1863) saw only glaciers.

Valleys Formed by Rivers.

One strong voice before 1860 appears to have called Americans back to truths expounded by Desmarest and Hutton. Dana in 1850[18] amply demonstrated that valleys on the Pacific Islands owe neither their origin,

position or form to the sea or to structural factors.
They are the work of existing streams which have eaten
their way headwards. Even the valleys of Australia
cited by Darwin as type examples of ocean work are
shown to be products of normal stream work. Dana
went further and gave a permanent place to the Huttonian idea that many bays, inlets, and fiords are but the
drowned mouths of stream-made valleys. In the same
volume in which these conclusions appeared, Hubbard
(1850)[19] announced that in New Hampshire the "deepest
valleys are but valleys of erosion." The theory that
valleys are excavated by streams which occupy them
was all but universally accepted after F. V. Hayden's
description[20] of Rocky Mountain gorges (1862) and Newberry's interpretation of the canyons of Arizona (1862);
but the scientific world was poorly prepared for Newberry's statement:[21]

"Like the great canons of the Colorado, the broad valleys
bounded by high and perpendicular walls *belong to a vast system
of erosion, and are wholly due to the action of water.* . . . The
first and most plausible explanation of the striking surface features of this region will be to refer them to that embodiment of
resistless power—the sword that cuts so many geological knots—
volcanic force. The Great Cañon of the Colorado would be
considered a vast fissure or rent in the earth's crust, and the
abrupt termination of the steps of the table-lands as marking
lines of displacement. This theory though so plausible, and so
entirely adequate to explain all the striking phenomena, lacks
a single requisite to acceptance, and that is *truth.*"

With such stupendous examples in mind, the dictum
of Hutton seemed reasonable: "there is no spot on which
rivers may not formerly have run."

Denudation by Rivers.

The general recognition of the competency of streams
to form valleys was a necessary prelude to the broader
view expressed by Jukes (1862)[22]

"The surfaces of our present lands are as much carved and
sculptured surfaces as the medallion carved from the slab, or the
statue sculptured from the block. They have been gradually
reached by the removal of the rock that once covered them, and
are themselves but of transient duration, always slowly wasting
from decay."

Contributions to the Journal between 1850 and 1870 reveal a tendency to accept greater degrees of erosion by rivers, but the necessary end-product of subaërial erosion—a plain—is first clearly defined by Powell in 1875.[23] In formulating his ideas Powell introduced the term "base-level," which may be called the germ word out of which has grown the "cycle of erosion," the master key of modern physiographers. The original definition of base-level follows:

"We may consider the level of the sea to be a grand base-level, below which the dry lands cannot be eroded; but we may also have, for local and temporary purposes, other base-levels of erosion, which are the levels of the beds of the principal streams which carry away the products of erosion. (I take some liberty in using the term 'level' in this connection, as the action of a running stream in wearing its channel ceases, for all practical purposes, before its bed has quite reached the level of the lower end of the stream. What I have called the base-level would, in fact, be an imaginary surface, inclining slightly in all its parts toward the lower end of the principal stream draining the area through which the level is supposed to extend, or having the inclination of its parts varied in direction as determined by tributary streams.)"

Analysis of Powell's view has given definiteness to the distinction between "base-level," an imaginary plane, and "a nearly featureless plain," the actual land surface produced in the last stage of subaërial erosion.

Following their discovery in the Colorado Plateau Province, denudation surfaces were recognized on the Atlantic slope and discussed by McGee (1888),[24] in a paper notable for the demonstration of the use of physiographic methods and criteria in the solution of stratigraphic problems. Davis (1889)[25] described the upland of southern New England developed during Cretaceous time, introducing the term "peneplain," "a nearly featureless plain." The short-lived opposition to the theory of peneplanation indicates that in America at least the idea needed only formulation to insure acceptance.

It is interesting to note that surfaces now classed as peneplains were fully described by Percival (1842),[26] who assigned them to structure, and by Kerr (1880),[27] who considered glaciers the agent. In Europe "plains of denudation" have been clearly recognized by Ramsay (1846), Jukes (1862), A. Geikie (1865), Foster and Topley (1865), Maw (1866), Wynne (1867), Whitaker (1867), Macintosh (1869), Green (1882), Richthofen (1882), but all of them were looked upon as products of marine work, and writers of more recent date in England seem reluctant to give a subordinate place to the erosive power of waves. Americans, on the other hand, have been thinking in terms of rivers, and the great contribution of the American school is not that peneplains exist, but that they are the result of normal subaërial erosion. More precise field methods during the past decade have revealed the fact that no one agent is responsible for the land forms classed as peneplains; that not only rivers and ocean, but ice, wind, structure, and topographic position must be taken into account.

The recognition of rivers as valley-makers and of the final result of stream work necessarily preceded an analysis of the process of subaërial erosion. The first and last terms were known, the intermediate terms and the sequence remained to be established. A significant contribution to this problem was made by Jukes (1862).[22]

". . . I believe that the lateral valleys are those which were first formed by the drainage running directly from the crests of the chains, the longitudinal ones being subsequently elaborated along the strike of the softer or more erodable beds exposed on the flanks of those chains."

Powell's discussion of antecedent and consequent drainage (1875) and Gilbert's chapter on land sculpture in the Henry Mountain report (1880) are classics, and McGee's contribution[28] contains significant suggestions. but the master papers are by Davis,[29] who introduces an analysis of land forms based on structure and age by the statement:

"Being fully persuaded of the gradual and systematic evolution of topographical forms it is now desired . . . to seek the causes of the location of streams in their present courses; to go back if possible to the early date when central Pennsylvania was first raised from the sea, and trace the development of the several river systems then implanted upon it from their ancient beginning to the present time."

That such a task could have been undertaken a quarter of a century ago and to-day considered a part of everyday field work shows how completely the lost ground of a

half-century has been regained and how rapid the advance in the knowledge of land sculpture since the canyons of the Colorado Plateau were interpreted.

FEATURES RESULTING FROM GLACIATION.

The Problem Stated.

Early in the 19th century when speculation regarding the interior of the earth gave place in part to observations of the surface of the earth, geologists were confronted with perhaps the most difficult problem in the history of the science. As stated by the editor of the Journal in 1821:[30]

"The almost universal existence of rolled pebbles, and boulders of rock, not only on the margin of the oceans, seas, lakes, and rivers; but their existence, often in enormous quantities, in situations quite removed from large waters; inland,—in high banks, imbedded in strata, or scattered, occasionally, in profusion, on the face of almost every region, and sometimes on the tops and declivities of mountains, as well as in the vallies between them; their entire difference, in many cases, from the rocks in the country where they lie—rounded masses and pebbles of primitive rocks being deposited in secondary and alluvial regions, and vice versa; these and a multitude of similar facts have ever struck us as being among the most interesting of geological occurrences, and as being very inadequately accounted for by existing theories."

The phenomena demanding explanation — jumbled masses of "diluvium," polished and striated rock, bowlders distributed with apparent disregard of topography—were indeed startling. Even Lyell, the great exponent of uniformitarianism, appears to have lost faith in his theories when confronted with facts for which known causes seemed inadequate. The interest aroused is attested by 31 titles in the Journal during its first two decades, articles which include speculations unsupported by logic or fact, field observation unaccompanied by explanation, field observation with fantastic explanation, *ex-cathedra* pronouncements by prominent men, sound reasoning from insufficient data, and unclouded recognition of cause and effect by both obscure and prominent men. With little knowledge of glaciers, areal geology, or of structure and composition of drift, all known forces were called in: normal weathering, catastrophic floods, ocean currents, waves, icebergs, glaciers, wind, and even depositions from a primordial atmosphere (Chabier, 1823). Human agencies were not discarded. Speaking of a granite bowlder at North Salem, New York, described by Cornelius (1820)[31] as resting on limestone, Finch (1824)[32] says: "it is a magnificent cromlech and the most ancient and venerable monument which America possesses." In the absence of a known cause, catastrophic agencies seem reasonable.

The Deluge.

In the seventh volume of the Journal (1824)[33] we read:

"After the production of these regular strata of sand, clay, limestone, &c. came a terrible irruption of water from the north, or north-west, which in many places covered the preceding formations with diluvial gravel, and carried along with it those immense masses of granite, and the older rocks, which attest to the present day the destruction and ruin of a former world."

Another author remarks:

"We find a mantle as it were of sand and gravel indifferently covering all the solid strata, and evidently derived from some convulsion which has lacerated and partly broken up those strata. . . ."

The catastrophe favored by most geologists was floods of water violently released—"we believe," says the editor, "that all geologists agree in imputing . . . the diluvium to the agency of a deluge at one period or another."[34] Such conclusions rested in no small way upon Hayden's well-known treatise on surficial deposits (1821),[35] a volume which deserves a prominent place in American geological literature. Hayden clearly distinguished the topographic and structural features of the drift but found an adequate cause in general wide-spread currents which "flowed impetuously across the whole continent . . . from north east to south west." In reviewing Hayden's book Silliman remarks:

"The general cause of these currents Mr. Hayden concludes to be the deluge of Noah. While no one will object to the propriety of ascribing very many, probably most of our alluvial features, to that catastrophe, we conceive that neither Mr. Hayden, nor any other man, is bound to prove the immediate physical cause of that vindictive infliction.

16

We would beg leave to suggest the following as a cause which *may* have aided in deluging the earth, and which, were there occasion, *might* do it again.

The existence of enormous caverns in the bowels of the earth, (so often imagined by authors,) appears to be no very extravagant assumption. It is true it cannot be proved, but in a sphere of eight thousand miles in diameter, it would appear in no way extraordinary, that many cavities might exist, which collectively, or even singly, might well contain much more than all our oceans, seas, and other superficial waters, none of which are probably more than a few miles in depth. If these cavities communicate in any manner with the oceans, and are (as if they exist at all, they probably are,) filled with water, there exist, we conceive, agents very competent to expel the water of these cavities, and thus to deluge, at any time, the dry land.''

The teachings of Hayden were favorably received by Hitchcock, Struder, and Hubbard, and many Europeans. They found a champion in Jackson, who states (1839) :[36]

''From the observations made upon Mount Ktaadn, it is proved, that the current did rush over the summit of that lofty mountain, and consequently the diluvial waters rose to the height of more than 5,000 feet. Hence we are enabled to prove, that the ancient ocean, which rushed over the surface of the State, was at least a mile in depth, and its transporting power must have been greatly increased by its enormous pressure.''

Gibson, a student of western geology, reaches the same conclusion (1836) :[37]

''That a wide-spread current, although not, as imagined, fed from an inland sea, once swept over the entire region between the Alleghany and the Rocky Mountains is established by plenary proof.''

Professor Sedgwick (1831) thought the sudden upheaval of mountains sufficient to have caused floods again and again. The strength of the belief in the Biblical flood, during the first quarter of the 19th century, may be represented by the following remarks of Phillips (1832) :[38]

''Of many important facts which come under the consideration of geologists, the 'Deluge' is, perhaps, the most remarkable; and it is established by such clear and positive arguments, that if any one point of natural history may be considered as proved, the deluge must be admitted to have happened, because it has left full evidence in plain and characteristic effects *upon the surface of the earth.*''

17

However, the theory of deluges, whether of ocean or land streams, did not hold the field unopposed. In 1823, Granger,[39] an observer whose contributions to science total only six pages, speaks of the striæ on the shore of Lake Erie as

"having been formed by the powerful and continued attrition of some hard body. . . . To me, it does not seem possible that water under any circumstances, could have effected it. The flutings in width, depth, and direction, are as regular as if they had been cut out by a grooving plane. This, running water could not effect, nor could its operation have produced that glassy smoothness, which, in many parts, it still retains."

Hayes and also Conrad expressed similar views in the Journal 16 years later.

The idea that ice was in some way concerned with the transportation of drift has had a curious history. The first unequivocal statement, based on reading and keen observation, was made in the Journal by Dobson in 1826:[40]

"I have had occasion to dig up a great number of bowlders, of red sandstone, and of the conglomerate kind, in erecting a cotton manufactory; and it was not uncommon to find them worn smooth on the under side, as if done by their having been dragged over rocks and gravelly earth, in one steady position. On examination, they exhibit scratches and furrows on the abraded part; and if among the minerals composing the rock, there happened to be pebbles of feldspar, or quartz, (which was not uncommon,) they usually appeared not to be worn so much as the rest of the stone, preserving their more tender parts in a ridge, extending some inches. When several of these pebbles happen to be in one block, the preserved ridges were on the same side of the pebbles, so that it is easy to determine which part of the stone moved forward, in the act of wearing.

These bowlders are found, not only on the surface, but I have discovered them a number of feet deep, in the earth, in the hard compound of clay, sand, and gravel. . . .

I think we cannot account for these appearances, unless we call in the aid of ice along with water, and that they have been worn by being suspended and carried in ice, over rocks and earth, under water."

In Dobson's day the hypothesis of "gigantic floods," "debacles," "resistless world-wide currents," was so firmly entrenched that the voice of the observant layman found no hearers, and a letter from Dobson to Hitchcock written in 1837 and containing additional evidence and argument remained unpublished until Murchison, in 1842,[41] paid his respects to the remarkable work of a remarkable man.*

"I take leave of the glacial theory in congratulating American science in having possessed the original author of the best glacial theory, though his name had escaped notice; and in recommending to you the terse argument of Peter Dobson, a previous acquaintance with which might have saved volumes of disputation on both sides of the Atlantic."

[The remainder of this discussion of glaciers and glaciation, p. 117-127, was deleted.]

CONCLUSION.

During the past century many principles of land sculpture have emerged from the fog of intellectual speculation and unorganized observation and taken their place among generally accepted truths. Many of them are no longer subjects of controversy. Erosion has found its place as a major geologic agent and has given a new conception of natural scenery. Lofty mountains are no longer "ancient as the sun," they are youthful features in process of dissection; valleys and canyons are the work of streams and glaciers; fiords are erosion forms; waterfalls and lakes are features in process of elimination; many plains and plateaus owe their form and position to long-continued denudation. Modern landscapes are no longer viewed as original features or the product of a single agent acting at a particular time, but as ephemeral forms which owe their present appearance to their age and the particular forces at work upon them as well as to their original structure.

It is interesting to note the halting steps leading to the present viewpoint, to find that decades elapsed between the formulation of a theory or the recording of significant facts and their final acceptance or rejection, and to realize that the organization of principles and observations into a science of physiography has been the work

* Peter Dobson (1784-1878) came to this country from Preston, England, in 1809 and established a cotton factory at Vernon, Conn.

19

of the present generation. Progress has been conditioned by a number of factors besides the intellectual
ability of individual workers.

The influence of locality is plainly seen. Convincing
evidence of river erosion was obtained in central France,
the Pacific Islands, and the Colorado Plateau—regions
in which other causes were easily eliminated. Sculpture
by glaciers passed beyond the theoretical stage when the
simple forms of the Sierras and New Zealand Alps were
described. The origin of loess was first discerned in a
region where glacial phenomena did not obscure the
vision. The complexity of the Glacial period asserted by
geologists of the Middle West was denied by eastern
students. The work of waves on the English coast
impressed British geologists to such an extent that plains
of denudation and inland valleys were ascribed to
ocean work.

In the establishment of principles, the friendly interchange of ideas has yielded large returns. Many of the
fundamental conceptions of earth sculpture have come
from groups of men so situated as to facilitate criticism.
It is impossible, even if desirable, to award individual
credit to Venetz, Charpentier, and Agassiz in the formulation of the glacial theory; and the close association of
Agassiz and Dana in New England and of Chamberlin
and Irving in Wisconsin was undoubtedly helpful in
establishing the theory of continental glaciation. From
the intimate companionship in field and laboratory of
Hutton, Playfair and Hope, arose the profound influence
of the Edinburgh school, and the sympathetic coöperation
of Powell, Gilbert, and Dutton has given to the world its
classics in the genetic study of land forms.

The influence of ideas has been closely associated with
clarity, conciseness, and attractiveness of presentation.
Hutton is known through Playfair, Agassiz's contributions to glacial geology are known to every student, while
Venetz, Charpentier, and Hugi are only names. Cuvier's
discourses on dynamical geology were reprinted and
translated into English and German, but Lamarck's
"Hydrogéologie" is known only to book collectors. The
verbose works of Guettard, although carrying the same
message as Playfair's "Illustrations" and Desmarest's
"Memoirs," are practically unknown, as is also Horace
H. Hayden's treatise (1821) on the drift of eastern

North America. It has been well said that the world-wide influence of American physiographic teaching is due in no small part to the masterly presentations of Gilbert and Davis.

It is surprising to note the delays, the backward steps, and the duplication of effort resulting from lack of familiarity with the work of the pioneers. Sabine says in 1864:[73]

"It often happens, not unnaturally, that those who are most occupied with the questions of the day in an advancing science retain but an imperfect recollection of the obligations due to those who laid the first foundations of our subsequent knowledge."

The product of intellectual effort appears to be conditioned by time of planting and character of soil as well as by quantity of seed. For example: Erosion by rivers was as clearly shown by Desmarest as by Dana and Newberry 50 years later. Criteria for the recognition of ancient fluviatile deposits were established by James Deane in 1847 in a study of the Connecticut Valley Triassic. Agassiz's proof that ice is an essential factor in the formation of till is substantially a duplication of Dobson's observations (1826).

The volumes of the Journal with their very large number of articles and reviews dealing with geology show that the interpretation of land forms as products of subaërial erosion began in France and French Switzerland during the later part of the 18th century as a phase of the intellectual emancipation following the Revolution. Scotland and England assumed the leadership for the first half of the 19th century, and the first 100 volumes of the Journal show the profound influence of English and French teaching. In America, independent thinking, early exercised by the few, became general with the establishment of the Federal survey, the increase in university departments, geological societies and periodicals, and has given to Americans the responsibilities of teachers.

Am. Jour. Sci.—Fourth Series, Vol. XLVI, No. 271.—July, 1918.
5

BIBLIOGRAPHY.

[1] Wilson, J. W., Bursting of lakes through mountains, this Journal, 3, 253, 1821.

[2] Whitney, J. D., Progress of the Geological Survey of California, this Journal, 38, 263-264, 1864.

[3] Playfair, John, Illustrations of the Huttonian theory of the earth, Edinburgh, 1802.

[4] Kain, J. H., Remarks on the mineralogy and geology of northwestern Virginia and eastern Tennessee, this Journal, 1, 60-67, 1819.

[5] Hitchcock, Edward, Geology, etc., of regions contiguous to the Connecticut, this Journal, 7, 1-30, 1824.

[6] Buckland, Wm., Reliquiæ diluvianæ, this Journal, 8, 150, 317, 1824.

[7] Phillips, John, Geology of Yorkshire, this Journal, 21, 17-20, 1832.

[8] Scrope, G. P., Excavation of valleys, Geol. Soc., London, No. 14, 1830.

[9] Hayes, G. E., Remarks on geology and topography of western New York, this Journal, 35, 88-91, 1839.

[10] Seventh Meeting of the British Association for the Advancement of Science, this Journal, 33, 288, 1838.

[11] Darwin, Charles, Geological observations on the volcanic islands and parts of South America, etc., second part of the Voyage of the ''Beagle,'' during 1832-1836. London, 1844.

[12] Hildreth, S. P., Observations, etc., valley of the Ohio, this Journal, 29, 1-148, 1836.

[13] Geddes, James, Observations on the geological features of the south side of Ontario valley, this Journal, 11, 213-218, 1826.

[14] Conrad, T. A., Notes on American geology, this Journal, 35, 237-251, 1839.

[15] Warren, G. K., Preliminary report of explorations in Nebraska and Dakota, this Journal, 27, 380, 1859.

[16] Lesley, J. P., Observations on the Appalachian region of southern Virginia, this Journal, 34, review, 413-415, 1862.

[17] Hitchcock, Edward, First anniversary address before the Association of American Geologists, this Journal, 41, 232-275, 1841.

[18] Dana, J. D., On denudation in the Pacific, this Journal, 9, 48-62, 1850.
————, On the degradation of the rocks of New South Wales and formation of valleys, this Journal, 9, 289-294, 1850.

[19] Hubbard, O. P., On the condition of trap dikes in New Hampshire an evidence and measure of erosion, this Journal, 9, 158-171, 1850.

[20] Hayden, F. V., Some remarks in regard to the period of elevation of the Rocky Mountains, this Journal, 33, 305-313, 1862.

[21] Newberry, J. S., Colorado River of the West, this Journal, 33, review, 387-403, 1862.

[22] Jukes, J. B., Address to the Geological Section of the British Association at Cambridge, Quart. Jour. Geol. Soc., 18, 1862, this Journal, 34, 439, 1862.

[23] Powell, J. W., Exploration of the Colorado River of the West, 1875. For Powell's preliminary article see this Journal, 5, 456-465, 1873.

[24] McGee, W. J., Three formations of the Middle Atlantic slope, this Journal, 35, 120, 328, 367, 448, 1888.

[25] Davis, W. M., Topographic development of the Triassic formation of the Connecticut Valley, this Journal, 37, 423-434, 1889.

[26] Percival, J. G., Geology of Connecticut, 1842.

[27] Kerr, W. C., Origin of some new points in the topography of North Carolina, this Journal, 21, 216-219, 1881.

[28] McGee, W. J., The classification of geographic forms by genesis, Nat. Geogr. Mag., 1, 27-36, 1888.

[29] Davis, W. M., The rivers and valleys of Pennsylvania, Nat. Geogr. Mag., 1, 183-253, 1889.
————, The rivers of northern New Jersey with notes on the classification of rivers in general, ibid., 2, 81-110, 1890.

[29] Silliman, Benjamin, Notice of Horace H. Hayden's geological essays, this Journal, 3, 49, 1821.

[31] Cornelius, Elias, Account of a singular position of a granite rock, this Journal, 2, 200-201, 1820.

[32] Finch, John, On the Celtic antiquities of America, this Journal, 7, 149-161, 1824.

[33] Finch, John, Geological essay on the Tertiary formations in America, this Journal, 7, 31-43, 1824.

[34] Conybeare and Phillips, Outlines of the geology of England and Wales, this Journal, 7, 210, 211, 1824.

[35] Hayden, Horace H., Geological essays, 1-412, 1821, this Journal, 3, 47-57, 1821.

[36] Jackson, C. T., Reports on the geology of the State of Maine, and on the public lands belonging to Maine and Massachusetts, this Journal, 36, 153, 1839.

[37] Gibson, J. B., Remarks on the geology of the lakes and the valley of the Mississippi, this Journal, 29, 201-213, 1836.

[38] Phillips, John, Geology of Yorkshire, this Journal, 21, 14-15, 1832.

[39] Granger, Ebenezer, Notice of a curious fluted rock at Sandusky Bay, Ohio, this Journal, 6, 180, 1823.

[40] Dobson, Peter, Remarks on bowlders, this Journal, 10, 217-218, 1826.

[41] Murchison, R. I., Address at anniversary meeting of the Geological Society of London, this Journal, 43, 200-201, 1842.

[73] Sabine, Sir Edward, Address of the president of the Royal Society, this Journal, 37, 108, 1864.

American Journal of Science, (Series 2), 1850, Vol..9, pp. 48–62

2

On Denudation in the Pacific

J. D. DANA

Art. X.—*On Denudation in the Pacific;* by James D. Dana.

The following pages are extracted from different chapters in
the Geological Report of the Exploring Expedition under Capt.
Wilkes.*

The valleys of the Pacific Islands have usually a course from
the interior of the island towards the shores; or when the island
consists of two or more distinct summits or heights (like Maui)
they extend nearly radiately from the centre of each division of
the island.   They are of three kinds:

I. A narrow gorge, with barely a pathway for a streamlet at
bottom, the enclosing sides diverging upward at an angle of thirty
to sixty degrees.   Such valleys have a rapid descent, and are
bounded by declivities from one hundred to two thousand feet or
more in elevation, which are covered with vegetation, though
striped nearly horizontally by parallel lines of black rock.   There
are frequent cascades along their course; and at head, they often
abut against the sides of the central inaccessible heights of the
island.   The streamlet has frequently its source in one or more
thready cascades that make an unbroken descent of one or two
thousand feet down the precipitous yet verdant walls of the amphitheatre around.

II. A narrow gorge, having the walls vertical or nearly so, and
a flat strip of land at bottom more or less uneven, with a streamlet sporting along, first on this side, and then on that, now in rapids, and now with smoother and deeper waters.   The walls may
be from one hundred to one thousand feet or more in height; they
are richly overgrown, yet the rocks are often exposed, though
every where more than half concealed by the green drapery.

These gorges vary in character according to their position on
the island.   Where they cut through the lower plains, (as the
dividing plain of Oahu,) they are deep channels with a somewhat
even character to the nearly vertical walls, and an open riband of
land at bottom.   The depth is from one to three hundred feet, and
the breadth as many yards.   Farther towards the interior, where
the mountain slopes and vegetation have begun, the walls are
deeply fluted or furrowed, the verdure is more varied and abundant, and cascades are numerous.

This second kind of gorge, still farther towards the interior,
changes in character, and becomes a gorge of the first kind, narrowing at bottom to a torrent's course, along which are occasional
precipices which only a torrent could descend.

---

* U. S. Exploring Expedition during the years 1838–1842, under the command
of C. Wilkes, U. S. N.—Geology by James D. Dana, A.M., Geologist of the Expedition.   750 pp. 4to, with a folio Atlas of 21 plates of fossils.   Philadelphia: 1849.

III. Valleys of the *third* kind have an extensive plain at bottom quite unlike the strip of land just described. They sometimes abut at head against vertical walls, but oftener terminate in a wide break in the mountains.

The ridges of land which intervene between the valleys, have a flat or barely undulated surface, where these valleys intersect the lower plains or slopes; but in the mountains, they are narrow at top, and sometimes scarcely passable along their knife-edge summits. Some of them as they extend inward, become more and more narrow, and terminate in a thin wall, which runs up to the central peaks. Others stop short of these central peaks, and the valleys either side consequently coalesce at their head, or are separated only by a low wall, into which the before lofty ridge had dwindled. The crest is often jagged, or rises in sharp serratures.

The main valleys, which we have more particularly alluded to above, have their subordinate branches; and so the ridges in necessary correspondence, have their subordinate spurs.

As examples of the valleys and ridges here described, we introduce a brief account of an excursion in the Hanapepe valley on Kauai, one of the Hawaiian Islands, and a second up the mountains of Tahiti.

Hanapepe Valley, Kauai.—We reached its enclosing walls, about four miles from the sea, where the sloping plain of the coast was just losing its smooth, undulating surface, and changing into the broken and wooded declivities of the interior. The valley, which had been a channel through the grassy plain, a few hundred feet in depth, was becoming a narrow defile through the mountains. A strip of land lay below, between the rocky walls, covered with deep-green garden-like patches of taro, through which a small stream was hastening on to the sea.

We found a place of descent, and three hundred feet down, reached the banks of the stream, along which we pursued our course. The mountains, as we proceeded, closed rapidly upon us, and we were soon in a narrow gorge, between walls one thousand feet in height, and with a mere line of sky over head. The stream dashed along by us, now on this side of the green strip of land, and then on that; occasionally compelling us to climb up, and cling among the crevices of the walls to avoid its waters, where too deep or rapid to be conveniently forded. Its bed was often rocky, but there was no slope of debris at the base of the walls on either side, and for the greater part of the distance it was bordered by plantations of taro. The style of mountain architecture, observed on the island of Oahu, was exhibited in this shaded defile on a still grander scale. The mural surfaces enclosing it had been wrought, in some places, into a series of semi-

circular alcoves or recesses, which extended to the distant summits over head : more commonly, the walls were formed of a
series of semicircular columns of vast size, collected together like
the clustered shafts of a Gothic structure, and terminating several hundred feet above, in low conical summits.   Although the
sides were erect or nearly so, there was a profuse decoration of
vines and flowers, ferns, and shrubbery ; and where more inclined,
forests covered densely the slopes.

These peculiar architectural features proceed from the wear of
rills of waters, streaming down the bold sides of the gorge : they
channel the surface, leaving the intermediate parts prominent.
The rock is uniformly stratified, and the layers consist of gray
basalt or basaltic lava, alternating with basaltic conglomerate.

Cascades were frequently met with ; at one place, a dozen
were playing around us at the same time, pouring down the high
walls, appearing and disappearing, at intervals, amid the foliage,
some in white foamy threads, and others in parted strands im-
perfectly concealing the black surface of rock beneath.

A rough ramble of four miles brought us to the *falls* of the
Hanapepe.   The precipice, sweeping around with a curve, abruptly closed the defile, and all farther progress was therefore
intercepted.   We were in an amphitheatre of surpassing grandeur,
to which the long defile, with its fluted or Gothic walls, decorated
with leaves and flowers and living cascades, seemed a fit porch
or entrance-way.   The sides around were lofty, and the profuse
vegetation was almost as varied in its tints of green as in its
forms.   On the left stood apart from the walls an inclined columnar peak or leaning tower, overhanging the valley.   Its abrupt
sides were bare, excepting some tufts of ferns and mosses, while
the top was crowned with a clump of bushes.   To complete the
decorations of the place,—from a gorge on the right, in the verdant mountains above, where the basaltic rocks stood out in
curved ascending columns on either side, as if about to meet in a
Gothic arch, a stream leaped the precipice and fell in dripping
foam to the depths below : where, gathering its strength again,
it went on its shaded way down the gorge.

The *mountains of Tahiti* commence their slopes from the
sea or a narrow sea-shore plain, and gradually rise on all sides
towards the central peaks, the ridges of the north and west terminating in the towering summits of Orohena and Aorai, while
the eastern and southern, though reaching towards the same
peaks, are partly intercepted by the valley of Papenoo.   Aorai is
seven thousand feet in height and Orohena not less than eight
thousand feet.

We commenced the ascent of Mount Aorai by the ridge on the
west side of the Matavai Valley, and, by the skillfulness of our
guide, were generally, able to keep the elevated parts of the ridge

without descending into the deep valleys which bordered our path. An occasional descent, and a climb on the opposite side of the valley were undertaken; and although the sides were nearly perpendicular, it was accomplished, without much difficulty, by clinging from tree to tree, with the assistance of ropes, at times, where the mural front was otherwise impassable. By noon of the second day, we had reached an elevation of five thousand feet and stood on an area twelve feet square, the summit of an isolated crest in the ridge on which we were travelling. To the east, we looked down two thousand feet into the Matavai Valley; to the west a thousand feet into a branch of the Papaua Valley, the slopes either way, being from sixty to eighty degrees, or within thirty degrees of perpendicular. On the side of our ascent, and beyond, on the opposite side, our peak was united with the adjoining summit by a thin ridge, reached by a steep descent of three hundred feet. This ridge was described, by our natives, as no wider at top than a man's arm, and a fog coming on, they refused to attempt it that day. The next morning being clear, we pursued our course. For a hundred rods, the ridge on which we walked was two to four feet wide, and from it, we looked down, on either side a thousand feet or more, of almost perpendicular descent. Beyond this the ridge continued narrow, though less dangerous, until we approached the high peak of Aorai. This peak had appeared to be conical and equally accessible on different sides, but it proved to have but one place of approach, and that along a wall with precipices of two to three thousand feet, and seldom exceeding two feet in width at top. In one place we sat on it as on the back of a horse, for it was no wider, and pushed ourselves along till we reached a spot where its width was doubled to two feet, and numerous bushes again affording us some security, we dared to walk erect. We at last stood perched on the summit edge, not six feet broad. The ridge continued beyond for a short distance, with the same sharp, knife-edge character, and was then broken off by the Punaavia Valley. Our height afforded a near view of Orohena; it was separated from us only by the Valley of Matavai, from whose profound depths it rose with nearly erect sides. The peak has a saddle shape, and the northern of the two points is called Pitohiti. These summits, and the ridge which stretches from them toward Matavai, intercept the view to the southward. In other directions, the rapid succession of gorge and ridge that characterizes Tahitian scenery, was open before us. At the western foot of Aorai, appeared the Crown. Beyond it extended the Punaavia Valley, the only level spot in sight; and far away, in the same direction, steep ridges, rising behind one another with jagged outline, stood against the western horizon. To the north, deep valleys gorge the country, with narrow precipitous ridges between; and these melt away into ridgy hills and valleys, and finally into the palm-covered plains bordering the sea.

On our descent, we followed the western side of the Papaua Valley, along a narrow ridge such as we have described, but two or three feet wide at top, and enclosed by precipices of not less than a thousand feet. Proceeding thus for two hours, holding to the bushes which served as a kind of balustrade, though occasionally startled by a slip of the foot one side or the other—our path suddenly narrowed to a mere edge of naked rock, and, moreover, the ridge was inclined a little to the east, like a tottering wall. Taking the upper side of the sloping wall, and trusting our feet to the bushes while clinging to the rocks above, carefully dividing our weight lest we should precipitate the rocks and ourselves to the depths below, we continued on till we came to an abrupt break in the ridge of twenty feet, half of which was perpendicular. By means of ropes doubled around the rocks above, we in turn let ourselves down, and soon reached again a width of three feet, where we could walk in safety. Two hours more at last brought us to slopes and ridges where we could breathe freely.

The peculiarities here described characterize all parts of the island. Towards the high peaks of the interior, the ridges which radiate from, or connect with them, become mere mountain walls with inaccessible slopes, and the valleys are from one to three thousand feet in depth. The central peaks themselves have the same wall-like character. It is thus with Orohena and Pitohiti, as well as Aorai; and owing to the sharpness of the summit edge, rather than the steepness of the ascent, Orohena is said to be quite inaccessible. Dr. Pickering and Mr. Couthony, in an excursion to a height of five thousand feet on this ridge, met with difficulties of the same character we have described.

Without citing other examples, we continue with the author's remarks on the origin of these valleys.

The causes operating in the Pacific, which may have contributed to valley-making, are the following:

1. Convulsions from internal forces, or volcanic action.
2. Degradation from the action of the sea.
3. Gradual wear from running water derived from the rains.
4. Gradual decomposition through the agency of the elements and growing vegetation.

The *action of volcanic forces* in the formation of valleys, is finely illustrated in the great rupture in the summit of Hale-a-kala on Maui. The two valleys formed by the eruption are as extensive as any in the Hawaiian Group, being two thousand feet deep at their highest part, and one to two miles wide. They extend from the interior outward towards the sea. Above, they open into

29

a common amphitheatre, the remains of the former crater, the walls of which are two thousand feet high.

As other examples of volcanic action, we may refer to the pit craters of Mount Loa, among which ·Kilauea stands preëminent. This great corral, if we may use a Madeira word, is a thousand feet deep, one to two miles wide, and over three long, so that it forms a cavity which may compare advantageously with many valleys; and were the walls on one side removed, it might become the head of a valley like that of Hale-a-kala on Maui.

As an example of this kind of valley upon islands which have lost their original volcanic form, we venture to refer to the wide Nunanu, back of Honolulu, island of Oahu,) which has at its head on either side, a peak rising above it to a height of two thousand four hundred feet, or four thousand feet above the sea.

The immense amphitheatre to the west of the lofty Orohena and Aorai, on the island of 'Tahiti, is remarkable for its great breadth, and the towering summits which overhang it; and if not a parallel case to that of Maui, that is, if the head was not originally the great crater, there must have been a subsidence or removal of a large tract by internal forces.

The precipice of the eastern mountain of Oahu, is another example of the effect of convulsion in altering the features of islands, causing either a removal or subsidence.

The many fissures which are opened by the action of Kilanea, might be looked upon as valleys on a smaller scale, and the germs of more extensive ones. But with few exceptions, these fissures as soon as made are closed by the ejected lava, and the mountain is here no weaker than before. Those which remain open, may be the means of determining the direction of valleys afterwards formed.

Action of the sea.—The action of the sea in valley-making, is supposed to have been exerted during the rise of the land; and as such changes of level have taken place in the Pacific, this cause it would seem, must have had as extensive operation in this vast ocean as any where in the world, especially as the lands are small and encircled by the sea, and there is, therefore, a large amount of coast exposed, in proportion to the whole area.

But in order to apprehend the full effect of this mode of degradation, we should refer to its action on existing shores.* At the outset we are surprised at finding little evidence of any such action now in progress along lines of coast. The islands, and the shores of continents have occasional bays, but none that are deepening by the action of the sea. The waves tend rather to fill up the bays and remove by degradation the prominent capes, thus rendering the coast more even, and at the same time, accu-

---

* The view here presented is sustained in De la Beche's Geological Researches, page 192.

mulating beaches that protect it from wear. If this is the case on shores where there are deep bays, what should it be on submarine slopes successively becoming the shores, in which the surface is quite even compared with the present outline of the islands? Instead of making bays and channels, it can only give greater regularity to the line of coast.

Upon the North American coast, from Long Island to Florida there are no valleys in progress from the action of the sea. On the contrary, we ascertain by soundings that the bottom is singularly even; and the bays, as that of New York, are so acted upon by the sea, that were it not, in the case mentioned, for the action of the current of the Hudson River, its limits would continue gradually to contract. Around Tahiti there are no submarine valleys. The valleys of the land are often two thousand feet deep; but they die out towards the shores. Thus over the world, scarcely an instance can be pointed out of valley making from the action of the sea. During the slow rise of a country, the condition would not be more favorable for this effect than in a time of perfect quiet. If America were to be elevated, would the action make valleys in the shores just referred to? If England were slowly to rise, would this favor the scooping of valleys through its beaches? Would not beach formations continue to be the legitimate production of the sea along its line of wave action; and where the rocks should favor the opening of a deep cove, would not the same action go on as now, causing a wear of the headlands and a filling up of the cove at its head? Were Tahiti now to continue rising, could the waves make valleys on the coast? The increasing height of the mountains would give the streams of the land greater eroding force, and more copious waters; but the levelling waves would continue to act as at the present time. The effects of the sea in making valleys have been much exaggerated, as is obvious from this appeal to existing operations, the appropriate test of truth in geology.

The action of a rush of waters in a few great waves over the land, such as might attend a convulsive elevation, though generally having a levelling effect, might produce some excavations, as is readily conceived; yet it is obvious on a moment's consideration, that such waves could not make the deep valleys, miles in length, that intersect the rocks and mountains of our globe.

But it is supposed that there may be fissures about volcanic islands in which the sea could ply its force. Yet even in these cases, unless the fissures were large, the seashore accumulations would be most likely to fill and obstruct them. To try this hypothesis by facts, we remark that there are no such shore fissures around Mount Loa, nor any of the other Hawaiian Islands. The fissures formed by volcanic action immediately about a volcano, are generally filled at once with lavas as we have stated, and the vent is mended by the force which made it. It is, therefore, a gratuitous assumption that such fissures have been common. The existence, however, of large valleys such as have been attributed above to convulsions cannot be doubted; but the sea would exert its power in such places, nearly as now in Fangaloa Bay, Tutuila, and other bays in continents;—a beach forms, and a shore plain, and afterwards there is a little action from the sea in these confined areas of water.

In the Illawarra district, New South Wales, there are several places where dikes of basalt have been removed by the sea, and channels one hundred yards in depth, of the width of the dike (six feet), now exist, cutting straight into the rocky land. This is an example of the action of the sea where everything is most favorable for it. And we observe that there is little resemblance in this narrow channel with but a trifling wear of the inclosing rocks, to the valleys which are to be accounted for in the Pacific; and little authority to be derived from it for attributing much efficacy to the sea in wearing out valleys. The reason of this is apparent in the fact that the sea rolls up a coast in great swells, and cannot parcel itself off, and act like a set of gouges: this latter effect it leaves for the streams and streamlets of the shores which are gouges of all dimensions.

Although the sea can accomplish little along coasts towards excavating valleys, yet when the land is wholly submerged, or only the mountain summits peer out as islands, the great oceanic currents sweeping over the surface and through channels between the islands, would wear away the rocks or earth beneath. From the breadth and character of such marine sweepings, we learn that the excavations formed would be very broad rounded valleys; and their courses would correspond in some degree with the probable direction which the currents of the ocean would have, over the region in case of a submergence. Moreover where there are different open channels for the ingress of the sea, having free intercommunication, there are often strong currents connected with the tides, and consequently much erosion. It is obvious that the valleys of the Pacific islands have nothing in their features or positions attributable to such a cause.

Running water of the land, and gradual decomposition.—Of the causes of valleys mentioned in the outset we are forced to rely for explanations principally upon running streams: and they are not only gouges of all dimensions, but of great power, and in constant action. There are several classes of facts which support us in this conclusion.

a. We observe that Mount Loa, whose sides are still flooded with lavas at intervals, has but one or two streamlets over all its slopes, and the surface has none of the deep valleys common about other summits. Here volcanic action has had a smoothing effect, and by its continuation to this time, the waters have had scarcely a chance to make a beginning in denudation.

Mount Kea, which has been extinct for a long period, has a succession of valleys on its windward or rainy side, which are several hundred feet deep at the coast and gradually diminish upward, extending in general about half or two-thirds of the way to the summit. But to the westward it has dry declivities, which are comparatively even at base, with little running water. A direct connection is thus evinced between a windward exposure, and the existence of valleys: and we observe also that the time since volcanic action ceased is approximately or relatively indicated, for it has been long enough for the valleys to have advanced only part way to the summit. Degradation from running water would of course commence at the foot of the mountain, where the waters are necessarily more abundant and more powerful in denuding action, in consequence of their gradual accumulation on their descent. Mount Kea, like Mount Loa, is nearly 14,000 feet high, and the average slope is 7 to 8 degrees.

Hale-a-kala on Maui offers the same facts as Mount Kea, indicating the same relation between the features of the surface and the climate of the different sides of the island. On Eastern Oahu the valleys are still more extensive; yet the slopes of the original mountains may be in part distinguished. And thus we are gradually led to Kauai, the westernmost of the Hawaiian Islands, where the valleys are very profound and the former slopes can hardly be made out. The facts are so progressive in character, that we must attribute all equally to the running waters of the land.

The valleys of Mount Kea alone, extending some thousands of feet up its sides, sustain us in saying, that time only is required for the formation of similar valleys elsewhere in the Pacific. As in Tahiti, so in other islands. these valleys take the direction of the former slopes; and though they may be of great depth and commence even under the central summits, they *terminate at the sea level, instead of continuing beneath it.*

The fluting of the walls of the Hanapepe Valley, a thousand feet or more in height, has been described on a preceding page. It cannot be doubted here that water was the agent; for the rills are seen at work. The contrast between the same valley near the sea, and in the mountains, (the walls in the former case being nearly unworn vertically,) is explained on the same principle: for the mountains are a region of frequent rains and almost constant clouds, and therefore abound in streams and streamlets and threads of water; while below, there are grassy plains instead of forest declivities, and but little rain. These furrowings vary from a few yards in width and depth to many furlongs.

The long and lofty precipice of Eastern Oahu, is an excellent place for studying farther this action. It is fluted in the same style as the Hanapepe Valley. In the distant view the vertical channels appear very narrow; but when closely examined they are found to be deep and often winding passages. The precipice faces to the windward, and is directly under the whole line of peaks in the mountain range, both of which facts account for an abundance of water. Going to the westward along the range, the precipice changes to a sloping declivity, and these passages become deeper and longer, and more winding, just in proportion to the increasing length of the slopes: moreover at the same time they decrease in number. Where there is no slope to collect the waters, the rills act independently, and their furrowings like themselves are small, narrow, and numerous; but as the declivity becomes gradual, the rills flow on and collect into larger streams, and the furrowings become deeper and more distant. Over this region, no distinction can be drawn as regards origin between these flutings and the gorges: and in respect to features, only this difference appears, that the size of the excavations is less and the number greater, the steeper the declivity. If a fissure be appealed to as the commencement of the longer valleys, it should also be admitted for each of the flutings. But this idea is wholly inadmissible.

A brief review of the action of flowing waters with reference to the different results described may place this subject in a clear light.

a. Suppose a mountain, sloping around like one of the volcanic domes of the Pacific.—The excavating power at work proceeds from the rains or condensed vapor, and depends upon the amount of water and rapidity of slope.

b. The transporting force of flowing water* increases as the sixth power of the velocity,—double the velocity giving sixty-four times the transporting power.—The eroding force will be greater than this on a mountain declivity, where the waters add their own gravity to the direct action of a progressive movement.

c. Hence, if the slopes are steep, the water gathering into rills excavates so rapidly, that every growing streamlet ploughs out a gorge or furrow; and consequently the number of separate gorges is very large, and their sizes comparatively small, though of great depth.

---

* It has been shown by W. Hopkins, Esq., that the moving force of running water, (this force being estimated by the volume or weight of a mass of any given form which it is just capable of moving,) varies as the *sixth* power of the velocity. He says, "if a stream of ten miles an hour would just move a block of five tons weight, a current of fifteen miles an hour would move a block of similar form upwards of fifty-five tons; a current of twenty miles an hour would, according to the same law, move a block of three hundred and twenty tons: again, according to the same law, a current of two miles an hour would move a pebble of similar form of only a few ounces in weight."—*On the Transport of Erratic Blocks,* Trans. Camb. Phil. Soc., 1844, viii, 221, 233.

Second Series, Vol. IX, No. 25.—Jan., 1850. 8

d. But if the slopes are gradual, the rills flow into one another from a broad area, and enlarge a central trunk, which continues on towards the sea, with frequent additions from either side. The excavation above, for a while, is small; for the greater abundance of water below, during the rainy seasons, causes the denudation to be greatest there, and in this part the gorge or valley most rapidly forms. In its progress, it enlarges from below upward, though also increasing above; at the same time, the many tributaries are making lateral branches.

e. Towards the foot of the mountain, the excavating power ceases whenever the stream has no longer in this part a rapid descent,—that is whenever the slope is not above one or two feet to the mile. The stream *then consists of two parts, the torrent of the mountains and the slower waters below*, and the latter is gradually lengthening at the expense of the former.

f. After the lower waters have nearly ceased excavation, a new process commences in this part,—that of widening the valley. The stream which here effects little change at low water, is flooded in certain seasons, and the abundant waters act *laterally* against the enclosing rocks. Gradually, through this undermining and denuding operation, the *narrow bed becomes a flat strip of land, between lofty precipices*, through which, in the rainy season, the streamlet flows in a winding course. The streamlet, as the flat bottom of the valley is made, deposits detritus on its banks, which in some places so accumulates as to prevent an overflow of the banks by any ordinary freshet. Such is the origin of the deep channels with a riband of land at bottom that cut through the "dividing plain" of Oahu, and which are common towards the shores of many of the Pacific islands.

g. The torrent part of the stream, as it goes on excavating, is gradually becoming more and more steep. The rock-material operated upon, consists of layers of unequal hardness, varying but little from horizontality and dipping towards the sea, and this occasions the formation of cascades. Whenever a softer layer wears more rapidly than one above, it causes an abrupt fall in the stream: it may be at first but a few feet in height; but the process begun, it goes on with accumulating power. The descending waters in this spot add their whole weight, as well as a greatly increased velocity, to their ordinary force, and the excavation below goes on rapidly, removing even the harder layers. The consequences are, a fall of increasing height, and a basin-like excavation directly beneath the fall. Often, for a short distance below, the stream moves quietly before rushing again on its torrent course, and when this result is attained by the action, the height of the fall has nearly reached its limit as far as excavation below is concerned;—though it may continue to increase from the gradual wear and removal of the rocks over which it descends.

h. As the gorge increases in steepness, the excavations above deepen rapidly,—the more rapid descent more than compensating, it may be, for any difference in the amount of water. Moreover, as the rains are generally most frequent at the very summits, the rills in this part are kept in almost constant action through the year, while a few miles nearer the sea they are often dried up or absorbed among the cavernous rocks. The denudation is consequently at all times great about the higher parts of the gorge, (especially after the slopes have become steep by previous degradation;) thus finally a steep precipice forms the head of the valley.

i. The waters descending the ridges either side of the valley or gorge, are also removing these barriers between adjacent valleys, and are producing as a *first* effect, a thinning of the ridge at summit to a mere edge; and as a *second*, its partial or entire removal, so that the two valleys may at last be separated only by a low wall, or even terminate in a common head,—a wide amphitheatre enclosed by the lofty mountains. In one case, the ridge between the two valleys, which towards the shores of the island has rather a broad back, high up in the region of mists and frequent rains becomes a narrow wall, and thus connects with the central summit. In the second, the ridge finally terminates abruptly, and a deep valley separates it from the main mountain.

The following sketch may assist the mind in conceiving of the action upon the Pacific mountains. It represents one of the val-

leys of Tahiti from the centre to the shore, excepting its irregularities of direction and descent, and the uneven character of its walls, arising from lateral valleys and minor denudations. The height of Tahiti is about eight thousand feet; its radius *c s* is ten geographical miles. The head of the valley at *a* is three thousand feet below the summit peak *p*. The descent along the air-line from *a* to *s*, averages five hundred feet to the mile. If *a* be four thousand feet below the summit, (the exact depth was not ascertained,) it would still give four hundred feet to the mile.

This subject is beautifully illustrated in some of the tufa cones of Oahu, where, on a smaller scale, we have the same kind of gorge and valley; and in this case, there is no doubt that denudation was the cause by which they were produced. The valleys have the direction of the slopes, and are similar in form and winding character to those of the mountains. The intervening ridges are also similar. Many of them become very thin at summit as they rise towards the crest of the volcanic cone, and others have this upper part adjoining the crest wanting, owing to the extent of the degradation, so that two valleys have a common head against the vertical bluff. A better model of the mountain gorges could hardly be made, and it stands near by, convenient for comparison. Diamond Hill, one of these cones, is 800 feet high.

We need add little, in this place, on the capabilities of running water, after the statement, based on mathematics, that the transporting force varies as the sixth power of the velocity. If we remember that these mountain streams at times increase their violence a million fold when the rains swell the waters to a flood, all incredibility on this point must be removed.

A few thousand feet in depth, even in the solid rocks, is no great affair for an agent of such ceaseless activity, during the periods which have elapsed since the lands became exposed to their influence. And when we take into view the lofty heights of the Pacific islands, their rapid declivities giving speed to the waters and transported stones and earth, we must admit that of all lands, these are especially fitted for denudation by torrents.

The nature of the rocks also favors wear and removal. They are in successive layers, soft conglomerates or tufas frequently alternating with the harder basalt or basaltic lava. Moreover, the rock is commonly much fissured, owing to a tendency to a columnar structure; besides, they are often cellular. The waters thus find admission, promoting decomposition and also degradation. There are, also, frequent caverns between layers, which contribute to the same end.

There is every thing favorable for degradation which can exist in a land of perpetual summer: and there is a full balance against the frosts of colder regions in the exuberance of vegetable life, since it occasions rapid decomposition of the surface, covering even the face of a precipice with a thick layer of altered rock, and with spots of soil wherever there is a chink or shelf for its lodgment. The traveler on one of these islands ascending a valley on a summer day, when the streams are reduced to a mere creeping rill which half the time burrows out of sight, seeing the rich foliage around, vines and flowers in profusion covering the declivities and festooning the trees, and observing scarcely a bare rock or stone excepting a few it may be along the bottom of the gorge, might naturally inquire with some degree of wonder, where are the mighty agents which have channeled the lofty mountains to their base? But though silent, the agents are still on every side at work; decomposition is in slow, but constant progress; the percolating waters are acting internally, if not at the surface. Moreover, at another season, he would find the scene changed to one of noisy waters, careering along over rocks and plunging down heights with frightful velocity; and then the power of the stream would not be disputed.*

But if the waters have been thus efficient in causing denudation and opening valleys, may not fissures or dikes have determined their courses? The only test of truth, an appeal to facts, may answer the question. Mount Loa is a mountain yet unchanged. It has its dikes in great numbers: but over these dikes the country is more apt to be *raised* a little from the overflow of lavas than depressed, and this would turn off the water. Again, we see no instances of dikes yielding, and offering a course for a stream. As to unfilled fissures, there are few of them, and these, with rare exceptions, are immediately about the active vents. Is either supposition then sustained by the facts presented? We know the tendency of water to take the lowest parts of a surface, and will it not follow these parts, whether or not there be a dike or fissure? It is obvious that whatever ravines or depressions the floods of lava may have left, would be the courses of the waters; and these depressions would be followed to the sea, and ultimately become valleys. We may believe that the waters would not wait till there was a convenient fissure; they would go where *inclination* led, and make valleys with little difficulty, if there were no guiding or aiding fissures. Were the dikes filled by a rock more decomposable or more easily eroded than those enclosing it, as is the case in some granitic regions, we should expect that they would frequently become water courses: but this is seldom the fact in the Pacific islands.

The valleys in some of the Canary Islands, extend from the shores part way to the summit, as on Mount Kea and Hale-a-kala, and evidently for the reason already explained. We can detect

---

* The rise of the streams, from the rains of the mountains, is often so rapid that in some instances, the native villages of the coast become flooded, before they have time even to move their property.—*Miss. Herald.* xxiii, 207.

Mr. Coan, who has often traversed the coast of Hawaii, north of Hilo, and during the drier seasons, (which, however, are of short duration on this, the windward coast,) fords the shallow streams without difficulty, gives the following account of his journey during a time of rains. "Great and continued rains fell during my absence, and the numerous rivers became so swollen and furious that the very sight of them was fearful. These raging streams crossed my path about *once in half a mile* for a distance of about thirty miles, and I was compelled to cross them to return home. Most of them run at a rate of twenty or thirty miles an hour, and in their course there are numerous cataracts from ten to a hundred and fifty feet in perpendicular descent. Though the torrents were so fearful as to make one almost quail at the thought of struggling with their fury, ropes were provided, and several men employed for the adventurous task. Great calmness and presence of mind, and great energy and muscular effort, were required to retain one's grasp of the rope, and buffet with the foaming flood. We at last succeeded, though at imminent peril. At one of the rivers, we spent three hours in finding a place where we might, with any degree of safety, extend our hawser across, and transfer our party to the opposite bank. The streams are at the bottom of narrow ravines, with the banks exceedingly precipitous, and often perpendicular bluffs of basaltic rock."—*Miss. Herald,* xxxviii, 157.

in regions of a similar kind, no evidence that the valleys have depended for their origin on the mountain's being a "crater of elevation," as von Buch urges.* The regular stratification of the sides of these valleys; the absence of all tiltings; their situation, as related to the rains; and the absence of fissures ready for making valleys on the leeward declivities, are points which favor no such theory: and, moreover, it is an unnecessary hypothesis.

We are thus led to conclude that between convulsions from subterranean forces, and degradation from waters supplied by the rains and attending decomposition, a lofty volcanic dome may be changed to a skeleton island like Tahiti. We have referred to Mount Loa as still unfurrowed; to Mount Kea and Hale-a-kala as having only the lower slopes deeply channeled with narrow gorges; and to other islands, as exemplifying all gradations in these effects to those in which the original features are no longer to be traced: we have pointed out the difference in the windward and leeward slopes, and have shown a relation between the quantity of rain and the amount of degradation :—we have exhibited a model of the mountains, an undeniable result of denudation, placed at their very base, as if for illustration :—and thus we have traced out and elucidated all the steps in the valley-making process, and have also shown them to be a necessary result from the action of running water.

Again, examples of convulsions from igneous forces have been pointed out in the great gorges of Hale-a-kala, and in Kilauea and other Hawaiian craters; in the mountain wall of Oahu, and similar scenes on other islands; in the wide amphitheatre of central Tahiti: and the importance of this means of change has thus been exhibited. Yet few such changes are apparent on any one island, and these are marked by decided characters not often to be mistaken. It has also been shown that although fissures made by volcanic forces, may in some cases have given the direction to valleys, yet they are by no means necessary in order that valleys should commence to form.

With literal truth may we speak of the valleys of the Pacific Islands, as the furrowings of time, and read in them marks of age. Our former conclusion with regard to the different periods which have passed over the several Hawaiian Islands since the fires ceased and wear begun, is fully substantiated. We also learn how completely the features of an island may be obliterated by this simple process, and even a cluster of peaks like Orohena, Pitohiti and Aorai of Tahiti, be derived from a simple volcanic dome or cone. Mount Loa, alone, contains within itself the material from which an island like Tahiti might be modeled, that should have near twice its height and four times its geographical extent.

---

* See Iles Canaries, p. 285.

Directions

II

Once the eroding power of rivers was accepted, their study was destined to follow two disparate routes, one engineering in approach (open-channel hydraulics, and river mechanics), the other historically oriented (geomorphic). Obviously the behavior of modern rivers cannot be fully appreciated without knowledge of their history nor can the history be correctly interpreted without an understanding of fluid flow and sediment transport in open channels. A science of potamology should have developed encompassing both branches, but the engineers followed their pragmatic paths while the geomorphologist dallied with description and classification. If anyone could have saved the situation it would have been the eminent geologist, G. K. Gilbert (Davis, 1926). Portions of chapter 5 of his classic work on the geology of the Henry Mountains, Utah are reprinted (see Gregory's reference to this, p. 112). This long (52 pages) chapter is a treasury of research ideas and problems. Although his discussion of sediment transport and open-channel hydraulics is qualitative, Gilbert in this report showed how landform studies might have developed by an integration of the engineering and geomorphic approaches.

Gilbert's innate ability was enhanced by exposure to the geology of the West. His powers of observation and synthesis led him to anticipate the work of many modern investigators. For example, he described the condition of dynamic equilibrium in a drainage basin and considered a river or a drainage basin as a system rather than a cluster of independent components (p. 118). His conception of the graded stream, and certainly his example (p. 121) is analogous to that of Mackin (this volume). In addition, he described pediments, superimposed streams, and the interrelations among discharge, gradient, and sediment transport. This is an outstanding 19th century contribution only fully appreciated in this past quarter century. Gilbert continued his work on fluvial processes as part of a study of the effect of hydraulic mining in the Sierra Nevadas. He later performed experiments on sediment transport

(Gilbert, 1914), the results of which are still quoted in the geologic and engineering literature. Among other works of the time, that of De La Noe and Margerie (1888) was outstanding.

Following hard on this work of Gilbert was the prolific output of W. M. Davis. It is fair to say that his impact was decisive, and his influence persisted for half a century. Davis' contribution was great (Daly, 1945), but his explanatory description of landforms and their history led to qualitative descriptions that contributed little to an understanding of the erosional and depositional phenomena involved in land-form development and evolution. Nevertheless, his work is a basic part of most geomorphology texts, and a common application of the descriptive approach is the interpretation of geologic structure from drainage patterns (Zernitz, 1932; Howard, 1967). Although Davis' personal contribution was exceptional, many of his followers did not ask themselves important questions about the landscape. To illustrate this, a review paper by Douglas Johnson is reprinted as a contrast to Gilbert's much earlier contribution. The paper is also of interest because it reveals the semantic problems that concerned geomorphologists during the first half of the 20th century. Douglas Johnson was Professor of Geology at Columbia University, and his contributions in other areas of geomorphology and geology were significant. He also collected and republished Davis' important papers in a volume of reprints (1954).

DEPARTMENT OF THE INTERIOR
U. S. GEOGRAPHICAL AND GEOLOGICAL SURVEY OF THE ROCKY MOUNTAIN REGION
J. W POWELL IN CHARGE

REPORT

ON THE

GEOLOGY OF THE HENRY MOUNTAINS

3

BY G. K. GILBERT

SECOND EDITION

WASHINGTON
GOVERNMENT PRINTING OFFICE
1880

43

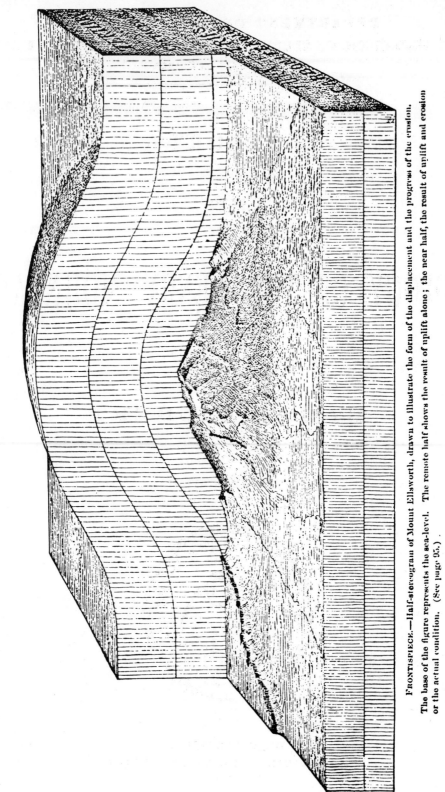

FRONTISPIECE.—Half-stereogram of Mount Ellsworth, drawn to illustrate the form of the displacement and the progress of the erosion. The base of the figure represents the sea-level. The remote half shows the result of uplift alone; the near half, the result of uplift and erosion or the actual condition. (See page 95.)

CHAPTER V.

LAND SCULPTURE.

The Basin of the Colorado offers peculiar facilities for the study of the origin of topographic forms, and its marvelous sculpture has excited the interest of every observer. It has already made notable contributions to the principles of earth sculpture*, and its resources are far from exhausted. The study of the Henry Mountains has not proved entirely unfruitful, and for the sake of showing the bearing of its peculiar features upon the general subject, I shall take the liberty to restate certain principles of erosion which have been derived or enforced by the study of the Colorado Plateaus.

I.—EROSION.

The sculpture and degradation of the land are performed partly by shore-waves, partly by glaciers, partly by wind; but chiefly by rain and running water. The last mentioned agencies only will be here discussed.

The erosion which they accomplish will be considered (A) as consisting of parts, and (B) as modified by conditions.

A. PROCESSES OF EROSION.

All indurated rocks and most earths are bound together by a force of cohesion which must be overcome before they can be divided and re-

---

* Geology of the "Colorado Exploring Expedition", by J. S. Newberry, p. 45.
"Exploration of the Colorado River of the West", by J. W. Powell, p. 152.
"Geology of the Uinta Mountains", by J. W. Powell, p. 181.
"Explorations West of the 100th Meridian", Vol. III, Part I, by G. K. Gilbert, pp. 67 and 554.
"The Colorado Plateau Region" in American Journal of Science for August, 1876, by G. K. Gilbert.
A portion of the last paper is repeated, after modification, in the first section of this chapter.

moved. The natural processes by which the division and removal are accomplished make up erosion. They are called disintegration and transportation.

Transportation is chiefly performed by running water.

Disintegration is naturally divided into two parts. So much of it as is accomplished by running water is called corrasion, and that which is not, is called weathering.

Stated in their natural order, the three general divisions of the process of erosion are (1) *weathering*, (2) *transportation*, and (3) *corrasion*. The rocks of the general surface of the land are disintegrated by *weathering*. The material thus loosened is *transported* by streams to the ocean or other receptacle. In transit it helps to *corrade* from the channels of the streams other material, which joins with it to be transported to the same goal.

Weathering.

In weathering the chief agents of disintegration are solution, change of temperature, the beating of rain, gravity, and vegetation.

The great solvent of rocks is water, but it receives aid from some other substances of which it becomes the vehicle. These substances are chiefly products of the formation and decomposition of vegetable tissues. Some rocks are disintegrated by their complete solution, but the great majority are divided into grains by the solution of a portion; and fragmental rocks usually lose by solution the cement merely, and are thus reduced to their original incoherent condition.

The most rigid rocks are cracked by sudden changes of temperature; and the crevices thus begun are opened by the freezing of the water within them. The coherence of the more porous rocks is impaired and often destroyed by the same expansive force of freezing water.

The beating of the rain overcomes the feeble coherence of earths, and assists solution and frost by detaching the particles which they have partially loosened.

When the base of a cliff is eroded so as to remove or diminish the support of the upper part, the rock thus deprived of support is broken off in blocks by gravity. The process of which this is a part is called cliff-erosion or *sapping*.

Plants often pry apart rocks by the growth of their roots, but their chief aid to erosion is by increasing the solvent power of percolating water.

In general soft rocks weather more rapidly than hard.

Transportation.

A portion of the water of rains flows over the surface and is quickly gathered into streams. A second portion is absorbed by the earth or rock on which it falls, and after a slow underground circulation reissues in springs. Both transport the products of weathering, the latter carrying dissolved minerals and the former chiefly undissolved.

Transportation is also performed by the direct action of gravity. In sapping, the blocks which are detached by gravity are by the same agency carried to the base of the cliff.

Corrasion.

In corrasion the agents of disintegration are solution and mechanical wear. Wherever the two are combined, the superior efficiency of the latter is evident; and in all fields of rapid corrasion the part played by solution is so small that it may be disregarded.

The mechanical wear of streams is performed by the aid of hard mineral fragments which are carried along by the current. The effective force is that of the current; the tools are mud, sand, and bowlders. The most important of them is sand; it is chiefly by the impact and friction of grains of sand that the rocky beds of streams are disintegrated.

Streams of clear water corrade their beds by solution. Muddy streams act partly by solution, but chiefly by attrition.

Streams transport the combined products of corrasion and weathering. A part of the *débris* is carried in solution, and a part mechanically. The finest of the undissolved detritus is held in suspension; the coarsest is rolled along the bottom; and there is a gradation between the two modes. There is a constant comminution of all the material as it moves, and the work of transportation is thereby accelerated. Bowlders and pebbles, while they wear the stream-bed by pounding and rubbing, are worn still more rapidly themselves. Sand grains are worn and broken by the continued jostling, and their fragments join the suspended mud. Finally the detritus is all more or less dissolved by the water, the finest the most rapidly.

In brief, weathering is performed by solution; by change of temperature, including frost; by rain beating; by gravity; and by vegetation. Transportation is performed chiefly by running water. Corrasion is performed by solution, and by mechanical wear.

Corrasion is distinguished from weathering chiefly by including mechanical wear among its agencies, and the importance of the distinction will be apparent when we come to consider how greatly and peculiarly this process is affected by modifying conditions.

B. CONDITIONS CONTROLLING EROSION.

The chief conditions which affect the rapidity of erosion are (1) declivity, (2) character of rock, and (3) climate

Rate of Erosion and Declivity.

In general *erosion is most rapid where the slope is steepest;* but weathering, transportation, and corrasion are affected in different ways and in different degrees.

With increase of slope goes increase in the velocity of running water, and with that goes increase in its power to transport undissolved detritus.

The ability of a stream to corrade by solution is not notably enhanced by great velocity; but its ability to corrade by mechanical wear keeps pace with its ability to transport, or may even increase more rapidly. For not only does the bottom receive more blows in proportion as the quantity of transient detritus increases, but the blows acquire greater force from the accelerated current, and from the greater size of the moving fragments. It is necessary however to distinguish the ability to corrade from the rate of corrasion, which will be seen further on to depend largely on other conditions.

Weathering is not directly influenced by slope, but it is reached indirectly through transportation. Solution and frost, the chief agents of rock decay, are both retarded by the excessive accumulation of disintegrated rock. Frost action ceases altogether at a few feet below the surface, and solution gradually decreases as the zone of its activity descends and the circulation on which it depends becomes more sluggish. Hence the rapid removal of the products of weathering stimulates its action, and especially that portion of its action which depends upon frost. If however the power of transportation is so great as to remove completely th‿ products of weathering, the work of disintegration is thereby checked; for the soil which weathering tends to accumulate is a reservoir to catch rain as it reaches the earth and store it up for the work of solution and frost, instead of letting it run off at once unused.

Sapping is directly favored by great declivity.

In brief, a steep declivity favors transportation and thereby favors corrasion. The rapid, but partial, transportation of weathered rock accelerates weathering; but the complete removal of its products retards weathering.

Rate of Erosion and Rock Texture.

Other things being equal, *erosion is most rapid when the eroded rock offers least resistance;* but the rocks which are most favorable to one portion of the process of erosion do not necessarily stand in the same relation to the others. Disintegration by solution depends in large part on the solubility of the rocks, but it proceeds most rapidly with those fragmental rocks of which the cement is soluble, and of which the texture is open. Disintegration by frost is most rapid in rocks which absorb a large percentage of water and are feebly coherent. Disintegration by mechanical wear is most rapid in soft rocks.

Transportation is most favored by those rocks which yield by disintegration the most finely comminuted *débris*.

[A brief discussion on the influence of climate on erosion and land forms, p. 97-99, was deleted.]

Transportation and Comminution.

A stream of water flowing down its bed expends an amount of energy that is measured by the quantity of water and the vertical distance through which it descends. If there were no friction of the water upon its channel the velocity of the current would continually increase; but if, as is the usual case, there is no increase of velocity, then the whole of the energy is consumed in friction. The friction produces inequalities in the motion of the water, and especially induces subsidiary currents more or less oblique to the general onward movement. Some of these subsidiary currents have an upward tendency, and by them is performed the chief work of transportation. They lift small particles from the bottom and hold them in suspension while they move forward with the general current. The finest particles sink most slowly and are carried farthest before they fall. Larger ones are barely lifted, and are dropped at once. Still larger are only half lifted; that is, they are lifted on the side of the current and rolled over without quitting the bottom. And finally there is a limit to the power of every current, and the largest fragments of its bed are not moved at all.

There is a definite relation between the velocity of a current and the size of the largest bowlder it will roll. It has been shown by Hopkins that the weight of the bowlder is proportioned to the sixth power of the velocity. It is easily shown also that the weight of a suspended particle is proportioned to the sixth power of the velocity of the upward current that will prevent its sinking. But it must not be inferred that the total load of detritus that a stream will transport bears any such relation to the rapidity of its current. The true inference is, that the velocity determines the size-limit of the detritus that a stream can move by rolling, or can hold in suspension.

Every particle which a stream lifts and sustains is a draft upon its energy, and the measure of the draft is the weight (weighed in water) of the particle, multiplied by the distance it would sink in still water in the time during which it is suspended. If for the sake of simplicity we suppose the whole load of a stream to be of uniform particles, then the measure of the energy consumed in their transportation is their total weight multiplied by the distance one of them would sink in the time occupied in their transportation. Since fine particles sink more slowly than coarse, the same consumption of energy will convey a greater load of fine than of coarse.

Again, the energy of a clear stream is entirely consumed in the friction of flow; and the friction bears a direct relation to its velocity. But if detritus be added to the water, then a portion of its energy is diverted to the transportation of the load; and this is done at the expense of the friction of flow, and hence at the expense of velocity. As the energy expended in transportation increases, the velocity diminishes. If the detritus be composed of uniform particles, then we may also say that as the load increases the velocity diminishes. But the diminishing velocity will finally reach a point at which it can barely transport particles of the given size, and when this point is attained, the stream has its maximum load of detritus of the given size. But fine detritus requires less velocity for its transportation than coarse, and will not so soon reduce the current to the limit of its efficiency. A greater percentage of the total energy of the stream can hence be employed by fine detritus than by coarse.

(It should be explained that the friction of flow is in itself a complex affair. The water in contact with the bottom and walls of the channel develops friction by flowing past them, and that which is farther away by flowing past that which is near. The inequality of motion gives rise to cross currents and there is a friction of these upon each other. The ratio or coefficient of friction of water against the substance of the bed, the coefficient of friction of water against water, or the viscosity of water, and the form of the bed, all conspire to determine the resistance of flow and together make up what may be called the coefficient of the friction of flow. The friction depends on its coefficient and on the velocity.)

Thus the capacity of a stream for transportation is enhanced by comminution in two ways. Fine detritus, on the one hand, consumes less energy for the transportation of the same weight, and on the other, it can utilize a greater portion of the stream's energy.

It follows, as a corollary, that the velocity of a fully loaded stream depends (ceteris paribus) on the comminution of the material of the load. When a stream has its maximum load of fine detritus, its velocity will be less than when carrying its maximum load of coarse detritus; and the greater load corresponds to the less velocity.

It follows also that a stream which is supplied with heterogeneous *débris* will select the finest. If the finest is sufficient in quantity the current will be so checked by it that the coarser cannot be moved. If the finest is not sufficient the next grade will be taken, and so on.

Transportation and Declivity.

To consider now the relation of declivity to transportation we will assume all other conditions to be constant. Let us suppose that two streams have the same length, the same quantity of water, flow over beds of the same character, and are supplied to their full capacities with detritus of the same kind; but differ in the total amount of fall. Their declivities or rates of fall are proportional to their falls. Since the energy of a stream is measured by the product of its volume and its fall, the relative energies of the two streams are proportional to their falls, and hence proportional to their declivities. The velocities of the two streams, depending, as we have seen above, on the character of the detritus which loads them, are the same; and hence the same amount of energy is consumed by each in the friction of flow. And since the energy which each stream expends in transportation is the residual after deducting what it spends in friction from its total energy, it is evident that the stream with the greater declivity will not merely have the greater energy, but will expend a less percentage of it in friction and a greater percentage in transportation.

Hence declivity favors transportation in a degree that is greater than its simple ratio.

There are two elements of which no account is taken in the preceding discussion, but which need to be mentioned to prevent misapprehension, although they detract in no way from the conclusions.

The first is the addition which the transported detritus makes to the energy of the stream. A stream of water charged with detritus is at once a compound and an unstable fluid. It has been treated merely as an unstable fluid requiring a constant expenditure of energy to maintain its constitution; but looking at it as a compound fluid, it is plain that the energy it develops by its descent is greater than the energy pertaining to the water alone, in the precise ratio of the mass of the mixture to the mass of the simple water.

The second element is the addition which the detritus makes to the friction of flow. The coefficient of friction of the compound stream upon its bottom will always be greater than that of the simple stream of water, and the coefficient of internal friction or the viscosity will be greater than that of pure water, and hence for the same velocity a greater amount of energy will be consumed.

It may be noted in passing, that the energy which is consumed in the friction of the detritus on the stream bed, accomplishes as part of its work the mechanical corrasion of the bed.

Transportation and Quantity of Water.

A stream's friction of flow depends mainly on the character of the bed, on the area of the surface of contact, and on the velocity of the current. When the other elements are constant, the friction varies approximately with the area of contact. The area of contact depends on the length and form of the channel, and on the quantity of water. For streams of the same length and same form of cross-section, but differing in size of cross-section, the area of contact varies directly as the square root of the quantity of water. Hence, *ceteris paribus*, the friction of a stream on its bed is proportioned to the square root of the quantity of water. But as stated above, the total energy of a stream is proportioned directly to the quantity of water; and the total energy is equal to the energy spent in friction, plus the energy spent in transportation. Whence it follows that if a stream change its quantity of water without changing its velocity or other accidents, the total energy will change at the same rate as the quantity of water; the energy spent in friction will change at a less rate, and the energy remaining for transportation will change at a greater rate.

Hence increase in quantity of water favors transportation in a degree that is greater than its simple ratio.

It follows as a corollary that the running water which carries the *débris* of a district loses power by subdivision toward its sources; and that, unless there is a compensating increment of declivity, the tributaries of a river will fail to supply it with the full load it is able to carry.

It is noteworthy also that the obstruction which vegetation opposes to transportation is especially effective in that it is applied at the infinitesimal sources of streams, where the force of the running water is least.

A stream which can transport *débris* of a given size, may be said to be *competent* to such *débris*. Since the maximum particles which streams are able to move are proportioned to the sixth powers of their velocities, competence depends on velocity. Velocity, in turn, depends on declivity and volume, and (inversely) on load.

In brief, the capacity of a stream for transportation is greater for fine *débris* than for coarse.

Its capacity for the transportation of a given kind of *débris* is enlarged in more than simple ratio by increase of declivity; and it is enlarged in more than simple ratio by increase of volume.

The competence of a stream for the transport of *débris* of a given fineness, is limited by a corresponding velocity.

The *rate* of transportation of *débris* of a given fineness may equal the capacity of the transporting stream, or it may be less. When it is less, it is always from the insufficiency of supply. The supply furnished by weathering is never available unless the degree of fineness of the *débris* brings it within the competence of the stream at the point of supply.

The chief point of supply is at the very head of the flowing water. The rain which falls on material that has been disintegrated by weathering, begins after it has saturated the immediate surface to flow off. But it forms a very thin sheet; its friction is great; its velocity is small; and it is competent to pick up only particles of exceeding fineness. If the material is heterogeneous, it discriminates and leaves the coarser particles. As the sheet moves on it becomes deeper and soon begins to gather itself into rills. As the deepening and concentration of water progresses, either its *capacity* increases and the load of fine particles is augmented, or, if fine particles are not in sufficient force, its *competence* increases, and larger ones are lifted. In either case the load is augmented, and as rill joins rill it steadily grows, until the accumulated water finally passes beyond the zone of disintegrated material.

The particles which the feeble initial currents are not competent to move, have to wait either until they are subdivided by the agencies of weathering, or until the deepening of the channels of the rills so far increases the declivities that the currents acquire the requisite velocity, or until some fiercer storm floods the ground with a deeper sheet of water.

Thus rate of transportation, as well as capacity for transportation, is favored by fineness of *débris*, by declivity, and by quantity of water. It is opposed chiefly by vegetation, which holds together that which is loosened by weathering, and shields it from the agent of transportation in the very place where that agent is weakest.

When the current of a stream gradually diminishes in its course—as for example in approaching the ocean—the capacity for transportation also diminishes; and so soon as the capacity becomes less than the load, precipitation begins—the coarser particles being deposited first.

Corrasion and Transportation.

Where a stream has all the load of a given degree of comminution which it is capable of carrying, the entire energy of the descending water and load is consumed in the translation of the water and load and there is none applied to corrasion. If it has an excess of load its velocity is thereby diminished so as to lessen its competence and a portion is dropped. If it has less than a full load it is in condition to receive more and it corrades its bottom.

A fully loaded stream is on the verge between corrasion and deposition. As will be explained in another place, it may wear the walls of its channel, but its wear of one wall will be accompanied by an addition to the opposite wall.

The work of transportation may thus monopolize a stream to the exclusion of corrasion, or the two works may be carried forward at the same time.

Corrasion and Declivity.

The rapidity of mechanical corrasion depends on the hardness, size, and number of the transient fragments, on the hardness of the rock-bed, and on the velocity of the stream. The blows which the moving fragments deal upon the stream-bed are hard in proportion as the fragments are large and the current is swift. They are most effective when the fragments are hard and the bed-rock is soft. They are more numerous and harder upon the bottom of the channel than upon the sides because of the constant tendency of the particles to sink in water. Their number is increased up to a certain limit by the increase of the load of the stream; but when the fragments become greatly crowded at the bottom of a stream their force is partially spent among themselves, and the bed-rock is in the same degree protected. For this reason, and because increase of load causes retardation of current, it is probable that the maximum work of corrasion is performed when the load is far within the transporting capacity.

The element of velocity is of double importance since it determines not only the speed, but to a great extent the size of the pestles which grind the rocks. The coefficients upon which it in turn depends, namely, declivity and quantity of water, have the same importance in corrasion that they have in transportation.

Let us suppose that a stream endowed with a constant volume of water, is at some point continuously supplied with as great a load as it is capable of carrying. For so great a distance as its velocity remains the same, it will neither corrade (downward) nor deposit, but will leave the grade of its bed unchanged. But if in its progress it reaches a place where a less declivity of bed gives a diminished velocity, its capacity for transportation will become less than the load and part of the load will be deposited. Or if in its progress it reaches a place where a greater declivity of bed gives an increased velocity, the capacity for transportation will become greater than the load and there will be corrasion of the bed. In this way a stream which has a supply of *débris* equal to its capacity, tends to build up the gentler slopes of its bed and cut away the steeper. It tends to establish a single, uniform grade.

Let us now suppose that the stream after having obliterated all the inequalities of the grade of its bed loses nearly the whole of its load. Its velocity is at once accelerated and vertical corrasion begins through its whole length. Since the stream has the same declivity and consequently the same velocity at all points, its capacity for corrasion is everywhere the same. Its rate of corrasion however will depend on the character of its bed. Where the rock is hard corrasion will be less rapid than where it is soft, and there will result inequalities of grade. But so soon as there is inequality of grade there is inequality of velocity, and inequality of capacity for corrasion; and where hard rocks have produced declivities, there the capacity for corrasion will be increased. The differentiation will proceed until the capacity for corrasion is everywhere proportioned to the resistance, and no further,—that is, until there is an equilibrium of action.

In general, we may say that a stream tends to equalize its work in all parts of its course. Its power inheres in its fall, and each foot of fall has the same power. When its work is to corrade and the resistance is unequal, it concentrates its energy where the resistance is great by crowding many feet of descent into a small space, and diffuses it where the resistance is small by using but a small fall in a long distance. When its work is to transport, the resistance is constant and the fall is evenly distributed by a uniform grade. When its work includes both transportation and corrasion, as in the usual case, its grades are somewhat unequal; and the inequality is greatest when the load is least.

It is to be remarked that in the case of most streams it is the flood stage which determines the grades of the channel. The load of detritus is usually greatest during the highest floods, and power is conferred so rapidly with increase of quantity of water, that in any event the influence of the stream during its high stage will overpower any influence which may have been exerted at a low stage. That relation of transportation to corrasion which subsists when the water is high will determine the grades of the water-way.

Declivity and Quantity of Water.

The conclusions reached in regard to the relations of corrasion and declivity depend on the assumption that the volume of the stream is the same throughout its whole course, and they consequently apply directly to such portions only of streams as are not increased by tributaries. A simple modification will include the more general case of branching streams.

Let us suppose that two equal streams which join, have the same declivity, and are both fully loaded with detritus of the same kind. If the channel down which they flow after union has also the same declivity, then the joint stream will have a greater velocity than its branches, its capacity for transportation will be more than adequate for the joint load, and it will corrade its bottom. By its corrasion it will diminish the declivity of its bed, and consequently its velocity and capacity for transportation, until its capacity is equal to the total capacity of its tributaries. When an equilibrium of action is reached, the declivity of the main stream will be less than the declivities of its branches. This result does not depend on the assumed equality of the branches, nor upon their number. It is equally true that in any river system which is fully supplied with material for transportation and which has attained a condition of equal action, the declivity of the smaller streams is greater than that of the larger.

Let us further suppose that two equal streams which join, are only partially loaded, and are corrading at a common rate a common rock. If the channel down which they flow after union is in the same rock and has the same declivity, then the joint river will have a greater velocity, and will corrade more rapidly than its branches By its more rapid corrasion it will diminish the declivity of its bed, until as before there is an equilibrium of action,—the branch having a greater declivity than the main. This result also is independent of the number and equality of the branches: and it is equally true that in any river system which traverses and corrades rock of equal resistance throughout, and which has reached a condition of equal action, the declivity of the smaller streams is greater than that of the larger.

In general we may say that, *ceteris paribus, declivity bears an inverse relation to quantity of water.*

(There is an apparent exception to this law, which is specially noteworthy in the sculpture of bad-lands, and will be described in another place).

[The material here deleted, p. 109-116, is not concerned with rivers, but it is, nevertheless a classic discussion of landscape erosion.]

Equal Action and Interdependence.

The tendency to equality of action, or to the establishment of a dynamic equilibrium, has already been pointed out in the discussion of the principles of erosion and of sculpture, but one of its most important results has not been noticed.

Of the main conditions which determine the rate of erosion, namely, quantity of running water, vegetation, texture of rock, and declivity, only the last is reciprocally determined by rate of erosion. Declivity originates in upheaval, or in the displacements of the earth's crust by which mountains and continents are formed; but it receives its distribution in detail in accordance with the laws of erosion. Wherever by reason of change in any of the conditions the erosive agents come to have locally exceptional power, that power is steadily diminished by the reaction of rate of erosion upon declivity. Every slope is a member of a series, receiving the water and the waste of the slope above it, and discharging its own water and waste upon the slope below. If one member of the series is eroded with exceptional rapidity, two things immediately result: first, the member above has its level of discharge lowered, and its rate of erosion is thereby increased; and second, the member below, being clogged by an exceptional load of detritus, has its rate of erosion diminished. The acceleration above and the retardation below, diminish the declivity of the member in which the disturbance originated; and as the declivity is reduced the rate of erosion is likewise reduced.

But the effect does not stop here. The disturbance which has been transferred from one member of the series to the two which adjoin it, is by them transmitted to others, and does not cease until it has reached the confines of the drainage basin. For in each basin all lines of drainage unite in a main line, and a disturbance upon any line is communicated through it to the main line and thence to every tributary. And as any member of

59

the system may influence all the others, so each member is influenced by every other. There is an interdependence throughout the system.

III.—SYSTEMS OF DRAINAGE.

To know well the drainage of a region two systems of lines must be ascertained—the drainage lines and the divides. The maxima of surface on which waters part, and the minima of surface in which waters join, are alike intimately associated with the sculpture of the earth and with the history of the earth's structure; and the student of either sculpture or history can well afford to study them. In the following pages certain conditions which affect their permanence and transformations are discussed.

THE STABILITY OF DRAINAGE LINES.

In corrasion the chief work is performed by the impact and friction of hard and heavy particles moved forward by running water. They are driven against all sides of the channel, but their tendency to sink in water brings them against the bottom with greater frequency and force than against the walls. If the rate of wear be rapid, by far the greater part of it is applied to the bottom, and the downward corrasion is so much more powerful than the lateral that the effect of the latter is practically lost, and the channel of the stream, without varying the position of its banks, carves its way vertically into the rock beneath. It is only when corrasion is exceedingly slow that the lateral wear becomes of importance; and hence as a rule the position of a stream bed is permanent.

The stability of drainage lines is especially illustrated in regions of displacement. If a mountain is slowly lifted athwart the course of a stream, the corrasion of the latter is accelerated by the increase of declivity, and instead of being turned aside by the uplift, it persistently holds its place and carves a channel into the mountain as the mountain rises. For example the deep clefts which intersect the Wasatch range owe their existence to the fact that at the time of the beginning of the uplift which has made the range, there were streams flowing across the line of its trend which were too powerful to be turned back by the growing ridge. The same relation has been shown by Professor Powell where the Green River crosses the uplift of the Uinta Mountains, and in many instances throughout the Rocky Mountain region it may be said that rivers have cut their way through mountains merely because they had established their courses before the inception of the displacement, and could not be diverted by an obstruction which was thrown up with the slowness of mountain uplift.

THE INSTABILITY OF DRAINAGE LINES.

The stability of waterways being the rule, every case of instability requires an explanation; and in the study of such exceptional cases there have been found a number of different methods by which the courses of streams are shifted. The more important will be noted.

Ponding.

When a mountain uplift crosses the course of a stream, it often happens that the rate of uplift is too rapid to be equaled by the corrasion of the stream, and the uprising rock becomes a dam over which the water still runs, but above which there is accumulated a pond or lake. Whenever this takes place, the pond catches all the *débris* of the upper course of the stream, and the water which overflows at the outlet having been relieved of its load is almost powerless for corrasion, and cannot continue its contest with the uplift unless the pond is silted up with detritus. As the uplift progresses the level of the pond is raised higher and higher, until finally it finds a new outlet at some other point. The original outlet is at once abandoned, and the new one becomes a permanent part of the course of the stream. As a rule it is only large streams which hold their courses while mountains rise; the smaller are turned back by ponding, and are usually diverted so as to join the larger.

The disturbances which divert drainage lines are not always of the sort which produce mountains. The same results may follow the most gentle undulations of plains. It required a movement of a few feet only to change the outlet of Lakes Michigan, Huron, and Superior from the Illinois River to the St. Clair; and in the tilting which turned Lake Winipeg from

FIG. 55.—The Crest of Mount Ellen, as seen from Ellen Peak.

FIG. 56.—The Crest of Mount Holmes.

the Mississippi to the Nelson no abrupt slopes were produced. If the entire history of the latter case were worked out, it would probably appear that the Saskatchewan River which rises in the Rocky Mountains beyond our northern boundary, was formerly the upper course of the Mississippi, and that when, by the rising of land in Minnesota or its sinking at the north, a barrier was formed, the water was ponded and Lake Winipeg came into existence. By the continuance of the movement of the land the lake was increased until it overflowed into Hudson's Bay; and by its further continuance, combined with the corrasion of the outlet, the lake has been again diminished. When eventually the lake disappears the revolution will be complete, and the Saskatchewan will flow directly to Hudson's Bay, as it once flowed directly to the Gulf of Mexico. (See the "*Physical Features of the Valley of the Minnesota River*," by General G. K. Warren.)

Planation.

It has been shown in the discussion of the relations of transportation and corrasion that downward wear ceases when the load equals the capacity for transportation. Whenever the load reduces the downward corrasion to little or nothing, lateral corrasion becomes relatively and actually of importance. The first result of the wearing of the walls of a stream's channel is the formation of a flood-plain. As an effect of momentum the current is always swiftest along the outside of a curve of the channel, and it is there that the wearing is performed; while at the inner side of the curve the current is so slow that part of the load is deposited. In this way the width of the channel remains the same while its position is shifted, and every part of the valley which it has crossed in its shiftings comes to be covered by a deposit which does not rise above the highest level of the water. The surface of this deposit is hence appropriately called the *flood-plain* of the stream. The deposit is of nearly uniform depth, descending no lower than the bottom of the water-channel, and it rests upon a tolerably even surface of the rock or other material which is corraded by the stream. The process of carving away the rock so as to produce an even surface, and

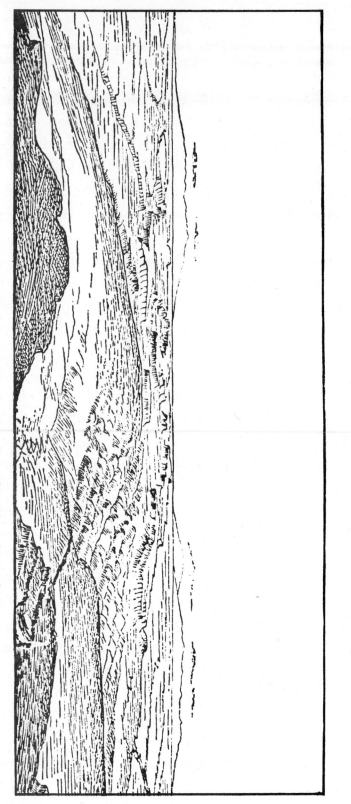

FIG. 57.—General view of the Plateaus lying East of the Henry Mountains.

64

at the same time covering it with an alluvial deposit, is the process of *planation*.

It sometimes happens that two adjacent streams by extending their areas of planation eat through the dividing ridge and join their channels. The stream which has the higher surface at the point of contact, quickly abandons the lower part of its channel and becomes a branch of the other, having shifted its course by planation

The slopes of the Henry Mountains illustrate the process in a peculiarly striking manner. The streams which flow down them are limited in their rate of degradation at both ends. At their sources, erosion is opposed by the hardness of the rocks; the trachytes and metamorphics of the mountain tops are carved very slowly. At their mouths, they discharge into the Colorado and the Fremont, and cannot sink their channels more rapidly than do those rivers. Between the mountains and the rivers, they cross rocks which are soft in comparison with the trachyte, but they can deepen their channels with no greater rapidity than at their ends. The grades have adjusted themselves accordingly. Among the hard rocks of the mountains the declivities are great, so as to give efficiency to the eroding water. Among the sedimentary rocks of the base they are small in comparison, the chief work of the streams being the transportation of the trachyte *débris*. So greatly are the streams concerned in transportation, and so little in downward corrasion (outside the trachyte region), that their grades are almost unaffected by the differences of rock texture, and they pass through sandstone and shale with nearly the same declivity.

The rate of downward corrasion being thus limited by extraneous conditions, and the instrument of corrasion—the *débris* of the hard trachyte—being efficient, lateral corrasion is limited only by the resistance which the banks of the streams oppose. Where the material of the banks is a firm sandstone, narrow flood-plains are formed; and where it is a shale, broad ones. In the Gray Cliff and Vermilion Cliff sandstones flat-bottomed cañons are excavated; but in the great shale beds broad valleys are opened, and the flood-plains of adjacent streams coalesce to form continuous plains. The broadest plains are as a rule carved from the thickest beds of shale, and these are found at the top of the Jura-Trias and near the base of the Cretaceous. Where the streams from the mountains cross the Blue Gate, the Tununk, or the Flaming Gorge shale at a favorable angle, a plain is the result.

The plain which lies at the southern and western bases of Mount Hillers is carved chiefly from the Tununk shale (see Figure 27). The plain sloping eastward from Mount Pennell (Figure 36) is carved from the Blue Gate and Tununk shales. The Lewis Creek plain, which lies at the western base of Mount Ellen, is formed from the Blue Gate, Tununk, and Masuk shales, and the planation which produced it has so perfectly truncated the Tununk and Blue Gate sandstones that their outcrops cannot be traced (Figures 61, 39, and 42). The plain which truncates the Crescent arch (Figure 49) is carved in chief part from the Flaming Gorge shale. Toward the east it is limited by the outcrops of the Henry's Fork conglomerate, but toward the mountain it cuts across the edge of the same conglomerate and extends over Tununk shale to the margin of the trachyte.

The streams which made these plains and which maintain them, accomplish their work by a continual shifting of their channels; and where the plains are best developed they employ another method of shifting—a method which in its proper logical order must be treated in the discussion of alluvial cones, but which is practically combined in the Henry Mountains with the method of planation. The supply of detritus derived from the erosion of the trachyte is not entirely constant. Not only is more carried out in one season than another and in one year than another, but the work is accomplished in part by sudden storms which create great floods and as suddenly cease. It results from this irregularity that the chan-

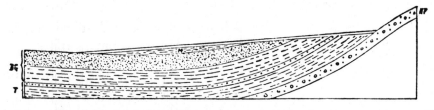

FIG. 61.—Cross-section of the Lewis Creek Plain. M, Masuk Shale. BG, Blue-Gate Group. T, Tununk Group. HF, Henry's Fork conglomerate. Scale, 1 inch = 4,000 feet.

nels are sometimes choked by *débris,* and that by the choking of the channels the streams are turned aside to seek new courses upon the general
plain.   The abandoned courses remain plainly marked, and one who looks
down on them from some commanding eminence can often trace out many
stages in the history of the drainage.   Where a series of streams emerge
from adjacent mountain gorges upon a common plain, their shiftings bring
about frequent unions and separations, and produce a variety of combinations.

The accompanying sketch, Figure 62, is not from nature, but it serves to
illustrate the character of the changes.   The streams which issue from the
mountain gorges a and b join and flow to $z;$ while that which issues at c
flows alone to x.   An abandoned channel, n, shows that the stream from b
was formerly united with that from c, and flowed to $x;$ and another channel,
m, shows that it has at some time maintained an independent course to y.
By such shiftings streams are sometimes changed from one drainage system
to another; the hypothetical courses, x, y, and z, may lead to different rivers, and to different oceans.

FIG. 62.—Ideal sketch to illustrate the Shifting of waterways on a slope of Planation.

An instance occurs on the western flank of the mountains. One of the principal heads of Pine Alcove Creek rises on the south slope of Mount Ellen and another on the northwest slope of Mount Pennell. The two unite and flow southward to the Colorado River. They do not now cross an area of planation, but at an earlier stage of the degradation they did; and the portions of that plain which survive, indicate by the direction of their slopes that one or both of the streams may have then discharged its water into Lewis Creek, which runs northward to the Fremont River.

As the general degradation of the region progresses the streams and their plains sink lower, and eventually each plain is sunk completely through the shale whose softness made it possible. So soon as the streams reach harder rock their lateral corrasion is checked, and they are no longer free to change their ways. Wherever they chance to run at that time, there they stay and carve for themselves cañons. Portions of the deserted plains remain between the cañons, and having a durable capping of trachyte gravel are long preserved. Such stranded fragments abound on the slopes of the mountains, and in them one may read many pages of the history of the degradation. They form tabular hills with sloping tops and even profiles. The top of each hill is covered with a uniform layer of gravel, beneath which the solid rock is smoothly truncated. The slope of the hill depends on the grade of the ancient stream, and is independent of the hardness and dip of the strata.

The illustration represents a *hill of planation* on the north slope of Mount Ellsworth. It is built of the Gray Cliff sandstone and Flaming Gorge shale, inclined at angles varying from 25° to 45°; but notwithstanding their variety of texture and dip the edges of the strata are evenly cut away, so that their upper surface constitutes a plane. The stream which performed this truncation afterward cut deeper into the strata and carved the lower table which forms the foreground of the sketch. It has now abandoned this plain also and flows through a still deeper channel on the opposite side of the hill.

68

FIG. 63.—A Hill of Planation.

The phenomena of planation are further illustrated in the region which lies to the northwest of the Henry Mountains. Tantalus and Temple Creeks, rising under the edge of the Aquarius Plateau, transport the trachyte of the plateau across the region of the Waterpocket Flexure to the Fremont River. Their flood-plains are not now of great extent, but when their drainage lines ran a few hundred feet higher they appear to have carved into a single plain a broad exposure of the Flaming Gorge shale, which then lay between the Waterpocket and Blue Gate Flexures.

[A discussion of river terraces, alluvial cones, and the effect of structure on divide stability, p. 126-137, was deleted.]

CONSEQUENT AND INCONSEQUENT DRAINAGE.

If a series of sediments accumulated in an ocean or lake be subjected to a system of displacements while still under water, and then be converted to dry land by elevation *en masse* or by the retirement of the water, the rains which fall on them will inaugurate a drainage system perfectly conformable with the system of displacements. Streams will rise along the crest of each anticlinal, will flow from it in the direction of the steepest dip, will unite in the synclinals, and will follow them lengthwise. The axis of each synclinal will be marked by a watercourse; the axis of each anticlinal by a watershed. Such a system is said to be *consequent* on the structure.

If however a rock series is affected by a system of displacements after the series has become continental, it will have already acquired a system of waterways, and *provided the displacements are produced slowly* the waters will not be diverted from their accustomed ways. The effect of local elevation will be to stimulate local corrasion, and each river that crosses a line of uplift will inch by inch as the land rises deepen its channel and valorously maintain its original course. It will result that the directions of the drainage lines will be independent of the displacements. Such a drainage system is said to be *antecedent* to the structure.

But if in the latter case the displacements are produced rapidly the drainage system will be rearranged and will become consequent to the structure. It has frequently happened that displacements formed with moderate rapidity have given rise to a drainage system of mixed character in which the courses of the larger streams are antecedent and those of the smaller are consequent.

There is a fourth case. Suppose a rock series that has been folded and eroded to be again submerged, and to receive a new accumulation of unconforming sediments. Suppose further that it once more emerges and that the new sediments are eroded from its surface. Then the drainage system will have been given by the form of the upper surface of the superior strata, but will be independent of the structure of the inferior series, into which it will descend vertically as the degradation progresses. Such a drainage system is said to be *superimposed by sedimentation* upon the structure of the older series of strata.

Fifth. The drainage of an alluvial cone or of a delta is independent of the structure of the bed-rock beneath; and if in the course of time erosion takes the place of deposition and the alluvial formation is cut through, the drainage system which is acquired by the rocks beneath is not consequent upon their structure but is *superimposed by alluviation.*

Sixth. The drainage of a district of planation is independent of the structure of the rock from which it is carved; and when in the progress of degradation the beds favorable to lateral corrasion are destroyed and the waterways become permanent, their system may be said to be *superimposed by planation.*

In brief, systems of drainage, in their relation to structure, are

    (A) *consequent*

        (a) by emergence, when the displacements are subaqueous, and

        (b) by sudden displacement;

    (B) *antecedent*; and

    (C) *superimposed*

        (a) by sedimentation, or subaqueous deposition,

        (b) by alluviation, or subaërial deposition, and

        (c) by planation.

THE DRAINAGE OF THE HENRY MOUNTAINS

is consequent on the laccolitic displacements. The uplifting of a laccolite, like the upbuilding of a volcanic cone, is an event of so rapid progress that the corrasion of a stream bed cannot keep pace with it. We do not know that the site of the mountains was dry land at the time of their elevation; but if it was, then whatever streams crossed it were obstructed and turned from their courses. If it was not, there were no preëxistent waterways, and the new ones, formed by the first rain which fell upon the domes of strata, radiated from the crests in all directions. The result in either case would be the same, and we cannot determine from the present drainage system whether the domes were lifted from the bed of the Tertiary lake or arose after its subsidence.

But while the drainage of the Henry Mountains is consequent as a whole, it is not consequent in all its details, and the character of its partial inconsequence is worthy of examination.

Let us begin with the simplest case. The drainage system of Mount Ellsworth is more purely consequent than any other with which I am acquainted. In the accompanying chart the point c marks the crest of the Ellsworth dome; the inner circle represents the line of maximum dip of the

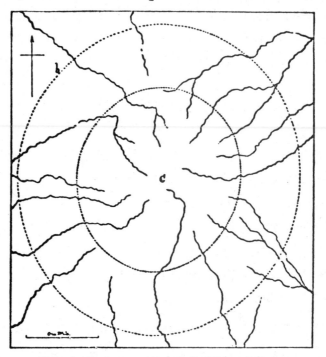

Fig. 71.—Drainage system of the Ellsworth Arch.

arching strata and the outer circle the limit of the disturbance. It will be seen that all the waterways radiate from the crest and follow closely the directions in which the strata incline. At a the Ellsworth arch touches that of Mount Holmes and at b that of Mount Hillers; and the effect of the compound inclination is to modify the directions of a few of the waterways.

Turning now to Mount Holmes, we find that its two domes are not
equally respected by the drainage lines. The crest of the Greater arch (see
Figure 72) is the center of a radiating system, but the crest of the Lesser

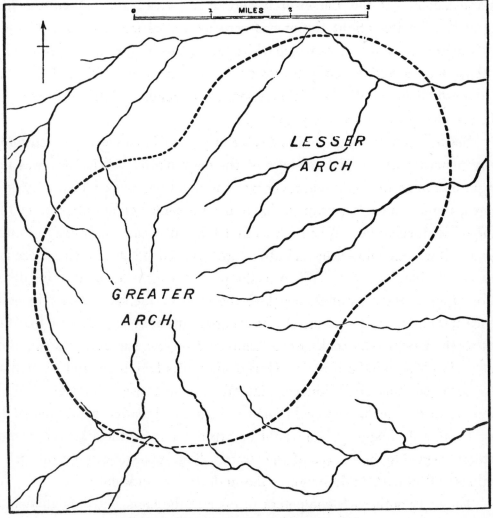

Fig. 72.—Drainage system of the Holmes Arches.

arch is not; and waterways arising on the Greater traverse the Lesser from
side to side. More than this, a waterway after following the margin of the
Lesser arch turns toward it and penetrates the flank of the arch for some
distance. In a word, the drainage of the Greater arch is consequent on the
structure, while the drainage of the Lesser arch is inconsequent.

There are at least two ways in which this state of affairs may have
arisen.

First, the Greater arch may have been lifted so long before the Lesser that its waterways were carved too deeply to be diverted by the gentle flexure of the latter. The drainage of the Lesser would in that case be classed as antecedent. If the Lesser arch were first formed and carved, the lifting of the Greater might throw a stream across its summit; but it could not initiate the waterways which skirt the slopes of the Lesser, especially if those slopes were already furrowed by streams which descended them. If the establishment of the drainage system depended on the order of uplift, the Greater arch is surely the older.

Second, the drainage of the Lesser arch may have been imposed upon it by planation at a very late stage of the degradation. Whatever was the origin of the arches, and whatever was the depth of cover which they sustained, the Greater is certain to have been a center of drainage from the time of its formation. When it was first lifted it became a drainage center because it was an eminence; and afterward it remained an eminence because it was a drainage center. When in the progress of the denudation its dikes were exposed, their hardness checked the wear of the summit and its eminence became more pronounced. It was perhaps at about this time that the last of the Cretaceous rocks were removed from the summits and slopes of the two arches and the Flaming Gorge shale was laid bare, and so soon as this occurred the conditions for lateral corrasion were complete. With trachyte in the peaks and shale upon the slopes planation would naturally result, and a drainage system would be arranged about the dikes as a center without regard to the curves of the strata. The subsequent removal of the shale would impart its drainage to the underlying sandstones.

Either hypothesis is competent to explain the facts, but the data do not warrant the adoption of one to the exclusion of the other. The waterways of the Lesser arch may be either antecedent, or superimposed by planation. The Greater arch may have been the first to rise or the last.

The drainage of Mount Hillers is consequent to the main uplift and to the majority of the minor, but to the Pulpit arch it is inconsequent. In this case there is no question that the arch has been truncated by planation. (Figure 73.) The Hillers dome, rising five times as high as the Pulpit, became the center of drainage for the cluster, and the trachyte-laden streams which it sent forth were able to pare away completely the lower arch while it was still unprotected by the hardness of its nucleus. The foot-plain of Mount Hillers, which extends unbroken to the outcrop of the Henry's Fork conglomerate, is continued on several lines across the Pulpit arch, although in the intervals the central area is deeply excavated. The planation stage is just completed, and an epoch of fixed waterways is inaugurated.

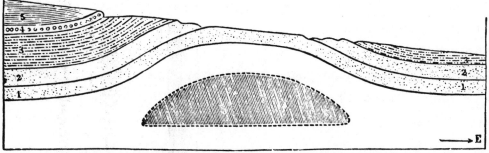

Fig. 73.—Cross-section of the Pulpit Arch, showing its truncation.

The drainage of Mount Pennell is consequent in regard to the main uplift, but inconsequent to some of the minor. A stream which rises on the north flank not merely runs across one of the upper series of laccolites,—a companion to the Sentinel,—but has cut into it and divided it nearly to the base. It is probable that the position of the waterway was fixed by planation, but no remnant of the plain was seen.

Too little is known of the structure of the central area of Mount Ellen to assert its relation to the drainage. About its base there are five laccolites which have lost all or nearly all their cover, and each of these is a local center of drainage, avoided by the streams which head in the mountain crest. Four others have been laid bare at a few points only, and these are each crossed by one or two streams from higher levels. The remainder are not exposed at all, and their arches are crossed by numerous parallel streams. The Crescent arch is freshly truncated by planation, and the Dana and Maze bear proof that they have at some time been truncated. The laccolites which stand highest with reference to the general surface are exempt from cross-drainage, and the arches which lie low are completely overrun.

If we go back in imagination to a time when the erosion of the mount-

75

ain was so little advanced that the stream-beds were three thousand feet
higher than they now are, we may suppose that very little trachyte was
laid bare. As the surface was degraded and a few laccolites were exposed,
it would probably happen that some of the then-existing streams would be
so placed as to run across the trachyte. But being unarmed as yet by the
débris of similar material they would ·corrade it very slowly; and the
adjoining streams having only shale to encounter, would so far outstrip
them as eventually to divert them by the process of "abstraction". In this
way the first-bared laccolites might be freed from cross-drainage and permitted to acquire such radiating systems of waterways as we find them to
possess. At a later stage when trachyte was exposed at many points and
all streams were loaded with its waste, the power to corrade was increased,
and the lower-lying laccolites could not turn aside the streams which overran them.

The work of planation is so frequently seen about the flanks of the
Henry Mountains that there seems no violence in referring all the cross-
drainage of lateral arches to its action; and if that is done the history of
the erosion of the mountains takes the following form :

When the laccolites were intruded, the mounds which they uplifted
either rose from the bed of a lake or else turned back all streams which
crossed their sites ; and in either case they established upon their flanks a
new and "consequent" set of waterways. The highest mounds became
centers of drainage, and sent their streams either across or between the
lower. All the streams of the disturbed region rose within it and flowed
outward. The degradation of the mounds probably began before the
uplift was complete, but of this there is no evidence. As it proceeded the
convex forms of the mounds were quickly obliterated and concave profiles
were substituted. The rocks which were first excavated were not uniform
in texture, but they were all sedimentary and were soft as compared to the
trachyte. The Tertiary and probably the Upper Cretaceous were removed
from the summits before any of the igneous rocks were brought to light,
and during their removal the tendency of divides to permanence kept the
drainage centers or maxima of surface at substantially the same points.
When at length the trachyte was reached its hardness introduced a new

factor. The eminences which contained it were established more firmly as maxima, and their rate of degradation was checked. With the checking of summit degradation and the addition of trachyte to the transported material, planation began upon the flanks, and by its action the whole drainage has been reformed. One by one the lower laccolites are unearthed, and each one adds to the complexity and to the permanence of the drainage.

If the displacements were completed before the erosion began, the mountains were then of greater magnitude than at any later date. Before the igneous nuclei were laid bare and while sedimentary rocks only were subject to erosion, the rate of degradation was more rapid than it has been since the hardness and toughness of the trachyte have opposed it. If the surrounding plain has been worn away at a uniform rate, the height of the mountains (above the plain) must have first diminished to a minimum and afterward increased. The minimum occurred at the beginning of the erosion of the trachyte, and at that time the mountains may even have been reduced to the rank of hills. They owe their present magnitude, not to the uplifting of the land in Middle Tertiary time, but to the contrast between the incoherence of the sandstones and shales of the Mesozoic series and the extreme durability of the laccolites which their destruction has laid bare. And if the waste of the plain shall continue at a like uniform rate in the future, it is safe to prophesy that the mountains will for a while continue to increase in relative altitude. The phase which will give the maximum resistance to degradation has been reached in none of the mountains, except perhaps Mount Hillers. In Mount Ellen the laccolites of the upper zone only have been denuded; the greater masses which underlie them will hold their place more stubbornly. The main bodies of Mounts Ellsworth, Holmes, and Pennell are unassailed, and the present prominence of their forms has been accomplished simply by the valor of their skirmish lines of dikes and spurs. In attaching to the least of the peaks the name of my friend Mr. Holmes, I am confident that I commemorate his attainments by a monument which will be more conspicuous to future generations and races than it is to the present.

VOLUME XL   NUMBER 6

THE

JOURNAL OF GEOLOGY

4 August-September 1932

STREAMS AND THEIR SIGNIFICANCE

DOUGLAS JOHNSON

Columbia University

ABSTRACT

In the following pages there is presented (*a*) a review of the classification of streams according to stages of development, in which the criteria for discriminating different stages are discussed, and some misconceptions regarding stream behavior are corrected. (*b*) The classification of streams according to genesis is then considered, and an attempt made to define with greater precision certain terms regarding the significance of which differences of opinion appear to exist. (*c*) The classifications of streams with respect to genetically associated structures, and (*d*) with respect to structures not concerned with the origin of the streams, are more concisely presented, as is also (*e*) the classification of streams with respect to past changes of level. (*f*) Drainage patterns are briefly referred to, but the discussion of this subject is left to a companion paper subsequent to this article in the *Journal of Geology*.

INTRODUCTION

The members of a complex drainage system may record many events in the past geologic history of a region, some recent and trivial, others ancient and of major importance. It is, therefore, important that the student of geomorphology should give more than passing attention to streams and their significance. The literature of the subject is voluminous, and any adequate treatment of its contents would require a comprehensive volume. The purpose of this paper is much more modest. Instead of reviewing and analyzing the progress of our knowledge concerning streams and their behavior, and in the light of such review proposing a full and consistent treatment of the subject, it is intended in these pages to set forth quite briefly some general conceptions which the writer has been in the habit of placing

481

before his students each year as a sort of introduction to the more detailed study of streams. The reader will, of course, recognize in what follows much that is old and familiar; for the conceptions of stream action held today represent the accumulated knowledge of a long past in which the names of Playfair, Philippson, Powell, Davis, and others are landmarks indicating specific stages of progress in our understanding of the work of running water. But if most of what I have to say is the common heritage of present-day students, it is hoped that the manner of its presentation, the comments on disputed points, and certain original contributions will render the whole of some help to others who would know our rivers better. The prevalence of certain misconceptions in the literature of geology and geography suggests that even the mere restatement of some fundamental principles of stream development will not be out of place.

THE CLASSIFICATION OF STREAMS

One may classify streams according to a variety of different principles. Depending on the purpose in view, the classification may be according to (a) stage of development in the cycle, (b) method of origin, or genesis, (c) relation to genetically associated structures, (d) relation to foreign structures, (e) relation to past changes of level, (f) pattern of the drainage lines. Given a hundred streams, all might find an appropriate place under most of these six methods of grouping; but in each case any particular stream might find itself grouped with an entirely different set of individuals. For the methods of classification, while indirectly related in some cases, are in their essence mutually independent.

STAGES OF STREAM DEVELOPMENT

Classification of streams according to stages of development into young, sub-mature, mature, late-mature, and old streams is a common procedure, but there is some disagreement regarding the significance of each age term, and regarding the essential criteria for distinguishing different stages and substages of development. The trouble arises in part from early failure to distinguish clearly between the stage of the landmass being dissected by streams, and the stage of the streams accomplishing that dissection. A certain part

79

of the Allegheny Plateau in West Virginia has been called a "mature region." The term is ambiguous, for the "region" consists, as far as surface form is concerned, of the slopes of countless narrow, steep-sided valleys, many of which are still in their youth. But the stage of the plateau, the thing being dissected, may properly be designated as mature. It will help toward clarity of understanding and expression if one remembers that we may have young valleys in a mature plateau, and mature valleys in a young plateau, just as well as mature valleys in a mature plateau, or young valleys in a young plateau. In other words, there is no necessary relation between stage of landmass dissection and stage of streams dissecting that landmass.

It will be noted that I have used the terms "young valley" and "young stream" interchangeably. This is because the stream, which consists of both water and waste streaming toward the sea, cannot profitably be treated as independent of the depression caused by the streaming water and waste. Depressions not due to stream action, such for example as synclinal troughs and fault-block basins, are better classified as basins and not as valleys, although the geomorphologist recognizes that the uninitiated will continue to speak of the "Great Valley" of California. This will not worry him any more than it worries the astronomer when the man in the street continues to speak of the planets as "stars," but refuses to think of our sun as a star.

Criteria for discriminating stages.—The criteria for discriminating stages of stream development are matters of much importance. When two textbooks can figure exactly similar valleys, one labeled "young valley" and the other "mature valley," it behooves the student to give thought to this problem. It has seemed to the writer that there would be less disagreement in current usage if greater emphasis were placed upon the outstanding events of a stream's life-history.

What are these events? The elimination of lakes, by the combined processes of deposition of sediment to raise the floor of the basin and down-cutting of the outlet to lower the lake level, takes place rather rapidly under normal conditions. The stream now changes from a chain of beadlike expanses of water connected by segments of thread-

80

like current, to a continuous thread of water. Falls and rapids are the opposites of lakes; for just as the latter occur where the longitudinal profile slopes too steeply upstream, so falls and rapids occur where this profile slopes too steeply downstream. The elimination of these last irregularities of the profile normally proceeds more slowly than the elimination of lakes, while new falls and rapids may develop as streams cut rapidly downward into diverse rock structures. Yet the elimination of falls and rapids may for the most part be accomplished before the slower down-cutting of later time brings the stream to the perfect profile next to be discussed.

Significance of the profile of equilibrium.—The establishment of the profile of equilibrium, when approximately perfect balance is reached between the capacity of the stream for work and the work given the stream to do, is beyond all question the most important event in the life-history of any stream. It is comparable in importance to the passing of adolescence in man, the most important event in the life of the human being. And just as in man adolescence marks the transition from youth to maturity, so we may best accept the establishment of the profile of equilibrium in a stream as marking the passage from its youth to its maturity. Prior to this time the proportion of down-cutting to lateral corrasion has been great; so great in fact that the effect of lateral corrasion is commonly not prominently registered in the valley form, unless it be as a greater or less asymmetry of valley slopes. Hereafter the proportion of down-cutting to lateral corrasion will be so small that the effect of the former may escape attention, while lateral corrasion becomes apparent in the opening out of a valley floor of progressively increasing breadth.

The contrast in conditions just sketched has been responsible for a widespread misconception, frequently encountered in the literature in some such form as the following: "The stream now ceases to cut down, and begins to cut laterally." While the first part of the quoted statement may be true temporarily, it is not true as a generality, and hence is misleading. But the error involved in the phrase "and begins to cut laterally" implies a more serious and fundamental misconception of stream processes. Lateral cutting is at a maximum during the early stages of stream development, when the current is

81

most vigorous and provided with the most effective cutting tools. Normally the lateral migration of a stream will always exceed its vertical incision, in youth as well as in maturity and old age. This will be true, not only for the outsides of particular bends, but for the stream course as a whole, due to the fact that the bends, like meanders, sweep downstream. Exceptional chasms, where for special reasons and for a short time vertical cutting undoubtedly has exceeded lateral cutting, should not blind us to the more usual conditions. Neither should the fact that the stream in Figure 1 has a narrow, steep-sided valley cause us to lose sight of the fact that in

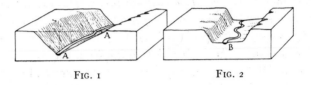

FIG. 1   FIG. 2

sinking its course from *A* to *A'* it has cut laterally twice as great a distance as it has cut vertically; and has cut laterally much more than stream *B*, Figure 2, which possesses an open valley floor.

It is the *proportion* of vertical to lateral cutting which undergoes such a far-reaching change when the stream reaches equilibrium. Lateral cutting is henceforth slightly less effective than formerly; but vertical cutting is enormously reduced. This is why the effect of lateral cutting now first becomes prominent in the production of a relatively flat valley floor. The beginnings of such a floor, with its floodplain cover, afford evidence that the profile of equilibrium has at last been established.

Significance of valley width.—What is the next important change in the river's history? Obviously it comes when the valley floor has been broadened until the stream can freely develop meanders appropriate to its volume. We express this by saying that the valley has acquired a width equal to the width of its normal meander belt, which in turn is ordinarily from ten to twenty times the width of the stream itself. From now on the stream is free to meander at will on its floodplain; but the meander belt as a whole is restrained from shifting its position freely until continued lateral corrasion has given the valley a width several times greater than the width of the meander belt. With the achievement of this condition the last great change in the river's history has taken place. The meander belt may now shift freely over a broad floodplain, the valley may widen indefinitely, the valley walls may become more gently sloping, the shifting stream may continue slowly to consume its floodplain and to reduce the level of its valley floor, at the same time depositing alluvium at the new levels; but in the normal course of events no such striking changes will again take place as characterized its earlier history. The river has entered the last stage of its evolution, old age.

When attempting to compare valley widths with widths of meander belts as a basis for discriminating stages of development, one encounters the practical difficulty that for certain reasons some streams on broad floodplains do not meander. In such a case it is perhaps fair to estimate the appropriate meander belt as being approximately fifteen times the width of the stream, and to use this imaginary meander belt in the desired comparisons. Experience shows that while the width of a given stream may vary within fairly wide limits, and the meander belt of a given stream similarly varies in width, there is normally an approximate relation between stream volume and stream width, and between stream width and width of meander belt, which enables us to make comparisons, only roughly approximate to be sure, yet sufficient for the purpose in view. One cannot give precise criteria for discriminating stages of development, nor divide stages by clean-cut partitions, whether dealing with a river or with men. Passage from one stage to another is normally a gradual transition, and approximate criteria serve the purpose of making approximate divisions and subdivisions.

"*Misfit streams.*"—From the brief analysis given in the preceding pages it should be evident that there is no limit to the size of valley which a given stream may develop for itself. Given sufficient time, even a small stream may acquire a valley of the greatest width. If the small stream happens to be located on a broad belt of weak rock, it may acquire a valley of enormous proportions, while a great river traversing resistant rocks near by still flows in a narrow gorge. Thus time and rock resistance are two factors which, quite apart from stream volume, play a major rôle in determining valley widths. There is no such thing as a valley's being "too broad to have been

formed by the stream which occupies it." Yet one may count by
scores the pages in the literature of geology and geography on which
this misconception appears in print. Not infrequently doubtful
drainage modifications are predicated on the erroneous assumption
that a very small stream cannot have a very broad valley, unless
that valley was carved for it by some great stream which has since
disappeared. The term "misfit stream" is often wrongly applied to
a small stream in a large valley, whereas it can properly apply only
to streams the meanders of which are obviously out of harmony—

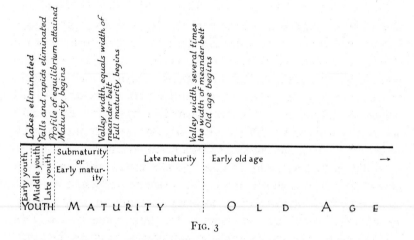

FIG. 3

whether too small or too large—with the meanders of the valley itself, or with meander scarps preserved in the valley wall.

Meander scarps, where these are found with sufficiently large arc
of curvature to prove clearly that they represent the dimensions of
former stream meanders, and not merely curved cliffs cut during the
down-valley migration of shifting bends of smaller size, give us our
best indication of former stream volumes. Where these are lacking,
one cannot reason directly from size of valley to size of former
stream, although one may under certain conditions make deductions
based on a comparison of sizes of valleys and sizes of streams where
erosion has operated for the same period of time on rocks of the same
resistance.

Duration of stages.—If we represent the ideal life-history of any
river by a horizontal line as in Figure 3, we may sum up the salient

events in such history, and show their significance as criteria for distinguishing stages of development in the manner portrayed in that figure. It is intended to represent maturity as enduring longer than the stage of youth, and old age as a much longer stage than maturity; but the limits of the page make it impossible to give these differences proper relative values. In terms of percentages of the whole life-history of a river, one might assign 5 per cent to youth, 25 per cent to maturity, and 70 per cent to old age, although this at best is but a scientific guess, designed merely to emphasize the fact that stream evolution proceeds rapidly in its early stages, ever more and more slowly in its later stages.

THE GENESIS OF STREAMS

An anlysis of stream development shows that the various causes of valley locations may be reduced to this simple formula: The position of every valley is determined by inequalities of surface slope, or by inequalities of rock resistance. Valleys falling into the first group might all be termed consequent, those of the second group might all be called subsequent. But such a simple classification does not reveal all that we need to know about the genesis of streams. Hence, further subdivisions have been suggested from time to time, the terminology most employed for this particular classification being that devised by Davis. Not all the terms proposed by him filled a constant need, even in his own writings, and one hears little today of "antogenetic consequents," "complex and compound drainage," and certain other terms appearing in his earlier papers. But some of the concepts elucidated by Davis are indispensable to the student of geomorphology, and no one has ever devised a more acceptable terminology than that proposed by him. We may review the genetic classification of streams and their valleys, making brief comments on some of the terms employed.

Consequent streams.—A stream which has its course determined by, or which is "consequent upon," the initial slope of the land is called a "consequent" stream. In defining such a stream it is fatal to omit the adjective qualifying the noun "slope," as is sometimes done; for merely to say that a stream is "determined by the slope of the land" does little more than tell us that water runs downhill.

85

Even to specify the "general slope" or "regional slope" is insufficient, since several classes of streams of different origin would be included by so broad a term. One must make clear the fact that by consequent stream is meant a stream which flows or did flow down the initial slope, the original slope, the constructional slope, of the land. If the streams actually take their rise on the initial or constructional slope, as, for example, the radial streams of a volcano or streams born on a newly uplifted coastal plain, they are called "initial consequents." If they are merely extensions, across the initial slope, of streams already existing on an earlier land surface, as in the case of a river in an oldland area flowing out across a recently elevated coastal plain, they are called "extended consequents."[1]

Subsequent streams.—A stream which develops by headward erosion along a belt of weak rock is called a "subsequent" stream. The weak rock belt may be the outcrop of some nonresistant stratum, a dike which is less resistant than the country rock penetrated by it, the crushed zone along a fault, or the weathered zone bordering a joint plane. Notwithstanding the excellent authority for such usage, it is undoubtedly confusing and misleading to define the term "subsequent" as meaning following after, or developed after, the consequent stream. If "subsequent" be employed in geomorphology in the sense of "later in time," it fails to designate any single type of stream, but applies equally to all the other genetic types mentioned below; for all of these normally develop after the consequent drainage is established. The student will best get the conception of the originator of the term, and will keep essential distinctions more clearly in mind, if he will think of a subsequent stream as one which follows along or is *sequent* to the underlying or *sub*structure.

Obsequent streams.—A stream which flows in a direction opposite that of the consequent drainage is called an "obsequent" stream (opposite consequent = op(posite con)sequent = obsequent). The

[1] Miss Charlotte Preuss, graduate student in physiography at Columbia University, has called my attention to the fact that the term "extended consequent" is ambiguous, since it may be taken to imply that the stream was a consequent on the oldland, and has merely been extended across the coastal plain. The objection is valid, since a subsequent or any other genetic type of stream on the oldland may be extended across the newly raised sea-bottom; but I have not found a term which seemed to me sufficiently good to replace the one already in use.

term has occasionally been applied to the "inverted stream" developing after capture; but since all other genetic types of streams, as well as consequent streams, may suffer capture, such usage introduces confusion into what should be, and may be, a clear and logical terminology.

It need hardly be pointed out that, when obsequent streams are said to flow "in the direction opposite that of the consequent drainage," the student must understand that the phrase "in the same area" is by implication a part of the definition. On a slightly tilted fault block mountain (Fig. 4) there is normally a series of long consequent streams, *ab*, descending the gentle backslope of the block. A series of shorter streams, *ac*, flow in the opposite direction, down the

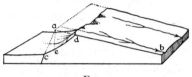

FIG. 4

fault face; but these are not obsequent streams. They are likewise consequents—consequent on the initial slope of the fault scarp. Later, when these steeper, shorter consequents have pushed the divide, *d* (between them and the opposing consequents), some distance down the backslope of the range, their lengthened upper courses, *ed*, will be truly obsequent, since they will flow in a direction opposite to that in which the consequent drainage "in the same area" formerly flowed.

Resequent streams.—A stream which flows in a direction identical with that of the consequent drainage, but which develops at a lower level than the initial slope, is called a "resequent" stream. We may think of such a stream as having "retaken a consequent direction" (hence re-consequent = re(con)sequent = resequent). The essential elements in the conception of this stream type are the "renewed" development of drainage in a consequent direction, after other drainage has intervened for a time, and the fact that this renewed development takes place at a *lower horizon* than that on which the drainage initially developed. It is, therefore, not quite sufficient to say that resequent streams are those which flow in the direction of the consequent drainage; for such a definition is broad enough to include both consequents and resequents. Since consequents themselves may persist in initial courses while cutting down to lower levels, or some parts of consequents may so persist while other parts are lost by capture, it is not safe to regard as a resequent any stream flowing in a consequent direction at a low horizon. We must know that the stream developed at the lower horizon before we can so classify it. In practice it is frequently difficult or impossible to distinguish in particular cases between resequents and inherited consequents, even when we know that there must be many resequents present in the area. But realization of the fact that a stream may be a resequent will often prevent an erroneous interpretation of geomorphic history.

Insequent streams.—Streams the courses of which are not due to (consequent upon) determinable factors are called "insequent" streams (in(con)sequent = insequent). While the term literally means "not consequent," it should not be interpreted to mean any stream which does not belong in the class of consequents. "Not consequent" must here rather be interpreted "not due to." It is essential, also, to complete the phrase by adding "determinable factors," since it is not intended to imply that the courses of these streams are without structural or topographic control. On the contrary, the location of each part of an insequent drainage system was doubtless determined in the first instance by inequalities of surface slope or inequalities of rock resistance. But these inequalities were so slight, or so obscure, or have been so completely effaced by later erosion, that it is not possible, when surveying the irregularly branching stream, to say why it ran this way, or bent in that direction, or branched at those angles. A faint dip in the surface of plain or plateau, an inconspicuous joint plane, a local increase in lime content of a given stratum, may have been sufficient to guide the growing ravine which later became the present valley, such guidance persisting for but a few feet, or a few hundred feet, when some other control perhaps came into play.

Only in the horizontal rocks of a level plain or plateau, or in massive crystallines, which have been planed by earlier erosion, do we ordinarily get that close approach to equality of surface slope and rock resistance in all horizontal directions which permits the best development of insequent drainage. Hence good insequent drainage, like good consequent, subsequent, resequent, and obsequent drainage, may tell us something, though not everything, about the original external form and the internal structure of a landmass.

It will appear, on consideration, that in certain geologic structures streams may develop which partake of the characters of more than one of the foregoing genetic types. Thus in Figure 5 if we imagine a stream *CC*, which is consequent on an inclined coastal plain, to be superposed on underlying folded structures, we have no difficulty in recognizing ordinary subsequents *S,S*, developed on belts of weak rock. Nor is there any complication about the obsequents *O,O*, which flow down the flanks of resistant ridges in directions opposite that of the lateral consequents, the latter having formerly descended the sides of bordering anticlines to join a longitudinal consequent which must originally have flowed toward us in the trough of the pitching syncline. The resequents *R,R*, have the directions of the former lateral consequents, although it is obvious that they represent a new development of drainage at a lower level than the original surface of the syncline.

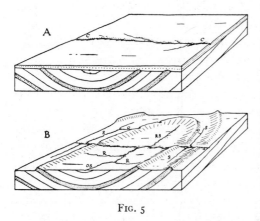

FIG. 5

But when we consider the streams *RS* and *OS* in the center of the eroded syncline, we encounter a new complication. Both of these streams are subsequents, for they have developed by headward erosion along the belt of weak shales in the center of the syncline exposed when the overlying coastal plain beds were stripped off. In addition the stream *RS* is a resequent, for it flows in the same direction as the former longitudinal consequent, referred to above, and has obviously developed at a horizon far below the initial surface of the fold. We may call it a resequent-subsequent. The stream *OS*, flowing in a direction opposite to that of the former longitudinal consequent, is obsequent as well as subsequent, and may be called an obsequent-subsequent stream.

Some may find the foregoing genetic classification of streams too refined for their use. To these the terminology will be confusing, and the task of memorizing the names and their significance will be a burden. Such a task should never be undertaken. The fact that it constitutes a task is sufficient proof that those who find it so do not have serious need for the classification. If a few simple terms such as "longitudinal stream," "transverse stream," "dip-slope stream," or more roundabout descriptive phrases will serve the needs of the geologist or geographer, let such terms suffice for him. But the geomorphologist who deals constantly and intimately with drainage problems cannot do his work with such crude tools. He makes frequent and close acquaintance with streams of diverse genesis, he has a clear image of the typical history of each, and he must have clean-cut, precise terms by which to designate the various types. For him the terminology given above is not confusing, but clarifying; it does not have to be memorized, because it is largely self-explanatory and neatly fits conceptions with which he is already familiar; it is convenient, because it avoids the ambiguity of loose terms of more general application, and the cumbrous circumlocutions of descriptive phrases; and it is practical, for experience teaches him that precise terminology is an aid to that precision of thought which is essential to the successful solution of complicated drainage histories of past geologic time. That some of the terms have been wrongly used is not so much an evidence of inherent lack of precision in the terms themselves, as it is an indication of the need for care on the part of those who employ them.

RELATIONS OF STREAMS TO GENETICALLY ASSOCIATED STRUCTURES

We often find it convenient to employ a simple classification of stream valleys based on their relations to the geological structures with which their development was associated. Longitudinal or strike valleys, parallel to the well-marked structural belts of a tilted or folded region, may be "monoclinal" valleys, "anticlinal" valleys, or "synclinal" valleys. In the first two cases the streams will normally be subsequents; in the last case they may be consequents, resequent-subsequents, or obsequent-subsequents. Transverse valleys have been called "cataclinal" where the direction of stream flow is in the direction of the dip, as is the case with consequents and resequents; and "anaclinal" where the direction of flow is against the dip, as in the case of obsequents. The last two terms are less commonly employed than are the other three, possibly in part because the terms "consequent," "resequent," and "obsequent" indicate relation to dip and at the same time convey additional information about the origin of the valleys; and perhaps also in part because the terms "cataclinal" and "anaclinal" are less significant than the others, applying as they do to many streams belonging in some of the classes considered below.

Valleys which have their locations determined by faults are called "fault" valleys if the stream is consequent on the faulted surface, "fault-line" valleys if the stream develops as a subsequent, either on the crushed zone or on an infaulted strip of weaker rock. "Joint" valleys may develop as subsequents along weakened joint planes.

RELATIONS OF STREAMS TO FOREIGN STRUCTURES

It was early recognized that a distinction must be made between streams genetically related to the structures on which they flow, and streams which traverse structures quite foreign to those on which they originated. Streams of the latter group are divided into two main classes: those in which the stream course antedates the foreign structure, and those in which the foreign structure antedates the stream course. In the first case a stream of any genetic type, developing in response to any given geological structure, may at some time in its history have a new and wholly extraneous structure developed across its course. The new structure, quite foreign to that which guided the stream's development, may be a gradually growing anticline, a slowly down-warped basin, or an uplifted fault block. If the stream is able to maintain its original course despite the growing obstacle, it is called an "antecedent" stream, because it acquired its course antecedent to the development of the new structure.

The reverse situation occurs when the foreign structure is already in existence, but blanked by overlying deposits on which streams acquire courses in harmony with the constructional surface or internal structures of the overlying formation. If, later, these streams cut through the overlying deposits, and thus have their courses "imposed from above" upon the underlying structure, such streams are called "superimposed," or more simply "superposed." We may speak of superposed consequents, superposed subsequents, and so on, provided we keep clearly in mind that the words "consequent," "subsequent," etc., refer to the stream's genetic relation to the overlying beds, whereas the word "superposed" in each case refers to the same stream's relation to the underlying structures, wholly foreign to the stream's normal evolution. In Figure 5 the transverse master stream is a superposed consequent; consequent upon the constructional slope of the coastal plain which buried the beveled fold, and superposed upon the underlying syncline, a structure quite foreign to that which determined the genesis of the stream.

Not infrequently the term "superimposed" (or "superposed") has been broadened to include streams let down upon lower parts of the very same structure that determined the genesis of the stream. Thus a subsequent stream entrenched in a resistant underlying stratum of the coastal plain on which the stream originated, a radial consequent incised in the core of the laccolith upon which the stream took its rise, and a horseshoe-shaped subsequent stranded across the nose of a hard layer plunging underground at the end of an anticline have all been called "superimposed streams." It is true that in each of these cases the stream has been "let down from above" upon underlying beds. But if incision from above be made the sole criterion of a superposed stream, the term becomes so broad as to include most streams, and so becomes practically meaningless. It is better to speak of the streams in question as having "inherited" consequent or subsequent courses from higher levels, and to restrict the term "superposed" to streams imposed upon foreign structures. It may help us to keep the desired distinction in mind if we think of inheritance as something normally taking place within the family, while imposition from above implies something outside the normal course of events.

92

RELATIONS OF STREAMS TO PAST CHANGES OF LEVEL

Where regional uplift or depression, or both, have taken place, it is desirable to classify those streams which show the effects of either change of level. Uplift causes renewed incision of streams, often with such accompanying changes as the development of falls and rapids, an inner gorge, rock benches or terraces, incised or entrenched meanders, and certain less striking features. Such a stream is said to be *rejuvenated* or revived. As the latter term has been used in a slightly different sense, for streams not now showing evidence of the uplift, it is perhaps wiser to employ the former term. It should further be noted that depression of one part of a continent with respect to another which remains quiescent; or depression of both parts, but of one part more than the other; or a drop in sea level with no change in land level, may all cause stream incision in certain areas, with the production of the associated phenomena described above. The term "rejuvenation" is satisfactory, because it connotes the change in the stream's condition without implying the nature of the change of level, or even what it was that changed.

Depression of the land, or rise of sea level, causes the lower parts of valleys near the coast to be invaded by the sea. A stream which has suffered this history is said to be *drowned*. If the influx of fresh water be great, the upper parts of the drowned area may be fresh instead of salt; and if bars separate the drowned valley from the open ocean, as in Pamlico and Albemarle Sound, most of the drowned area may contain water which is fresh or only brackish.

One defect of this classification remains to be noted. The term "rejuvenated" applies not alone to streams affected by changes of level but to streams which experience similar alterations in character due to changes of climate, stream piracy, and certain other events. There is no satisfactory term indicating rejuvenation due to changes of level alone; and even if there were, we should be confronted by the awkward fact that in the present state of our knowledge it is often impossible to say, for example, whether the streams of a given area owe their rejuvenated characteristics to a change of level or to a change of climate. Perhaps the classification will be improved as our knowledge of the criteria and causes of rejuvenation increases.

93

Regime Theory and Hydraulic Geometry

III

In distinct contrast to the qualitative descriptive treatment of rivers and valleys by geologists, engineers were attempting to relate velocity and discharge to channel morphology for design purposes. For example, a body of literature developed, as a result of British engineers' efforts to design stable irrigation canals in India and Egypt, but it was generally ignored by earth scientists. "Regime theory" for the design of stable alluvial channels is reviewed in Leliavsky (1955) and Raudkivi (1967). There are many papers that could have been selected for inclusion here, but Lane's paper is representative and provides a review of the earlier work. Papers by Kennedy (1895) and Lacey (1930) are classic, but they are difficult to read unless one is familiar with canal design problems.

Lane's paper is valuable for it demonstrates clearly how empirical equations as well as the qualitative conclusions reached in one part of the world do not necessarily apply elsewhere because of different climatic and geologic conditions. The controversy involving the validity of equations developed locally but applied generally resembles some geologic controversies that were resolved when the investigators visited their opponents' field areas. Lane's recognition of the importance of sediment size and quantity of sediment load is also significant. One needs to read Lane's paper with the understanding that silt means sediment, and does not refer to silt-size particles alone. Lane was Professor of Hydraulic Engineering at Iowa State University.

As data accumulated on the hydrology and morphology of rivers, it was inevitable that the "regime" approach would be applied to rivers, and this was done by Leopold and Maddock. This paper had an immediate impact on geomorphology, primarily because it and Horton's (1945) earlier paper demonstrated quantitatively that there is order in landform development, and a series of papers demonstrating similar relations in other areas followed its publication (Brush, 1961; Wolman, 1955; Leopold and Miller, 1956; Nixon, 1959; Miller, 1958; Carlston, 1969; Tricart, 1960). The

95

paper has been widely cited, and its contents are treated in detail in Leopold, Wolman, and Miller's book (1964); therefore, only a brief part of the more extensive treatment is included here. Again a word of caution—width and depth are not bankfull depths of channels, rather they are the width and depth of the flow of water in the channel at a given discharge. Furthermore, the reader should examine figures 5, 6, and 7 with some care, for in some of the examples downstream increases of width, depth, and velocity do not occur. (See Mackin's 1963 discussion of this paper.)

AMERICAN SOCIETY OF CIVIL ENGINEERS

Founded November 5, 1852

TRANSACTIONS

5   Paper No. 1957

STABLE CHANNELS IN ERODIBLE MATERIAL

By E. W. Lane,[1] M. Am. Soc. C. E.

Synopsis

The design of the All-American Canal, which will divert 15 000 cu ft per sec from the Colorado River, required a thorough study of stable channel shapes. Data from various sources were conflicting and unsuitable for the unusual conditions on this canal. These data were analyzed and conclusions were drawn regarding the various factors controlling stable channel shapes, and the relation between them.

Introduction

For a canal to be stable the banks must not slough or slide, and the bottom and sides must neither silt nor scour. To establish these conditions the engineer must consider a number of factors.

The problem of controlling sloughing or sliding is not treated in detail in this paper, since stable slopes for the various soils are comparatively well known. To prevent scouring or the accumulation of silt in the bed, it is necessary that the velocity along the bed is sufficient to move all the material brought into the canal, and yet not be so high as to cause the subgrade of the canal to scour. Flowing water will not attack the subgrade unless its velocity is more than sufficient to move the material brought into the canal. The excess of velocity over that required to move this material, which will attack the canal subgrade, depends upon the material of which the subgrade is composed.

In order that the banks may neither silt nor scour, the velocities along them must be sufficient to prevent deposition but not sufficient to cause the material of which they are composed to scour. From a practical standpoint

Note.—Published in November, 1935, *Proceedings*.

[1] Prof. of Hydr. Eng., State Univ. of Iowa, Iowa City, Iowa.

a slight degree of silting on the sides is not especially detrimental, so that the important requirement is the prevention of scour and excessive deposition. The maximum allowable velocity along the banks depends upon the material of which they are composed. The material on the sides is also acted upon by the force of gravity, which assists the water in tending to cause motion. The sides, therefore, will scour under velocities less than would be permissible along the bottom.

The ratio between the velocity acting on the sides and that on the bottom depends upon the ratio of the bed width of the canal to the depth. The greater this latter ratio the greater will be the ratio of the velocity acting on the bottom to that acting on the sides. The bed width-depth ratio required for a stable channel is that which will bring the proper ratio of velocity acting on the bottom to that acting on the sides. Conditions that require high velocities acting on the bottom, as compared with those that may be permitted to act on the sides, require high ratios of bed width to depth. For example, canals that carry a heavy bed load in friable material require high velocities on the bed to move the load and low velocities along the banks to prevent cutting them; in other words, such channels require a high ratio of bottom velocity to side velocity, and, therefore, a high bed width-depth ratio. Canals with small bed loads in friable material do not require such high velocities along the bottom to transport the bed load and, therefore, the ratio of this lower velocity, V_B, to the permissible side velocity, V_S, can be smaller. The correct ratios for other conditions can be determined by the application of these principles. This paper records an attempt to outline the major principles that control stable channel shapes and velocities.

THE ALL-AMERICAN CANAL

The All-American Canal is planned to take water from the Lower Colorado River and carry it to the lands lying in the Imperial and Coachella Valleys by a route lying entirely within the United States. The Imperial Valley is now (1935) irrigated from the Colorado River by a publicly owned canal system, of which a large part of the main canal lies within the Republic of Mexico. The difficulties of international administration. and the undesirable silt conditions connected with the existing canal has led to the instigation by the United States Bureau of Reclamation of the new All-American Canal project to be built entirely within the United States, which has been approved by Congress.

The Colorado River is a very silt-laden stream. It has a discharge varying from 2 500 to 190 000 cu ft per sec and a suspended silt content near the intake of the proposed canal averaging 0.90% by weight, and, at times, reaching 5.40 per cent. The suspended silt is extremely fine and the bed silt averages about 0.10 mm (0.004 in.) in diameter. The river slope is approximately 1.2 ft per mile. The use of this very silty water in the Imperial Valley has led to great difficulty and an expense estimated at approximately $1 400 000 per yr for dredging, canal cleaning, and land leveling.

Before the All-American Canal is finished, it is expected that the Boulder Dam, 303 miles above the proposed head-works, will be completed. This dam will be 725 ft high and will form a reservoir, with a maximum capacity of 30 500 000 acre-ft, in which all the silt brought down to the reservoir will be deposited. Another dam will be built 155 miles above the intake, which will stop practically all the silt coming from above that point. The silt that reaches the intake, therefore, will be only that picked up from the banks and bed of the river below the lower dam, and the small quantity brought in by the tributaries to the river between the lower dam and the intake. An elaborate desilting works will be built to remove the coarser part of the silt load which will be carried into the canal. Consequently, the silt load in the canal will differ greatly from that now (1935) carried, and will create different stable channel shapes. To determine the shape best adapted to the new condition a thorough study of the subject was made, the results of which are described herein.

NOTATION

The symbols introduced in this paper are defined as follows (the English system of units being used unless otherwise stated):

a = a subscript denoting "average";

d = depth of flow; d_a = average depth;

f = silt factor = $8 \sqrt{D}$;

m = a subscript denoting "mean";

n = exponent in a formula of the Kennedy type;

s = a subscript denoting "near the sides";

A = area of water cross-section;

B = breadth, or width of channel; B_s = width at the bottom; B_m = mean channel width; as a subscript, B, denotes "at or near the bottom";

C = coefficient in a formula of the Kennedy type;

D = diameter of particles;

L = length;

P = wetted perimeter (not including water surface);

Q = flow, or rate of discharge;

R = hydraulic radius = $\dfrac{A}{P}$;

S = slope = $\dfrac{\text{fall}}{L}$

V = velocity; average velocity in a section; V_s = velocity near the bottom; V_s = velocity near the sides; and V_o = critical velocity from the standpoint of silting.

HISTORY OF NON-SILTING CANAL SECTION STUDIES

Most of the study of the problem of non-silting canal sections has been made by the British engineers in India, in connection with the large irrigation projects of that country. A certain amount has also been done in Egypt, in connection with the irrigation work on the Nile. Thus far, little has been contributed by the United States. In the last few years, however, a surprising interest in silt problems has developed in this country and it is now (1935) being attacked from many angles by a number of research engineers. From this interest, no doubt, future progress will become considerably more marked.

The first study of non-silting canal sections was made by Mr. R. G. Kennedy (1)[2]. His work is a classic in this field, and has resulted in the saving of millions of dollars in reducing the cost of cleaning irrigation canals in India and elsewhere. Unfortunately, like most outstanding studies, it came to have such prestige that for many years little further progress along this line was made.

Kennedy gave the result of measurements of bed widths and "full supply" depths on about twenty-two canals in the Lower Bari Doab Canal System, in which the channels had become stable and several more which had nearly reached this condition. He also gave the "full supply" discharge and the velocity computed from this discharge and the full supply area. From these data he developed a formula of the type:

$$V_0 = C\,d^n \dots\dots\dots\dots\dots\dots\dots\dots(1)$$

which expressed, with reasonable accuracy, the relation between the critical mean velocity, V_0, and the depth, d, as indicated by the results of the measurements. For the Lower Bari Doab Canal, C was 0.84 and n was 0.64. Kennedy expected C to vary with the quality and quantity of silt, but thought n would be nearly constant. On Fig. 1 (with reference to Table 1) is shown a line giving the velocities corresponding to the various depths according to Equation (1). The local conditions influencing these observations and Kennedy's conclusions will be given more in detail subsequently.

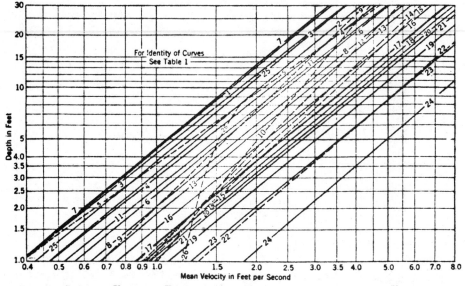

FIG. 1.—CRITICAL VELOCITY FORMULAS FOR NON-SILTING, NON-SCOURING VELOCITIES.

In 1895 Kennedy issued a set of hydraulic diagrams to aid in the design of non-silting channels. In 1904, he gave a rough rule for the relation of width to depth in non-silting canals (5). A second edition of "Hydraulic Diagrams" (6) was issued in 1907, in which Kennedy reprinted the original paper and added an extended discussion to clarify some of the obscure points and to give the results of his experience since the first paper was printed.

[2] For reference to figures in parentheses see "Bibliography."

TABLE 1.—Values of C and n, Equation (1), for Non-Silting, Non-Scouring Velocities

Curve No. (see Fig. 1)	Factors Applying to Equation (1) (in English Units)		Locality	Authority	Limit *	Reference
	Coefficient C	Exponent n				
1	0.381	0.64	Egypt.........	Buckley........	Lower...	Irrig. Dept. of Egypt.
2	0.46	0.64	Egypt.........	Buckley........	Upper...	
3	0.39	2/3	Egypt.........	Molesworth and	Lower...	"Irrigation Practice," p. 207.
4	0.475	2/3	Egypt.........	Yenidunia.....	Upper...	
5	0.391	0.727	Egypt.........	K. D. Ghaleb...	....	Minutes of Proceedings, Inst.. C. E., p. 260, Vol. 229; also p. 285, Vol. 223.
6	0.56	0.64	Egypt.........			U. S. Dept. of Agri., Technical Bulletin No. 67, p. 44.
7	0.38	0.64	Mozaffargorih D. Punjab, India.	G. W. Duthy...	Lower...	Proceedings, Punjab Eng. Congress, pp. 44 and 48, 1919.
8	{ 0.63	0.64		G. W. Duthy...	Upper...	
	0.63	0.64	Sind..........	F. W. Woods...		Engineer, p. 648, Vol. 143; Parker, "Control of Water," p. 678.
9	0.67	0.55	Godavari Western Delta, Madras.	Kennedy........		Minutes of Proceedings, Inst. C. E., p. 260, Vol. 229; Madras Public Works Dept., Oct. 9, 1912, Dist. 1872.
10	1.01	0.44	Rio Negro, Argentina	R. E. Ballester..	....	Minutes of Proceedings, Inst.C. E., p. 280, Vol. 223.
11	0.52	0.66	Siam..........			U. S. Dept. of Agri., Technical Bulletin No. 67, p. 44.
12	0.93	0.52	Madras (Kistna)	Kennedy........	....	Minutes of Proceedings, Inst. C. E., p. 260, Vol. 229.
13	0.67	0.64	Sutlej, India....	F. W. Woods...		Engineer, June 17, 1927, p. 648.
14	0.91†	0.571	Burma (Shwebo)	Kennedy........		Minutes of Proceedings, Inst. C. E., p. 260, Vol. 229 (1929–30); Parker, "Control of Water."
15	0.95	0.57	Chenab, Punjab.	Lindley........	....	Minutes of Proceedings, Inst. C. E., p. 260, Vol. 229; Punjab Eng. Congress, Proceedings, 1919, p. 63.
16	0.756	0.64	Sirhind, Punjab.	W. B. Harvey...	....	Proceedings Punjab Eng. Congress, 1919, p. 58.
17	0.84	0.64	Bari Doab......	Kennedy........	....	Hydraulic Diagrams, Kennedy, Public Works Dept.,India,1907.
18	{ 0.924	0.64	Penner River...	J. M. Lacey....	Lower...	Minutes of Proceedings, Inst. C. E., p. 333, Vol. 229.
	0.924	0.64	Cauvery Delta..	J. M. Lacey....	Lower...	
19	1.09	0.64	Penner River...	J. M. Lacey....	Upper...	Minutes of Proceedings, Inst. C. E., p. 333, Vol. 229.
20	0.966	0.64	Cauvery Delta..	J. M. Lacey....	Upper...	
21	0.98	0.64	Imperial Valley.	Rothery........		Minutes of Proceedings, Inst. C. E., p. 179, Vol. CCXVI.
22	1.26	0.64	Cauvery Delta..	J. M. Lacey....	Extreme Upper...	Minutes of Proceedings, Inst. C. E., p. 333, Vol. 229.
23	1.33	0.61	Imperial Valley..	Collings........	Lower...	Transactions, Am. Soc. C. E., Vol. 99 (1934), p. 549.
24	1.83	0.61	Imperial Valley..	Collings........	Upper...	Proceedings, Punjab Eng. Congress, 1919, p. 74j.
25	0.42	0.64	Bebera Delta...	R. G. Kinder...	....	
26	‡	‡	Jamrao, Sind....	W. L. C. Trench.	....	Minutes of Proceedings, Inst C. E., p. 307, Vol. 223, 1926–27.

* "Limit" refers to the upper or lower limit of the data observed, which may spread over a considerable range.

† Approximate.

‡ $V_o = (1.1+)\ 0.095\ d$.

Kennedy's work soon became extensively used throughout India; observations were made on the ditches of other irrigation systems and a number of other equations of the same type as those of Kennedy, were developed, suitable to the various local conditions. One of these was for the Godavari Western Delta and the Kistna Western Delta, in Madras (7). In 1913 a set of hydraulic diagrams for the design of channels was presented by Capt. A. Garrett which deals with non-silting channels (8), and which is used extensively in the United Provinces.

In 1917, Mr. F. W. Woods proposed (2) the use of definite ratios of depth to width, based on an analysis of data from the Lower Chenab Canal System. In 1919, the results of an extensive analysis of canal dimensions of the Lower Chenab Canal, by E. S. Lindley, M. Am. Soc. C. E., was published (3). For these canals, Mr. Lindley found a critical velocity relation such that, in Equation (1), $C = 0.95$ and $n = 0.57$. He also found a relation of bed width to depth of $B_s = 3.8\ d^{1.61}$.

In 1927, Woods (4) proposed a general formula covering velocity, average depth, mean width, and slope, as follows:

$$d_a = B_m^{0.434} \dots\dots\dots\dots\dots\dots\dots\dots\dots (2)$$

$$V_0 = 1.434\ \log_{10} B_m \dots\dots\dots\dots\dots\dots (3)$$

and,

$$S = \frac{1}{2 \times \log_{10} Q \times 1\,000} \dots\dots\dots\dots\dots (4)$$

Equations (2), (3), and (4) cover not only the depth and width, but also the discharge and slope. According to them for a given discharge there is a single condition of depth, width, and slope that will produce a stable channel.

In 1928, Mr. W. T. Bottomley (9) advanced the idea that irrigation channels would be non-silting and non-scouring if the slope of the canal was of the same order as that of the parent river, regardless of the relation of width to depth and the shape of the channel. In 1930, an excellent paper on this subject (18) was presented by Mr. Gerald Lacey in which he advanced the proposition that the wetted perimeter of stable channel was a simple function of the square root of the discharge; or,

$$P = 2.668\ Q^{0.5} \dots\dots\dots\dots\dots\dots\dots\dots (5)$$

and that the shape of the section depended upon the fineness of the silt carried, coarse silt giving rise to wide, shallow sections and fine silt to narrow, deep ones. He developed the formulas,

$$Q\ f^2 = 3.8\ V_0^6 \dots\dots\dots\dots\dots\dots\dots\dots (6)$$

and,

$$V_0 = 1.17\ \sqrt{f\ R} \dots\dots\dots\dots\dots\dots\dots (7)$$

in which f is a silt factor, related to the diameter of the bed material by the expression:

$$f = 8\ \sqrt{D} \dots\dots\dots\dots\dots\dots\dots\dots (8)$$

In Equation (8) D is in inches. From Equations (6), (7), and (8), knowing the flow, Q, in the ditch, V_0, A, and R can be computed.

Lacey also stated that the shape of a stable channel approximated an ellipse, with its major axis horizontal, the ratio of the major to the minor axis being larger as the silt became coarser. Lacey's ideas have been widely accepted in India, and extensive observations are under way to study the effect of various conditions on his silt factor, f.

The aforementioned authorities have developed their ideas almost entirely from experience in India. The result of experience on canals in Egypt is given by Messrs. Molesworth and Yenidunia (10). They give a general formula in English units:

$$d = (9\,060\ S + 0.725)\ \sqrt{B_s} \quad \ldots \ldots \ldots \ldots \ldots \ldots (9)$$

as developed from a careful examination of a large number of recognized good Egyptian canals. As a result of further experience, Mr. A. B. Buckley (11), develops the adjustment of Equation (9) for canals of depths of 1.6 m (5.26 ft) and less, as follows:

$$d = \frac{0.0025\ (100\,000\ S + 8)^2\ E_B}{1.62} \quad \ldots \ldots \ldots \ldots \ldots (10)$$

Equation (10) is in English units. In addition to the general formulas proposed by various investigators, a large number of special formulas of the Kennedy type have been developed. These formulas are listed on Table 1.

Summary of Previous Stable-Channel Formulas

The formulas developed for stable channels fall into two classifications: (a) Those giving an expression for velocity; and (b) those giving stable channel shapes. Those in the first class are similar to the Kennedy formula, Equation (1). In most of these formulas n has been taken as 0.64, the value developed by Kennedy. In all cases the value of C was constant for a given locality or canal system. Kennedy believed that C would vary with both the size and quantity of silt, but did not emphasize the effect of the quantity of silt as much as the quality, and, as a result, it has been largely lost sight of by other students of the subject. He did not believe that the value of n would change greatly.

A formula of the Kennedy type indicates that the critical velocity increases with the depth, but experience shows that as the depth is increased a velocity is finally reached at which the banks begin to erode. Kennedy believed that the limiting velocity was a matter of experience, and gave limiting values which correspond to depths of about 10 ft. This had the effect of limiting the depths of canals designed according to his rules to these values. No data on this limitation are available for the conditions under which any of the other formulas of the Kennedy type were developed.

Of the formulas of the second type, Lindley gives a relation of critical velocity to depth and bed width, but suggests no modifications for the quality or quantity of silt. Woods gives relations for mean depth, velocity, and slope, but like Lindley makes no suggestion that these relations might be influenced by the quantity or the quality of the silt. Lacey gives channel shapes and velocities. introducing the effect of the size of the silt grain, but does not consider the quantity of material to be transported.

Comparison of Critical Velocities

In order to determine what velocities could be used safely in the All-American Canal, Fig. 1 was prepared, showing the relation of depth to critical velocity, as determined from all available observations on actual ditches. These show at a glance that for a given depth of flow there is a tremendous variation in critical velocity. The line representing Kennedy's data is shown heavier than the others. The variations range approximately from 46 to 208% of Kennedy's results, or the highest value over 450% of the lowest.

The local conditions under which most of these formulas were developed are not known in detail. In general, however, it is believed that the silt of the Nile River is finer than that of Ravi River, from which water is drawn for the Lower Bari Doab Canal, on which Kennedy's observations were made. The lower velocities found for the Egyptian canals, as compared with those given by Kennedy are, therefore, consistent with the relation of Lacey's formula (Equation (6)), that finer material results in lower critical velocities. It is also known, however, that the silt of the Colorado River and the tributary Imperial Valley canals is finer than that of the Ravi, but the critical velocities are higher in the case of the Imperial Valley canals. This is contrary to the relation given by Lacey.

COMPARISON OF FORMULAS FOR WIDTH-DEPTH RELATION

A comparison similar to that of the critical velocity relations was also made of the various formulas for the relation of bed width to depth. The results are shown on Fig. 2, which gives the relation of bed width for the principal formulas and some of the data. The Woods' formula was expressed in terms of mean width, and has been changed to terms of bed width by assuming side

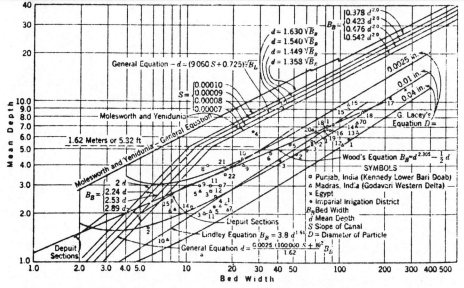

FIG. 2.—BED WIDTH-DEPTH RELATION FOR A NON-SILTING NON-SCOURING CANAL.

slopes of 1 on 2. The data for channels as proposed by Lacey (using side slopes of 1 on 2) for three sizes of material, are also shown. The finest of these, 0.0025 in. in diameter, is for material roughly corresponding in size to that composing the bottom of the Imperial Valley canals.

The Punjab (Kennedy) data are computed from those given by Kennedy for the Lower Bari Doab Canal, using vertical side slopes, as reported by him. Data are also given on canals in the Godavari Western Delta and some values obtained from canals in the Imperial Valley. The data from Egypt were in the form of a general equation by Molesworth and Yenidunia, which is independent of the slope, and an equation which is dependent on the slope, four slopes being given. For depths less than 1.62 m (5.32 ft), a modification of the Molesworth-Yenidunia, formula given by Buckley has been used, based on data which have been collected since the other formula was proposed. The Depuit Section, said to be widely used in Egypt, is also shown.

These data for the bed width-depth relation show even greater variation than the depth critical-velocity relations shown on Fig. 2. For a 5-ft depth, the Molesworth-Yenidunia formula without the slope factor, gives a bed width of 6.4 ft and the Lindley equation gives 50.0 ft, or a ratio of maximum to minimum of 781 per cent. Some of the Imperial Valley data indicate even higher ratios than those given by the Lindley formula. The wide range does not seem to be due to variation in the size of the silt because, although the Egyptian data are believed to be for finer silt than the Indian data of Woods and Lindley, most of the Imperial Valley data, which are also for fine silt, give even higher bed width-depth ratios than those of either Lindley or Wood.

FACTORS AFFECTING STABLE CHANNEL SHAPES

As a result of the wide range of critical velocities and bed width-depth relations found on the canals in the different parts of the world, and the lack of any readily apparent consistency in the variations, it was clear that if the factors controlling this variation could not be determined it would not be safe to adopt any of the relations given by existing formulas for the design of the sections of the All-American Canal. Although these formulas no doubt provide workable relations for the conditions for which they were developed, these conditions have not been delineated sufficiently to enable them to be applied elsewhere. In general, also, they were developed empirically from a very limited range of conditions, and in most cases they omit important factors from consideration.

To develop a rational design for the sections of the All-American Canal, it was necessary, therefore, to attempt to go back to the fundamentals and try to make an analysis of the factors controlling the shape of a stream channel in erodible material, and their relations to each other.

The following is a list of factors that may enter into a determination of stable channel shapes: (a) Hydraulic factors (slope, roughness, hydraulic radius or depth, mean velocity, velocity distribution, and temperature); (b) channel shape (width, depth, and side slopes); (c) nature of material transported (size, shape, specific gravity, dispersion, quantity, and bank and subgrade material); and, (d) miscellaneous (alignment, uniformity of flow, and aging).

In arriving at a rational solution of the problem of stable channels it is necessary to consider all these factors, and to determine as accurately as possible which of them are of major importance, and which are minor or negligible. By determining first the relation between major factors, it may be possible later to study the effect of minor factors, but until the major relations are known, the data available are only a collection of miscellaneous facts of limited value.

Of the hydraulic factors, the slope, roughness, hydraulic radius, and mean velocity are interdependent and with reasonable certainty their relation is known quantitatively through the ordinary velocity formulas. It is true that the effect of the movement of material in suspension and by traction upon the roughness is not definitely known and more information on this point is needed, but compared to the uncertainty in other phases of the problem, the relations of these four items is so well known that for the purposes of this study further investigation along these lines was probably unjustified. The relation between these factors and scouring or transportation of solids in channels is not well established and must be studied further.

As will be shown subsequently, it is believed that the velocity distribution, as well as the mean velocity, is of primary importance to the problem and that it, together with the channel shape factors of width and depth, exercise an important influence on stable shapes. The side slopes are relatively unimportant except as regards sloughing.

Temperature has been suggested as having an important effect because it influences the viscosity of the water and, consequently, the rate at which solid particles settle. That temperature might have some effect cannot be questioned, but it is probably small, from the standpoint of stable channel shapes. Most of the data were collected in warm countries, comparable to the locality of the All-American Canal, and the temperature variation although it might cause some difference in settlement rate would not, ordinarily, be enough, when averaged over the year, to cause major effects. For many sizes of silt the effect of temperature on settling rate is small. Moreover, it is possible that the tractive force, which is not appreciably affected by temperature, is the most important factor in stable channel shapes, and, therefore, temperature effects are relatively unimportant. In any event temperature data, which would enable an analysis of its effect to be made, are not available.

Nearly all students of the problem have admitted that the size of the material transported is of major importance. The shape no doubt has an effect, but it is believed to be of secondary importance as laboratory experiments show that angular particles are moved by only slightly higher velocities than rounded ones. In any event, no data on it are available for any of the localities, so that its influence could not be investigated, even if it was desirable to do so. Specific gravity of the transported material also has its effect, but since it rarely varies much from 2.65 it is of secondary importance. No data on this subject would be available, even if it were desirable to study them. The dispersion of the material by virtue of the electrical charges carried by the particles is important in some phases of sedimentation, but it is probably active only in the case of very fine material which is ordinarily not much of a factor in stable channel sections. In this case, again, no data for further study are available.

The quantity of solids in motion is an important factor in the shape of stable channel shapes, and has not received the attention that its importance warrants. Cases illustrating its importance are numerous. For example, it is a common occurrence in some irrigation systems to have the upper section of the ditch fill during periods of high silt content in the streams from which they draw, and for this fill to scour out later during periods of clear-water flow. In other words, the ditch is unstable, at times being unable to transport all the material brought to it, hence filling up, and at other times transporting more material than brought to it, and, therefore, cutting down its bed. Over long periods the ditches are approximately stable because the two actions counteract one another. Another common example is the change from unstable to stable condition which results when an effective sand trap is applied to a ditch that is becoming filled. There are also numerous cases in which the channel of a natural stream is stable but begins to scour severely when a dam is built on it and cuts off the supply of solid material which formerly came down to renew that which was moved forward by the flowing water.

One of the most important factors controlling stable channel shapes is the nature of the material composing the banks and subgrade. If these materials are resistant to scour, higher velocities can be used than if the material is friable. Alignment is another factor to be considered, because bank scour is more likely to occur on curves. If a canal is apt to be operated a large proportion of the time at part capacity, this must also be considered in the design.

Another factor that influences the stability of an irrigation channel is what is commonly termed "aging." After water has run for some time in a channel, the particles composing the bed arrange themselves in such a manner that they are more difficult to move than when the water is first turned in. If the water is silty, this material forms a kind of weak cement which binds the bed material together and makes it more resistant.

In addition to the items listed herein under the heading "Factors Affecting Stable Channel Shapes," another set of relations enters into the selection of the best channel section in any instance, which depends upon the conditions which the canal is designed to meet.

Canals for conveying water for irrigation or power are usually designed to meet one of three sets of conditions. The first type is encountered when it is desired to use the lowest practicable velocity, in order that the slope may be reduced to a minimum. In the case of power canals this is done to obtain the greatest feasible power head, and, in irrigation canals, it is done to enable the ditch to command as much irrigable area as possible for a given length. A second type of conditions is met in both power and irrigation canals where it is desired to reduce the size of the canal to a minimum, in order to make the cost as small as possible without making the slope steeper than necessary. This requires that the velocity be made as great as can be carried without scouring the banks or bed. A third condition is met in irrigation canals where it is desired to carry the ditch on an alignment that has a slope as steep as possible, in order to reduce the cost of drops. The first of these conditions aims at securing the minimum practical velocity within the limitations of cost and silting. The second aims to secure the highest velocity that the ditch will stand with a shape which will convey the water with a reasonable loss of head. The third aims to dissipate as much head as possible by making the canal wide and shallow, thus reducing the hydraulic radius to a minimum and the slope for a given velocity to a maximum. The group into which any particular canal falls, therefore, indicates limitations which are likely to control the best channel shape, which must not be exceeded while still being subject to the influence of the aforementioned factors.

Conditions Required for Stable Channels

For a channel to be perfectly stable, it must not fill or scour on either the banks or bed. The banks must also be stable against sloughing or sliding. To meet the non-filling requirement, the velocity must be enough to flush away all the solid material brought into the section by the flowing water. To fulfill the non-scouring requirement, the velocity at the bed or at the banks must not be great enough to scour the material of which they are composed. To determine a stable section for a set of conditions it is necessary to determine the various relations which will cause velocities at the banks and along the bed that will bring about these conditions.

The silt carried into a section of canal may be composed entirely of fine material, which is easily moved by the water, or it may be composed entirely of coarse material, which is moved only at relatively high velocities. Usually, however, it has a graded composition varying from coarse to fine. If all the material is very fine, ordinarily it offers little practical difficulty because the velocities required in the ditch to meet conditions of economy are sufficient to keep it in motion. If the material is graded, the fine material moved depends upon the velocity near the bed, to obtain a stable channel the the material is coarse, all of it may be dragged along the bed, and little if any be carried in suspension. Since the quantity of the bed material that can be moved depends upon the velocity near the bed, to obtain a stable channel the velocity along the bed must be greater for larger bed loads. This may require a higher velocity along the bed than the material in which the channel was built would stand from clear water, the entire energy of the water on the bottom being expended in dragging along the bottom the material which has been brought down by the water from above. However, if the velocity along the bottom exceeds that necessary to move the bed load, it will act on the subgrade of the channel. To have a stable channel, the subgrade material must be sufficiently tenacious to resist this scour. Summarizing this relation, it may be stated that the velocity along the bottom of a stable channel must be sufficient to move the quantity of material supplied to it, but not so great as to scour the subgrade.

The material composing the banks of the canal is acted upon by two forces tending to produce motion. One of these is gravity, which tends to make the material roll or slide down the sides of the ditch. The effective gravity force is the component that acts downward along the side slopes of the ditch. The other force acting is that due to the motion of the water through the canal, which tends to drag or to push the material in a down-stream direction. The magnitude of this force depends upon the velocity adjacent to the bank.

The force of gravity and the force of the stream both act together when water is flowing in the canal, and when the resultant of the two forces is sufficient to dislodge material from the sides, it moves in a diagonal direction to the bed of the stream, or if fine enough, is carried off in suspension by the water. The slope of the bank must be sufficiently flat so that the component along it, of the force of gravity, when combined with the force of the water, is insufficient to dislodge the particles. Since flat side slopes cause a smaller component of gravity, therefore, they have less tendency to scour from this cause.

Stable Channels for Clear Water

The simplest cases involving the determination of stable channel sections are those required to convey clear water. When the water carries silt in suspension or drags a load along the bottom, there are added complications. Therefore, the simplest cases, with clear water, will be considered first. When the smallest practical slope is desired, it is usually considered that the cheapest channel is secured when the wetted perimeter is least in proportion to the area. In trapezoidal channels this occurs with a ratio of bed width to depth ranging from 2.0 to 0.472 for side slopes between the vertical and 1 on 2. These values give the most efficient hydraulic section, but since this consideration neglects any excavation above the water line the flattest slope for a given quantity of excavation for a channel in cut is given by cross-sections where the ratio of bed width to depth is less than the foregoing. Thus, maximum economy will result from very low $\frac{B}{d}$ -ratios. In earth, however, experience has shown that such channels are not stable.

A stable channel for clear water must have banks with sufficiently flat side slopes to keep the material from sloughing or rolling in, and sufficiently low velocities to keep the banks and bed from scouring. As previously stated, since the material on the banks is acted upon by the force of gravity, as well as that due to the motion of the water, it will not resist as high a force from the motion of the water as the bottom, where gravity does not tend to produce motion.

If the mean velocity in a narrow, deep channel is low enough so that the forces acting on the side material are insufficient to move it, and the sides are stable from sloughing, the channel will be stable. In other words, narrow, deep channels can be used with clear water and low velocities. Ordinarily, however, considerations of cost prevent the use of the large canals necessary to produce low velocities. For such a channel a cross-section must be selected that will give velocities along the bottom which will not move the bottom material, and velocities along the sides which will not move the side material. Since the side material, due to the action of gravity, will move at a lower velocity than that on the bottom, to obtain the maximum possible mean velocity without scour the velocity along the sides must be enough less than that along the bottom to offset the gravity effect. This reduction of side velocity, as compared with bottom velocity, is secured by increasing the ratio of bed width to depth.

In Fig. 3 are shown the velocity distributions in a number of rectangular channels having the same cross-sectional area. Most of these data were secured from the results of the experiments of D'Arcy and Bazin. The velocities are indicated by the "isovels" (also called "isotacks"), or lines of equal velocity expressed in terms of the mean velocity. (These data were obtained with different discharges for many of the examples. Although it is probable that the positions of the isovels would change somewhat with different velocities, such changes would be relatively small and would not change the main relations.) Since the areas of all water cross-sections are equal, the lines giving the same ratio to mean velocity in all the diagrams represent the same

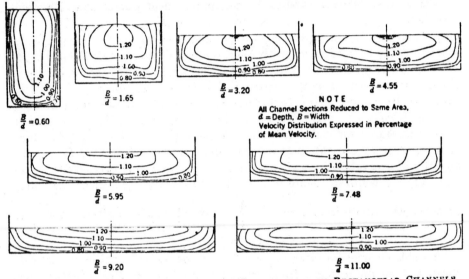

FIG. 3.—RELATION OF WIDTH TO VELOCITY DISTRIBUTION IN RECTANGULAR CHANNELS.

velocity for any given discharge. A study of the velocity distribution in these sections will show that high velocities extend closer toward the sides in the narrow, deep cross-sections than in the broad, shallow ones. The science of hydrodynamics has not yet progressed to the point where the relation between the velocity distribution adjacent to a surface can be related quantitatively to the drag of the water along the surface or to the velocity "gradient" adjacent to the surface; but progress along this line is rapid, and the near future may bring sufficient advancement in this field to enable more exact analysis to be made. For the present, however, it is sufficient to state that when the high velocities extend close to a surface the pushing or dragging force of water on the surface is greater than if these velocities close to the surface are low.

In a very narrow, deep section, the velocities close to the sides are as high as, or higher than, those close to the bottom. If the velocity in such a channel is increased gradually, due to the added force of gravity on the side material, motion would occur first on the sides.

The design of a channel to convey clear water where it is desired to obtain the smallest practicable slope, therefore, consists, from the hydraulic standpoint, of securing the smallest ratio of bed width-to depth that will not produce scour on the sides, provided such ratio is not less than that which will give the smallest wetted perimeter for a given earthwork quantity. This latter qualification will probably rarely control. The design of a channel for the second type of conditions, where the highest practicable mean velocity is to be secured, is obtained by proportioning the ratio of width to depth so that the forces tending to produce movement, both on the sides and bottom, are the maximum they will stand without motion. For canals in the third class, where it is desired to make the ditch as steep as possible without producing scour, it is customary to make the section wide and shallow in order to reduce the hydraulic radius and thus lower the velocity. For such very wide ditches the scour would be greatest on the bottom, and this condition would, control the slope that might be used. Theoretically, there is no limit to the slope a ditch might be given because the velocity could be reduced to any desired value by making it sufficiently wide and shallow. As a practical matter, however, it has been found that when the depth is made very small, the irregularities of construction are such that scour starts in the slightly deeper parts of the channel and enlarges them, causing a progressively greater concentration and scour until the beneficial effect of the widening is lost. This action has been noted in ditches with steep slopes 8 to 10 ft wide and 0.6 to 0.8 ft deep.

CHANNELS CARRYING SOLIDS IN SUSPENSION

It is quite generally agreed that material can be carried in suspension by a stream because of the vertical currents that occur in flowing water and carry the solid particles upward at a greater rate than the force of gravity causes them to fall. A promising hypothesis for the capacity of a stream to transport material in suspension, therefore, should be that the capacity is proportional to its turbulence, which, in turn, is probably proportional to the energy expended. The concentration of a given quality of solids which a stream could support, therefore, would be proportional to the energy expended per unit of volume of the water. This energy is proportional to the rate of fall of the water, which is equal to the product of the velocity and the slope.

This is a kind of over-all relation, however, and silting may occur in one part of a ditch cross-section while other parts may be scouring. Because the velocity near the edge of a stream flowing in a trapezoidal section is low, in a channel carrying silt in suspension there is a tendency to deposit at that point. This is aided by the growth of vegetation, and usually a berm is formed which creates steeper sides to the section than were originally constructed. This material is quite resistant to scour, and forms more or less evenly even in ditches where there are high velocities. This action is not ordinarily very detrimental, and is often anticipated and allowed for by computing the capacity of the channel with the slopes which it is expected the silt will cause, rather than the slopes to which it is first excavated.

It is probably not feasible to prevent entirely the deposition of suspended material along the edges of channels in earth, although it may be reduced by using higher velocities. The greatest difficulties from suspended matter occur in ditches where the slopes are so slight that the energy being dissipated in the water is insufficient to prevent deposit. The remedy in these cases is to increase the velocity, or to remove the suspended material in some kind of desilting device.

CHANNELS CARRYING BED LOAD

Irrigation channels frequently carry considerable solid matter by dragging or pushing it along the bed, with either clear or silt-laden water flowing above. The quantity of material depends upon the velocity near the bottom of the channel. Higher velocity is probably necessary to move the same quantity of coarse material as fine material. If a channel is supplied with a heavy bed load, in order to be stable it must move this load along; otherwise, the channel will become filled. This requires a high velocity along the bottom, as compared with a channel carrying clear water. For a given quality of material in the banks, the velocities that could act on the banks in the two cases would be the same. To be stable, the channel carrying bed loads, therefore, should have a higher velocity along the bed, but the same velocity along the banks, and this could only occur with a wider, shallower section. Heavily loaded channels in easily scoured material therefore, should have high ratios of bed width to depth. If the banks of the loaded channel are of material which is resistant to scour, the ratio of bed width to depth can be less than in friable material without scouring the banks.

COLLOIDS

Colloids carried in the water exercise a considerable effect on the shape of the channel cross-section. They cement the fine particles which collect along the sides of the ditch and are responsible for the vertical or nearly vertical banks which exist in many canals. This colloid cemented material along the sides is more resistant to scour than the size of material would indicate, and thus permits higher velocities along the banks than would otherwise be allowable. To a certain extent also colloids may cement the particles composing the bed and make it more resistant to scour. It is believed, however, that some of the effects ascribed to colloids are really due to the presence of a high silt load. The ability of the canals of the Imperial Valley, which are constructed in fine silt, to carry velocities of 4 or 5 ft per sec without scour has been ascribed to colloids, but the writer believes that a large part of it is due to the presence of the high silt load. When these canals are supplied by the All-American Canal with desilted water, their beds will scour considerably, and this would not be prevented by the colloids.

RECENT CONCEPTIONS OF FLOW NOT USED

To engineers who are familiar with the latest theories of stream mechanics and hydrodynamics, the foregoing analysis of the factors controlling stable channel shapes may seem somewhat crude, and in ignoring the drag theory of bed-load movement and the conception of velocity gradient, it may appear that the writer has not taken advantage of the best available information.

In making the study outlined herein, the most recent pertinent literature in stream mechanics and hydrodynamics has been analyzed to determine all the material that was applicable to the problem. A list of these references is included in the "Bibliography" contained in this paper. Since many engineers are not familiar with recent ideas, however and since a knowledge of them is not necessary to understand the relations developed regarding stable channel shapes, it was believed to be better to explain these relations in terms of conceptions with which all engineers are familiar, rather than to make it unnecessarily confusing to some by adding the other new ideas.

AGREEMENT OF SUGGESTED RELATIONS WITH OBSERVED DATA

The relations suggested in this paper seem to agree with the observed data, as shown on Figs. 1 and 2. The critical velocity shown for the Nile River on Fig 1 is much less than that found by Kennedy in India and also less than that for the Imperial Valley canals. The quantity as well as quality of silt is an important factor in these cases. The silt in both the Nile and Colorado Rivers is fine, but the Imperial canals require a much higher velocity than the canals of Egypt because the quantity of silt is much greater in the Imperial canals. The critical velocity for the canals observed by Kennedy is higher than those in Egypt, probably because the particles moved on the bed were larger, and, therefore, required higher velocities to move them. The Imperial canals require more velocity than the canals observed by Kennedy, although the latter have coarser loads, because the velocity required to transport the immense bed load of the fine Imperial Valley sand is greater than that necessary for the lesser quantity of coarser sand of the canals mentioned by Kennedy.

A similar agreement of the relations previously discussed in found in the data on bed width-depth ratios as shown on Fig. 2. In the canals of Egypt the velocities are low and, therefore, the velocities along the sides, although relatively high because the channels are narrow and deep, are still below those that will move the side material. The bed load is fine and small in quantity and, therefore, the low velocities along the bottom are sufficient to move it all.

The Indian canals shown on the diagram (Fig. 2) carry medium loads of rather coarse material and, therefore, require rather wide sections. The Imperial Valley canals carry immense loads of fine sand, which require high velocities to transport. In order that the velocities along the sides may be low enough so that the banks do not scour, the bed width-depth ratio must be high. In three of the four canals on which data are available, this relation is higher than that indicated by the equations of either Woods or Lindley. These had readily erodible sides. The fourth, which had a lower bottom width-depth ratio, had sides composed of material which had considerable resistance. The three sections with easily erodible banks gave widths considerably greater than is indicated by Lacey's formula for the type of silt which they contained. It is believed that Lacey's formula was based on data from canals which carry loads of considerably less magnitude.

STABLE CHANNEL SHAPES

The only investigator who has attempted a closer definition of the shape of stable channels than the bed width-depth relation is Lacey. He states (18):

"That natural silt-transporting channels have a tendency to assume a semi-elliptical section is confirmed by an inspection of a large number of channels in final regime and an examination of cross-sections of discharge sites of rivers in well-defined straight reaches of known stability."

He concluded that stable channels would be semi-elliptical, with the major axis horizontal, and with the ratio of the major axis to the semi-minor axis depending on the nature of the silt carried, being greater for coarser silt.

The results of the writer's investigations do not support this conclusion. A convenient way of comparing channel cross-sections is by means of a ratio, which may be called the "form factor," between the area of the channel section, up to the water surface, and the area of the enclosing rectangle. For an ellipse this ratio would be $\dfrac{\pi}{4} = 0.79$; for a parabola, 0.67; for a triangle, 0.50; and for a rectangle, 1.00. A study of a large number of cross-sections of channels has disclosed ratios from 0.56 to 0.92. The stable channels observed by Kennedy were reported to have practically vertical sides and horizontal bottoms, which would give a form factor of 1.00.

Just what shapes for stable channels are produced by all varieties of conditions has not yet been determined, but the writer has observed that for channels carrying a heavy load of graded silt, ranging from colloids to fine sand, the sections have nearly horizontal beds composed of the fine sand and nearly vertical sides of silts and clays. Such channels have form factors of about 0.90. This is the condition on the canals of the Imperial Valley. This difference between the composition of the bed and bank material has also been observed in India. Similar conditions result in channels carrying considerable bed load and a moderate quantity of fine silt. For a channel carrying water containing a small quantity of silt at high velocity in a material containing a considerable number of cobbles, the cross-section is distinctly saucer-shaped, most of the section being covered with cobbles, but with a small silt berm at each edge. This condition was observed on some of the ditches on the Uncompahgre Project, in Colorado, and in the San Luis Valley, in Colorado. One ditch that was carefully measured, had a form factor of 0.85. It is believed that further study will disclose typical shapes for a number of common conditions and the reasons therefor.

VARIATION IN DISCHARGE

The design of the best section for many canals is complicated by variation in the flow they are to carry. Some canals fill at one time and scour out at another, a substantially stable channel resulting from the balance of scour and fill. Many of the data which can be secured on stable shapes are complicated by this discharge variation. No rules can be given for the treatment of such cases. Until the problem of the simple case of relatively uniform flow is obtained, the more complex case of variable flow can be attacked only by the application of engineering judgment based on a knowledge of existing conditions and available information regarding shapes required for uniform flow.

ACKNOWLEDGMENTS

In the investigation leading to this paper many discussions of the problem were studied and many helpful suggestions were thus secured. With these the writer has combined his own ideas. It is not always possible to state definitely which were original and which were secured from literature. The papers on the subject which have been found most useful have been incorporated in the "Bibliography." To the authors and discussers of those papers the writer is particularly indebted. He is also indebted to C. A. Wright, H. F. Blaney, W. M. Griffith, F. C. Scobey, J. C. Stevens, and S. P. Wing, Members, Am. Soc. C. E., and to the General Board of Irrigation of India, for valuable data and suggestions.

As previously stated, this paper gives the results of studies for the selection of stable channels for the All-American Canal. This canal is being designed by, and constructed under, the direction of the U. S. Bureau of Reclamation.

All designs and investigations of the Bureau of Reclamation are under the direction of J. L. Savage, M. Am. Soc. C. E. All engineering and construction work is under the general direction of R. F. Walter, M. Am. Soc. C. E., and all activities of the Bureau are under Elwood Mead, M. Am. Soc. C. E.[3] The writer wishes to express his appreciation to the authorities of the Bureau of Reclamation for permission to publish these data.

BIBLIOGRAPHY

(1) **Hydraulic Diagram for Canals in Earth**, by R. G. Kennedy, *Minutes of Proceedings,* Inst. C. E., Vol. 119 (1895), p. 281.

(2) **Normal Data of Design for Kennedy Channels**, by F. W. Woods, Chf. Engr., Irrig. Works, Punjab, July 28, 1917.

(3) **Regime Channels**, by E. S. Lindley, M. Am. Soc. C. E., *Proceedings,* Punjab Eng. Congress, 1919, p. 63.

(4) **A New Hydraulic Formula (for Silting Velocity—Kennedy's Data)**, by F. W. Woods, *The Engineer,* Vol. 143, June 17, 1927, p. 646.

(5) **Instructions for Grading and Designing Irrigation Canals**, by R. G. Kennedy, *Punjab Irrigation Paper No. 10.*

(6) **Hydraulic Diagrams for Channels in Earth**, by R. G. Kennedy, Public Works Dept., India. (A new edition of this work is available.) Also, *Engineering News-Record,* Vol. 106, 1931, p. 370.

(7) **Critical Velocity Observations**, Madras Public Works Dept., October 9, 1912.

(8) **Hydraulic Diagrams for Design of Channels in Earth by Kutter's Formula**, by Capt. A. Garrett, Second Edition, 1913. (The data and contents of the first edition are not known.)

(9) **A New Theory of Silt and Scour**, by W. T. Bottomley, *Engineering,* Vol. 125, March 16, 1928, p. 307.

(10) **Irrigation Practice in Egypt**, by Molesworth and Yenidunia, 1922.

[3] Dr. Mead died on January 26, 1936.

(11) **Silt Investigations,** by A. B. Buckley, *Paper No. 4,* Irrig. Projects Dept. of Egypt.

(12) **Some Problems Connected with Rivers and the Canals in Southern India,** by J. M. Lacey, *Minutes of Proceedings,* Inst. C. E., Vol. 216, p. 150.

(13) **The Influence of Silt on the Velocity of Water Flowing in Open Channels,** by A. B. Buckley, *Minutes of Proceedings,* Inst. C. E., Vol. 216, p. 183.

(14) **Irrigation Project of the Californias,** by S. L. Rothery, M. Am. Soc. C. E., *Minutes of Proceedings,* Inst. C. E., Vol. 216, p. 161.

(15) **Note on Silt Investigation No. 1,** by A. B. Buckley and Hughen, Cairo, 1919.

(16) **Influence of Silt on the Velocity of Water Flowing in Open Channels,** by R. B. Buckley, *Engineering,* Vol. 115, 1923, p. 311.

(17) **A Theory of Silt and Scour,** by W. M. Griffith, *Minutes of Proceedings,* Inst. C. E., Vol. 223, January 25, 1927. (Abstracted, *Engineering,* Vol. 123, January 21, 1927, p. 72; and Vol. 125, March 16, 1928, p. 307.)

(18) **Stable Channels in Alluvium,** by Gerald Lacey, *Minutes of Proceedings,* Inst. C. E., Vol. 229; also *Engineering,* Vol. 129, February 7, 1930, pp. 179–180.

(19) **The Transportation of Debris by Running Water,** by G. K. Gilbert, *Professional Paper No. 86,* U. S. Geological Survey.

Mechanics and Hydrodynamics

(20) **Modern Development in Study of Turbulence,** by L. Prandtl, *Memorandum No. 720,* National Advisory Committee for Aeronautics.

(21) **The Present State of the Turbulence Problem,** *Applied Mechanics,* A. S. M. E., Vol. 1, No. 1.

(22) **Review of the Theory of Turbulent Flow and Its Relation to Sediment Transportation,** by M. P. O'Brien, Assoc. M. Am. Soc. C. E., *Transactions,* Am. Geophysical Union, April, 1933.

(23) **Towards a Theory of the Morphologic Significance of Turbulence in the Flow of Water in Streams,** by J. B. Leighly, Univ, of California Geographical Publications, Vol. 6, No. 1, 1932.

(24) **Hydraulic and Sedimentary Characteristics of Rivers,** by L. G. Straub, Assoc. M. Am. Soc. C. E., *Transactions,* Am. Geophysical Union, April, 1932.

The Hydraulic Geometry of Stream Channels and Some Physiographic Implications

By LUNA B. LEOPOLD *and* THOMAS MADDOCK, Jr.

GEOLOGICAL SURVEY PROFESSIONAL PAPER 252

Quantitative measurement of some of the hydraulic factors that help to determine the shape of natural stream channels: depth, width, velocity, and suspended load, and how they vary with discharge as simple power functions. Their interrelations are described by the term "hydraulic geometry."

UNITED STATES GOVERNMENT PRINTING OFFICE, WASHINGTON : 1953

GENERAL STATEMENT

Geomorphology, that branch of geology dealing with land forms, their genesis and history, has been classically treated almost exclusively in a qualitative manner. William Morris Davis, for pedagogic reasons, invented words and contrived similes which were descriptive and easy to remember, but were supported by intricately developed general argument rather than by field data. The qualitative approach to geomorphology has indeed been constructive, but it would be desirable to analyze some of the concepts quantitatively.

There is available a mass of data on streamflow collected over a period of seventy years representing rivers all over the United States. The field procedure used by engineers to measure the rate of water discharge in a river furnishes concurrent measurements of mean velocity, width, shape and area of the cross section, as well as discharge. Moreover, in the last decade the systematic collection of data on suspended sediment has begun though the number of stations collecting is as yet few.

The present paper reports on analyses of some of these data, keeping in mind possible application to geomorphic problems. The available data are not necessarily the best type for an analysis of stream processes. The parameters measured are perhaps not the most meaningful for such analysis. Nevertheless, the available data do provide some generalized relations of interest to the geomorphologist.

The plan of the paper is as follows:

The characteristics of channel shape in certain river cross sections are examined. At a given cross section, the width and depth of the channel and, therefore, the velocity change with the amount of water flowing in the cross section. The changes in width, depth, and velocity in response to changes in discharge are observed to have certain characteristics which apply to many natural river cross sections, and these similarities are described in the first part of the paper.

These same characteristics are then examined downstream along the length of natural channels in order to determine how they change there. Changes in slope and roughness, which help determine the observed variations, are reserved for later discussion.

The data used are those collected at regular river measurement stations for purposes of determining river discharge. Such data are obtained for purposes other than a study of fluvial morphology and are, for the writers' purposes, incomplete. Particularly, data on river slope and bed roughness are meager but some useful ideas may be obtained even from the incomplete operational data.

It is emphasized that the present study should be considered preliminary in character. Data on stream-gaging and suspended load discussed here are clearly imperfect measures of the variables of specific interest to the geomorphologist. Moreover, the present analysis deals primarily with general trends in the relations among measured variables, and much further work is necessary to explain the deviations from these trends. And finally, the suspended-load data available are primarily derived from Western streams. Comparable data on streams in humid areas are most meager. These many restrictions are recognized by the authors who attempt continuously to keep before the mind of the reader the limitations of the data, while emphasizing the general trends rather than the innumerable individual variations.

Explanation of these individual variations and refinement of the general concepts must await further work.

THE HYDRAULIC GEOMETRY OF STREAM CHANNELS

CONCEPT OF FREQUENCY OF DISCHARGE

Before describing the channel characteristics at a given river cross section and how those characteristics change downstream, it appears desirable to discuss by way of definition, frequency of discharge and cumulative frequency, or flow-duration, curves. The hydrologist to whom these conceptions are everyday tools will pardon the inclusion here of a brief discussion aimed at providing the geologist a picture of frequency relations which is essential to an understanding of what will follow.

The procedure used in making stream measurements is well described in the literature (Corbett, 1943; Linsley, Kohler, and Paulhus, 1949, pp. 182–198).

The daily mean discharge is the average of all rates for a day, and is expressed in cubic feet per second. The mean rate of discharge for each day of the year at measuring stations on many rivers is published by the U. S. Geological Survey in the annual Water-Supply Papers.

118

The frequency of a daily mean discharge at a given river gaging station, is determined by counting the number of occurrences of this rate throughout a period of record. In hydrologic practice the number of occurrences is usually presented in the form of a cumulative frequency, or flow-duration, curve, an example of which is presented in figure 1 (after Hembree, Colby, Swenson, and Davis, 1952, fig. 30). To construct such a curve, a number of categories of rates of discharge are arbitrarily chosen. The number of days on which the measured daily mean discharge fell in each category is determined by tallying the data. The numbers in each category are then accumulated from the largest discharge category to the smallest, and each cumulative figure is divided by the total number of days of record. The resultant quotients represent the percent of time given discharges are equalled or exceeded at the station.

These figures representing percent of time are then plotted against discharge to provide the flow-duration curve of which figure 1 is a sample. On it a discharge of 1,000 cfs or more occurs about 8 percent of the time. This means that through a long period, 8 percent of the days, or on the average 8 days in every 100, experienced a discharge of 1,000 cfs or more.

The cumulative frequency, or duration, of a given daily discharge is expressed as the percent of time that this rate is equalled or exceeded. Discharge rates of the same cumulative frequency may differ, depending on the streams being considered. For example, a point on a large trunk river and a point on a small tributary may have discharge rates of the same cumulative frequency—or frequency, as it is ordinarily expressed; but discharge in the tributary may be only a few cubic feet per second, and in the trunk river it may be thousands of cubic feet per second.

The median discharge is that discharge which is equalled or exceeded 50 percent of the time; that is, half the days have flow greater than the median, and half less. At Arvada the median flow is about 160 cfs. The mean annual discharge, or the arithmetic mean of the flow of all individual days at Arvada is about 430 cfs, or almost three times the median. Mean annual discharge is generally greater than median, and the mean rate of discharge is equalled or exceeded on somewhat less than half the number of days at most points on a river.

As a rough generalization, it may be stated that the mean annual rates of discharge at all points on a large number of rivers are equalled or exceeded about the same percent of time.

The values of average annual discharge at measuring stations on many rivers in the United States are readily available in the Water-Supply Papers of the U. S. Geological Survey. For example, the average discharge for the Powder River at Arvada, Wyo., for the period 1916–47 is published with the description of the station in Water-Supply Paper 1086 (1950) on page 237.

For purposes of definition the conception of a varying discharge at a given river cross section and downstream will now be explained. In figure 2 cross sections A and B represent two points on a river at low discharge; C and D are the same sections at higher discharge. These sections are shown at the right, as *A*, *B*, *C*, and *D*, in their relation to the full length of the river and to its watershed at both low and high discharge. Though the highest discharge may flow over bank, this paper is not concerned with discharges above bankful.

These diagrams illustrate the conception that the width and depth of the channel increase at a given river cross section with increase in discharge. Variations in discharge follow a pattern in time that is peculiar to the position of the cross section and to the river. The different discharges at a given cross section vary in frequency. Frequency is a function of the watershed and its hydrologic and physical characteristics.

Under the condition of low discharge represented by the diagram in the upper right corner of figure 2, it is postulated that every point along the river is experiencing a discharge that is small for that point; or, if all points along a river system are experiencing a relatively low discharge, the frequency of the rate of discharge at any one point is about the same as the frequency of the rate at any other point. Of course the rate of discharge, not its frequency, will generally be much

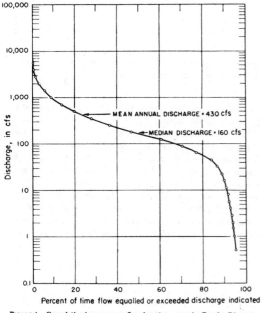

FIGURE 1.—Cumulative frequency, or flow-duration, curve for Powder River at Arvada, Wyo., 1917–50.

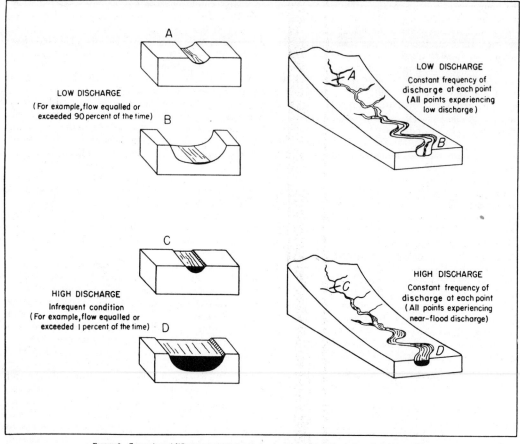

LOW DISCHARGE
(For example, flow equalled or
exceeded 90 percent of the time)

LOW DISCHARGE
Constant frequency of
discharge at each point
(All points experiencing
low discharge)

HIGH DISCHARGE
Infrequent condition
(For example, flow equalled or
exceeded I percent of the time)

HIGH DISCHARGE
Constant frequency of
discharge at each point
(All points experiencing
near-flood discharge)

FIGURE 2.—Comparison of different rates of discharge at a given river cross section and at points downstream.

greater near the mouth of a river draining a large area than at some headwater point. The same postulation is made for the condition of high discharge, as represented by the diagram in the lower right.

The two diagrams of the watershed are introduced to emphasize the points, first, that at a given cross section different discharges have different frequencies; and second, that at cross sections situated at various points along the stream the rates of discharge are usually different, one from another. Comparison of the various cross sections along a stream is made in this paper only under the assumed condition that they are experiencing equal frequency of discharge.

The term "at a station" is used in this paper to mean at a given cross section, and the term "in a downstream direction" refers to cross sections situated along the length of a stream. "Change of discharge downstream" means different discharges of the same frequency at cross sections situated along the length of a stream.

The differences in discharge both at a station and in a downstream direction are associated with differences in width, depth, and velocity, as will be shown later.

[A discussion of changes of water depth, width, and velocity with discharge at a single station, p. 4-9 was deleted.]

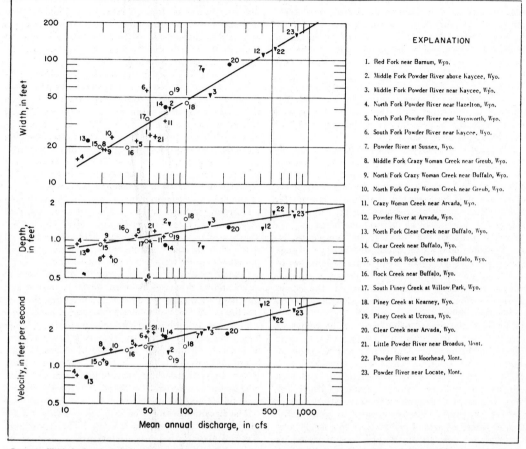

EXPLANATION

1. Red Fork near Barnum, Wyo.

2. Middle Fork Powder River above Kaycee, Wyo.

3. Middle Fork Powder River near Kaycee, Wyo.

4. North Fork Powder River near Hazelton, Wyo.

5. North Fork Powder River near Mayoworth, Wyo.

6. South Fork Powder River near Kaycee, Wyo.

7. Powder River at Sussex, Wyo.

8. Middle Fork Crazy Woman Creek near Greub, Wyo.

9. North Fork Crazy Woman Creek near Buffalo, Wyo.

10. North Fork Crazy Woman Creek near Greub, Wyo.

11. Crazy Woman Creek near Arvada, Wyo.

12. Powder River at Arvada, Wyo.

13. North Fork Clear Creek near Buffalo, Wyo.

14. Clear Creek near Buffalo, Wyo.

15. South Fork Rock Creek near Buffalo, Wyo.

16. Rock Creek near Buffalo, Wyo.

17. South Piney Creek at Willow Park, Wyo.

18. Piney Creek at Kearney, Wyo.

19. Piney Creek at Ucross, Wyo.

20. Clear Creek near Arvada, Wyo.

21. Little Powder River near Broadus, Mont.

22. Powder River at Moorhead, Mont.

23. Powder River near Locate, Mont.

FIGURE 5.—Width, depth, and velocity in relation to mean annual discharge as discharge increases downstream, Powder River and tributaries, Wyoming and Montana.

VARIATION OF HYDRAULIC CHARACTERISTICS IN A DOWNSTREAM DIRECTION

Frequency of discharge is especially important in an understanding of the hydraulic geometry of river systems and how the width, depth, and velocity of natural rivers change in a downstream direction.

As already emphasized, comparison of various cross sections along the length of a river is valid only under the condition of constant frequency of discharge at all cross sections.

The mean annual discharge is equalled or exceeded about the same percent of time on a large number of rivers. It represents roughly the discharge equalled or exceeded 1 day in every 4 over a long period. Though exactly the mean annual discharge may not occur at all points on any given day of record, it is closely approximated for a large number of days each year.

The data forming the basis of the discussion which follows are again current-meter measurements made at gaging stations of the Geological Survey.

The width, depth, and velocity corresponding to the mean discharge are plotted against mean discharge in figure 5 for all the gaging stations on all tributaries to the Powder River in Wyoming and Montana for which adequate data were available. Each gaging station provides one point in each of the plotted diagrams. Throughout the figure the abscissa value for each gaging station is its mean annual discharge.

For purposes of comparison, similar graphs representing the change of width, depth, and velocity with average annual discharge downstream are presented in figures 6–8. These represent the Bighorn River and tributaries in Wyoming and Montana, the Arikaree, Republican, Smoky Hill, and Kansas Rivers in the Kansas-Nebraska region, and gaging stations along the main trunk of the Missouri and lower Mississippi Rivers.

Proceeding downstream in a given river, the discharge tends to increase because of the progressively increasing drainage area, though of course there are some streams in which discharge decreases downstream, particularly in arid areas. It can be seen that for all the rivers plotted, the depth, width, and velocity tend to increase progressively as power functions of discharge. There is again considerable scatter of points in the graphs. There are reaches of the rivers represented in figures 5–8 on which either width, or depth, or velocity decreases downstream. The present paper, however, is concerned with the general trends and further work will be necessary to explain the details of deviations from these trends.

The graphs of figures 5–8 are referred to as the changes in width, depth, and velocity with increasing discharge in the downstream direction. It will be understood that a small tributary having a relatively low mean annual discharge may enter the main trunk far downstream, but its plotted position on the abscissa scale will be determined by its mean discharge.

Strictly speaking, the "downstream" graphs in figures 5–8 show how width, depth, and velocity change with discharges of equal frequency. Discharges of equal frequency tend to increase downstream with increasing drainage area. The phrase "in the downstream direction" is merely used as a short designation for this conception.

By use of the graph, tributaries can be compared directly with the trunk stream. On figure 5 the gaging stations on the main trunk of the Powder River (as an example, point 7) and a single large headwater fork (Middle Fork, point 2) are designated by the solid triangles. Stations on a single tributary, Clear Creek (point 14), and its headwater tributary, North Fork of Clear Creek (point 13), are designated by solid circles. Each of these two sets of points describe a single river stem and are downstream graphs uncomplicated by tributaries. It can be seen that were lines to be drawn through those two sets of points, separately, there would be a difference from the lines on the graphs representing the Powder River basin as a whole. Yet the difference is astonishingly small.

The general alinement of points on the downstream graphs indicates that in a given river basin where all cross sections are experiencing the same frequency of discharge, the corresponding values of depth, width, and velocity at different cross sections having the same discharge tend to be similar, regardless of where in the watershed or on what tributary the cross sections may be.

The graphs presented are examples chosen from a large number drawn for various river systems in the United States. Figure 9, with the plotted points through which the mean lines were drawn eliminated, presents similar graphs for selected river basins. Rivers were chosen to represent a diversity of geographic location, and physiographic and geologic types. The basins are also considerably different in size. To indicate this diversity of size of drainage area, the stations used to represent the Tombigbee River in Alabama have mean annual discharges from 700 to 35,000 cfs, whereas the Belle Fourche basin in Wyoming has mean annual discharges ranging from 40 to 600 cfs.

The mean lines through the points representing individual gaging stations (figures 5–8 are examples) were fitted by eye. There is considerable scatter of points about the respective mean lines. Moreover, as discussed previously, the points on the graphs represent values of depth, width, and velocity at stream-gaging stations situated at positions not uniformly representative of the average river cross sections. Despite the possible variations that might be introduced by these considerations, there is a tendency toward parallelism of the lines on the graphs in figure 9. As a rough generalization, it may be stated that in a downstream direction the rates of increase in width, depth, and velocity relative to discharge are of the same order of magnitude for rivers of different sized drainage basins and of widely different physiographic settings.

Some river basins studied have too small a range of mean annual discharge between small tributaries and the main stem to allow determination of the slope of the lines. A few river systems studied provide lines with slopes quite different from the majority. Figure 9 includes one such anomaly, the Loup River system, in order to demonstrate the range of slopes of lines found in the data studied. In the example of the Loup River, the ground-water contribution from the sand hills at the headwaters is believed to be partly responsible for its anomalous behavior.

The streams chosen to be included in figure 9 differ markedly in physiographic setting. The Tombigbee River of Alabama is a coastal-plain stream, narrow and deep. At a discharge of 1,000 cfs its depth is about 7.5 ft and its width 110 ft. The Republican and Kansas Rivers are typical streams of the Great Plains. They are relatively wide and shallow. At 1,000 cfs the lines representing these streams indicate a mean depth of 2.3 ft and a width of about 250 ft. In other words, the intercepts of the graphs on figure 9 differ greatly among rivers but the slopes of the lines are similar in magnitude. The rates of increase in depth, width, and velocity with discharge downstream may be similar among rivers despite marked differences in the width to depth ratio at any particular discharge.

From the data in figure 9 and other similar data it appears that the velocity tends to increase with mean annual discharge downstream in all the rivers studied. It must be remembered that this generalization is

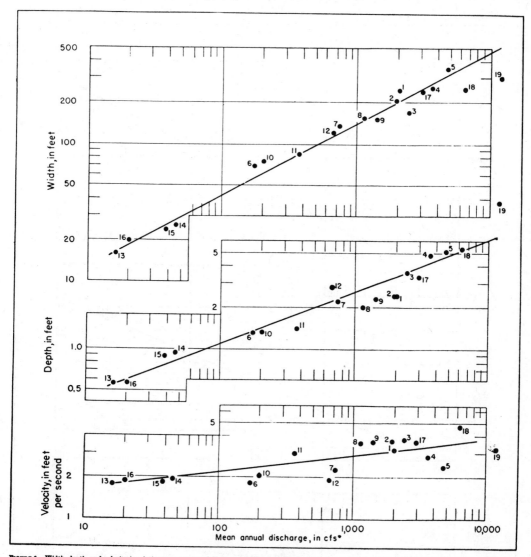

FIGURE 6.—Width, depth, and velocity in relation to mean annual discharge as discharge increases downstream, Bighorn River and tributaries, Wyoming, and Montana, and Yellowstone River, Montana.

EXPLANATION

1. Bighorn River at Manderson, Wyo.
2. Bighorn River at Thermopolis, Wyo.
3. Bighorn River at Kane, Wyo.
4. Bighorn River St. Xavier, Wyo.
5. Bighorn River near Custer (Hardin), Mont.
6. Wind River near Dubois, Wyo.
7. Wind River near Burris, Wyo.

8. Wind River at Riverton, Wyo.
9. Wind River near Crowheart, Wyo.
10. Greybull River near Basin, Wyo.
11. Greybull River at Meeteetsee, Wyo.
12. Popo Agie River near Riverton, Wyo.
13. North Fork Owl Creek near Anchor, Wyo.
14. Owl Creek near Thermopolis, Wyo.

15. Medicine Lodge Creek near Hyattville, Wyo.
16. Gooseberry Creek near Grass Creek, Wyo.
17. Yellowstone River at Corwin Springs, Mont.
18. Yellowstone River at Billings, Mont.
19. Yellowstone River near Sidney, Mont.

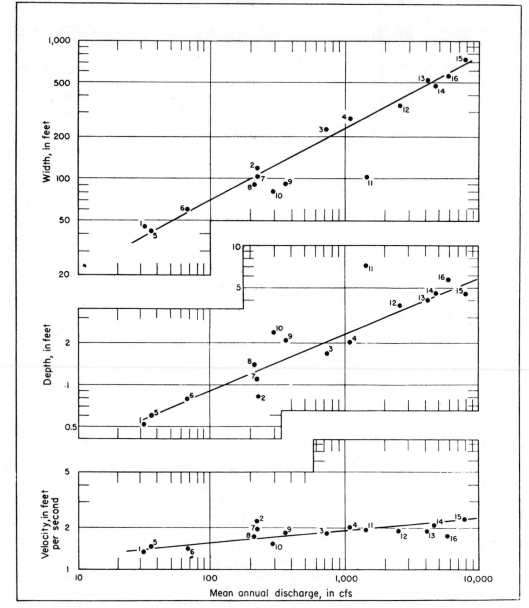

FIGURE 7.—Width, depth, and velocity in relation to mean annual discharge as discharge increases downstream, Arikaree, Republican, Smoky Hill, and Kansas Rivers in the Kansas River system, Kansas and Nebraska.

EXPLANATION

1. Arikaree River at Haigler, Nebr.
2. Republican River at Culbertson, Nebr.
3. Republican River near Bloomington, Nebr.
4. Republican River at Clay Center, Kans.
5. Smoky Hill River at Elkader, Kans.
6. Smoky Hill River at Ellis, Kans.

7. Smoky Hill River at Russell, Kans.
8. Smoky Hill River at Ellsworth, Kans.
9. Smoky Hill River near Langley, Kans.
10. Smoky Hill River at Linsborg, Kans.
11. Smoky Hill River at Enterprise, Kans.
12. Kansas River at Ogden, Kans.

13. Kansas River at Wamego, Kans.
14. Kansas River at Topeka, Kans.
15. Kansas River at Lecompton, Kans.
16. Kansas River at Bonner Springs, Kans.

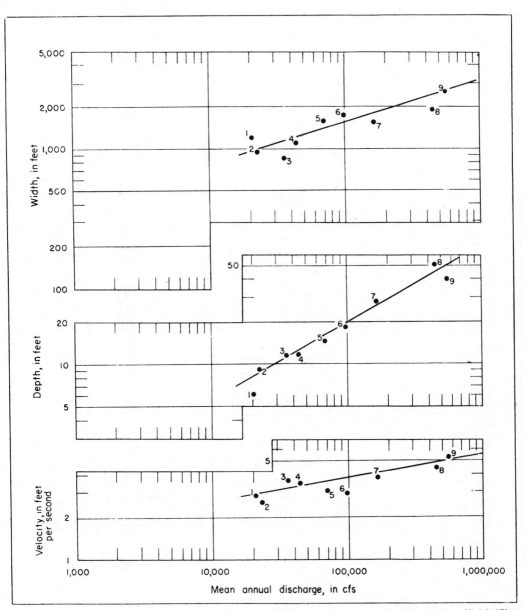

FIGURE 8.—Width, depth, and velocity in relation to mean annual discharge as discharge increases downstream, main trunk of Missouri and lower Mississippi Rivers.

EXPLANATION

1. Missouri River at Bismarck, N. Dak.
2. Missouri River at Pierre, S. Dak.
3. Missouri River at St. Joseph, Mo.

4. Missouri River at Kansas City, Mo.
5. Missouri River at Hermann, Mo.
6. Mississippi River at Alton, Ill.

7. Mississippi River at St. Louis, Mo.
8. Mississippi River at Memphis, Tenn.
9. Mississippi River near Vicksburg, Miss.

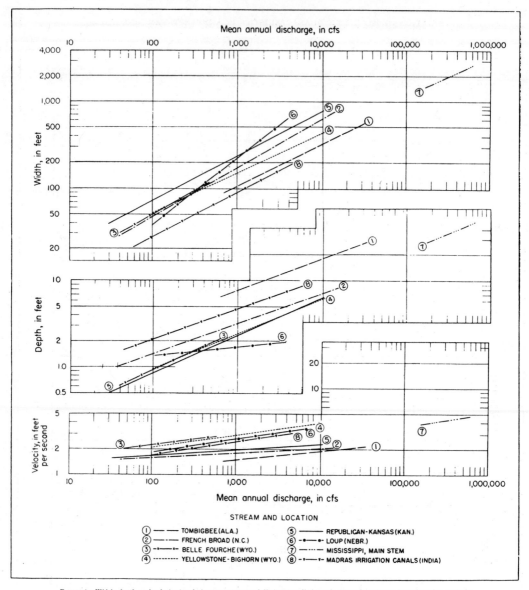

FIGURE 9.—Width, depth, and velocity in relation to mean annual discharge as discharge increases downstream in various river systems.

restricted to the situation in which discharge at all points along the river is of similar frequency.

Most geomorphologists are under the impression that the velocity of a stream is greater in the headwaters than in the lower reaches. The appearance of a mountain stream, of course, gives the impression of greater kineticity than that observed in a large river downstream. The impression of greater velocity upstream stems in part from a consideration of river slopes which obviously are steeper in the upper than in

126

the lower reaches. It will be recalled, however, that velocity depends on depth as well as on slope, as shown in the Manning equation

$$v = \frac{1.5}{n} d^{\frac{2}{3}} s^{\frac{1}{2}} \qquad (4)$$

where depth, d, is approximately equal to hydraulic radius for natural river sections, v is mean velocity, n is channel roughness, and s is slope. It is recognized that slope, s, in equation (4) is the slope of the energy grade line. For practical purposes throughout most of the discussion in the present paper, slope of the river profile sufficiently approximates the energy gradient for equation (4) to be used as if the slopes were identical.

The fact that velocity increases downstream with mean annual discharge in the rivers studied indicates that the increase in depth overcompensates for the decreasing river slope. The magnitude of this rate of change becomes clear by comparison of the exponents of depth and slope. In equation (4) the velocity depends on depth to the power $\frac{2}{3}$ and on slope to the power $\frac{1}{2}$. Increasing depth tends to increase velocity in a downstream direction. A variation of roughness in the downstream direction will also affect the rate of change of velocity and will be discussed later.

In summary, the rate of increase of depth downstream tends to overcompensate for the decreasing slope and tends to provide a net increase of velocity at mean annual discharge in the downstream direction of a river.

The straight-line relations on logarithmic paper show, just as they do for a particular river cross section, that width, depth, and velocity increase downstream with discharge in the form of simple power functions,

$$w = aQ^b \qquad (1)$$
$$d = cQ^f \qquad (2)$$
$$r = kQ^m \qquad (3)$$

The coefficients and exponents are assigned the same letters as for a given cross section of a river, but the values will be different for points in a downstream direction from those for the given section. Average values of the exponents for river basins studied are

$$b = 0.5$$
$$f = 0.4$$
$$m = 0.1$$

To recapitulate, both at a given river cross section and in the downstream direction at mean annual discharge, width, depth, and velocity increase with discharge. The functions representing these relations are similar but involve different exponents and numerical constants.

[Discussions of relations between channel shape and discharge, the hydraulic geometry of stream channels in relation to sediment load, channel shape adjustment during floods, stable irrigation canals, p. 16-52, were deleted.]

References

Corbett, D. M. and others, 1943, Stream gaging procedure: *U.S. Geol. Survey Water-Supply Paper 888.*

Hembree, C. H., Colby, B. R., Swanson, H. A. and Davis, J. R., 1952, Progress report, sedimentation and chemical quality of water in the Powder River drainage basin, Wyo. and Mont.: *U. S. Geol. Survey* (in preparation).

Linsley, R. K., Kohler, M. A., and Paulhus, J. L. H., 1949, *Applied hydrology,* McGraw-Hill Book Co., New York, 689 p.

The Graded River
and its Adjustment

IV

While engineers were attempting to design stable irrigation canals, geologists were puzzling over the possibility that rivers were stable over long periods of time. This controversy was essentially resolved by the appearance of Mackin's paper, which defined a graded stream in a manner acceptable to those concerned with both the long- and short-term behavior of rivers. It was an effort to reconcile the geologist's long-term view of rivers with the engineer's short-term view. For a discussion of grade and the concept of time in river morphology see Dury (1966) and Schumm and Lichty (1965). Mackin also emphasized that the river channel is part of a drainage system and that it cannot be understood apart from the system. Of considerable importance was Mackin's attempt to introduce the geomorphologist to the engineering literature on rivers and regime canals; in addition the paper summarizes the work of other investigators, notably Gilbert (1914) and Rubey (1933; see also 1955), whose papers are classics in the field. For another interpretation of the Cody Terrace see Moss and Bonini (1961). J. H. Mackin was Professor of Geology at the University of Washington and the University of Texas.

The second paper selected for inclusion in this section is another of Lane's papers that is still frequently cited in the engineering literature and which attempts to introduce the engineer to the geomorphic literature on rivers. After a short review of geomorphic research which will be repetitive to the geologist, Lane presents an equation relating sediment load to discharge and gradient. This simple relation helps organize one's thinking about river response to changes of load and discharge; however, the only morphologic variable is gradient and as indicated by Mackin many other morphologic factors can be altered during river adjustment (e.g., shape, pattern, channel roughness).

129

BULLETIN OF THE GEOLOGICAL SOCIETY OF AMERICA
VOL. 59, PP. 463-512, 1 FIG.   MAY 1948

7   CONCEPT OF THE GRADED RIVER

BY J. HOOVER MACKIN

CONTENTS

ILLUSTRATIONS

ABSTRACT

Grade is a condition of equilibrium in streams as agents of transportation. The validity of the concept has been questioned, but it is indispensable in any genetic study of fluvial erosional features and deposits. This paper modifies and extends the theory of grade originally set forth by Gilbert and Davis.

A graded stream is one in which, over a period of years, slope is delicately adjusted to provide, with available discharge and the prevailing channel characteristics, just the velocity required for transportation of all of the load supplied from above. Slope usually decreases in a downvalley direction, but because discharge, channel characteristics, and load do not vary systematically along the stream, the graded profile is not a simple mathematical curve. Corrasive power and bed rock resistance to corrasion determine the slope of the ungraded profile, but have no direct influence on the graded profile. Chiefly because of a difference in rate of downvalley decrease in caliber of load, the aggrading profile differs in form from the graded profile; the aggrading profile is, and the graded profile is not, asymptotic with respect to a horizontal line passing through base level. It is critical in any analysis of stream profiles to recognize the difference in slope-controlling factors in parts of the overall profile that are (1) graded, (2) ungraded, and (3) aggrading.

A graded stream responds to a change in conditions in accordance with Le Chatelier's general law:—"if a stress is brought to bear on a system in equilibrium, a reaction occurs, displacing the equilibrium in a direction that tends to absorb the effect of the stress." Readjustment is effected primarily by appropriate modification of slope by upbuilding or downcutting, and only to a minor extent or not at all by concomitant changes in channel characteristics. · Paired examples illustrate (1) the almost telegraphic rapidity with which the first phases of the reaction of a graded stream to a number of artificial changes are propagated upvalley and downvalley and, (2) the more or less complete readjustment that is effected over a period of thousands of years to analogous natural changes.

The engineer is necessarily concerned chiefly with short-term and quantitative aspects of the reaction of a graded stream to changes in control, while the attention of the geologist is usually focused on the long-term and genetic aspects of the stream's response to changes. But the basic problems are the same, and a pooling of ideas and data may enable the engineer to improve his long range planning of river control measures and permit the geologist to interpret, in quantitative terms, the deposits of ancient streams.

INTRODUCTION

The concept of grade, as a condition of equilibrium in streams as agents of transportation, has been the fundamental basis for the understanding of fluvial landforms for the last half century. The geologic literature contains, however, a number of markedly different definitions of the concept, and many geologists have been troubled by its defects and inconsistencies. An analysis of some of these difficulties leads Kesseli (1941) to conclude that the views of Gilbert (1877) and Davis (1902) regarding the equilibrium relationship are untenable and that the concept of grade must be abandoned. This article is an outgrowth of studies of stream planation surfaces in Wyoming (Mackin, 1936, 1937), was started several years before Kesseli's critique was published, and is a revision of the concept rather than a defense of the writings of Gilbert and Davis.

The engineering literature provides a counterpart for the concept of grade in the idea of the "adjusted" or "regime" condition in streams. The engineer is concerned primarily with short-term reactions of adjusted streams to damming, shortening, and deepening operations and other river training measures. The geologist sees erosional and depositional features in valleys as records of the long-term response of the graded stream to various natural changes in conditions controlling its activity. These natural changes in control are in many instances closely comparable with those introduced by man. Because they are a good test of the concept of the graded or adjusted condition, a number of paired examples of long- and short-term reactions of streams to analogous changes are brought together here; citations are drawn about equally from geologic and engineering writings.

There is much of common interest in this type of synthesis, but the geologist and the engineer differ widely in background and habits of thought, and an attempt to bridge the gap requires certain compromises in use of terms and manner of treatment. General policies are as follows:

(1) Future advances in knowledge of stream processes will certainly be based increasingly on quantitative measurement and mathematical analysis. But the quantitative aspects of transportation by running water are controversial and are not essential for an evaluation of the concept of grade; the treatment here is qualitative. If, by clarifying some of the genetic aspects of the problem in qualitative terms, or focusing attention on them, the article clears the way for more rapid quantitative advances, it will have served part of its purpose.

(2) There are two possible approaches to the study of streams as agents of transportation, (A) in terms of relationships between slope, discharge, channel form, and the size of grains comprising the load, and (B) in terms of energy transformations. Preferably, the two should not be combined. But they *are* combined in most of the papers cited, and, while the thesis of this article depends wholly on the first approach, some discussion of energy transformations is necessary. The manner in which the term energy is used is well established in the literature; it may be regarded by the specialist as loose, but he will be merely irritated rather than misled.

(3) Transporting power is considered to be a function of *velocity*, rather than the

depth-slope (tractive force) *relationship* that forms the basis for many mathematical treatments of transportation. This usage has the advantage of simplicity and, for present purposes, the differences are negligible (for analysis of these alternative theories see Rubey (1938) and discussion of Kramer (1935) by outstanding engineers, especially Matthes and Straub (p. 867–868).

(4) Partly in deference to the inveterate equation-skippers, but chiefly because critical differences between causes and effects do not appear in an equation, mathematical methods of expressing relationships are generally avoided.

ACKNOWLEDGMENTS

After the 15-year period during which the views outlined here were developed it is difficult for me to distinguish between ideas that were arrived at independently and those gleaned from reading, discussions with numerous geologists and engineers, and lectures in the classrooms of Douglas Johnson and W. M. Davis. An effort has been made to credit other workers with specific points made by them, but the 80-odd citations certainly do not cover all of the cases in which the same thoughts have been expressed before, especially in the writings of Baulig (1926), Davis (1902), Gilbert (1877, 1914), and Rubey (1933, 1938) among the geologists, and Lane (1937), Salisbury (1937), Schoklitsch (1937) and Sonderegger (1935) among the engineers. Early papers, chiefly of historic interest, are not included in the bibliography (in this connection see Baulig, 1926).

I am indebted to W. W. Rubey and Lee Stokes (U. S. Geological Survey), Stafford C. Happ and Allen S. Cary (U. S. Army Engineers), and Robert C. Hennes (Engineering, University of Washington) for critical comments on the manuscript.

VELOCITY AND LOAD

GENERAL STATEMENT

This section is a brief review of certain general principles of stream transportation, drawn chiefly from the works of Gilbert, Rubey and Hjulström. The principles are are based largely on laboratory studies and apply equally to graded streams and streams that are not graded. As outlined here they provide a basis for understanding observed behavior of graded streams; the concept of grade depends, not on any particular theory of transportation nor any special manner of apportioning energy losses, but on the form of the longitudinal profile developed by the debris-carrying stream under stable controlling conditions, and on profile changes that automatically readjust the stream to any change in controls.

ENERGY AND VELOCITY

The energy of a stream between any two points is proportional to the product of the mass and the total fall between the two points. This is, hereafter, the "total energy"; it increases with increase in discharge or slope but is increased also, negligibly for present purposes, by the presence of debris in motion in the water.

The energy is dissipated largely, or in some circumstances wholly, as heat developed by viscous shear within the stream. A rather artificial but useful distinction can be made between (1) energy dissipated in friction along the wetted perimeter of the channel (external frictional losses), (2) energy dissipated in friction between the diverse threads of the turbulent current (internal frictional losses), and (3) energy consumed in the transportation of load. The external and internal frictional losses occur whether or not the stream is engaged in transportation; these losses increase with increase in roughness of the channel, with irregularity in the trend or alignment of the channel, and with any departure from the ideal semicircular cross-sectional form that provides the shortest length of wetted perimeter per unit of cross-sectional area. Roughness, alignment, and cross-sectional form are referred to as "channel characteristics"; they determine the "hydraulic efficiency" of the channel. On the basis of an analysis of Gilbert's experimental results and other data, Rubey estimates that the frictional energy losses account for 96% to 97.5% of the total energy in some debris-carrying streams, and that the remaining energy is utilized in transportation (Rubey, 1933, p. 503). The point emphasized here is that the share of the total energy that is utilized in transportation is very small.

Transportation of boulders and pebbles that move only if they are rolled or dragged along the stream bed, and of smaller grains that must be lifted again and again by turbulent currents consumes energy. These pebbles and grains move slower than the water—the energy required to put them in motion and keep them in motion varies with grain size and quantity. Transportation of ultra-fine or colloidal particles with negligible settling velocities (in still water) does not tax the energy of the stream.

If the energy in a given segment were not utilized within that segment an acceleration in the rate of flow would result. Since this is usually not the case it appears that the energy in most segments is equal to the energy dissipated within those segments (Gilbert, 1877, p. 106). This conclusion taken together with the fact that the energy dissipated in internal and external friction is overwhelmingly greater than that consumed in transportation means that, total energy determined by slope and discharge remaining the same, relatively slight changes in the channel characteristics cause very marked changes in transporting power. The practical engineer concerned, for example, with design of non-silting and non-eroding canals is well aware of this relationship (Lane, 1937). It is not given due emphasis in geologic textbook discussion of stream transportation.

The several factors that enter into this energy balance in streams may be recast in terms of velocity:

Velocity increases with increase in slope of the water surface.

Increase in discharge is accompanied by increase in (a) the cross-sectional area and (b) the wetted perimeter of the channel. Since the natural channel is approximately rectangular in section the cross-sectional area increases approximately as the product of width and depth, while the wetted perimeter increases approximately as the sum of the width and twice the depth. Cross-sectional area therefore increases relatively to wetted perimeter with increase in discharge, and this change results in a relative decrease in frictional retardation of flow. Primarily for this reason, velocity varies with discharge.

As the channel departs from the ideal cross-sectional form, or as the floor and walls vary from smooth to rough, or as the trend varies from straight to tortuous, there is an increase in external frictional retardation of flow due to increased length of the wetted perimeter relative to cross-sectional area, and also an increase in internal frictional retardation of flow due to increased turbulence. For these reasons, velocity varies with variation in the channel characteristics.

Velocity is, then, a measure of the energy content of the stream. It varies with any change in the total energy resulting from change in slope or discharge, and, total energy remaining the same, it varies with any change in the energy dissipated in external or internal friction, as defined earlier. To complete the picture of energy-velocity interrelations for the case of the debris-laden stream we have Gilbert's experimental data indicating that velocity varies inversely with the amount of energy consumed in the transportation of load (1914, p. 225–230).

COMPETENCE

Competence is defined by Gilbert as a measure of the ability of the stream to transport debris in terms of particle size; the familiar statement is that the weight of the largest particles moved by a stream varies as the sixth power of the velocity. It is well known that there are notable differences in velocity in different parts of the cross section of a stream; the term, as used in the expression above, is usually interpreted as the average velocity. Rubey states that competence actually varies as the sixth power of the "bed velocity", and that the bed-velocity formula gives "reasonably close estimates of the maximum size of particles transported by some large natural streams for which adequate data are available" (Rubey, 1938, p. 137). For purposes of the present discussion, the significance of Rubey's analysis and of the experimental data presented by Gilbert and numerous other workers in this field is simply that velocity required for transportation of detritus increases very markedly with increase in particle size.

The "sixth-power law" was formulated to express the velocity requirements of that fraction of the load of a stream which moves by sliding, rolling, and bouncing along the stream's bed, i.e. the tractional load or bed load. But a large part of the load of most natural streams is transported in suspension. The size of the largest particles that can be carried in suspension depends, not on velocity directly, but upon the intensity of turbulence within the stream (Leighly, 1934). Turbulence itself is, however, a function of velocity among other factors; intensity of turbulence increases with increase in velocity. Thus, while Rubey's sixth-power law does not apply to the transportation of suspended load, the decrease in velocity requirements with decrease in grain size probably continues through the range of the larger grain sizes that are normally carried in suspension. A considerable fraction of the suspended load may consist of ultra-fine or colloidal particles with negligible setting velocities; maintenance of these ultra-fine materials in suspension depends only negligibly upon velocity.

CAPACITY

"Capacity", as defined by Gilbert (1914, p. 35), refers to "the maximum load a stream can carry". The experimental data on which the competence principle was based demonstrate also that, in a stream of given discharge, the velocity required for transportation varies with the quantity of any one grain size, the velocity requirements increasing with increase in the quantity or total weight of the material shed into the stream.

Gilbert used "capacity" in discussing data relating to transportation of weighed amounts of particles in the sand gravel size range under laboratory conditions. In spite of his explicit warning that his concept of capacity does not necessarily apply to natural streams (Gilbert, 1914, 223–230; see also Quirke, 1945) there has been a tendency so to apply it; the expressions "loaded to capacity", or "fully loaded", or "saturated with load" are frequently used in discussion of the graded condition in streams. These expressions are of course meaningless unless accompanied by some statement of the grain sizes or range in grade sizes which constitute the load. A stream "loaded to capacity" with coarse sand and pebbles could carry an enormously greater tonnage of material without change in velocity if the materials making up the load were crushed to silt size.

The capacity principle, like the competence principle, probably does not apply to the transportation of very small particles. Since the maintenance in suspension of ultra-fine clay particles and colloids (particles with negligible settling velocities) does not depend upon velocity, there is no theoretical upper limit to the amount of these materials that a stream of a given size and velocity can carry. A stream "loaded to capacity" with exceedingly fine particles would be a mud flow (Hjulström, 1935, p. 344–345).

There probably is in nature every gradation between normal streams and mud flows. Even the low concentrations of colloidal and ultra-fine particles that occur in normal streams undoubtedly tend slightly to increase carrying power by increasing the specific gravity of the water, and tend slightly to increase external and internal frictional energy losses by increasing the viscosity of the water. With higher and higher concentrations of these materials, particles of silt and sand and finally pebbles and boulders come to have negligible settling velocities in the medium until, in a mud flow, great blocks of rock can be carried buoyantly in a plastic mass that may move only a few feet an hour. These effects are negligible in normal streams.

THE TOTAL LOAD

Depending upon the lithologic characteristics, relief, and erosional processes in its drainage basin, and on processes in operation within the stream itself (as sorting), the range in grain sizes in the total load supplied to a given segment of a stream may vary widely. Moreover, the proportions of the several grain sizes in the total load may differ markedly in streams in which the range in grain size is the same. There is always, in normal streams, a decided "deficiency" in the supply of colloidal and ultra-fine materials.

Frequently the alluvial materials beneath and marginal to a stream channel include such an assortment of grain sizes that, as the velocity of the stream increases with seasonal increase in discharge, it is free to put in motion progressively coarser grain sizes up to the limits of its competence. There will be in this case a reasonably close relationship between the *quantity* of the debris in motion and the *largest grain sizes* that are in motion at a given time.   Partly on this basis, and using an expression for the "average settling velocity of all of the debris particles being transported", Rubey has developed a means for evaluating both competence and capacity relationships in terms of bed velocity: "in a stream free to pick up much sand and gravel as its velocity is increased, the unit width load will vary roughly as the third power of the 'bed' velocity" (Rubey, 1938, p. 139).

Rubey points out that this third-power principle applies only approximately in even those streams to which a fair proportion of the several movable grain sizes (excepting the ultra-fines) are available.   In this case both competence and capacity might be said to be a function of velocity.   But a stream completely adjusted to the transport of a large amount of sand and silt may carry no pebbles at all, due to a deficiency in supply, although gravel sizes are well within its competence.   Gilbert's experimental proof that the quantity of load increases as the grain size decreases suggests that in this special case the total load per unit width of stream varies as a power of the bed velocity higher than the third power; it might be said that "capacity" is the critical factor in this case.   A stream may, on the other hand, be supplied with a load consisting predominantly of pebbles and boulders, with a notably small proportion of sand.   It appears that in this circumstance the total load per unit width of channel may vary as a power of the bed velocity lower than the third power; competence might be said to be the critical factor.   (For an example of the significance of this point in a practical problem of design *see* Whipple's discussion of Missouri River slope, 1942, p. 1191–1200, 1212–1214.)

These numerical values, as such, are not important for purposes of the discussion to follow.   But the possibility of notable variations in the proportions of the several grain sizes making up the total load, and the bearing of these variations (qualitatively) on the velocity requirements in the transporting stream, are important. Hereafter the expression "increase (or decrease) in load" means increase (or decrease) in the quantity and average grain size, in accordance with the case treated by Rubey. The expression "increase (or decrease) in calibre of load" means increase (or decrease) in particle size, the total load remaining the same.

THE CONCEPT OF GRADE

A graded stream is not then, strictly speaking, one in which there is "a balance between total energy and the work given the stream to do", or in which "energy supplied equals energy consumed"; a non-accelerating flow of water carrying no load in a flume or a bed-rock channel fulfills these requirements, but would hardly be considered graded in the geologic sense.   It is not a stream in which "slope is adjusted to load"; the carrying power of a stream is a function of velocity, and slope is only one of the factors which bear on velocity.   One of the attributes of a graded stream is a "balance between erosion and deposition", but definition of the condition of grade in terms of this balance, and emphasis on the "constant shifting" of the balance, is unfortunate because it focuses attention on incidental short-term changes in the activity of the stream and loses sight of the long-term balance which is the distinctive characteristic of the stream at grade.   A graded stream is not a stream "loaded to capacity" because streams never carry a capacity load (by Gilbert's definition). These definitions are partly or basically sound, but all of them include half-truths that are sources of confusion.

A graded stream is not in any sense a stream which is unable to abrade its bed because "all of its energy is used in transportation", or because "transporting the load requires all the energy that was formerly (during youth) applied to downcutting". The particles comprising the load are the tools used in abrasion, and since abrasion does not involve a dissipation of energy independent of that consumed in the propulsion of the tools, abrasion may be regarded as an incidental result of the bouncing, sliding and rolling motion of the particles.

A graded stream is one in which, over a period of years, slope is delicately adjusted to provide, with available discharge and with prevailing channel characteristics, just the velocity required for the transportation of the load supplied from the drainage basin. The graded stream is a system in equilibrium; its diagnostic characteristic is that any change in any of the controlling factors will cause a displacement of the equilibrium in a direction that will tend to absorb the effect of the change.

By *stream* we mean, of course, that particular segment with which we are directly concerned; many rivers have both graded and ungraded parts. The expression *over a period of years* rules out seasonal and other short-term fluctuations on the one hand and, on the other, the exceedingly slow changes that accompany the progress of the erosion cycle. *Load* and *discharge* deserve the prominence given in the definition not because they are the only or even necessarily the most important factors controlling slope, but because they are the only factors which are, *in origin*, wholly independent of the stream. *Slope* stands alone because it appears to be the only factor in the equilibrium which is automatically adjustable by the stream itself in such a direction as to accomodate changes in external controls that call for changes in velocity.

The balance involved in the condition of grade can be stated in an equation, but this method of expression is inadequate for present purposes because the terms of an equation are transposable. As set up in an equation, for example, load is a function of velocity. In answer to a query as to which is the cause and which is the effect, the average engineer will assert that velocity controls or determines the load that is carried by a stream; and he may have misgivings as to the sanity of the party who raised the question. In a flume or rock-floored torrent velocity does, in a sense, determine the load that can be carried. But, over a period of years, the load supplied to a stream is actually dependent, not on the velocity of the stream, but on the lithology, relief, vegetative cover, and erosional processes in operation in its drainage basin, and, in the graded stream, that particular slope is maintained which will provide just the velocity required to transport all of the supplied load. In this very real sense velocity is determined by, or adjusted to, the load. In the graded stream, load is a cause, and velocity is an effect: this relationship is not transposable.

The sections that follow approach the question raised by Kesseli as to the validity of the concept of grade by considering (1) typical examples of streams at grade, (2) factors that control the slope of the profile under stable conditions, and (3) reactions of graded streams to natural and artificial changes.

139

EXAMPLES OF STREAMS AT GRADE

A 50-mile segment of the Shoshone Valley east of Cody, Wyoming, contains a striking assemblage of river terraces, ranging from a few feet to several hundred feet above the stream.   Inter-terrace scarps and the valleys of cross-cutting tributaries

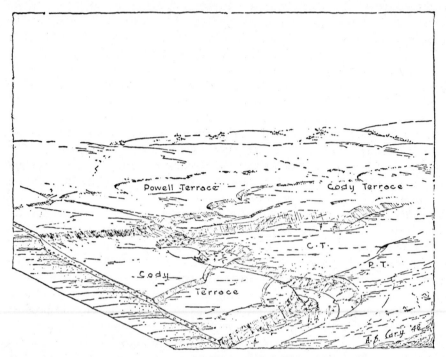

FIGURE 1.—*River terraces near Cody, Wyoming*

Drawn by Allen S. Cary from photographs taken from Cedar Mountain looking eastward down the Shoshone Valley. The alluvial veneer shown on the front of the block includes Shoshone River channel gravel and overbank silts, and side stream fan deposits; these materials are wholly different in origin and appearance but cannot be distinguished on the scale of the drawing.   Note truncation of bed rock structure along the terrace scarps.   The rear scarp of the Powell Terrace is about 90 feet high, but is largely covered by alluvial fans and slope wash.

provide linear miles of exposures indicating that each terrace tread consists of a channeled and fluted rock floor, essentially flat in cross-valley profile, mantled by a uniformly thin (15 to 25 feet) sheet of alluvium.   The rock floor of each terrace bevels inclined strata of varied types (Fig. 1).   The mantle is made up largely of stream rounded pebbles wholly different lithologically from the local bedrock, and identical in composition with the detritus now being handled by the Shoshone River.   The terrace surfaces and their planed rock floors exhibit smooth, concave-upward longitudinal profiles similar to that of the flood plain (Mackin, 1937, p. 825–837).

The manner of origin of the terraces is indicated by the present activity of the stream, which is meandering on its valley floor.   Some curves are slicing laterally at the base of vertical to overhanging rock walls, and some are shifting down-valley from similar cut banks.   As each meander shifts it leaves behind a gravelly surface exposed at low-water stage—it is safe to infer that the thickness of this channel gravel is at least equal to the depth of the channel. It is evident that the gravel deposit grows by lateral accretion as the stream shifts, and if, as seems likely, it rests on a rock floor, then this floor must have been cut by the shifting stream, *pari passu* with the deposition of the gravel. The gravel sheet represents the bed load; it is soon covered by fine silt and sand representing the finer fractions of the suspended load deposited by slow-moving or ponded overbank waters, and later by slope wash and side-stream alluvial fans. We do not *know* that the valley floor gravel sheet rests on bedrock because we canot see its base. But the gravel sheet on each terrace does rest on beveled bedrock, and edges laterally against the base of scarps with the same systematic curvature in plan as those being cut by the stream (Fig. 1).

These relations, taken together, indicate that the terraces are remnants of valley floors cut in bedrock by the lateral planation of the Shoshone River during earlier periods of very slow downcutting or pauses in downcutting (Mackin, 1937). They are altogether different in origin and structure from the equally valid type of terrace formed by partial filling of a valley and later trenching of the fill. And they most certainly were not formed by incidental deposition of gravel (as by floods?) on surfaces produced by other erosional process (successive downstepping peneplanes?); in that they were formed by the same agency at the same time, the gravel veneers are related directly, not incidentally, to the planed surfaces on which they rest.

Individual terrace remnants in the Shoshone Valley are more than half a mile wide and a higher Shoshone valley floor (Pole Cat Bench) is over 2 miles wide and essentially flat in cross profile. In the opening out of valley floors of such great breadth the river must have shifted repeatedly from side to side, trimming back first one valley side and then the other. As indicated above, the stream is now engaged in the same activity on a valley floor with an average declivity of more than 30 feet per mile; the slope of the earlier valley floors is (and was) of the same order of magnitude. Since streams of similar discharge and channel characteristics are now vigorously cutting downward in rock with much lower slopes, the question arises as to what held in check the downcutting of the high-gradient Shoshone during the very long period of planation. Bedrock resistance can be readily ruled out as a controlling factor, for the valley is underlain by sandstones and shales, and such contrasts in resistance as do occur are not reflected in the profiles of the present stream or the terraces. Even more compelling is the fact that the river has repeatedly opened out very broad valley floors by lateral corrasion in the same bedrock during periods when its downcutting was negligible.

The Shoshone failed to trench its valley floor during the terrace-cutting stages, and the present stream fails to trench its present valley floor because its high gradient is perfectly adjusted to provide, with available discharge and with the prevailing channel characteristics, just the velocity required for transportation of a large load of coarse rock waste continuously supplied to it from ramifying headwaters in the rugged Absaroka Range. Adjacent ephemeral streams that head on the arid floor of the Bighorn Basin and are supplied only with fine-textured detritus maintain lower slopes than the master streams that head in the mountains, although their discharge is only a small fraction of that of the master streams (Mackin, 1936; see also Rich, 1935, and Hunt, 1946, for parallel cases in Utah).   Water diverted from the Shoshone River and freed of bed load must be conducted down the terrace surfaces in concrete canals or in canals interrupted by concrete dams; it would otherwise entrench itself below the headgates of the laterals.   The "velocity required for transportation" is such that the river rolls and bounces 8 to 12 inch boulders along its bed.   The river bed is so efficient a grinding mill that boulders of such rock types as dense andesite are reduced in diameter by one-half within a few tens of miles.   But the velocity requirements for transportation are so definitely fixed that the river, flowing over sandstone and shale, could not lower its slope by downcutting during the planation stages, and is not able to cut down at the present time.   If the slope were altered, as by warping, the river would be forced to restore it by cutting or filling as the case might be.   The Shoshone east of Cody was during the planation stages, and probably is at the present time, a typical graded stream.

Valleys of tributaries of the Columbia River system, particularly those of the Clark Fork and Spokane rivers, illustrate the same additional relationships even more strikingly than the Shoshone Valley.   These Columbia Basin valleys were partly filled with glacial, glacio-fluvial, and glacio-lacustrine deposits during the Pleistocene and have since been partly re-excavated. · Here again, we look to terrace remnants of higher valley floors because exposures in the dissected terraces supply morphological data that could be obtained from the present valley floor only by hundreds of borings. The postglacial stream terraces (not to be confused with a wide variety of other types of terraces produced during the period of ice occupancy) usually consist of a sheet of channel gravel, 10 to 30 feet thick, overlain by typical overbank silt plus loess and slopewash from higher valley sides.   The gravel sheet rests on a channeled and fluted surface which truncates disordered structures in till, lake clays and silts, older gravels, and bedrock; deposition of the gravels accompanied the cutting of the surface on which they lie.   The longitudinal slopes of the terraces and of the present valley floors range from 5 feet per mile upward and the larger common pebble sizes in the terrace gravels and the present river bars approximate 6 inches in diameter.   It is useful to consider how rapidly, in so far as scouring power is concerned, large streams carrying coarse gravel on these high slopes could trench downward in silt, and at the same time to note that the streams opened out broad valley floors by lateral planation in silt and bed rock in adjoining segments of their valleys, without trenching.   The high longitudinal slopes were maintained during the planation stages simply because these slopes were required to provide the velocity needed for transportation of detritus continuously supplied to the streams; for emphasis through hyperbole, one might say that they would have been so maintained had the subjacent materials been cream cheese.

These high-gradient streams were selected as examples to indicate at the outset that the term grade carries no connotation of low declivity.   The low-gradient Illinois River is, as Rubey states, an excellent example of a stream in equilibrium (1931) but it is no more excellent than the Columbia tributaries, the Shoshone, the Mesa-stage Rock Creek (Montana) with a slope of about 90 feet per mile (Mackin, 1937, p. 848–850), or many Southwestern pediment streams with much higher slopes (Bryan,

1922). The classic examples are, of course, the wet-weather streams that carved Gilbert's planation surfaces around the flanks of the Henry Mountains in Utah (1877). If, as suggested by some engineering articles, the adjusted stream is one that is stable in channel form and position (Pickels, 1941, p. 166) then the (engineering) adjusted stream is only one special type of the (geologic) graded stream, which is stable only in slope.

The Columbia tributaries are useful also as·examples because these streams are at many points locally superposed from the fill onto rock knobs and spurs, some of which have caused falls or rapids now and during earlier planation stages. These streams consist, in other words, of graded segments separated by segments that are not graded, but this circumstance is certainly no defect in the theory of grade.

THE GRADED STREAM AS A SYSTEM IN EQUILIBRIUM

The idea that a balanced or adjusted condition in streams is an expression of an equilibrium relationship, and that the graded profile is a slope of equilibrium is one of the oldest and most useful of geological concepts relating to streams. Many geologists seem to try to make their treatment of the balanced condition conform to the rigid definition of equilibrium used in the sciences of physics and chemistry. This point of view is reflected in the stock statement that the equilibrium is constantly shifting, approached, but rarely or never attained in the seasonally varying stream. It reaches its logical climax in Kesseli's argument that since discharge, velocity, and other factors are not literally constant in natural streams, no equilibrium can exist.

The requisite conditions for chemical equilibria (as between water and water vapor in a closed container) are; (1) absolute constancy of external controlling conditions (as temperature), and (2) a literally perfect balance between opposed tendencies (as the hail of molecules leaving and returning to the surface of the water). If the water-water vapor apparatus is housed in a laboratory where it is affected by constantly varying diurnal temperature changes, then, strictly speaking, the system rarely or never attains the perfect equivalence between opposed processes which is the essential mark of chemical equilibria. There is, moreover, in the precise chemical sense, a shifting between different states of equilibrium, but there is no such thing as a shifting equilibrium.

(1) *Constancy of controlling conditions* is certainly absent in any segment of a graded stream if attention is focused on its activity during any short period of time, as a year or part of a year. All natural streams vary in discharge, and in many the ratio of high-water to low-water discharge is several hundred to one. In some fully graded stream-transportation systems (in the geologic sense) there may be no discharge at all for most of the year. Velocity, load and all the other factors which enter into the economy of the balanced stream vary markedly with variations in discharge.

(2) *The perfect balance between opposed tendencies*, as an interchange between particles at rest on the bed and in motion in the stream, is not maintained in natural streams. In general, a stream flowing over alluvial materials within its competence tends to enlarge the channel during high-water stages, not only by increase in the height of the water surface, but also by scouring the bed. With decrease in discharge

143

and slackening in velocity as the high-water stage recedes, the stream deposits that part of the load which it is no longer able to carry. Indeed, the same change in controlling conditions may give rise to opposite changes in different parts of the same channel at the same time; increase in discharge and velocity usually causes, for instance, scouring on bends and filling on "crossings" in meandering streams (Straub, 1942, p. 619).

Kesseli, implying (1941, p. 580) that Davis was not aware of seasonal variations in discharge and velocity in natural streams, misses the point. Davis considered the stream as an agent of transportation over a period of years—he was concerned with the forest rather than the trees. Over a period of years sufficiently long to include all the vagaries of the stream, the two independent controls (discharge and supplied load) may be essentially constant. Whatever the conclusions from *a priori* reasoning as to whether constancy of these conditions *should be* maintained in nature, *a posteriori* reasoning based upon the existence of widespread corrasion surfaces of the type represented by the Shoshone terraces indicates that they *are* so maintained long enough to produce distinctive land forms.

Scouring and filling with seasonal fluctuations in discharge and velocity occur in all streams; it is the peculiar and distinctive characteristic of the graded stream that after hundreds or thousands of such short-period fluctuations, entailing an enormous total footage of scouring and filling, the stream shows no change in altitude or declivity. Here again the extensive stream-planed rock surfaces of the Shoshone Valley, with their thin veneers of alluvium, are a case in point. In this long-term sense, there is an equivalence of opposed tendencies in the graded stream.

The concept of equilibrium is the basis for modern quantitative treatments of stream transportation; Rubey's mathematical analysis of "capacity" is appropriately entitled *Equilibrium conditions in debris-laden streams* (1933). The origin and significance of slope variations in the longitudinal profile of the graded stream under stable conditions can be understood only in terms of equilibrium relations. In its sensitivity to change, and its tendency to readjust itself to the changed conditions, the graded stream exhibits the chief and diagnostic mark of a system in equilibrium. It is, in other words, useful and necessary to consider a graded stream as a system in equilibrium, and it is altogether proper so to consider it, provided that it is stated explicitly that the type of equilibrium is different in mechanism and detail from the types treated by the chemist and the physicist, and from the equally valid types recognized by the zoologist and the botanist.[1]

Recognition of these differences eliminates the need for apologetic statements, seemingly made in deference to the chemical usage, to the effect that the stream shifts with every short-period fluctuation from one state of equilibrium to another, or toward another which it never quite attains. To the extent that this view has been the vogue, Kesseli's statement that the condition of grade is "elusive" is amply justified. Distribution of discharge over a short period of time, whether essentially uniform or largely concentrated in rare floods, has much significance with regard to the charac-

---

[1] For discussion of equilibrium as a "universal law" of wide application *see* W. D. Bancroft's Presidential Address to the American Chemical Society (1911). *See also* "The principle of dynamic equilibrium" as applied in Oceanography (Sverdrup *et al.*, 1942, p. 160).

teristics of the stream, and it is true that the greater part of the work of all streams both in erosion and transportation is accomplished during high-water stages. But whether the slope of the profile is determined during a brief annual period of high water (Baulig, 1926, p. 59) during the longer period of low water, or during some "bedforming stage" (Schaffernak, cited by Schoklitsch, 1937, p. 144) need not concern us here. It is not the particular stage of the stream in flood or low water, but the stream operating "over a period of years" that is the natural unit; the balance automatically maintained in this unit is, in its own way, quite as perfect as that of the most delicate equilibria dealt with in the "precise sciences".[2]

THE SHIFTING EQUILIBRIUM

The expression "over a period of years" was used advisedly in the statement above regarding the essential constancy of controlling conditions; all of the conditions are subject to change over a period of geologic time. The changes may be sudden, or they may occur at a rate corresponding with the slow progress of the erosion cycle. Other things being equal, the manner in which the stream responds to changes is determined by the rate at which they occur.

A once-graded stream may, in response to a change tending to cause downcutting, (1) lower itself so slowly that each of its slightly lower profiles is maintained in *approximate* adjustment to that phase of the slowly changing conditions in existence at the time of its formation or, (2) be transformed by a relatively sudden change into a wholly unadjusted series of waterfalls and rapids, and re-establish a graded profile at a lower level only after a considerable lapse of time.

Similarly, a graded stream may (3) respond to slow uplift of a barrier across its path by upbuilding, each of its successively higher profiles being in *approximate* adjustment to the conditions at the time of its formation. Rate of uplift of the barrier may, on the other hand, (4) so far outstrip the rate of filling that a lake basin is formed. The stream will in this case develop a new graded profile only after a period of delta building following cessation of uplift.

In cases (2) and (4) the streams were clearly ungraded or out of equilibrium during the transitional periods. The sharply contrasted condition of the streams in cases (1) and (3) may be thought of as representing a *shifting equilibrium*. Use of this expression to indicate maintenance of approximate adjustment to a long-term change in control is justified by the fact that it describes what actually occurs.

In the discussion to follow it will be necessary to return again and again to the contrast between processes in operation in the stream in which the condition of equilibrium is maintained, the stream in which the equilibrium is shifting, and the stream in which there is no semblance of equilibrium. The landforms and deposits

---

[2] It is useful in this connection to look again at the water-water vapor system, this time focusing attention on the smallest conceivable surface area of water. It will be noted that *two* molecules may leave the water surface and only one return to it in any exceedingly short period of time. The level of the water surface is lowered. In the next unit of time two molecules return and only one leaves; the surface of the water returns to its former position. The point is that time and space relationships must enter into any consideration of equilibria. The time and space relations of the balance in graded streams are of a wholly different order of magnitude from those that obtain in the chemist's laboratory, but the perfection of equivalence of opposed tendencies is none the less perfect.

associated with these three conditions show differences that are of special significance to the geologist, but his terminology includes no simple and definitive terms for distinguishing them.   It is therefore suggested, in accordance with Davis' (1902, p. 107) original proposal that "graded" be used specifically for the stream in which equilibrium is maintained, and that "degrading" and "aggrading" be restricted to cases of the shifting equilibrium.   "Degrading" is downcutting approximately at grade, in contradistinction to such self-explanatory terms as trench or incise.   "Aggrading" is upbuilding approximately at grade.   "Regrading" refers to alteration in the form of the longitudinal profile by simultaneous aggrading and degrading in different parts (Johnson, 1932, p. 662).   The term "degrade" is still available, of course, to describe the modeling of waste slopes in interstream areas.

There is no justification or need for using either "aggrade" or "degrade" to describe short-period variations in stream activity, that is, as synonyms for "filling" or "scouring" (of a channel), or for the more general terms "erosion" and "deposition".   The following quotations from the last edition of an outstanding and most influential textbook illustrate, from the point of view of the present paper, a misuse of terms. The numbers in brackets are inserted for convenience in reference.

"(1) As downcutting reduces the gradient . . . a time comes when the increasing burden of transporting the load requires all of the energy that was formerly applied to downcutting. . . . The long profile has become a *profile of equilibrium* and the stream is said to be *graded*.   (2) When a part of a main stream reaches grade, the local tributaries soon become graded with respect to it.   (3) Any change in gradient, discharge, or load would upset the graded condition by altering the rate of erosion.   A flood, for example, might convert the graded stream into one actively degrading, but with subsidence of the flood the graded condition would be restored.   (4) Again, great increases in load are known to have converted graded streams into actively aggrading ones; for example, when glaciers appearing in their headwater regions poured great additional quantities of rock waste into them".   (Longwell, Knopf and Flint, 1939, p. 64–65).

The view expressed in (1) has been discussed earlier; downcutting, or abrasion in general, does not involve an expenditure of energy independent of that consumed in friction and transportation of load.   In (2) the term grade is used in what the present writer regards the proper long-term sense, but in (3) it is used in a wholly different short-term sense.   In (3) the term degrading is synonymous with deepening of the bed by scouring (this usage involves a situation in which the *surface of the water is raised* when the stream is said to be degrading!).   If a stream responds to a flood by degrading it presumably restores the graded condition by aggrading when the flood subsides.   But in (4) aggrading is used to describe the response of a stream to a completely different long-term change in controlling conditions.

While no importance attaches to the terms, as such, it is the writer's opinion that the usage illustrated by these quotations is at least partly responsible for the confusion that forms the basis for Kesseli's attack on the theory of the graded river.   The usage suggested here emphasizes the contrast between seasonal fluctuations in stream activity (or, indeed, the equally striking diurnal changes in certain proglacial streams) and such true shiftings of the equilibrium as those represented by epicycles of valley cutting and filling in the Southwest (Bryan, 1940; Bailey, 1935).   The distinction is analagous to that made by the meteorologist between weather and climate, and it is just as fundamental.   In addition, the proposed usage differentiates between the equilibrium that shifts in response to long-term change and the equilibrium that is

146

maintained long enough to permit the stream to produce the distinctive landforms mentioned earlier. A question may arise as to the exact line of demarkation, in terms of feet of degradation or aggradation during so many thousands or millions of years, between the graded stream and the stream that is degrading or aggrading very slowly. Argument on this score leads nowhere—we classify natural phenomena not to assign each member of a series to a numerical pidgeonhole, but to clarify our understanding of their interrelationships. The distinction between the graded and the slowly degrading stream must, and should properly, depend on the nature of the problem and the point of view of the investigator.

FACTORS CONTROLLING THE SLOPE OF THE GRADED PROFILE

GENERAL STATEMENT

Longitudinal profiles of graded streams are often considered to be smooth, "concave upward" curves, that is, curves that decrease systematically in slope in a downvalley direction. Systematic downvalley decrease in slope is, however, by no means an essential or necessary attribute of the graded profile. The stream receives contributions of water and debris from every part of its drainage basin, but the additions are concentrated largely at tributary junctions and the ratio of water to debris varies markedly from place to place, from the high-water ratio of a tributary issuing from a lake or other natural settling basin to the high-debris ratio represented by a talus slide. Superposed on, and in part the result of, the changes in load and discharge are changes in the channel characteristics; these affect the hydraulic efficiency of the channel and hence the slope of the stream.

Such changes along its length might seem to count against considering the graded stream a system in equilibrium, or to indicate that it should be regarded as a type of shifting equilibrium. Indeed, comparison of the manner in which a stream accomodates itself to changes in control from segment to segment under stable conditions with its reaction to a change in conditions (as warping or a climatic change) is a useful mental exercise. But these two types of changes are completely different in origin, and it would be fatal to confuse them in analysis of a given longitudinal profile. While the velocity of each unit segment of a graded stream under stable conditions differs from that of adjoining segments (being kept in balance with local variations in velocity requirements by appropriate adjustments in slope) the close interdependence between all of the segments is such that they are parts of one well-defined system. Factors bearing on the slope of the longitudinal profile that is *maintained* without change as long as conditions remain the same are considered in this section.

DOWNVALLEY INCREASE IN DISCHARGE

It is a matter of observation that large graded streams usually have lower slopes than smaller graded streams. Similarly, a graded stream formed by the confluence of two graded streams usually has, below the junction, a slope lower than that of either of the confluents. The essential reason for these relations, mentioned earlier, is that with increase in size of the channel there is usually an increase in cross-sectional area relative to wetted perimeter and a consequent relative decrease in frictional retardation of flow.   A result is that large streams commonly have higher velocities than smaller streams with the same slope, or, stated in terms of the profile of a single stream, a downvalley segment with large discharge can maintain a given velocity on a lower slope than an upvalley segment with small discharge.   In other words, a mere downvalley increase in discharge requires (or permits) a corresponding downvalley decrease in the slope of the graded profile.

DOWNVALLEY INCREASE IN RATIO OF LOAD TO DISCHARGE

Trunk streams often head in regions of high relief and flow in their lower portions through regions of relatively low relief.   Under these circumstances the ratio of total load to discharge in the contributions of tributaries may be larger in the lower than in the upper parts of the stream.   For the same reason, the caliber of the load supplied to the stream by tributaries, slope-washing, creep, and talus fall commonly decreases from head to mouth.   Downvalley decrease in total load relative to discharge and/or downvalley decrease in the caliber of load shed into the stream, to the extent that they occur, require a corresponding downvalley decrease in the slope of the graded profile.

DOWNVALLEY DECREASE IN RATIO OF LOAD TO DISCHARGE

The load of a graded stream may increase in a downvalley direction relative to its discharge because of evaporation or subsurface loss of water, or as a result of the entry of heavily loaded tributaries and various slower types of mass movement from its valley sides.   Kesseli particularly emphasizes the latter process as being incompatible with the concept of grade, his statement being that if a stream be "fully loaded" it is manifestly impossible for it to acquire additional load as, for instance, the material caving from banks undercut in the process of valley floor widening (1941, p. 578).   This statement is roughly equivalent to the contention that a given saturated solution, in the presence of excess of the solute, cannot take more of that substance into solution.   The solution can and must, of course, become more concentrated if any change in control, as an increase in temperature, displaces the equilibrium in the proper direction.   Similarly, the graded stream can accommodate itself to the transportation of increased load at any point; it usually does so by a local increase in declivity.

Steepening of the Missouri profile at and below the junction of the Platte River is a case in point. The average declivity of the Missouri for 31 miles above the mouth of the Platte was .74 feet per mile as measured in 1931, and the average slope for 44 miles below the junction was 1.24 feet per mile (Whipple, 1942, p. 1185—in the original report by Straub, cited by Whipple, slopes for unspecified distances above and below the junction are given as .68 and 1.16 feet per mile, respectively; Straub, 1935, p. 1145). The slope of the lower part of the Platte is 3.2 feet per mile.   Steepening of the Missouri profile is ascribed by Straub and Whipple to entry of the heavy gravel bed load of the Platte into the Missouri, which carries chiefly sand and silt above the junction.   On the basis of an extended study of Missouri slopes and load, Straub generalizes as follows: "As is to be expected, the steepest part of the Missouri River below the point of confluence of the Yellowstone is in the vicinity of the mouths of the tributaries adding the largest bed load" (Straub, 1935, p. 1145).

It should be emphasized that entry of the Platte gravels into the Missouri is not due to any recent change in conditions. The local steepening of the Missouri profile is *not* a matter of "deposition" of gravels by the Platte at its mouth because the Missouri is unable to carry the load. If this were so the streams would be upbuilding rapidly, which is not the case. The Missouri profile below the junction is just steep enough to permit the stream to carry *all* of the added load. The profile break has been and will be maintained without change as long as conditions remain the same, which is the same as saying that the Missouri is graded above and below the junction.

Additions to the load of a graded stream resulting from various types of mass movements of the type mentioned by Kesseli are accomodated in the same way. The fact that nearly all streams receive detritus from these sources and, nevertheless, usually maintain smooth concave-upward profiles past the individual caving banks means simply that these additions are usually so small, relative to the great bulk of rock waste in process of transport along the channel in any given period of time, that their effects on the longitudinal profile are usually lost to view in the general down-valley lowering of declivity resulting from the other changes discussed in this section.

Increased slope of the Missouri at and below the Platte junction is required to provide increased velocity needed for transportation of the increased bed load, but this is not the whole story. The Missouri, a meandering river above the Platte junction, is characterized at and below the junction by a broad irregular channel with numerous bars. This change in habits, a result of the added bed load, almost certainly increases frictional retardation and, hence, calls for a steepening in slope to permit development of any given velocity by the Missouri. In other words, the effect of the Platte is two-fold—the total steepening of the main stream profile represents the adjustment required to accomodate both the direct and the indirect effects of the influx of Platte gravels.

DOWNVALLEY DECREASE IN CALIBER OF LOAD

Graded profiles usually decrease in slope in a downvalley direction between tributary junctions, chiefly because of a downvalley decrease in caliber of load due to processes within the stream. The principle involved is that the velocity (and, other things being equal, the declivity) required for the transportation of the coarser fractions of a stream's load decreases with decrease in grain size, the total amount of the load remaining the same. The operation of this principle in natural streams is best illustrated by consideration of a graded segment without tributaries, in which additions and loss of water and detritus are negligible.

The lower portion of the Greybull River in the Bighorn Basin, Wyoming, approximates these ideal conditions. The river issues from the Absaroka Mountains and flows through the arid lowlands of the Basin to its junction with the Bighorn River, receiving its last perennial tributary (Wood River) about 50 miles above its mouth. A peculiar drainage pattern that delivers most of the intermittent drainage from immediately adjacent lowland areas to the Bighorn River by independent streams and an analysis of available discharge records provide reasonable assurance that there is no significant increase in the discharge of the Greybull in the 50-mile segment below Wood River. Throughout this segment the stream is meandering on a valley floor wider than the meander belt. Since the stream is neither aggrading nor degrading at a rate that would be appreciable over a period of years, the total load passing through all parts of the 50-mile segment in a given interval of time must be essentially the same, or may increase slightly downvalley as a result of bank erosion and other processes. In other words, variations in ratio of discharge to total load are of minor importance.

The profile of the Greybull valley floor decreases in slope from about 60 feet per mile at the head of the 50-mile segment to about 20 feet per mile at the lower end; that is, the profile is strongly "concave upward". Stream-cut rock terraces ranging from 50 to 1200 feet above the present stream show a similar eastward (downvalley) decrease in slope. The river was certainly in essentially perfect adjustment during the long periods of lateral planation recorded by the terraces and probably still is. The downvalley decrease in slope must in this case be ascribed largely to a decrease in caliber of load in transit; pebbles of the valley floor and terrace gravel sheets decrease notably in size in a downvalley direction (Mackin, 1937, p. 858–862).

Discussions of the form of the graded profile often neglect downvalley decrease in caliber of load as a control, or, what is worse, imply that this decrease is the *result* of the decrease in slope. Discussion of this point belongs in a later section; it is sufficient to state here that downvalley decrease in caliber of load is an important cause of downvalley decrease in the slope of the graded profile, and that, in the graded stream, the decrease in caliber is due primarily to attritional comminution of particles comprising the load.

The bearing of decrease in caliber of load due to attrition on the slope of the graded profile is particularly emphasized in the European literature. Schoklitsch, for example, cites Sternberg to the effect that certain central European rivers show a systematic decrease in the weight of particles comprising the bed load as a function of distance traveled. He then points out (1) that "An examination of the profiles of natural watercourses reveals the striking fact that, with few exceptions, the slope (like the size of the bed-sediment particles) decreases from source to mouth"; (2) that it is therefore "quite logical to attempt to ascertain a relation between this law [the Sternberg law of decrease in particle weight] and the shape of the profile, at least in the stretches in which the reduction in size of the particles is due to abrasion"; and finally, (3) that "study of a number of river profiles showed that the slope . . . is proportional to the particle size". On this basis Schoklitsch develops an equation for the river profile (1937, p. 153). Many other writers have advanced the theory that graded or adjusted river profiles are mathematical curves, often without Schoklitsch's qualifications as to the effect of tributaries. The most recent contribution in this country (Shulits, 1941) presents a so-called "Rational equation of river-bed profile". The theory that longitudinal profiles closely approximate simple logarithmic curves has been utilized in geomorphic studies, chiefly in England. (*See*, for example, Jones, 1924; and Green, 1936; for critical discussion see Miller, 1939; and Lewis, 1945.)

Analysis of the mathematics of the graded profile and its important geomorphic implications lies beyond the scope of this article. The following will indicate how the theory applies in this qualitative treatment of the concept of grade:

Rubey, discussing the Shulits article, points out (1) that the Shulits equation is empirical rather than "rational"; (2) that many factors other than caliber of load bear on the slope of the profile, and (3) that the profile of a stream could vary directly as a power of bed-load diameters only if there were some "complex and as yet unformulated interrelationships among the many other variables" (p. 630).

The fact is, of course, that there can be no such interrelationships because there is no interdependence of all the factors bearing on slope in a trunk stream. The contribution of each tributary to a main stream is conditioned by the rocks, relief, and climate in the tributary drainage basin and is not systematically related to relationships in the main stream above the point where the tributary happens to enter. Changes in slope such as that caused by the Platte occur elsewhere on the Missouri, as indicated by Straub's generalization; in high-gradient western streams with which the writer is familiar these changes are even more striking than on the Missouri. The effect of tributaries is only one of several types of change along the length of the stream which are neither interdependent nor systematic. Mathematics can be an exceedingly useful tool in the study of river profiles, but it seems to the writer that the attitude that considers the job to be done because an *approximate* overall fit is obtained in the matching of curves is basically wrong; slurring over the irregularities gives a false impression of simplicity. Some types of numerical values, as the percentages of the several grain sizes in samples of sand and gravel, yield significant averages. But precise altitudes of points along a river profile are not subject to sampling errors; insofar as any understanding of its origin is concerned, the *breaks* in a semi-log plat of the profile are the significant elements, and a single straight line drawn through scattered points has little meaning. Downvalley decrease in caliber of load by reason of attrition is more nearly systematic than any of the other factors bearing on the slope of the graded profile. But caliber of load does not vary systematically in graded streams joined by tributaries, nor in graded streams in which the rock types in the load differ notably in resistance to attrition; even if it did, caliber of load is only one of a number of partly or wholly independent factors controlling the graded slope.[3]

RELATIONSHIP BETWEEN CHANNEL CHARACTERISTICS AND SLOPE

As indicated earlier, the hydraulic efficiency of a channel varies with the channel characteristics; self-evident theoretical considerations and experimental data establish this point so clearly that it needs no discussion here. Close relationship between efficiency, as determined by channel characteristics, and slope of the graded stream is demonstrated compellingly by the reduction in slope from about .96 to about .69 feet per mile in a few years, as a result of artificial smoothing of tortuous curves and narrowing, and consequent automatic deepening, of parts of the Missouri channel (Whipple, 1942, p. 1199). The overall length of the channel was not significantly changed by the channel improvement measures. In terms of velocity the essential reason for the reduction in slope is that a reduction in frictional retardation of the current in the corrected channel permits the stream to develop the velocity required for transportation of its load on a lowered slope. In terms of energy the

---

[3] Slopes of ungraded stream segments are determined by the depth to which the stream has cut downward. In headwater basins in bed rock fairly uniform in resistance to corrasion the ungraded profile tends to decrease in declivity in a downvalley direction, the reason being downvalley increase in discharge and therefore corrasive power. Ungraded profiles of this type are superficially similar to graded profiles but they are completely different in origin; the ungraded profile is conditioned by the corrasive power of the stream, bed rock resistance to corrasion, and the length of time that the stream has been downcutting, while the graded profile is an adjusted slope of transportation that is influenced negligibly, if at all, by these factors. Mathematical analysis of a stream profile that fails to distinguish between graded and ungraded segments involves the fundamental error of mixing different types of data, and can lead only to frustration or to conclusions that are unsound.

explanation is that a reduction in "internal" and "external" energy losses in the improved channel causes an automatic adjustment of slope of such nature as to reduce the total energy of the stream, the energy utilized in transportation remaining the same.

Because different segments of graded streams vary widely in channel characteristics, these variations certainly bear on the overall form of the longitudinal profile. But before discussing these effects it is necessary to consider a fundamental question regarding the theory of grade.

THE CONCEPT OF ADJUSTMENT IN SECTION

The channel characteristics of a graded stream, like its slope, are developed by the stream itself. Both slope *and* channel characteristics vary from segment to segment, and any change in external controls usually results in changes in both of these variables. Because of the nature of his work the attention of the geologist is usually focused on slope; he knows, for example, that a graded stream responds to changes in load due to waxing and waning of glaciers in its drainage basin by appropriate adjustments in slope effected by upbuilding or downcutting. The attention of the engineer is, on the other hand, usually focused on the channel characteristics; he can, for example, enable an "adjusted" stream to transport an influx of mine waste that greatly increases its load by appropriate channel-improvement measures, without change in slope. A question arises, then, as to whether the foregoing definition which describes the graded stream as one "in which *slope* is delicately adjusted", etc., should not be revised to read, "in which *slope and channel characteristics* are delicately adjusted," etc.

That the question is a very real one is indicated by recent discussion of transportation by running water in the engineering literature which emphasizes especially the concept of the "adjusted", or "stable", or "regimen" (in the sense of equilibrium) cross-sectional form.[4] The discussion centers around problems of design of nonsilting and noneroding canals of various types. (Lane, 1937, with bibliography and discussion by 10 writers; important British papers include Griffith, 1927; and Lacey, 1930); but theoretical aspects of the relationship between cross-sectional form and transportation necessarily apply to natural streams. For example, Griffith observes (A) that natural streams with heavy bed load tend to flow in broad, shallow channels. He concludes (B) that the broad, shallow channel is the type of cross section best adapted for the transportation of heavy bed load. The general attitude of mind that makes (B) follow from (A) is expressed as follows: "A river fully charged with silt [meaning, in the geologic usage, debris without regard for particle size] *must obviously tend to adopt that form of section which will give it a maximum silt-carrying capacity*" (Griffith, 1927, p. 251) (italics mine).

---

[4] I am indebted to W. W. Rubey for calling my attention to the need for somewhat more extended discussion of the concept of adjusted cross sections than was accorded that concept in an early draft of this article examined by him. He kindly loaned me an unpublished manuscript on the Hardin-Brussels quadrangles in Illinois, in which the channel characteristics of the Illinois River are analyzed mathematically (for published abstract, *see* Rubey, 1931a), and subsequent correspondence with him clarified and extended my own views. These views do not parallel his in all respects, and he is not responsible for them. But I would like to emphasize that everything that may have lasting value in this section is an outgrowth of his council.

There is perhaps deductive ground for believing that all the characteristics of natural channels, if they are to be "permanent", must somehow contribute to the ability of the stream to transport debris. It might be argued in the same deductive vein that the principle of "least work" would lead one to expect that changes in channel characteristics caused by a change in controlling conditions must be "adjustments" in that they must be of such nature as to adapt the stream to the new conditions. Analysis of the extent to which channel characteristics *are* adjustable in this sense may begin by considering channel-modeling processes in a straight channel in which movement of coarse-textured debris depends on velocity.

ADJUSTMENT IN SECTION IN THE STRAIGHT CHANNEL

The semicircular section that would provide the least frictional retardation of flow for clear water or for water carrying only ultra-fine or colloidal particles is rarely or never developed or maintained by flowing water charged with coarse debris for many reasons, the more important of which are: (1) a large bed load requires high bed velocity and widening by bank erosion that must continue until velocity at the banks is reduced to the point where the resistance to erosion of the bank-forming materials equals the erosive force applied to them. (2) Shoaling by deposition will accompany widening of the narrow channel by erosion because the particles of the bed load tend to lodge, and move, and lodge again, the velocity required each time to set them in motion being greater than that required to keep them in motion, and because a higher velocity is required to set in motion a particle on the bed than one on the sloping banks. The operation of these processes results in a channel that is, under different circumstances, semielliptical (Lacey, 1930, p. 273; Lacey in discussion of Lane, 1937, p. 160) or parabolic (Pettis, in discussion of Lane, 1937, p. 149–151) in section, and this section, once developed by automatic modification of an originally too narrow or too wide section, will be stable, or in adjustment, or regimen as long as conditions remain the same. But it does not follow that the channel so formed will necessarily provide the "maximum silt-carrying capacity."

Widening causes (1) reduction in bed load moved per unit width of bed by reason of decrease in velocity that accompanies decrease in depth, and, at the same time, (2) increases the length of the cross section (that is, the number of width units) through which the bed load is moved. Tendencies (1) and (2) are opposed insofar as transportation of bed load is concerned; especially because of (2) the cross-sectional form that provides maximum efficiency for transportation of debris is wider and shallower than the semicircular section that gives maximum efficiency for movement of water. The form of the cross section most efficient for transportation varies with slope, with amount and caliber of the load, and especially with the proportions of the total load that are carried in suspension and moved along the bed. These factors are partly interdependent, and they certainly influence the form of cross section that is developed and maintained by the stream. But the form of the cross section depends also, for reasons indicated above, on a factor wholly independent of the stream, namely, resistance of the banks to erosion. For any one set of slope-debris charge factors there will be one critical degree of erodibility of the bank-forming materials such that an originally too narrow channel will quickly develop a cross section with depth-width relations that provide "the maximum silt-carrying capacity". If the bank-forming materials are less erodible than this critical degree the stream may tend to develop the maximum efficiency section over a period of time; that is, the final stable channel section, however long delayed, may approximate the ideal form for the given slope-debris-charge factors. But if the bank-forming materials are more erodible than the critical degree the stream will adopt and maintain a section that is wider and shallower than the ideal transportation section. In the case of the high-slope stream carrying coarse gravel between banks of incoherent sand, widening may continue until the channel disintegrates into a plexus of split channels and gravel bars that is the antithesis of efficiency for transportation. In this case, and generally, the operation of the "least work" principle is merely a matter of expediency and compromise with local conditions—the river braids because an arrangement of minor channels and bars is somewhat less inefficient than a single exceedingly wide and uniformly shallow channel.

It appears, therefore, that a statement to the effect that a flow of water charged with debris must necessarily develop for itself that form of section that will give it a "maximum debris-carrying capacity" is an invalid generalization because it ignores erodibility of the banks; the influence of this factor increases with increase in slope and caliber of debris. The cross-sectional form developed by a stream may be "stable" in that it is not subject to modification as long as conditions remain the same, but "stability" in section is no guarantee of maximum efficiency for transportation. There is no need to labor this point with examples; it suffices to say that in many instances on record, efficiency for transportation in streams and canals has been greatly increased by artificial modification of self-adopted sections.

ADJUSTMENT IN SECTION IN THE SHIFTING CHANNEL

The tendency for erosional widening along both banks in the straight channel is, in the curving channel, localized and greatly accentuated at the outside of the curves. Whatever the type of meandering involved (Melton, 1936), the inner parts of the curving channel are bar-ridden shoals if the meanders are actively shifting. The meandering channel is usually deepest at the outside of the curves, but even here, if lateral shifting is rapid and the subjacent materials are resistant, the channel does not continue to operate in one place long enough to permit deepening to the potential depth of flood-stage scour. If outward shifting were stopped and if the shallows were filled so as to concentrate the flow in a narrowed channel, deepening would result. Efficiency for transportation would be further increased if the tortuous curves of the channel were smoothed.

The first point to be made, then, is that lateral shifting is one of the most important factors responsible for the inefficiency of the natural channel. This holds for the meandering stream, and it is true also for the braided stream. In general, efficiency for transportation varies inversely with the rate of lateral shifting.

The second point is that, other things being equal, the rate of lateral shifting in the graded stream increases with velocity and load; high-velocity, gravel-carrying streams on piedmont slopes of semiarid mountains shift laterally far more rapidly than low-velocity, silt-carrying streams of humid lowlands.

Consider now how a meandering stream will react to a change in controlling conditions, as for example, an increase in load. The engineer might be able to accommodate the stream to the increased load by artificially increasing the efficiency of the channel without increase in slope. Under natural conditions there will usually be both change in the channel characteristics and increase in slope. The increase in slope will be effected automatically by aggradation, and aggradation will continue until the slope is steep enough to provide the velocity required to transport, with available discharge and the prevailing channel characteristics, *whatever they may be,* all the debris delivered to the stream. Modification of the channel characteristics, considered separately as a mechanism of readjustment, will, on the other hand, be self baffling because increase in velocity required by increase in load will itself entail an increase in lateral shifting which will, in turn, tend to decrease the efficiency of the channel, and hence the velocity of the stream.

A graded stream may react to an increase in load by a more drastic change in the channel characteristics, namely, by a change from a meandering to a braided habit. Braiding involves the choking of each functional channel by bar building; the resulting maze of shifting minor channels has a total overall proportionate depth much smaller than that of the corresponding meandering channel. Here again, the effect on velocity of a change in the channel characteristics is precisely the reverse of that called for by the original change in external controls. Eventual readjustment to the new conditions (including increased load *and* notably decreased channel efficiency) will be achieved by increase in slope effected through aggradation.

These examples are certainly not intended to establish a general rule to the effect that, with a change in control, channel characteristics necessarily shift in a manner opposite to that required to bring the stream into balance with the new conditions. In some instances the effects of changes in the channel characteristics may be negligible, and in other instances they may contribute notably to the readjustment. But the examples do serve to bring out a basic difference in the role of adjustments in section and adjustments in slope in the equilibrium of grade; while adjustments in section may or may not accommodate the effect of a change in control, slope is always modified, by the stream itself, in such a manner as to absorb the effect of the stress. This relationship, the tendency for one of a number of partly interdependent variables to act as the outstanding counterbalance in effecting a readjustment to new conditions, is familiar in many types of equilibria. In the case of grade it means simply that the stream normally reacts to a change in controls calling for an increase or decrease in energy required for transportation by increasing or decreasing the total energy through modification of slope rather than by effecting economies in the energy dissipated in friction. A graded stream is a system, prodigiously wasteful of energy at every bend and shoal, kept in a constant state of balance under stable conditions, and brought back into balance after any change in controls, primarily by appropriate adjustments in slope.

EFFECT OF VARIATION IN CHANNEL CHARACTERISTICS ON THE GRADED PROFILE

It has been indicated that changes in ratio of load to discharge, in caliber of load, and other factors, occur in the graded stream, and that, while none of these changes is necessarily systematic, they usually combine to cause a downvalley decrease in the slope of the profile. Variation in the channel characteristics from segment to segment under stable conditions is due, in part directly, to changes in these other factors—for example, decrease in the caliber of the load that is moved along the stream bed tends, other things being equal, to be accompanied by an increase in proportionate depth. But changes in the channel characteristics are due largely to change in the resultant of these other factors, namely, velocity, and, in turn, rate of lateral shifting. The paragraphs below are intended to show the nature of the changes that may be expected in an ideal case and how these will affect slope.

In the upper parts of the graded stream,[5] velocity, and therefore the power of the stream to cut laterally, is high, but the valley floor does not greatly exceed the width of the stream itself, and the rate of lateral shifting is inhibited by confining rock walls. In the absence of well-developed meanders, the channel is relatively straight. For these reasons the actual rate of lateral shifting in any representative segment is relatively slow, and the proportionate depth relatively large.

The middle parts of the graded stream are characterized by fully developed meanders and by decreased velocity and therefore decreased corrasive power. But the actual rate of lateral shifting may be increased because the tendency for lateral shifting increases with decrease in the radius of curves, and especially because the stream now operates largely in unconsolidated alluvium on a wide valley floor. Other things being equal, proportionate depth decreases with increase in the rate of lateral shifting.

Finally, in the lower parts of the stream, velocity and corrasive power may decrease until there is a notable decrease in the rate of lateral shifting even in alluvial materials, with a corresponding increase in proportionate depth. Degree of sinuousity of the channel may remain the same (as in the middle parts) or may decrease.

It follows from the earlier discussion that, in the measure that these changes in the channel characteristics affect velocity, they will result in departures from the theoretical profile adjusted to discharge and load, but with uniform channel characteristics throughout. The effect will be to decrease the slope required to provide the velocity needed for the transportation of load with available discharge in the upper parts, to increase the slope required etc., in the middle parts, and to decrease the slope required etc., in the lower parts.

Deductions as to the effects on slope of the contrasts between the upper and middle sets of conditions are verified by relations described by Gilbert on the Yuba River in California:

"Where the Yuba River passes from the Sierra Nevada to the broad Sacramento Valley its habit is rather abruptly changed. In the Narrows it is narrow and deep; a few miles downstream it has become wide and shallow. Its bed is of gravel, with slopes regulated by the river itself when in flood, and the same material composes the load it carries.

---

[5] The terms "upper", "middle", and "lower" are used here for convenience to designate contrasted sets of conditions that bear on actual (not potential) rate of lateral shifting of a graded stream. These contrasted sets of conditions usually occur in the geographic order suggested by the terms, but depending on the geology of the drainage basin, they may occur in any order along the part of the stream that is graded. The terms should not be confused with the upper (downcutting), middle (cutting and filling), and lower (upbuilding) parts of the overall profile recognized by many workers. These subdivisions of the profile as a whole are discussed later; they have no place in the present treatment of factors bearing on the graded slope.

"In the Narrows the form ratio during high flood is 0.06 and the slope is 0.10 percent. Two miles downstream the form ratio is 0.008 and the slope is 0.34 per cent. Thus the energy necessary to transport the load where the form ratio is 0.008 is more than three times that which suffices where the form ratio is 0.06; and it is evident that the larger ratio is much more efficient than the smaller" (Gilbert, 1914, p. 135).

Gilbert's "form ratio" is depth over width; it increases with increase in proportionate depth. While Gilbert does not say so, the abrupt change in depth-width relations on the Yuba is associated geographically with, and is certainly due in large part to, a change from a relatively low rate of lateral shifting in the rock-walled "Narrows" to a rapid rate of shifting on the piedmont alluvial plain. This downvalley *steepening* in slope at the point where a stream issues from a gorge is precisely the reverse of what we normally expect, and it is the reverse of what we usually find, because decrease in caliber of load, loss of water through infiltration and evaporation, and other factors, usually outweigh the effects of lateral shifting on channel characteristics and of channel characteristics on slope.

Factual relations at other California canyon mouths described by Sonderegger (1935, p. 296–300) indicate that the Yuba is not an isolated case; Sonderegger's reasoning as to the cause of the slope contrasts corresponds closely with that advanced here. These examples were not known to the writer when the deductions were set down in their present form—the examples therefore are "verification", by prediction of extraordinary or unique relationships, of the theory from which the deductions were drawn.

The effect of rate of lateral shifting on channel characteristics, and, in turn, of channel characteristics on slope in the middle and lower sets of conditions is strikingly illustrated by the Illinois River. This stream seems to exemplify the logical climax or end stage of the hypothetical sequence of downvalley changes in slope and channel characteristics outlined above.

According to Rubey the lower Illinois channel does not shift perceptibly, is much narrower but somewhat deeper than that of the adjacent part of the Mississippi, and is deepest at the inside rather than at the outside of its bends. The river has a slope of less than 2 inches per mile, actually lower than that of the Mississippi from Memphis to the Gulf.

An explanation of the remarkable habits of the Illinois, taken in part from Rubey's writings (Rubey, 1931a and the unpublished report mentioned earlier) and in part rationalized from factual relations described by him and shown on the topographic sheets, is as follows: The river flows in a valley formed by a much larger stream which served as the outlet of Lake Michigan during late-glacial times. Now, after several hundred feet of aggradation due in part to post-glacial aggradation of the Mississippi (which it enters), the lower Illinois is neither aggrading nor degrading at an appreciable rate. It is essentially graded (Rubey, 1931a, p. 366) and, as such, has a velocity adjusted to the transport of all of the debris shed into it. The slope of the stream is, in other words, adjusted to the present load under the prevailing conditions. The main stream is partly or wholly laked above the mouth of the Sangamon at Beardstown, and minor lateral tributaries below this point supply little coarse clastic debris. Under these circumstances the velocity required for transportation of the debris handled by the Illinois below Beardstown is very low—so low, in fact, that inertia fails to counteract the tendency of the principle current to follow the shortest and steepest route, which, in all curving streams, lies along the *inside* of the bends. This introduces a new factor tending to inhibit or halt lateral shifting (which would be very slow in any case because of low velocity) with the result that the stream maintains a relatively narrow and deep channel. The efficiency of this channel is so great, relative to that of actively shifting streams, that the Illinois develops the velocity required for the transportation of the load supplied to it on an exceptionally low slope.

The characteristics of the Illinois River are due largely to fortuitous circumstances (glacial drainage diversion, etc.), but the same type of regimen is approached in the lower flat reaches of many streams.   Flattening of slope in the lower reaches is, for example, accompanied by a decrease in the rate of lateral shifting and an increase in proportionate depth on the Mississippi River (see Humphreys and Abbott, 1876, p. 107, 122) and the Brazos River in Texas (Barton, 1928, p. 622).   It seems likely that this type of regimen, exceptional during the present epoch of crustal unrest and high-standing continents, may have been during earlier geologic periods a prevalent type in the lower parts of sluggish trunk streams draining areas of exceedingly low relief in the penultimate stages of the Davisian cycle of erosion.

LOCAL VARIATION FROM MEAN SLOPE

Detailed surveys based on reading of closely spaced gauges at the same river stage usually reveal what may be called local variations in the slopes of graded streams. These local departures from mean slope in any short segment may be fixed in position over a period of years, or they may shift along the stream; they usually vary in position with variation in discharge.   They are in most cases clearly related to local variations in proportionate depth or detailed roughness, or to sharp bends, split channels, and other irregularities in trend which increase frictional retardation of flow.   The fact that some of the local variations are obviously not associated with changes in load has led one student of streams to publish this rather remarkable nonsequitur: "the declivity of the adjusted stream is not a function of load".   The fact is, of course, that declivity is not controlled by load alone.

These local variations in slope merit only brief mention here for the same reason that seasonal variations in discharge, velocity, and load were left largely out of account in the discussion of equilibrium relationships.   Local changes in slope of the water surface, as such, are usually symptoms of some local "defect" in the channel; from the point of view of the geologist they are usually negligible because they are not reflected in the slopes of the valley floors produced by streams.

BACKWATER AND DRAW-DOWN EFFECTS

The usual downvalley decrease in the slope of the graded stream has led to the suggestion that the profile tends to be asymptotic with respect to a horizontal plane passing its base level.   Similarly, the profile of a tributary is sometimes supposed to approach the slope of the main stream near the junction.   It will be shown later that in a special case (aggradation) there is such a tendency.   But it is the essence of the concept of grade that declivity is controlled by velocity or energy requirements and, in the graded stream, base level, as long as it does not change, has no bearing on velocity or energy requirements.   Base level controls the *level* or *elevation* at which the profile is developed, but it does not influence the *slope* of the profile.   For this reason a generalization to the effect that the graded profile approaches base level asymptotically is not valid.

In detail, profile relations in the vicinity of downvalley control points (that is, either general or local base levels) differ markedly (1) where the stream enters still water, (2) where the downvalley control is the lip of a waterfall, and (3) where a tributary enters a trunk stream.   In (1) the lowermost part of the profile may show the "back-water effect" to a greater or less extent depending upon a number of factors; additional factors are involved if the "still water" is tidal, and/or if outbuilding of a delta is in progress.   In (2) the lowermost part of the profile will show a "draw-down curve," that is, a steepening in the slope of the water surface resulting from a decrease in cross-sectional area due to acceleration in velocity toward the point of free fall.   In (3) the backwater curve may affect either tributary or trunk stream or both depending upon their relative velocity and discharge and on the angle (in plan) between the streams at the confluence.   These three different types of "base level" and their contrasted effects on a transitional zone in the lowermost part of the profile qualify the statement made in the last paragraph with respect to the relation of the overall profile to base level.   But these relationships are local details having no direct bearing on the concept of grade.

EFFECTS OF DIFFERENCES IN ROCK RESISTANCE

Differential abrasion by streams tends to bring into relief differences in bedrock resistance; resistant rocks often form falls or rapids separating adjoining graded reaches.   But if the stream be graded across the barrier, differences in bedrock resistance have no direct influence on its slope; theoretically and actually, as indicated earlier, graded streams cross belts of such contrasted rock types as quartzite and shale without change in slope at the contacts. Differences in the rock types traversed by the graded stream may, of course, cause changes in slope if associated contrasts in topography or lithology alter the amount and caliber of the load supplied to the stream, or if associated contrasts in valley-floor width affect rate of lateral shifting or details of trend or cross-sectional shape of the channel.

SUMMARY

The longitudinal profile of a graded stream may be thought of as consisting of a number of segments, each differing from those that adjoin it but all closely related parts of one system.   Definition of the unit segment (in terms of length, permissible slope variation, etc.) depends on the purpose of the investigation.

Each segment has the slope that will provide the velocity required for transportation of all of the load supplied to it from above, and this slope is maintained without change as long as controlling conditions remain the same.   The graded profile is a slope of transportation; it is influenced directly neither by the corrasive power of the stream nor bed rock resistance to corrasion.

Some changes from segment to segment in factors controlling the slope of the graded profile are matters of geographic circumstance that are not systematic in any way; these include the downvalley increase in discharge, and the downvalley decrease in load relative to discharge, that characterize trunk streams flowing from highland areas through humid lowlands.   Other changes, as downvalley decrease in caliber of load by reason of attrition, may be more or less systematic between tributary junctions.   Still others, as change in channel characteristics, are partly dependent on changes in load and discharge; the channel characteristics are determined chiefly by caliber of load and rate of lateral shifting of the channel, and the rate of channel shifting is itself dependent on velocity and erodibility of the banks.

These changes are usually such as to decrease slope requirements in a downvalley direction but, because none of them is systematic, the graded profile cannot be a simple mathematical curve in anything more than a loose or superficial sense. We can proceed toward an understanding of the graded profile, not by "curve matching", but by rigorous analysis of adequate sets of data for unit segments of natural and laboratory streams numerous and varied enough to reveal the effect of variation of each of the factors separately. An essential prerequisite for efficiency in the gathering and analysis of the data is recognition of the difference between the graded profile that is maintained without change, and the ungraded profile that is being modified by upbuilding or downcutting.

RESPONSE OF THE GRADED STREAM TO CHANGES IN CONTROL

GENERAL STATEMENT

The response of a graded stream to any change in control is systematic in that it is predictable in terms of Le Chatelier's general law: "If any stress is brought to bear on a system in equilibrium, a reaction occurs, displacing the equilibrium in a direction which tends to absorb the effect of the stress." This section outlines the manner in which a graded stream, as a system in equilibrium, reacts to "stresses" by considering the nature of its response to changes in some of the controlling conditions which were, in the preceding section, held constant.

The method of presentation adopted to some extent above but used more particularly here involves deduction, from the general concept, of specific reactions that should be expected as results of a number of changes in control, and the matching of these "expected consequences" with field examples. This method of testing the theory is neither superior nor inferior to the laboratory model method; it is simply different from the experimental method which it supplements but certainly cannot replace. Its validity as a test depends on (1) whether the deductions are logical, (2) whether the effects are specifically related to the stated causes, and (3) whether the examples are representative. Obviously, in some cases, the reasoning is inductive; the deductive method of presentation (Johnson, 1940) is not followed rigorously in most of these instances. But it is worth nothing that many of the reactions were in fact predicted purely on the basis of deduction, and later verified by reference to the record, and that a survey of factual relations set forth in the literature has failed to discover any effect of a given cause that does not fit the concept.

Examples are not cited, or are mentioned briefly, where relationships are clear cut or generally familiar. In some instances scores of examples bear out the deductive analysis, each differing from the others in nice detail; some selection was therefore necessary. In general, examples were selected in which a given cause can be related to a definite effect with the least explanatory argument. If alternative examples occur to the reader that illustrate a point more clearly than those cited, that is good; if, on the other hand, there are cases that fail to conform to the general thesis a description of them will be a contribution to our understanding of streams.

Engineering examples are usually intended to show the almost telegraphic rapidity with which preliminary reactions are propagated upvalley and/or downvalley from the point where a change has been introduced by man; some of the geologic examples show the nature of the response to analogous natural changes over a period of time in which more or less complete readjustment may be attained.

Discussion in the paragraphs below is confined to the general mechanism by which readjustment is effected. Contrasted methods of aggradation, the bearing of certain secondary cause-and-effect couples on the slope of the final readjusted profile, and the contrast between the form of the adjusted (or readjusted) profile of the graded stream and the disadjusted profile of the aggrading or degrading stream are treated later.

INCREASE IN LOAD

A once-graded stream responds to an increase in load primarily by steepening its declivity below the point of influx. The steepening is accomplished by deposition of part of the excess load in the channel at the point of influx with a consequent up-building of the channel at that point and the formation of a steepened part immediately below.[6] Steepening of any segment permits increased transport of load through that segment to the next segment which is in turn the site of deposition and steepening. Thus the effect of an increase in load is registered by the down-valley movement of a wave of deposition, large or small depending on the rate and manner of addition of the load, and deposition must continue throughout the stream below the point of influx until the slope is everywhere adjusted to the transport of all of the debris delivered to it.

The classic example of marked and immediate response of streams to increase in load associated with works of man is the aggradation and resulting widespread destruction of agricultural lands along the eastern side of the Great Valley of California caused by hydraulic mining on the western slopes of the Sierra Nevada between 1855 and 1884, when court decisions halted discharge of mining debris into the Sierra streams (Gilbert, 1917). Various surveys to 1894 are summarized as follows:

"the deposit . . . was 20 miles long, had a maximum width of three miles, covering 16,000 acres and containing 600,000,000 cu. yd. It was 20 feet deep at the river's mouth, 35 feet deep at the edge of the foothills, and 80 feet deep 5 miles higher up on the Yuba River. The grade of the original bed was 5 feet per mile. After the fill was made, the grade per mile was 2½ feet at the mouth, 10 feet at the middle zone, and 20 feet on the upper reaches" (Waggoner, in discussion of Stevens, 1936, p. 271).

The effect of increase in load due to natural causes is most strikingly exemplified by the aggradation that commonly occurs when river valleys are invaded by glaciers. Automatic steepening of the declivity of the proglacial stream is not necessarily proof that great additional *quantities* of debris are being shed into them. The detritus carried from upvalley and delivered to the stream at the terminus of the glacier is usually much coarser than that formerly delivered to the same point from upvalley by running water, and increase in caliber may be more important than increase in quantity of load as a cause of the profile steepening.

---

[6] A stream affected by a change in controls of any type "deposits part of its load" or "picks up more load" by appropriate modifications in the amount of material deposited and picked up in the course of its normal seasonal fluctuations, and the net differences are usually very small compared with the great bulk of material moved and relaid during these fluctuations.

Because glaciation is usually a relatively brief episode in the life history of the drainage basin, with the main cycle of advance and recession interrupted by numerous minor pulsations, and with continual change in topographic relations governing discharge of water and debris from the ice front, proglacial streams rarely or never attain adjustment. Their profiles therefore differ from the more or less completely adjusted pre-glacial and post-glacial profiles not only in overall slope, but also in form. (*See,* for example, MacClintock, 1922, p. 575, 681.)

DECREASE IN LOAD

A decrease in load may be thought of as occurring at any point in the stream. It may be stated for the time being that the stream simply makes up for deficiency in the load supplied from above by picking up additional load from its channel floor. The net result is downcutting, with a consequent lowering in declivity downvalley from the point where the change occurred. Downcutting must continue until the profile is reduced to that slope which will provide just the velocity required to transport the reduced load.

Because of the operation of the reservoir as a settling basin, the dam is the most common man-made cause of decrease in load. The downcutting that may result is typically shown by the Rio Grande below the Elephant Butte Reservoir and the Colorado below Lake Mead (Stevens, 1938) the Saalach River below the Reichenhall Reservoir (Schoklitsch, 1937, p. 157) and in many other cases (Lane and others, 1934). This effect of decrease in load due to damming is almost always complicated by elimination of peak discharges and velocities that results from the use of the reservoir as a water storage basin.

Terraces cut in earlier fill characterize Pleistocene outwash plains and valley trains. The usual downvalley convergence of terrace profiles cut during the period of deglaciation is probably due primarily to decrease in caliber of load reaching any given segment of the degrading stream as the distance between that segment and the receding ice front increases.

Davis (1902, p. 261) treated the very gradual decrease in stream slope that results from decrease in load due to reduction in relief during the humid erosion cycle; Johnson (1932) and others described analogous effects around the borders of shrinking desert ranges.

CHANGES IN DISCHARGE

If a segment of a graded stream receives all or most of its load at the upper end, changes in discharge call for readjustments in the slope in much the same way as changes in load. A decrease in discharge requires an increase in declivity because the load, remaining the same, must move faster through a smaller cross section, and because, as indicated earlier, decrease in the cross-sectional area of the channel involves a relative increase in frictional retardation of flow and, hence, a decrease in velocity. The stream affected by a decrease in discharge, being unable to transport all the load supplied to it on its former slope, deposits some of the load and thereby steepens the slope, the process continuing until the reduced stream is able, by reason of increased velocity on the steepened slope, to transport all the load shed into it. The opposite adjustment occurs in the case of increased discharge.

A special case of the operation of this principle is described by Salisbury (1937) in the lower Mississippi Valley. Subsequent to diversion of part of the Mississippi discharge into the Atchafalaya channel in 1882 there has been, downvalley from the point of diversion, silting of the bed of the reduced Mississippi, and lowering of the slope of the augmented Atchafalaya. Clearing of rafts on the Red River (the upper Atchafalaya), confinement of both the Mississippi and the Atchafalaya between levees, and other works of man have altered the regimen of both streams since the diversion. For these reasons, and particularly because of the exceedingly low slopes of the streams involved, the effects of the diversion are revealed only by careful evaluation of the evidence by Salisbury (chiefly in terms of variation in gauge heights) and by Lane (in discussion of Salisbury's paper, chiefly in terms of variation in discharge).

The distance from the point of diversion to the Gulf is about 125 miles along the Atchafalaya, and about 310 miles along the Mississippi. Deterioration of the discharge capacity of the Mississippi channel since the diversion began and concomitant increase in discharge through the steeper Atchafalaya suggest that we are viewing a type of deltaic drainage change, set in motion in this instance by man, which must have occurred repeatedly in the past under natural conditions. Salisbury's demonstration of silting in the trunk channel below the diversion provides an explanation of a mechanism by which deep-channel, slow-shifting streams like the Mississippi may transfer themselves to different radial positions as delta growth proceeds.

The principle and the general mechanics of readjustment are precisely the same in the more general case of a main stream which receives notable additions of debris from tributaries, but the effects on the form of the profile may be very different because loss of discharge in the main stream calls for local readjustments of slope at each tributary junction, usually enough steepening to permit the reduced main stream to transport the load supplied by the tributaries.

Aggradation of the trunk stream at and below tributary junctions is now in progress on the Rio Grande and the Colorado River below the Elephant and Boulder dams, due chiefly to elimination of peak discharges that formerly moved detritus delivered to the main channel by flash floods on the tributaries (Stevens, 1938). In these cases the effect of reduction of peak discharges locally outweighs the general tendency for downcutting due to retention in the reservoir of the bed load supplied from the upper parts of the trunk stream.

Recent widespread incision of valley floors by streams in the Southwest is ascribed by Bryan (1925; 1940) and Bailey (1935) to increase in peak discharge resulting from an increased rate of runoff due to reduction in vegetative cover. Assuming that this diagnosis is correct, whether the cause be climatic change (Bryan) or overgrazing (Bailey) the recent arroyo cutting is of special interest because, as in the examples last mentioned, a change in distribution of discharge through the year produces effects similar to those caused by a change in discharge, and because the downcutting, a preliminary result of deterioration in vegetative cover, may revert to upbuilding when and if increased load resulting from accelerated erosion of the denuded slopes begins to affect the streams.

The most common geologic cause of decrease in discharge is drainage diversion, and the most evident effect is the growth of side-stream fans in the valley of the reduced stream. The classic case is the partial blocking of the valley of the Petit Morin after capture of its headwaters by the Marne and the Aube; the marsh of St. Gond was caused by detrital accumulations which locally reversed the slope of the valley of the Petit Morin (Davis, 1896, p. 603, 604). Local slope reversals on a larger scale are represented by Lake Traverse and other lakes in the valley now occupied by the Minnesota River; this small postglacial stream has been unable to maintain the low-gradient valley cut during the Pleistocene by the very much larger "Warren River", which served as the outlet of Glacial Lake Agassiz. The final step in the blocking process is illustrated by an enormous accumulation of tributary fan detritus, possibly as much as 700 feet thick, in the gap cut by the former Shoshone River through the Pryor Mountains in Montana; in this case the discharge of the Shoshone was so greatly reduced by headwater diversion that the direction of flow of the beheaded trunk stream was completely reversed by tributary fans (Mackin, 1937, Fig. 6).

It appears, therefore, that reduction in discharge in a trunk stream joined by tributaries tends in general to cause profile changes that express the increased relative importance of the tributaries in the economy of the drainage system, and that, depending on how drastic is the reduction of the trunk stream, and how vigorous the tributaries, the main stream may respond by appropriate modification of its profile during a period of disadjustment or may disintegrate into a series of lakes and reversed segments.

163

RISE OF BASE LEVEL

A rise of base level is equivalent to the rising of a barrier across the path of the graded stream. Each unit of increase in the height of the barrier tends to flatten the declivity immediately upstream. The stream, unable because of decreased declivity to carry all of the load through the flattened segment, deposits in the segment, thus increasing the declivity and transferring the flattening upvalley. Continuation of the process results in upstream propagation of a wave or, better, of an infinite number of small waves of deposition.

If the barrier is raised slowly the stream may maintain itself in approximate adjustment during the process; its rate of aggradation is determined by the rate at which the barrier is elevated. If the barrier is raised rapidly or instantaneously a lake is formed; the distal part of the delta is then the "flattened part" of the profile, and the rate of aggradation is determined by the rate of delta building into the lake. In either case the successive profiles developed during the period of readjustment will differ markedly in form from the original profile and from the eventual completely readjusted profile. The final readjusted profile will tend toward parallelsim with the original profile, differing in this respect from the cases treated above. But, because of secondary effects of aggradation to be discussed later, precise parallelism will usually not be achieved; the only generalization that can be made is that the new profile will be everywhere adjusted to the new prevailing conditions.

Rapid upvalley propagation of a wave of deposition due to rise in base level is well shown by profile modifications brought about within a few years by erection of Debris Barrier #1 on the Yuba River (Gilbert, 1917, p. 52–63); Gilbert's figure 7 illustrates the typical wedging out upstream of the preliminary detrital accumulations. (See also Sonderegger, 1935, Fig. 2, p. 298).

The same effect, but on a much larger scale, is seen in aggradation on the Rio Grande above the Elephant Butte Reservoir (Eakin and Brown, 1939, p. 90–99). At San Marcial, a town near the head of the reservoir, the channel of the Rio Grande has been raised at least 10 feet since 1916, when the reservoir was completed, and the town site is largely buried in silt. Blaney states that surveys made in 1934 show a rise of the channel of 7 feet since 1918 at La Joya, and 2 to 4 feet at Albuquerque (Blaney, in discussion of Stevens, 1936, p. 266). La Joya and Albuquerque are about 50 and 100 miles (airline) above San Marcial, respectively, and Albuquerque is 500 feet above the level of the reservoir.[7]

The Elephant Butte Reservoir is about 40 miles long and the spillway crest is 193 feet above the original river bed. A statement to the effect that the eventual readjusted profile of the Rio Grande, long after complete filling of the reservoir, will be parallel with the original river bed and about 200 feet higher is, of course, wholly indefensible. It is, however, probably closer to the truth than the comfortable assumption that the final debris fill will wedge out to zero within a few tens of miles above the original head of the reservoir. The profile of the aggrading Rio Grande during the period of disadjustment will be less steep than the original profile, but the final readjusted profile may be less steep or steeper. It is not necessary to look so far into the future for trouble—a few tens of feet of upbuilding to the latitude of Albuquerque would destroy highways and railways, towns, irrigation works, and farmlands with an aggregate value that may exceed the cost of the dam.

---

[7] Stafford C. Happ points out (personal communication) that increased sedimentary loads of tributaries in the last 50 years have probably caused aggradation in the Rio Grande Valley independently of the influence of the Elephant Butte Reservoir. If quantitative evaluation of adequate data indicate that all of the upbuilding noted by Blaney at La Joya and Albuquerque is due to these "upvalley" influences it will mean simply that the effects of the reservoir have not yet reached these points. For definite evidence that aggradation had extended to a point at least 15 miles above the reservoir by 1941 see Happ, in discussion of Stevens (1945, p. 1298).

Aggradation of the Kickapoo River in Wisconsin is ascribed by Thwaites and Bates chiefly to Pleistocene upbuilding of the Wisconsin River, which it enters; it is in effect, therefore, a case of aggradation caused by a "geologic" rise of base level. As in all such cases, aggradation undoubtedly altered conditions controlling slope on the Kickapoo; it is interesting, nevertheless, to note that the modern profile for the first 100 miles above the mouth corresponds closely in slope with the original profile determined by well logs (Bates, 1939; Thwaites, 1928, p. 628).

In some respects analogous to the more or less adjusted Kickapoo and serving especially as an antidote for any idea that the readjusted stream *must* be less steep than the original stream is the striking case of aggradation above a debris barrier on the Bear River in California; the approximately adjusted profile of this river above the barrier is notably steeper than the original profile of the stream (Stevens, 1936, p. 219).

Johnson and Minaker (1945, p. 904) cite an unpublished report by Kaetz and Rich to the effect that study of profiles above 22 debris barriers shows that the slopes of the deposits average from 37 to 49 per cent of the original slope—these cases are recognized as not having reached "equilibrium conditions". They state further that in model studies slopes up to 90 per cent of the original streambed slopes were obtained. Their interpretation of the difference in the form of the original profile and the profiles developed during aggradation differs in detail from those advanced later in the present article, but their factual data, reasoning, and conclusions conform in all respects with the general theory of grade.

Loss of storage capacity by silting is one of the outstanding engineering problems of the century; the problem is many-sided, and the literature is extensive. (*See*, for example, Brown, 1944; Stevens, 1936, 1945; Witzig, 1944; and papers cited therein.) Two practical implications of the theory of grade bearing on special aspects of the problem follow so directly from the views and factual relations cited above as to merit brief mention in passing.

It seems to be common practice to determine the "useful life" of a reservoir (usually the time required for filling with debris to spillway level at the dam, but varying depending on the purpose of the reservoir) by dividing the yearly increment of debris into the capacity of the reservoir for water, with due allowance for compaction and related factors. This method is evidently based on the tacit assumption that, when the delta front has advanced any considerable distance toward the dam, the river will carry its detrital load from the original head of the reservoir to the delta front on a surface of no slope (i.e., the water level). Mere statement of this basic assumption in these terms demonstrates its absurdity. Remedial measures costing large sums are in part contingent on predicted rates of storage depletion; these predictions, particularly on high gradient streams carrying a coarse bed load, are subject to gross errors when they fail to take into account the progressive increase in the proportion of the stream's load that is deposited on the valley floor above the reservoir as aggradation proceeds. (*See* Eakin and Brown, 1939, p. 6, 7; Happ, in discussion of Stevens, 1945, p. 1298–1300.) Research on what may be called "the form of the aggrading profile" is much needed, and the results must of course be quantitative to be useful. It is the writer's conviction that some qualitative understanding of the complex interrelationships of the factors at play in aggrading streams is the essential prerequisite for such quantitative studies if they are to yield general "laws" rather than a set of empirical constants of the type that lead some engineers to conclude that each individual stream has its own rules of conduct.

Study of the form of the aggrading profile may be expected to pay dividends not only by increasing accuracy of the storage depletion rate but also by developing methods by which the rate may be decreased.   As indicated especially by the soil conservationists (Brown, 1944), a basic part of any comprehensive attack on the silting problem is reduction insofar as practicable of the debris shed into streams from uplands in the drainage area.   The next step is to decrease the load delivered by the streams to the reservoir; the trend of thought in this connection seems to favor use of debris dams.   But another method of holding debris out of the reservoir merits more attention than it has received.   Normal upvalley aggradational processes may be accelerated by use of groins and other temporary and inexpensive structures so placed as to cause the stream to decrease its transporting efficiency (perhaps it would be better to say—so placed as to accentuate the natural tendency of the meandering or braided channel to be exceedingly inefficient).   This method conforms with the well-recognized principle that, in dealing with rivers, better results may be achieved with less human effort by working with the water, rather than against it; river training to induce deposition is to impounding debris by damming as river training to maintain a navigable channel is to dredging.   Training measures intelligently planned to increase the rate of upbuilding of the channel by deposition of bed load, and to increase the rate of vertical accretion on the floodplain by overbank deposition of suspended load, combined with suitable types of agricultural utilization of the valley floor as upbuilding proceeds, may provide a partial answer to the problem of reservoir silting.   Quantitative data are needed to evaluate the practicability of contrólled upvalley aggradation as alternative or supplementary to the debris dam system.

These suggestions apply to the simple case (as that of Lake Mead on the Colorado) where protection of the reservoir is the primary concern.   The situation is quite different on the Rio Grande, where aggradation above the Elephant Butte reservoir will destroy valuable property on the valley floor.   The engineer charged with corrective measures on the Rio Grande will face an interesting dilemma.   He can, by increasing the efficiency of the channel, permit the stream to transport its load on a lower slope, thus delaying destruction of upvalley property and shortening the useful life of the reservoir, or he can, by decreasing the efficiency of the channel, force the river to develop a higher slope by aggradation, thus hastening destruction of upvalley property and lengthening the life of the reservoir.

LOWERING OF BASE LEVEL

Lowering in base level, is, insofar as the response of the stream is concerned, essentially the same as the lowering of a barrier in its path.   Each small lowering of the control point steepens the gradient immediately upstream.   Accelerated velocity in the steepened portion results in downcutting, and the steepening is propagated upvalley.   Downcutting must continue until the slope is again completely adjusted to supply just the velocity required to transport all of the debris shed into the stream; as in the last case, and with the same qualifications, the final readjusted profile will tend to parallel the original profile.

A man-made change which corresponds with a lowering in base level is the local shortening of a stream by the elimination of meander loops; the general trend of the upvalley effects is indicated or,

166

better, merely suggested by changes in the profile of the Mississippi River brought about by a series of artificial cutoffs and other channel improvements between 1929 and 1939. A generalized and more or less diagrammatic profile (Ferguson, 1939, p. 829) shows the new slope between the cutoffs essentially the same as the original slope, the changes in level resulting from the individual cutoffs being cumulative in an upvalley direction. At Arkansas City, at the head of the cutoffs, the river level was lowered about 15 feet. The effect was noted in 1939 at a gauge 107 miles above the head of the cutoffs, where there was a lowering of 2 or 3 feet in flood stage. The river has certainly not yet adjusted itself to the new conditions; the chief significance of the recorded profile changes to date is the sensitiveness of the stream to "lowering of base level", and the extremely rapid headward progression of the first effects of that lowering.

Macar, on the basis of studies of natural cutoffs in European and American rivers, concludes that the "steepened part" caused by a given cutoff moves headward in large streams several hundred times faster than the rate of downcutting of the stream; his profiles show subparallelism between the original and readjusted slopes (1934).

CLASSIFICATION OF CHANGES IN CONTROL

Changes of the type discussed above may be usefully divided into two catagories: (1) "upvalley", and (2) "downvalley" changes in controls; the terms are used, of course, with reference to a particular segment under consideration. As indicated in an earlier section the slope of the graded profile is determined primarily by load and discharge, which are "upvalley" factors; change in either or both of these factors calls for changes in *slope*. The level at which the profile is developed is determined by base level, which is a "downvalley" factor; change in base level calls for a change in the level of the profile but does not, directly, call for change in its slope. A single change usually affects the stream differently above and below the point where the change occurs; for example, if the load delivered by a tributary is greatly increased the effect on the trunk stream below the junction is increase in load, and above the junction rise in base level. The distinction between upvalley and downvalley changes in control is of special importance in interpreting the significance of parallel and converging terrace and valley-floor profiles.

Crustal movements, as tilting or warping of any segment of a graded stream, constitute a third category of changes. Such changes are neither upvalley nor downvalley, and they do not necessarily involve changes in load, discharge, or base level; they simply cause a forcible distortion of all earlier developed terrace and valley-floor profiles within the segment affected. The stream responds by building or downcutting or both. Except insofar as base level or factors which control slope are changed, either in consequence of the crustal movements directly or by reason of the upbuilding or downcutting of the stream, the completely readjusted profile will be developed at the same level and will have the same slope as the original profile.

REGRADING WITH PROGRESS OF THE EROSION CYCLE

A stream may lengthen during its life history by headward erosion, delta growth, and the development of meanders. Lengthening by the slow extension of ungraded headwaters and by capture involves additions of discharge and load to the stream. The contrasted effects of these additions have been treated earlier; their net effect on the graded portion of the stream is determined by their relative importance. The change, with the progress of the erosion cycle, from the relatively straight course of youth to the meandering course of maturity involves a systematic lengthening of the stream. This lengthening, together with that resulting from delta building, tends to decrease declivity and hence calls for aggradation to maintain the slope required for the transport of load. Whether aggradation will actually occur and how far up-valley its effects may be felt at any stage depends upon the relative rate of an accompanying opposed upvalley change, namely, the tendency for slow lowering of graded declivity resulting from decrease in load with advancement of the cycle. Green has developed an interesting mathematical treatment of the change in the form of the profile by which, with certain initial assumptions made, the past and future shifting of the zones of aggradation and degradation can be determined (Green, 1936; *see also* Miller, 1939; Lewis, 1945).

These changes may be difficult or impossible to detect in large, low-gradient streams of humid regions, especially because they tend to be masked by or confused with the effects of subsidence in the deltaic area and eustatic changes in sea level. Their effects are more clearly seen in high-declivity graded streams flowing from semiarid ranges to closed desert basins under such conditions that base level is raised *pari passu* with decrease in the declivity of the stream that accompanies reduction of the range. As shown by Johnson and others, the stream maintains its graded condition under these conditions by *regrading*, being engaged in aggradation in the lower levels at the same time that it is degrading on the rock-floored pediment, the line of demarcation between the contrasted zones shifting rangeward or basinward depending on the relative importance of the downvalley and upvalley factors (Johnson, 1932).

There is perhaps nothing seriously wrong with the statement that the stream maintains a graded condition while continuously lowering its slope during the process of the cycle of erosion; the statement is merely an oversimplification that is confusing because it is inconsistent. In a textbook discussion of the *cycle of erosion* it would seem preferable to state that, having developed an equilibrium slope under existing conditions at any given stage of the cycle, that is, having attained a condition of grade, the stream must continually alter its slope and its graded condition as controlling conditions change. The rate of change in controlling conditions is exceedingly slow, and the stream's adjustment to the controlling conditions is exceedingly delicate. The lag between change in conditions and adjustment is therefore so completely negligible that, viewed at any one time, the stream may be properly regarded as being graded. But if attention is focused on the orderly change in landforms during the erosion cycle, that is, *if the topic under discussion is the cycle*, then the emphasis should be not on the "static" equilibrium at any one time, but on the gradually shifting equilibrium over a long period of geologic time. In the course of the erosion cycle the stream maintains itself, not in any one graded condition, but in an infinite number of different graded states, each differing slightly from the last and each appropriate to the existing conditions.

If there is anything paradoxical or confusing in this relationship it escapes the writer. But even the best student may be hopelessly confused if the concept of grade and the wholly different concept of the erosion cycle are churned up together and administered in one dose. Grade must be explained in terms of channel processes

and thoroughly understood as a condition of equilibrium in the stream as a transporting agent before the fourth dimension, geologic time, is introduced in a consideration of the role of the stream in the cycle.

An understanding of grade is essential for any theoretical analysis of the erosion
cycle, but the principle geologic application of the concept is in interpretation of
erosional and depositional landforms produced directly by the work of streams.   The
field worker in most continental areas finds that he must deal with streams that have
at different times in the recent past engaged in episodes of downcutting and valley
filling, both proceeding at varying rates and punctuated by pauses.   The complex
history of most modern stream valleys is undoubtedly due largely to the climatic
fluctuations, crustal movements, and eustatic changes in sea level that characterize
the Pleistocene.   Valley floors and terrace remnants of several types and with various
slopes in the same valley record the automatic tendency of the streams to adjust
themselves to these changing conditions; even if equilibrium were never attained the
theory of grade would be indispensable for any understanding of these strivings toward it.   But, as shown by examples cited earlier, which could be multiplied a hundred fold, essential equilibrium is in fact often attained and maintained long enough
for the production of distinctive landforms by long-continued lateral planation at the
same level.

SHORT-TERM CHANGES

After the meandering habit is fully developed in any segment the length of the
stream is not significantly altered by continued shifting of the meanders; the shortening effect of occasional cutoffs is cumulative only in the pages of Mark Twain's "Life
on the Mississippi".   That these local shortenings are compensated, over a period of
years, by continued slow growth of all of the loops is indicated by the fact that, although 20 cutoffs between 1722 and 1884 shortened the Mississippi by about 249
miles, the river was by 1929 about the same as the original length (Pickels, 1941, p.
339).

Disturbance of equilibrium relations in the stream by sudden local shortenings and
slow general lengthening are not inconsistent with the concept of grade as defined
here.   If a cutoff results in a "significant" break in the longitudinal profile the stream
may be properly considered to be ungraded at that point; the height of the break that
is "significant" depends simply on the point of view of the investigator.   Schoklitsch's analysis of profile readjustments in the vicinity of a single cutoff, too long and
not sufficiently pertinent to be summarized here, is an excellent illustration of readjustment on a small scale (1937, p. 153, 154; see also Shulits, 1936).   The effect of a
number of cutoffs was cited above, also from the engineering literature, to illustrate
the very rapid headward propagation of a local steepening in the longitudinal profile.
But in most cutoffs in streams flowing in alluvium the resulting steepening in the
bed is less than its normal relief from bend to crossing, the break in the slope of the
water surface is less than the difference between high and low water levels, and the increased velocity in the steepened part is less than the seasonal variation in velocity.
Because breaks of this type usually leave no recognizable record in the valley-floor

169

features, they may in many types of geologic studies be properly neglected in considering whether the stream is graded. With other short-term fluctuations in velocity, discharge, and load, they are considered to be covered by the expression "over a period of years" which is an essential part of the definition of grade.

DEPOSITS OF GRADED AND AGGRADING STREAMS

The body of detritus that floors the valley of a graded stream usually consists of three types of material, unlike in origin: (1) sand and gravel originally carried as bed load and deposited in the shifting channel, (2) an overlying sheet of sand and silt deposited from suspension in slow moving or ponded overbank waters, and (3) detritus not directly related to the work of the main stream, as talus and slope wash from the valley sides, and loess and wind-blown sand.[8] The maximum potential thickness of the channel gravel sheet equals the maximum potential depth of scour in the shifting channel during high-water stages; a thickness of a few tens of feet does not necessarily indicate that the stream has aggraded or is aggrading. The maximum thickness attainable by the overbank silt is determined by the height to which it can be built by successive overspreadings of the valley floor by flood waters without long-term change in the river level; the natural levee, as such, is not an evidence of aggradation. There is no well-defined limiting thickness for deposits of type (3); for example, over 150 feet of fan wash accumulated over the main stream channel gravel sheet in the Shoshone Valley in Wyoming during a period when the Shoshone River was not aggrading (Mackin, 1937, Pl. 1, p. 827–833).

True aggradation, which involves a systematic long-term rise in the river level, may be effected by a thickening of deposits of types (1), (2), or (3), or any combination of them.

An aggrading stream may produce a thick fill that consists largely or wholly of channel deposits. Numerous examples occur in valleys marginal to glaciated ranges, where the fill was deposited by proglacial streams and subsequently trenched so that its internal structure can be seen; exposures in the frontal scarp of a great fill terrace in the Cle Elum Valley in Washington, for instance, show over 200 feet of uniformly bedded gravels. This preponderance of channel deposits certainly does not mean that the Pleistocene Cle Elum River carried no suspended load, nor does it mean that the successively higher valley floors formed during the period of aggradation carried no veneers of overbank silt.

Aggradation may, on the other hand, produce a fill made up largely of silt and lacustrine clay—the Oligocene White River deposits of the Great Plains are a case in point. The prevailing fine texture of the White River beds certainly does not represent the loads carried by the Oligocene streams; lenses and stringers of channel gravel, contrasting sharply with the overbank silts and clays, occur throughout the White River sediments (Osborn, 1929, p. 103–109).

The thick aggradational fill in the Kickapoo Valley in Wisconsin consists chiefly of slope wash derived from the local valley sides (Bates, 1939, p. 870–876). This is perhaps an exceptional case, but greater or less amounts of local wash, partly re-

---

[8] For a more elaborate classification of valley floor materials *see* Happ, Rittenhouse and Dobsen, 1940, p. 22–31.

worked and interfingering with main stream deposits, are to be expected in all valley fills.

Contrasts between aggradational fills of different types depend largely on contrasts in the rate of lateral shifting of the depositing stream relative to the rate of upbuilding of the deposit and, especially, on the mechanism of lateral shifting, whether by meander swing and sweep processes (Melton, 1936) or by avulsion as in the braided stream. These habits depend in turn on slope, discharge, load, channel characteristics, and the hydrographic regimen of the stream, resistance of the valley-floor materials to lateral cutting, vegetative cover on the valley-floor, distance from source of the detritus and from the mouth of the stream, relief and erosional processes on adjacent uplands, and other factors that cannot be evaluated here. The points to be made are simply: (1) that *deposits* formed by or associated with aggrading streams differ markedly from the *loads* carried by them, (2) that distinguishing between channel and overbank deposits is the first essential step in interpreting modern valley fills or ancient fluviatile sediments, and (3) that, even after this distinction is made it is virtually impossible to work directly from the grade sizes represented in the channel deposits to the characteristics of the depositing streams because there is no simple relationship between the deposits of an aggrading stream and such partly interdependent factors as slope, discharge, channel characteristics, velocity, and load. We cannot proceed directly from laboratory-determined laws relating to stream *transportation processes* to interpretation of ancient stream *deposits*. An alternative and promising route of attack on the problem is via study of deposits now being formed by natural streams of many types to determine whether the sum total of all of the characteristics of given deposits is uniquely related to the particular modern streams by which they are being formed, and to proceed thence to an understanding of the characteristics of ancient streams by comparison of their deposits with deposits of modern streams of known characteristics.

Here again, as in every phase of the study of streams, there is a broad field in which the interests of the geologist and the engineer overlap. For example, correct evaluation of the factors that control what proportion of overbank silts and channel gravels are incorporated in an aggrading valley fill under natural conditions may permit intelligent modification of these factors to alter, to the advantage of a reservoir, the ratio of bed load to suspended load in the debris charge delivered to the reservoir by the aggrading streams that enter it. The marked decrease in the rate of storage depletion in Lake Mac Millan brought about by accidental introduction and development of a dense growth of saltcedar (tamarisk) on the aggradational flood plain above the reservoir (Eakin and Brown, 1939, p. 17–18; Walter, in discussion of Taylor, 1929, p. 1722–1725) illustrates the effectiveness of modification of only one of the factors controlling silt deposition on the valley floor.

SECONDARY EFFECTS OF AGGRADATION

DECREASE IN SUPPLIED LOAD

Aggradation (for whatever reason) involves burial of the lower waste-shedding slopes of the valley sides, and a consequent reduction in the load supplied to the stream system as a whole. Usually far more important, back-filling in valleys tributary to the aggrading trunk stream tends to reduce the load delivered by the tributaries. In the extreme case, aggradation by the main stream may so far outstrip upbuilding by its tributaries that the lower portions of their valleys are ponded; settling basins formed in this manner serve to entrap all or most of the clastic waste carried by the tributaries. (For examples, see Lobeck, 1939.) In general, decrease in load calls for decrease in the slope of the main stream.

DECREASE IN DISCHARGE

A stream flowing in a valley cut in rock normally carries most of the runoff from its drainage basin as surface discharge. But in an aggraded valley a considerable part of the runoff may pass through the detrital filling as underflow, with a consequent reduction in surface discharge available for the transportation of load. In general, decrease in discharge calls for an increase in declivity.

CHANGE IN CHANNEL CHARACTERISTICS

Aggradation often involves a shoaling and widening of the channel, and it may cause very marked changes in the stream's characteristics, as from a meandering to a braided habit. These changes usually tend to reduce the efficiency of the channel and therefore to require an increase in declivity.

GENERAL STATEMENT

Changes of the types listed above are more or less incidental results of the reaction (aggradation) of a stream to a given "primary" change in control. Since they, in turn, call for modifications in declivity, they may be regarded as "secondary" controlling factors. They operate especially during the period of aggradation, but they may continue to affect the stream long after it has readjusted itself to the new conditions. Thus, while certain "downvalley" changes in control (as rise of base level) do not directly call for change in slope, the eventual readjusted profile may, under different circumstances, be steeper or less steep than the original profile because of secondary chain-reaction effects. Any attempt to predict the final form or slope of the readjusted profile by evaluating the effects of a given man-made primary change in controls which fails to take into account these secondary changes in slope-controlling factors is liable to serious error. In general, the net effect on declivity of any primary change in control will be the algebraic sum of the parallel or opposed effects of the primary change and the associated secondary changes.

PROFILES OF ADJUSTED AND DISADJUSTED STREAMS

SORTING IN THE GRADED STREAM

As the velocity of the graded stream increases with seasonal increase in discharge, progressively coarser grains are set in motion up to the limits of the competence of the current and the supply of detritus available in the bed and banks. As velocity decreases with passing of the high-water stage, the materials in motion are thrown down in order of decreasing grain size. Every part of the channel deposit that veneers the valley floor is worked over again and again as the stream shifts laterally, each time with selective deposition of the coarser materials and a winnowing out of the fines. For this reason the valley-floor channel deposits in any part of the valley contain notably higher proportions of coarse materials than the bed load in transit through that segment of the valley in any representative period of time. There is, in this sense, a sorting process in operation in the graded stream.

Because the finer grains in the bed load are set in motion earlier, move faster while in motion, and are retained in motion longer during each seasonal fluctuation in discharge, there is a "running ahead of the fines" in the channel of the graded stream. But this "running ahead of the fines" does not cause a downvalley decrease in the caliber of the load handled by the stream. The fines move faster toward and into any given segment, but they also move faster through and away from that segment; the average grain size in the bed load moving through any segment is the same as though all the grain sizes moved at the same rate. The primary cause of the downvalley decrease in caliber of load in the graded stream is attrition, not sorting.

The same conclusion holds for the channel gravel sheet which veneers the valley floor. Every boulder or pebble that is lodged in the valley-floor alluvium in any segment of the valley at any period of time is likely to be moved and lodged again farther downvalley in successive intervals of time. Downvalley decrease in the grain sizes making up the channel gravel sheet is due, not to sorting, but to attrition during stages of movement in the channel, possibly accentuated by weathering during periods of lodgement.

SORTING IN THE AGGRADING STREAM

It has been noted earlier that aggradation may be effected either by a downvalley movement of a wave or waves of steepened declivity, or by an upvalley propagation of a wave or waves of flattened declivity. The essential relationship in both cases is that of a given segment shedding debris into an adjacent (downvalley) segment that is not quite adjusted to the transportation of that debris. Under these circumstances the operation of the seasonally expanding and contracting channel combines with a deficiency in velocity to assure that the coarsest fractions of the load entering any disadjusted segment will be deposited in that segment. Since the channel of the stream is raised as aggradation proceeds, the materials so deposited will not be subject to reworking and continued downvalley movement. There is in the aggrading stream, in other words, a "permanent withdrawal from circulation" of the coarser fractions of the bed load, and the "running ahead of the fines" in this case makes for a real and substantial downvalley decrease in the caliber of the load in transit, and in the materials deposited by the stream as it aggrades.

EXCHANGE IN GRADED AND AGGRADING STREAMS

The channel of the graded stream, shifting back and forth in a valley-floor gravel sheet made up largely of channel deposits which may be somewhat coarser than the average bed load in transit, has little chance to decrease the caliber of its load by the process of exchange.   But the channel of the aggrading stream may shift laterally in alluvium consisting essentially of contemporaneous overbank deposits.   In this case the materials added to the load of the stream by scour and caving at the outside of a shifting bend may be largely fine silts and sands, but the coarser fractions of the bed load supplied from upvalley tend to be deposited and left behind as the channel shifts.   The term exchange as used here does not imply any equivalence in weight or bulk of the material set in motion and deposited; the stream simply cuts at the outside of its bends because inertia normally holds the strongest current against the outside bank; it deposits the coarsest fractions of the load in transit on its channel floor with every seasonal fluctuation and leaves some of these deposits behind as the channel shifts.   In the aggrading stream, in contrast to the graded stream, this type of exchange may result in a notable downvalley decrease in the caliber of load in transit.

EFFECT OF DOWNVALLEY CHANGE IN CALIBER OF LOAD ON THE FORM OF THE PROFILE

It has been repeatedly emphasized that the declivity of the graded stream is controlled by load (and other factors); the declivity is adjusted to furnish just the velocity required for the transportation of all the load supplied to the stream.   In the aggrading stream the supplied load does not control declivity in the same degree because, by definition, *all* of the supplied load is not transported.   But it is important to recognize that the amount of material moved through any segment of the channel of the aggrading stream in any interval of time is enormously greater than the amount deposited, and that even in the aggrading stream the declivity of each segment is *approximately* adjusted to the load in transit through that segment.   In general, with decrease in the discrepancy between the supplied load and the load in transit, the aggrading stream approaches the graded condition.

No generalization can be made with regard to the average steepness of the profiles of graded and aggrading streams as such; both may vary from a small fraction of a foot to hundreds of feet per mile.   But an exceedingly useful generalization can be made with regard to a contrast in the *form* of the profiles of graded and aggrading streams.   Since declivity is in general adjusted to caliber of load in transit, and since the downvalley decrease in caliber of load in aggrading streams (by attrition, sorting, and exchange) is much more rapid than the downvalley decrease in caliber of load in graded streams (by attrition), it follows that declivity should decrease in a downvalley direction much more rapidly in the aggrading stream than in the graded stream under otherwise similar conditions.   The profile of aggradation should be, in other words, more strongly "concave upward" than the graded profile.   Thus, while the profile of the graded stream usually shows no tendency to be asymptotic with respect to a horizontal plane passing through a downvalley control point, the profile of the aggrading stream should and usually does show a definite tendency in this direction.

The writer has found two "rules" that follow from the discussion above to be useful tools in field study and interpretation of terraces of many types in stream valleys: (1) If there is any considerable length of stream upvalley from a given segment, aggradational channel deposits in that segment are so consistently finer in grain size than earlier or later deposits formed when the stream was at grade that variation in grain size and sorting serves as a criterion, for example, in distinguishing between channel deposits laid down in a valley-filling stage and the channel gravel sheet that mantles terraces cut in the fill during a subsequent degradational stage. (2) Aggradational profiles (recorded by terrace remnants) are usually steeper than earlier or later graded profiles in the upper parts of proglacial valleys, but the contrast in slope decreases in a downvalley direction and may be reversed, so that the aggradational profile is less steep than the graded profile in the vicinity of a down-valley control point.

CONCLUSIONS

"Let us suppose that a stream endowed with a constant volume of water, is at some point continuously supplied with as great a load as it is capable of carrying. For so great a distance as its velocity remains the same, it will neither corrade (downward) nor deposit, but will leave the slope of its bed unchanged. But if in its progress it reaches a place where a less declivity of bed gives a diminished velocity, its capacity for transportation will become less than the load and part of the load will be deposited. Or if in its progress it reaches a place where a greater declivity of bed gives an increased velocity, the capacity for transportation will become greater than the load and there will be corrasion of the bed. In this way a stream which has a supply of debris equal to its capacity, tends to build up the gentler slopes of its bed and cut away the steeper. It tends to establish a single uniform slope. . . ."

"Every segment is a member of a series, receiving the water and waste of the segment above it, and discharging its own water and waste upon the segment below. If one member of the series is eroded with exceptional rapidity, two things immediately result; first, the member above has its level of discharge lowered, and its rate of erosion is thereby increased; and second, the member below, being clogged with an exceptional load of detritus, has its rate of erosion diminished. The acceleration above and the retardation below, diminish the declivity of the member in which the disturbance originated; and as the declivity is reduced the rate of erosion is likewise reduced.

"But the effect does not stop here. The disturbance which has been transferred from one member of the series to the two which adjoin it, is by them transmitted to others, and does not cease until it has reached the confines of the drainage basin. For in each basin all lines of drainage unite in a main line, and a disturbance on any line is communicated through it to the main line and thence to every tributary. And as any member of the system may influence all the others, so each member is influenced by every other. There is interdependence throughout the system."

These paragraphs, taken with minor changes in wording from the Henry Mountain report, dated 1877, set forth the essence of Gilbert's idea of grade in streams; additions and modifications discussed in the present paper are chiefly matters of qualifying detail. The principal conclusion, that the concept of the graded stream as a system in equilibrium is valid, is based on:

(1) Citation of broad valley floors cut by long-continued planation at the same level by high-gradient streams crossing rock types of varying resistance to corrasion;

(2) Analysis of the form of the longitudinal profile developed and maintained by the graded stream under stable conditions, demonstrating by citation of cases that, in each segment, slope is adjusted to provide, with available discharge and under prevailing channel conditions, just the velocity required for transportation of all of the load supplied to that segment without regard for variation in resistance to corrasion in the subjacent materials; and,

(3) an outline of the manner in which graded streams readjust themselves to natural and man-made changes in controlling conditions of several types, demonstrating that the stream responds to such changes always so as to "absorb the effect of the stress", and thus exhibits the chief and diagnostic characteristic of the equilibrium system.

A critical point in connection with (2) is that, because in a trunk stream conditions

175

controlling slope do not vary systematically from segment to segment, the longitudinal profile cannot be a simple mathematical curve. This conclusion is qualitative; if, in conformity with it, we cease to smooth out real departures from uniformity and center the attack on them, with an adequate understanding of the genetic relationships of the independent and interdependent factors involved, then mathematical analysis of longitudinal profiles will advance our knowledge of streams.

A second generalization, important because it has been so generally neglected in geologic writings, is that the slope of the graded profile is adjusted to, or controlled by, not only the classic "load and discharge" but also the cross-sectional form and alignment of the channel—the more efficient the channel, the lower the slope.

In connection with (3) the present study tends to confirm the standard geologic view that streams readjust themselves to new conditions primarily by adjustments in slope, and only in minor degree by modification of the channel section. This statement is so phrased as to avoid any semblance of a "law"—certainly no fetish attaches to slope, and each individual case must be judged on the basis of the evidence. But it does appear that, confronted by changed conditions that call for increased or decreased energy for transportation, the stream usually responds by increasing or decreasing its total energy by appropriate adjustments in slope rather than by effecting economies in the energy dissipated in friction.

Additional generalizations include the distinction between "upvalley" and "downvalley" changes in control and between "upvalley" and "downvalley" reactions of the stream to a given change, the contrast between the form of the disadjusted profile during the period of readjustment and the final readjusted profile, and the effect of secondary changes in control on the slope of the readjusted profile.

With a few minor lapses, this paper does not treat the practical implications of the concept of grade. In geology these ramify widely, ranging from the power of rivers to corrade laterally to interpretation of ancient fluvial sediments and the origin of unconformities beneath and within them. In connection with control of rivers by men, a safe general implication is that the engineer who alters natural equilibrium relations by diversion or damming or channel-improvement measures will often find that he has a bull by the tail and is unable to let go—as he continues to correct or suppress undesirable phases of the chain reaction of the stream to the initial "stress" he will necessarily place increasing emphasis on study of the genetic aspects of the equilibrium in order that he may work *with* rivers, rather than merely *on* them. It is certain that the long-term response of streams to the operations of the present generation of engineers will provide much employment for future generations of engineers and lawyers.

In this connection the most important point brought out by the study may well be the striking analogy between the streams' response to the works of man and to accidents and interruptions due to geologic causes. Nature has brought to bear on streams nearly all of the changes in controlling conditions that are involved in modern engineering works; the record of the long-term reaction of rivers to past geologic changes that is revealed by terraces and in dissected valley fills should contribute much to an understanding of the future of streams that man seeks to control, and will call for changes in design. Conversely, every advance in knowledge of erosional, transportation, and sedimentation processes deriving from engineering investigations will increase the geologist's ability to interpret the record of the past. As the engineer becomes more and more concerned with the genetic aspects of his especial problems (as he must), and as the geologist learns more about the quantitative aspects of his especial problems (as *he* must), it will become evident that the problems are in large measure the same. As Rubey (1931b) puts it, there is "a need for close cooperation among *students of stream-work.*"

REFERENCES CITED

Bailey, Reed W. (1935) *Epicycles of erosion in the valleys of the Colorado Plateau Province*, Jour. Geol., vol. 43, p. 337–355.

Bancroft, Wilder D. (1911) *A universal law*, Am. Chem. Soc., Jour., vol. 33, p. 91–120.

Barton, Donald C. (1928) *Meandering in tidal streams*, Jour. Geol., vol. 36, p. 615–629.

Bates, Robert E. (1939) *Geomorphic history of the Kickapoo region, Wisconsin*, Geol. Soc. Am., Bull., vol. 50, p. 819–879.

Baulig, M. H. (1926) *La notion de profil d'equilibre, histoire et critique*, Cong. Inter. Geog. (Le Claire, 1925), C. R., vol. 3, p. 51–63.

Brown, Carl B. (1944) *The control of reservoir silting*, U. S. Dept. Agric., Misc. Pub. 521.

Bryan, Kirk (1922) *Erosion and sedimentation in the Papago Country, Arizona*, U. S. Geol. Survey, Bull. 730.

———— (1925) *Date of channel trenching (arroyo cutting) in the arid Southwest*, Science, vol. 62, p. 338–344.

———— (1940) *Pre Columbian agriculture in the Southwest as conditioned by periods of alluviation*, 8th Am. Sci. Cong., Pr., vol. 2, p. 57–74.

Davis, W. M. (1896) *The Seine, the Meuse, and the Moselle*, Nat. Geog. Mag., vol. 7, p. 189–202, 228–238.

———— (1902) *Base level, grade and peneplain*, Jour. Geol., vol. 10, p. 77–111.

Eakin, Henry, and Brown, Carl B. (1939) *Silting in reservoirs*, U. S. Dept. Agric., Tech. Bull. 524.

Ferguson, Harley B. (1939) *Construction of Mississippi cut-offs: Effects of Mississippi cut-offs*, Civil Eng., vol. 8, p. 725–729, 826–829.

Gilbert, G. K. (1877) *Report on geology of the Henry Mountains*, U. S. Geog. Geol. Survey Rocky Mountain Region, 160 p.

———— (1914) *The transportation of debris by running water*, U. S. Geol. Survey, Prof. Paper 86.

———— (1917) *Hydraulic-mining debris in the Sierra Nevada*, U. S. Geol. Survey, Prof. Paper 105.

Green, J. F. N. (1936) *The terraces of southernmost England*, Geol. Soc. London, Quart. Jour., vol. 92, p. LVIII–LXXXVIII (Presidential address).

Griffith, W. M. (1927) *A theory of silt and scour*, Inst. Civil. Eng., Pr., vol. 223, p. 243–314.

Happ, Stafford C., Rittenhouse, Gordon, and Dobson, G. C. (1940) *Some principles of accelerated stream and valley sedimentation*, U. S. Dept. Agric., Tech. Bull. 695.

Hjulström, Filip (1935) *Studies of the morphological activity of rivers as illustrated by the River Fyris* Univ. Upsala, Geol. Inst., vol. 25, p. 221–527.

Humphreys, A. A., and Abbot, Henry L. (1876) *Report on the physics and hydraulics of the Mississippi River*, U. S. Army, Corps of Eng., Prof. Paper 13.

Hunt, Chas. B. (1946) *Guidebook to the geology and geography of the Henry Mountains region*, Utah Geol. Soc., Guidebook to the Geology of Utah, no. 1.

Johnson, Douglas (1932) *Rock planes of arid regions*, Geog. Rev., vol. 22, p. 656–665.

———— (1940) *Studies in scientific method; IV, The deductive method of presentation*, Jour. Geomorph. vol. 3, p. 59–64.

Johnson, J. W. and Minaker, W. L. (1945) *Movement and deposition of sediment in the vicinity of debris-barriers*, Am. Geophys. Union, Tr. 1944, p. 901–906.

Jones, O. T. (1924) *The upper Towy drainage-system*, Geol. Soc. London, Quart. Jour., vol. 80, p. 568–609.

Kesseli, John E. (1941) *The concept of the graded river*, Jour. Geol., vol. 49, p. 561–588.

Kramer, Hans (1935) *Sand mixtures and sand movement in fluvial models*, Am. Soc. Civ. Eng., Tr., vol. 100, p. 798–878.

Lacey, Gerald (1930) *Stable channels in alluvium*, Inst. Civil Eng., Pr., vol. 229, p. 259–384.

Lane, E. W. (1937) *Stable channels in erodible materials*, Am. Soc. Civil Eng., Tr., vol. 102, p. 123–194.

———— and others (1934) *Retrogression of levels in river beds below dams*, Eng. News-Record, vol. 112, p. 836–840.

Leighly, John (1934) *Turbulence and the transportation of rock debris by streams*, Geog. Rev., vol. 24, p. 453–464.

Lewis, W. V. (1945) *Nickpoints and the curve of water erosion*, Geol. Mag., vol. 82, p. 256–266.

Longwell, C. R., Knopf, A., and Flint, R. F. (1939) *Textbook of Geology, Part I, Physical Geology*, John Wiley and Sons, N. Y.

MacClintock, Paul (1922) *The Pleistocene history of the lower Wisconsin River*, Jour. Geol., vol. 30, p. 673–689.

Macar, Paul (1934) *Effects of cut-off meanders on the longitudinal profiles of rivers*, Jour. Geol., vol. 42, p. 523–536.

Mackin, J. Hoover (1936) *The capture of the Greybull River*, Am. Jour. Sci., 5th Ser., vol. 31, p. 373–385.

———— (1937) *Erosional history of the Big Horn Basin, Wyoming*, Geol. Soc. Am., Bull., vol. 48, p. 813–894.

Melton, F. A. (1936) *An empirical classification of flood-plain streams*, Geog. Rev., vol. 26, p. 593–609.

Miller, A. Austin (1939) *Attainable standards of accuracy in the determination of preglacial sea levels*, Jour. Geomorph., vol. 2, p. 95–115.

Osborn, Henry Fairfield (1929) *The titanotheres of ancient Wyoming, Dakota, and Nebraska*, U. S. Geol. Survey, Mon. 55.

Pickels, George W. (1941) *Drainage and flood-control engineering*, McGraw-Hill Book Co., N. Y.

Quirke, Terence T. (1945) *Velocity and load of a stream*, Jour. Geol., vol. 53, p. 125–132.

Rich, John L. (1935) *Origin and evolution of rock fans and pediments*, Geol. Soc. Am., Bull., vol. 46, p. 999–1024.

Rubey, W. W. (1931a) *The Illinois River, a problem in channel equilibrium* (Abstract) Wash. Acad. Sci., Jour., vol. 21, p. 366–367.

———— (1931b) *A need for closer cooperation among students of stream-work*, Am. Geophys. Union, Tr. 1931, p. 216–219.

———— (1933) *Equilibrium conditions in debris-laden streams*, Am. Geophys. Union, Tr. 1933, p. 497–505.

———— (1938) *The force required to move particles on a stream bed*, U. S. Geol. Survey, Prof. Paper 189E.

Salisbury, E. F. (1937) *Influence of diversion on the Mississippi and Atchafalaya Rivers*, Am. Soc. Civil Eng., Tr., vol. 102, p. 75–122.

Schoklitsch, Armin (1937) *Hydraulic structures (Der Wasserbau*—translated by Samuel Shulits), Am. Soc. Mech. Eng., N. Y.

Shulits, Samuel (1936) *Fluvial morphology in terms of slope, abrasion and bed-load*, Am. Geophys. Union, Tr. 1936, p. 440–444.

———— (1941) *Rational equation of river-bed profile*, Am. Geophys. Union, Tr. 1941, p. 622–629.

Sonderegger, A. L. (1935) *Modifying the physiographic balance by conservation measures*, Am. Soc. Civil Eng., Tr., vol. 100, p. 284–346.

Stevens, J. C. (1936) *The silt problem*, Am. Soc. Civil Eng., Tr., vol. 101, p. 207–288.

———— (1938) *The effect of silt removal and flow regulation on the regimen of the Rio Grande and Colorado Rivers*, Am. Geophys. Union, Tr., 1938, p. 653.

———— (1945) *Future of Lake Mead and Elephant Butte reservoir*, Am. Soc. Civil Eng., Tr. vol. 111 p. 1231–1342.

Straub, L. G. (1935) *Missouri River*, H. R. Doc. 238, 73rd Cong., 2nd Session, Appendix IV, p. 1032–1245.

——— (1942) *Mechanics of rivers*, in Meinzer, O. E. (editor) *Physics of the Earth, IX, Hydrology*, McGraw-Hill Book Co., N. Y., 712 p.

Sverdrup, H. U., Johnson, Martin W., and Fleming, Richard H. (1942), *The oceans*, Prentice-Hall, Inc., New York, 1087 p.

Taylor, T. U. (1929) *Silting of the Lake at Austin, Texas*, Am. Soc. Civil Eng., Tr., vol. 93, p. 1681–1735.

Thwaites, F. T. (1928) *Pre-Wisconsin terraces of the driftless area of Wisconsin*, Geol. Soc. Am., Bull., vol. 39, p. 621–642.

Whipple, William, Jr. (1942) *Missouri River slope and sediment*, Am. Soc. Civil Eng., Tr., vol. 107, p. 1178–1214.

Witzig, Berard J. (1944) *Sedimentation in reservoirs*, Am. Soc. Civil Eng., Tr., vol. 109, p. 1047–1106.

UNIVERSITY OF WASHINGTON, SEATTLE, WASHINGTON
MANUSCRIPT RECEIVED BY THE SECRETARY OF THE SOCIETY, JUNE 3, 1946.

American Society of Civil Engineering, Proceedings, 1955,
Vol 81, paper 795, pp. 1–17

8

The Importance of Fluvial Morphology in Hydraulic Engineering

E. W. LANE

THE IMPORTANCE OF FLUVIAL MORPHOLOGY
IN HYDRAULIC ENGINEERING

E. W. Lane,* M. ASCE

Morphology may be defined as "the science of structure or form" and fluvial may be defined as "produced by the action of flowing water." Since rivers can hardly be said to have structure, fluvial morphology is therefore the science of the form as produced by the action of flowing water. It is a branch of geomorphology, the science of the form of the earth's surface. Geomorphology has also been called physiography.

Fluvial morphology is particularly important to the hydraulic engineer because many of his greatest problems arise because of the form of streams brought about by the transportation and deposition of sediment by them. For the proper solution of these problems, a knowledge of the principles of fluvial morphology is often necessary. Among the problems in which fluvial morphology is a very important factor are many of those dealing with water resources development and include some of the most important river problems in the world. Among these are flood control on the Lower Mississippi and on the Lower Colorado Rivers (of California and Arizona), the development of the hydraulic resources of the Missouri and Arkansas Rivers in the United States, the Yellow and Huai River flood problems in China, the Kosi River floods in India, and many others. As streams become more highly developed, and changes in sediment movement due to stream developments slowly become evident, the importance of the morphological aspect of river control problems will be increasingly appreciated.

Early History

The science of fluvial morphology has developed from two roots which have been largely independent of each other. The most vigorous root is in the science of geomorphology where the principal originators were the geologists, J. W. Powell,[1] G. K. Gilbert,[2] and W. M. Davis,[3] who worked in the latter part of the past century and early part of the present one. The work of these men dealt chiefly with the form of the surface of the earth and the importance of flowing water in causing the present shape, but Gilbert also made extensive investigations into the quantitative aspects of sediment transportation. The other root is in engineering and goes back much further, to Dominique Guglielmini,[4] about 1697, who was probably the first writer on fluvial morphology. As early as 1750,[5] engineers were arguing about the advantages and disadvantages, from the standpoint of navigation, of dividing the Rhine into several channels and were constructing hydraulic models to prove their contentions. Very complete histories of the developments of this science in the field of engineering can be found in the summaries of Hooker[6] and Mavis.[7] Unfortunately for both engineering and geology, these two roots, except for the work of Gilbert, have remained largely separate down to the

*Cons. Hydr. Engr., Fort Collins, Colo.

present time; but it seems probable that in the future a closer coordination of the two fields will exist to the advantage of both.

Nomenclature of the Geomorphologists

One of the best contributions made by the geomorphologists to the science of fluvial morphology is the nomenclature which they have introduced. Rivers have been classified by them on two bases: 1) on the basis of the method of formation, i.e., whether the position of the river is as a consequence of the initial slope of the land area or as a result of other factors[8, p. 171] and 2) on the basis of the stage which has been reached in the development of the stream. From the standpoint of the approach of this paper, the first of these methods of classification has little usefulness; but classification on the basis of stage of development introduces ideas of major value. A number of the morphologist's descriptive terms for rivers, such as meandering and braided, have been generally adopted. The conception of "base level" and of a "graded river" are also very useful, as are also the terms "agrading" for the change of the level of a river whose bed is rising and "degrading" for change downward.

The Geomorphological Approach

As previously mentioned, the geomorphologist is interested in fluvial morphology principally as a tool in explaining the origin of the present form of the surface of the earth. The science appears to be of comparatively recent origin. Although many able men contributed to its early development, the outstanding work is that of W. M. Davis.[3] According to the Davis conception, the primary action in the formation of the earth by moving water is the geographical or geomorphic cycle which is a cycle of erosion passing through several stages. It starts with a nearly flat land surface which is gradually warped by movements of the earth's crust. This gives rise to increased erosive and transporting power of the water flowing from the land, the water beginning to carve the landscape into various forms. As time goes on, the forms of the land surface change, the various types of topography being characteristic of the various length of time during which the water has acted. Material is constantly being carried away from the land surface and deposited (usually in the sea); and the elevation of the land surface is gradually lowered and flattened until, after a very long period of time, the end of the cycle is reached when the whole surface has been reduced to a very gently sloping plain called a peneplain, and thus comes back to the condition in which the cycle started.

The various types of topography in the cycle were designated by Davis in terms of the stage reached in this cycle, using a terminology commonly adapted for designation of the age of a man. The stages began at the start of the cycle with youth, which passes into maturity and then into old age. The topographic forms typical of the first stage are spoken of as young or youthful, later ones as mature, and those of the last stage as old, with further subdivisions when desirable such as, for example, early and late maturity. The same set of terms are used to designate the stage of development of streams, and certain characteristics are typical of rivers of these various stages. Davis' designation by means of terms of age is somewhat confusing, as a mature stream may later become a youthful one. Also, although the stage reached by the stream usually corresponds with that of the surrounding topography, this is not necessarily the case. An entire river need not be at the same stage throughout; usually a stream is less youthful in character near the mouth than in the vicinity of its headwaters.

Fluvial morphology as developed by the geomorphologists is largely a qualitative or descriptive science and suffers somewhat from a lack of quantitative relations, but many keen minds have contributed to it. It is not the intention in this paper to present in detail the geomorphological approach to this subject but rather to present geomorphology from an engineering viewpoint in order that the engineer may have the advantage of the extensive work of the geomorphologist, and that the latter may possibly gain something from the engineering viewpoint. An engineer who wishes to become a specialist in this field of fluvial morphology should thoroughly study numerous books and original sources of this part of the sciences. (8, 24, 25, 26, 33, to 37 inc.)

Characteristics of the Various Stages of Development of Rivers

In the same way that a person rapidly forms an opinion of the age of another person from the presence or absence of certain features which are characteristic of the various ages, a geomorphologist forms his opinion of the stage of development of a river from the presence or absence of certain conditions which are characteristic of the various river stages. According to the classical conception, young rivers are characterized by their ability to cut their stream beds downward with, geologically speaking, considerable rapidity; and the characteristic features are those which result from this action. The valleys of young streams are usually V-shaped or are deep gorges or canyons. Waterfalls or rapids often exist in these streams because sufficient time has not passed since they were uplifted for the stream to cut down and thus eliminate them. There are frequent changes of the grade of the stream caused by the hardness of the strata over which the stream flows, and pot holes are sometimes found. Because the valleys are steep sided and narrow, there is very little flat land in their bottoms; and highway and railroad construction along them is accomplished with difficulty. Douglas Johnson(26) suggests that early youth ends when lakes are eliminated, and middle youth ends when falls and rapids are eliminated.

Late youth ends and early maturity begins in a stream when the stream ceases to cut down rapidly but continues to widen out the bottom of the valley. This occurs in any stretch of the river when the sediment supplied by the river upstream, the tributaries within the stretch, and the erosion of the banks and valley sides is equal to the transportation capacity of the river. It then ceases its rapid cutting down, but the valley widens out as the material from the banks and valley sides continues to be carried away. Normally, the river would continue to lower its bed as the whole drainage area is lowered; but this is a very much slower rate than the lowering in a youthful stream. Early maturity ends and late maturity begins when the valley width equals the width of the belt covered by meanders of the stream. Late maturity ends and early old age begins when the valley width reaches several times the meander belt width.

The features usually associated with maturity in streams are flood plains, no rapids or falls; and meanders with oxbow lakes, but no other kinds of lakes. There are no sharp divisions between the various stages, nor is there general agreement as to when the various stages end. For example, an old river is sometimes considered to be one in which all of whose tributaries have reached maturity. Also some consider that when the flood plain widens to the width occupied by the stream's meanders, so that these can move unrestrained by the valley walls, the end of the maturity stage is reached; and when the flood plain is wider than this, the river is old. These limits differ from those previously stated.

The foregoing classification represents the views of the classical or Davis school of geomorphologists; but a questioning of it has recently arisen, largely among those dealing with the Lower Mississippi River, who believe that the classical viewpoint puts too much emphasis on erosion and the formation of erosional peneplains and not enough on the depositional aspects. According to their view, the Lower Mississippi River with its meanders, oxbow lakes, and natural levees, and with a flood plain several times the meander belt width is still a comparatively young stream since it is building up the land along its course. There seems to be some justification for this new viewpoint. Obviously when an uplift occurs and streams start to cut down, there must soon be a part of their length, even though a relatively short one, along which at least part of the eroded material is deposited. This part of the stream is thus building up, and this process is as characteristic of a stream in the early part of the geographic cycle as is the cutting down of the high lands. It will thus be seen that the classical classification of age of a stream may be inexactly related to chronological age and that there is room for further work in classification to bring about a more logical system.

Base Level

Another of the concepts of the geomorphologist which is very useful to the engineer is that of base level. If the quantity of water in the ocean remained the same and no moving of the earth's crust took place, the dry surface of the earth would eventually be reduced nearly to sea level. Sea level is thus the ultimate base level toward which all streams tend to cut their beds. There are often certain local levels which, geologically speaking, temporarily are elevations toward which streams tend to cut their beds. Lakes, for example, for the period of their existence, control the level of streams entering them and thus form local or temporary base levels for such streams. Waterfalls and rapids often form local base levels. The bed of a large stream usually forms the temporary base level for its tributaries. There are here also borderline cases where it is difficult to establish the existence of a local or temporary base level, but usually they are quite evident.

Equilibrium in Natural Streams

The concept of equilibrium in streams as developed by the geomorphologist is also a very useful one to engineers. This concept is not unknown to engineers, but it has been more actively studied by geomorphologists. A variety of terminology has been used to express this condition. A stream in equilibrium is said to be a graded stream, a poised or balanced stream, or to be a regime stream or a stream in regime. Makin[25 p. 471] has given the following definition:

"A graded stream is one in which, over a period of years, slope is delicately adjusted to provide, with available discharge and with prevailing channel characteristics, just the velocity required for the transportation of the load supplied from the drainage basin. The graded stream is a system in equilibrium."

When a stream is capable of carrying more sediment than is supplied to it,

it carries away material from its bed and thus tends to lower the bed. This
cutting down increases the slope of the tributary streams which causes them
to bring down more material to the main stream. The more the stream cuts
down into the surrounding land, the greater becomes the load supplied to it.
Since most streams eventually reach either the ocean or some other base
level as they cut down their beds, their slopes decrease; and, therefore, their
ability to carry away the sediment brought to them is diminished. With the
amount of material brought down to the stream increasing and the stream's
ability to carry it away decreasing, a point is eventually reached where the
rate at which sediment is brought to the stream becomes substantially equal
to the rate at which it is carried away by the stream and a condition of equilibrium is reached. Under these conditions the bed neither cuts down nor
fills up.

Ordinarily in natural streams the flow of water is not constant but continually varies, the ratio of the high flows frequently being a hundred or more
times the low flows. Although the stream tends to pick up or deposit the bed
material until its load equals its capacity to transport the load, because of
the rapid variations of flow and sediment supply, a condition of equilibrium in
which the load exactly equals the capacity of the stream to transport rarely
exists except momentarily. Since the tendency of streams is to wear the land
surface down to sea level and hence to lower their beds, considering a very
long period, geologically speaking, the tendency is for more sediment to be
removed from a section of a stream than is supplied to it; and, therefore,
when long periods are considered, natural streams are rarely in equilibrium.
Normally, therefore, neither in very short or very long periods may natural
streams be considered to be in equilibrium.

Over long periods, historically speaking, however, it is true that the beds
of a large number of streams, for most practical engineering purposes, are
substantially in equilibrium; and accurate conclusions for many purposes
may be reached by assuming equilibrium to exist. In some streams the bed
may be slightly lowered in floods but fill back to their former level as the
flood recedes and, except during floods, be at practically the same elevation
even at the end of a long period of years as at the beginning of it. Although
exact equilibrium is only momentarily obtained and, geologically speaking, a
stream may be slowly degrading or agrading, for practical purposes it may
be considered to be in equilibrium. The term equilibrium in this case may be
likened to the term sea level, which for practical purposes is considered to be
a fixed level, although the surface of the sea is constantly fluctuating above
and below this level due to waves and tides; and, over very long periods of
time, the sea level may rise or fall scores of feet due to more or less water
being stored on the land surface in the form of glaciers.

For engineering purposes a section of a stream may, therefore, be said to
be in equilibrium if, although it may continually fluctuate between aggradation
and degradation, over a long period of years, in terms of human history, the
net amount of change is not sufficiently large to be detected by quantitative
measurements. It is believed that most alluvial streams, where not affected
by the works of men, may thus be said to be in this equilibrium or graded
condition.

If equilibrium exists in a reach of a river, a change of only one condition
at a single point which would upset the equilibrium at this point would, if no
other factors changed, eventually upset the conditions of equilibrium throughout the entire reach and bring about a new condition of equilibrium in this
reach. Except in short reaches, however, other changes probably occur

185

before the readjustment to any one change is complete; and in most streams on which man has built hydraulic works, several changes are going on at the same time. Not infrequently, however, one change is so large compared with the others that it overshadows the minor ones and appears as a single change.

Changes of the Profile of Natural Streams

As the science of sediment transportation and deposition develops, it will be possible to predict more and more closely the morphological changes which will take place in a river due to any set of conditions and the rate at which they will occur. In the future the necessity of making such predictions is likely to increase. Such quantitative predictions can often be made by means of the knowledge of sediment transportation now available if all of the factors are known with sufficient accuracy. Usually, however, the data is not sufficient for quantitative estimates; and only qualitative estimates are possible.

The following very general expression will be found useful in analyzing qualitatively many problems of stream morphology:

$$Q_S \, d \sim Q_w S$$

Here Q_S is the quantity of sediment, d is the particle diameter or size of the sediment, Q_w is the water discharge, and S is the slope of the stream. This is an equation of equilibrium and if any of the four variables is altered, it indicates the changes which are necessary in one or more of the others to restore equilibrium. For example, if a stream with its sediment load is flowing in a condition of equilibrium and its sediment load is decreased, equilibrium can be restored if the water discharge or the slope are decreased sufficiently or if the diameter of the sediment is increased the proper amount. This equation is not an exact mathematical equation as it will not give the quantitative values of the variables involved which bring about equilibrium, but it is helpful to indicate qualitatively the changes which will take place in a stream when a change of any one of the variables occurs.

The sediment discharge, Q_S, in this equation is the coarser part of the sediment load or more exactly the bed material load,* since this is the part of the load which largely molds the bed formation. In most cases, the quantity of the fine load of silt and clay sizes can change almost indefinitely without materially affecting the river profile. In the following discussions of profile changes, changes of sediment load will be considered to mean changes of bed material load.

Classes of Stream Profile Changes

The changes which take place in the profile of a graded stream in equilibrium, due to a change of one or more of the factors controlling equilibrium, usually fall into one of six classes. One of the most common classes (Class 1) is the change that takes place in a stream with an equilibrium Grade BA as shown on Figure 1-a which reaches a base level at A, due to a change of conditions in the channel. Suppose the change of conditions is an increase in the sediment load Q_S beginning at C without changing the size of the sediment diameter d or the water discharge Q. To re-establish equilibrium the slope

---

*Bed material load is sediment in transport of sizes readily available in considerable quantities in the stream bed.

S must be increased. Ordinarily after such a change of conditions a new equilibrium tends gradually to be established as follows: When the change of condition first occurs the stream between C and A cannot carry the increased load of sediment, and some of it is deposited on the bed downstream from C causing the bed to rise or aggrade to C'. At first this deposit may not extend down to base level but may end at E. As the deposit continues, the bed level may be increased to C", and the rise or aggradation may extend all the way to A. If the new condition continued a long enough time, a new equilibrium Grade C''' A would eventually be established; and no further rise or aggradation in the grade would take place.

The same changes would take place if instead of the sediment discharge Q_s increasing at C, the size of the sediment d was increased at C, leaving the sediment discharge Q_s and water discharge Q the same. A decrease of the water discharge Q leaving Q_s and d the same would produce the same result.

The foregoing changes also would cause a change of grade above the point C. The raising of the bed to C' would cause a decrease in the slope S upstream from the point C. The stream could not transport the sediment brought down on this flattened slope; and some of it would be deposited upstream from C, aggrading the stream bed upstream from C. As the stream bed below C aggraded, that above would also rise, approaching a final equilibrium Grade C'''B''' parallel to the original equilibrium Grade CB. The height of C'''B''' above CB would depend on the magnitude of the change of conditions which brought it about. The raising of the grade of the main stream in this way would also usually cause a rise in the grade of the tributaries entering the raised section, extending up the tributary a greater or less distance depending on the conditions in its bed.

Examples of Class 1

One of the common causes of a change in stream profile as in Class 1 is the decreasing of Q by taking the water out of the stream for irrigation, desilting the water, and returning the sediment to the river again, thus decreasing Q without changing Q_s or d. In the Rio Grande and in the Arkansas River in the United States, this has resulted in a rise in level of the river bed which causes many difficulties. A rise of the Yuba river bed in northern California, U.S.A., of about 20 feet started about 1850 due to the increase in the sediment load Q_s resulting from the discharge into the streams of large quantities of gravel wasted in the hydraulic mining of gold.[22] After hydraulic mining activity was greatly reduced, the height of this deposit gradually decreased, tending to restore the former levels. A similar case is the Serendah River in Malaya, where the river bed rose 21 feet in the years 1922-1933 due to the addition of sediment from the hydraulic mining of tin.[32] A very striking example is the Mu Kwa River in Formosa, the bed of which raised about 40 feet in 3 years due to the addition of sediment to the river from landslides. A two-story hydroelectric powerhouse along the side of the river was completely buried (Figure 2).

A rise of the stream bed may also occur due to the increase in sediment load brought into the stream by a tributary. The slope of the Missouri River for some distance upstream for the mouth of the Platte River is flatter; and below the mouth it is steeper than the slope of the remainder of the river in this vicinity, which is said to be due to the large quantity of coarse sediment brought in by the Platte River. The deposits brought in by a tributary may cause the stream bed downstream from the mouth of the tributary to build up so rapidly that the deposit upstream may not be rapid enough to keep the bed level upstream higher than that downstream. The deposits downstream then form a sort of dam which causes a lake to form upstream from the tributary mouth. An example of this condition is found at Lake Pepin which has been formed in the Upper Mississippi River by the great load of sand brought into it by the Chippewa River. Matthes reports that the sediment brought down the Yuba River previously mentioned temporarily formed a dam in the Feather River, into which the Yuba discharged, which caused a lake 10 miles or more long; and later the sediment coming down the Feather River formed another temporary dam in the Sacramento River, into which the Feather River discharged, which also produced a lake. Farther down the Sacramento River at the city of Sacramento, California, U.S.A., the low water stage was raised 10-1/2 feet by the deposits. This maximum stage was reached in 1890. The discharge of gravel into the streams was prohibited by law and the deposits decreased, restoring the original stage at Sacramento by 1920.

Examples of Class 2

Class 2 is similar to Class 1 but results in a lowering or degrading of the profile of the stream due to a decrease in the sediment load or its particle size or an increase in the water discharge. A reduction of the sediment load Q_s of the stream at point C (Figure 1-b) is brought into balance by a reduction of slope S from point C to the base level at A and upstream from C the bottom is lowered but retains the same slope as before. In this case, tributaries entering the stream usually have their beds lowered also.

A very common cause of such a lowering is the abstraction of part or all of the sediment load from a stream by the deposit of it in the quiet water upstream from a dam. Downstream from the dam the river bed is often considerably degraded because of the sediment carried away from the bed by the clarified water. This action caused the failure of an important dam in India. Many other changes of Class 2 have been observed on the Indus River.[29,30,31] A stream profile change of Class 2 necessitated the complete reconstruction of Fort Sumner Dam on the Pecos River in New Mexico. The extent of the degradation below this dam is shown in Figure 3. Stream profile changes of Class 2 have affected in some cases beneficially and other cases detrimentally a large number of water power plants. A knowledge of the magnitude of this action is an important factor in the design of the spillways of many dams, since failure to correctly estimate the lowering may in some cases cause failure of the spillway or even of the dam itself. A number of cases of degradation below dams have been described in technical literature.[13,27]

The increase of the flow Q_w has the same effect as a lowering of the quantity of sediment Q_s. A very striking case of stream bed lowering due to an increase in the flow has occurred in Five Mile Creek in Wyoming, U.S.A. The added flow is due to the waste water of an irrigation project constructed in the valley of this stream. Here the stream bed has degraded until it has uncovered rock ledges which were below bed level and produced waterfalls and rapids where the water flows over these ledges as shown in Figure 4. This degradation removed about 1,000 acre feet of sediment in a year from the stream bed and banks and which is depositing in and rapidly filling a reservoir a short distance downstream.

An interesting example of stream bed lowering due to a reduction of the quantity of sediment Q_s has occurred in Cherry Creek in Denver, Colorado. Large quantities of sand have been removed from the stream for building construction; and downstream from the point of removal, the bed degradation has extended to the mouth, a distance of about 5 miles. Figure 5 shows the magnitude of the lowering which took place at one point in about 2 years. The construction of a number of check dams was necessitated to hold up the bed level and prevent the undermining of walls, bridges, and sewers along this creek. A similar degrading has resulted on the Loup River near Bolus, Nebraska. A canal for hydroelectric power was constructed from one branch of the stream to a power plant on another branch. The increased flow in the branch below the power plant caused a lowering of the grade of the river above the plant and extended downstream 1-1/2 miles to the junction of the two streams below which the discharge is unchanged. The effect was beneficial to the power development as it increased the fall available for producing power by about 5 feet, but it caused damage to the foundations of bridges over this portion of the stream.

Usually the changes involved go on quite slowly but under certain conditions changes of surprising magnitude and rapidity can take place. Todd and Eliasson[11 p. 376] report that in a 30-mile stretch in the Yellow River, the bed was deepened an average of 15 feet. At Lungmen the bed was lowered approximately 30 feet over a width of 3,000 feet, the depth tapering off upstream and downstream removing an estimated quantity of 9,000,000 cubic yards in not more than 12 hours. The cause of this phenomenon is not indicated; but it was probably due to an increase in discharge, perhaps of less heavily sediment laden water.

Examples of Class 3

Class 3 changes of stream bed profile are those which occur when the grade of the stream is suddenly raised at one point. The most common cause of such a rise is the construction of a dam; but such changes also occur from natural causes, such as the damming of rivers by landslides, mud flows, lava flows, or the advance of a glacier. This class is represented by Figure 1-c which shows the changes which occur in the bed of a stream in equilibrium when the grade at one point is suddenly raised.

If the stream grade is raised suddenly enough, a lake is formed upstream from the point of rise; and this lake is then gradually filled with sediment brought down by the stream. The conditions during the filling period are represented by the profile ending at C' on Figure 1-c. The unusual shape of the stream profile is due to the coarse sediment being deposited at the upper end of the reservoir and the fine material being carried farther into the lake or flowing down the lake bottom as a density current. The reservoir is filled when the stream bottom is raised to point C'', and part of the sediment load passes over the obstruction. The grade continues to rise upstream from the dam and approaches a final equilibrium grade which is parallel to that before the grade was raised. This was probably first pointed out by Harris[28] over a half century ago. The changes discussed under Class 1, where lakes were formed upstream from the tributaries, are also occurrences of Class 3.

The length of the lake filling stage in this class depends largely on the volume of the lake and the rate at which sediment is brought down by the stream. When the reservoir volume is small and the rate at which sediment is brought down is great, the length of the filling period is short and the effects upstream from the lake may develop very rapidly. For example, the deposits above the Imperial Dam on the Lower Colorado River within 7 years were causing a rise of the stream bed 55 miles upstream from the dam, whereas the level pool above the dam originally extended only 15 miles upstream. The profile of the river upstream from the dam had already reached a gradient of three-fourths that of the original slope which was probably very close to the equilibrium grade. The bed 55 miles upstream would have continued to rise and the effect would have extended much farther upstream had it not been for the degradation effect, as discussed under Class 2, from another dam built farther upstream about the same time.

Another interesting example of similar action was observed on the Nan-shik-chi River in Formosa. This stream had a slope of about 1:120. A dam about 13 meters high was constructed on this stream 1.3 km below a hydro-electric power plant. In 7-8 years the lake above the dam was filled and the slope of the river bed extended upstream from the crest of the dam on a slope of 1:250, or about half that of the original river bed. This raised the river level so much at the hydroelectric plant that it was threatened with flooding, and it was necessary to blast off the top of the dam downstream to prevent it.

Extensive changes of level above dams have been investigated in India in connection with the great irrigation works in the Indus River basin.[29,30,31]

Examples of Class 4

Class 4 profile changes (Figure 1-d) result from the lowering of the temporary base level of the stream and causes effects somewhat similar to those upstream from point C in Class 2. This case often occurs when a reservoir, which is usually held at a constant level, is drawn down. The Salton Sea in California, U.S.A., was at one time filled to an elevation of 40 feet above sea level and the Whitewater River[12 p. 320] built a grade adjusted to this level. The sea has been cut off from the ocean and lowered by evaporation to 250 feet below sea level, and the Whitewater River is slowly adjusting itself to this new base level. The flow in the river is ordinarily very small so that the adjustment is slow; but in the rare large floods, scour proceeds rapidly upstream in a series of cataracts. Another example is the Mojave River which flowed into ancient Lake Manix. This lake drained itself by cutting through a barrier, and the stream is now adjusting itself to the new level. Over a long period of time such changes have taken place in many large rivers.

It is known that the level of the ocean during glacial times rose and fell several times as more or less ice was imprisoned on the earth surface in the form of glaciers. The lowerings reached as much as 325 feet below the present level. During these glacial changes, the beds of all of the streams which flowed in erodible deposits and entered the sea were probably adjusted to the lower level as they are now adjusted to the present level. Recent geological investigation[9] has shown that the Mississippi River was so adjusted.

Examples of Classes 5 and 6

Classes 5 and 6 (Figures 1-e and 1-f) result from the base level moving up or down the stream without a change of elevation. Illustrating Class 5 is the following set of circumstances: A railroad runs up the valley of the Missouri River in the United States and small tributaries of the river pass under the railroad in culverts. When the railroad was built at the point where one of these tributaries entered the river, the river flowed along the side of the valley near the railroad and the culvert was set to conform to the grade established by this situation. The Missouri River shifted to the other side of the valley and the distance from the culvert to base level in the river increased. This caused a raising of the grade of the tributary to such an extent that it was necessary to raise the grade of the railroad where it crossed the tributary. An illustration of Class 6 has occurred in the lower Mississippi Valley.[8] Here the Mississippi River has shifted from the west to the east side of the valley; and streams entering this river from the east, which were adjusted to the former position, have cut down their beds to the altered position of the base level.

190

The foregoing discussion of the six classes has assumed that the stream on which the changes occurred was in equilibrium before the change occurred. In applying the reasoning developed to the case of any particular river, it is necessary to know whether or not that stream is in equilibrium. For example, a change in the conditions on a stream in equilibrium which would produce an aggrading profile, might produce in a degrading stream only a slowing down of the rate of degrading. Similarly a change of conditions that would produce degradation in a stream in equilibrium might, in a stream which was aggrading, produce only a slowing down of the aggradation, unless the degrading effect of the change was greater than the present aggradation.

In the foregoing analysis only the vertical movements of the streams have been discussed, but horizontal changes accompany the vertical ones. These changes are also important, but comparatively little study has been given to this phase of the subject. A good start has been made by Leopold and Maddock,[37] who have investigated the shape of the cross-section of streams under various conditions. The writer is engaged in a quantitative study of the form of the plan of streams, such as meandering and braided, but much further study in this field is needed.

CONCLUSIONS

Fluvial morphology is the science of the forms of the earth's surface produced by flowing water. This science is of major importance to the hydraulic engineer, since many of his greatest problems arise because of such forms. Fluvial morphology has been studied most extensively as a part of geomorphology, which is a subdivision of the science of geology. The hydraulic engineer can learn much from the writings of the geomorphologists. Engineers have also contributed to progress in this field.

The concepts of 1) the stages of development of a river proposed by W. M. Davis, 2) of base level, to which streams tend to cut down and 3) of equilibrium in stream channels, will be of considerable assistance to hydraulic engineers in their analysis of plans for stream control.

Many problems arise because of the changes which take place in the profile of streams as the result of the works of man, or sometimes by natural causes. Because of the progressive nature of these changes, and the large number of hydraulic works that have been recently constructed, these problems are likely to be more frequent and important in the future than they have been in the past. In this paper an attempt has been made to classify these changes and to give illustrations of cases where they have occurred. It is believed that a study of this classification and the examples, will aid the hydraulic engineer in working out rational answers to some of his projects.

ACKNOWLEDGMENTS

The writer wishes to acknowledge helpful suggestions received in the preparation of this paper, from Professor John P. Miller, Division of Geological Sciences, Harvard University and David V. Harris, Professor of Geology, Colorado A & M College.

1. Powell, J. W.; 1875; Exploration of the Colorado River of the West.

2. Gilbert, G. K.; 1887; Report on the Geology of the Henry Mountains--U.S. Geographical and Geological Survey of the Rocky Mountain Region.

3. Davis, W. M.; 1909; Geographical Essays; Ginn and Company. Republished 1954; Dover Publications. New York, N.Y.

4. Guglielmini, Dominique; 1697; Della natura di fluni trattato fisico matematico.

5. Frizi, Paul; 1762; Treatise on Rivers and Torrents with Methods of Regulating their Courses and Channels (in Italian); Translated by Gen. Garstin; London; 1818. .

6. Hooker, E. H.; 1896; The Suspension of Solids in Flowing Water; Trans. ASCE; Vol. 36; 1896; pp. 239-340.

7. Mavis, F. T.; 1935; An Investigation of the Transportation of Bed Load by Flowing Water; Thesis at the University of Illinois.

8. Lobeck, A. L.; 1939; Geomorphology; McGraw-Hill Book Company.

9. Russell, R. J.; Quarternary History of Louisiana; Bulletin of the Geological Society of America; Vol. 51; August 1, 1940; pp. 1199-1234.

10. Dowd, M. J.; 1939; Silt Problems of Imperial Irrigation District as Affected by Completion of Boulder Dam; Civil Engineering; Vol. 9; October 1939; pp. 609-611.

11. Todd, O. J. and Eliassen, S.; 1940; The Yellow River Problem; Trans. ASCE; Vol. 105; pp. 346-453.

12. Soderegger, A. L.; 1935; Modifying the Physiolographical Balance by Conservation Measures; Trans. ASCE 1935; Vol. 100; pp. 284-346.

13. Lane, E. W.; 1934; Retregression of Levels in Riverbeds Below Dams; Engineering News Record; Vol. 112; June 28; p. 836.

14. Shulits, S.; 1934; Experience with Bed Degradation Below Dams on European Rivers; Engineering News Record; Vol. 112; June 28; p. 838.

15. Corey, N. T.; 1913; Irrigation and River Control in the Colorado River Delta; Trans. ASCE; Vol. 76; pp. 1204-1571.

16. Matthes, G. H.; 1941; Basic Aspects of Stream-Meanders; Trans. American Geophysical Union; Part III; p. 632.

17. Central Board of Irrigation of India; 1939-40; Annual Report (Technical).

18. Schoklitsch, A.; 1937; Hydraulic Structures; American Society of Mechanical Engineers.

19. Jefferson, M. S.; 1902; Limiting Width of Meander Belts; Nat. Geo. Mag. Vol. 13, pp. 373-384.

20. Bates, Robert E.; 1939; Geomorphic History of the Kickapoo Region, Wisconsin; Bull. Geol. Soc. Am. Vol. 50; pp. 819-880.

21. Kesseli, J. E.; 1941; The Concept of the Graded River; Journal of Geology; Vol. 49; August, September 1941; pp. 561-588.

22. Gilbert, G. K.; 1917; Hydraulic-Mining Debris in the Sierra Nevada; U.S. Geological Survey; Professional Paper No. 105.

23. Stabler, Herman; 1925; Does Desilting Affect Cutting Power of Streams; Eng. News Rec. Vol. 95; December 10; p. 969.

24. Worcester, P. G.; 1939; A Textbook of Geomorphology; D. Van Nostrand Company.

25. Mackin, J. Hoover; 1948; Concept of the Graded River; Bulletin of the Geological Society of America; Vol. 59; May 1948; pp. 463-512.

26. Johnson, Douglas; 1932; Streams and Their Significance; Journal of Geology; Vol. 40; August, September 1932; pp. 481-497.

27. Hathaway, G. A.; Observations on Channel Changes, Degradation, and Scour Below Dams; Report of the Second Meeting of the International Association of Hydraulic Research; 1948; pp. 297-307.

28. Harris, E. G.; Effect of Dams and Like Obstructions in Silt Bearing Streams; Engineering News; Vol. 46; August 15, 1901; pp. 110-111.

29. Foy, T.A.W.; Regime Level Changes on the Indus System, Punjab Irrigation Branch Paper No. 16.

30. Malhotra, S. L.; Effect of Barrages and Weirs on the Regime of Rivers; International Association for Hydraulic Research; Bombay; 1951.

31. Joglekar, D. V. and Wadekar, G. T.; The Effect of Weirs and Dams on the Regime of Rivers; International Association of Hydraulic Research; Bombay; 1951.

32. Dobby, E.H.G.; Southeast Asia; pp. 59-60.

33. Von Englen, 1942. Geomorphology. The MacMillan Co., New York.

34. Penk, Walter, 1924. Morphological Analysis of Land Forms. Translated 1953. MacMillan and Co., Ltd., London.

35. Fisk, N., 1944. Geological Investigation of the Alluvial Valley of the Mississippi River - Mississippi River Commission, Vicksburg, Miss.

36. Sonderegger, A. L., 1919-20. Physiography of Watersheds and Channels and Analysis of Stream Action of Southern California Rivers, ... Transactions, ASCE. Volume 83, pp. 1111-1148.

37. Leopold, L. B., & Maddock, Thomas, Jr., 1953. The Hydraulic Geometry of Stream Channels and Some Physiographic Implications. U. S. Geological Survey Professional Paper No. 252.

Errata:
Reference 8 should read: "Lobeck, A. K., . . ."
Reference 12 should read: "Sonderegger, . . ."

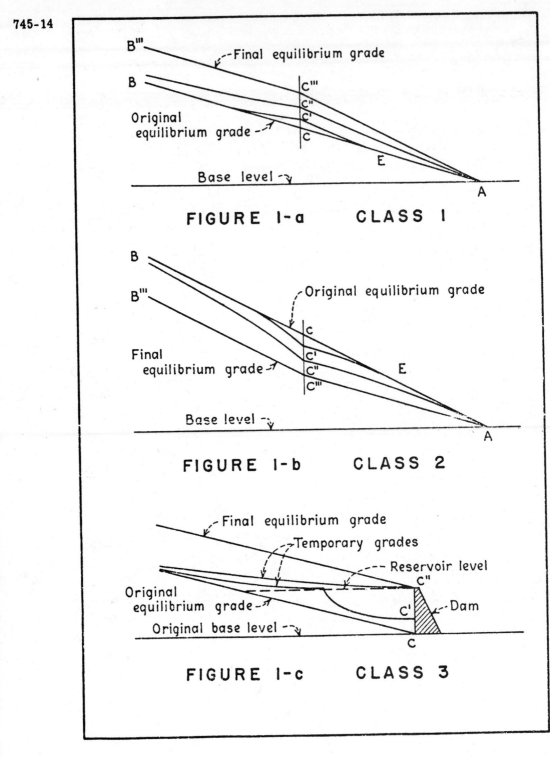

FIGURE I-a   CLASS 1

FIGURE I-b   CLASS 2

FIGURE I-c   CLASS 3

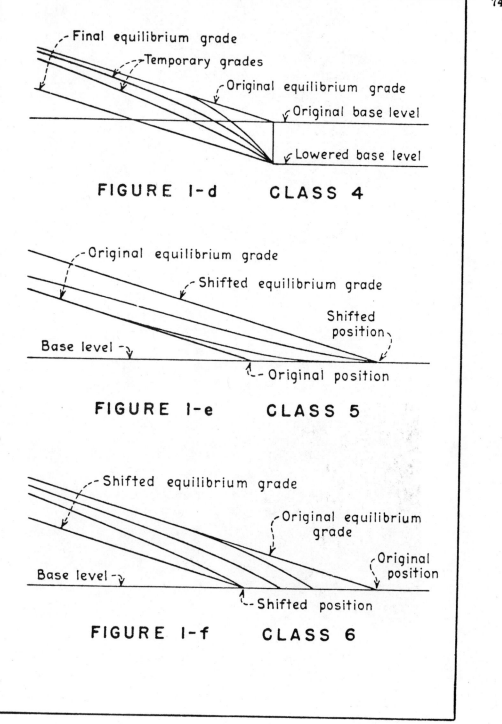

FIGURE I-d   CLASS 4

FIGURE I-e   CLASS 5

FIGURE I-f   CLASS 6

Figure 2. Roof of Powerplant
Buried by Rise of Bed of the
Mu Kwa River in Formosa

Figure 3. Degradation below
Ft. Sumner Dam on Pecos
River in New Mexico

196

Figure 4. Waterfall on Five
Mile Creek, Wyoming,
Resulting from Grade Reduction
Caused by Increase in
Discharge

Figure 5. Bed Lowering in
Cherry Creek, Denver,
Colorado, Caused by
Reduction of Sediment
Load

197

Longitudinal Profile and Gradient

V

As the discussions of Mackin and Lane have demonstrated, the gradient of rivers is of major interest to engineers and geomorphologists alike. In this section the papers consider the longitudinal river profile and gradient in more detail, and there is an attempt to investigate cause and effect.

Shulits uses the well-known downstream decrease in grain size to develop an equation for the longitudinal profile. (See Mackin's comments p. 482, p. 492.) Shulits is well aware of the complexity of the situation, and he suggests that perhaps his equation applies only to segments of a profile. He further states that the relation is not simply the result of abrasion of sedimentary grains during transport (p. 624).

Yatsu describes one of the unforeseen circumstances that may complicate a theoretical or empirical relationship such as that described by Shulits. A discontinuity in the downstream rate of reduction of sediment size results when cobbles or pebbles break down into their constituent grains. In Yatsu's example this causes a deficiency of particles in the 2 to 4 mm size range which produces a marked break in the long profile and, of course, an abrupt change of gradient.

Hack compares the gradient of streams draining from areas underlain by different lithologies and establishes that in this more complex situation variations in gradient can be explained by grain size and discharge. Only a few pages of Hack's longer text are included here. Descriptions of field sites and the shape of the long profile were deleted.

It is obvious that empirical equations of the type developed by these authors cannot be applied widely, and this recalls the development of the numerous regime equations, each applicable to only one limited area.

The brief selection from Strahler's paper on hill slopes is included because it reemphasizes the fact that the channel should not and cannot be considered separately from the drainage basin as a whole.

Two papers that review much of the literature on channel gradients and long profiles are by Woodford (1951) and Birot (1961).

American Geophysical Union Trans., 1941, V. 36, pp. 655–663

9

Rational Equation
of River Bed Profile

SAMUEL SHULITS

RATIONAL EQUATION OF RIVER-BED PROFILE

Samuel Shulits
(Presented by G. H. Matthes)

Introduction--River engineering has been faced for many years with the dilemma that, on the one hand, its accumulated experience is sometimes inadequate for reliable prediction of river behavior, while, on the other hand, there has been little attempt at systematic quantitative evaluations to "discover identity in difference"--all the above referring particularly to the form of river-channels, in cross-section, plan, and profile. The purpose of this paper is to review certain principles which afford a rational derivation of the profile of river-beds and to test the results on several American rivers.

Derivation of equation of river-bed profile--As particles of bed-load move downstream, their size or weight is reduced by abrasion or wear, collision, and solution. The most important of these factors is abrasion, for which Sternberg developed a law that has been verified experimentally by Schoklitsch [see 1 of "References" at end of paper]. The reduction in weight of a stone or particle, as it travels downstream, should be proportional to the work done against friction along the bed. If P is the weight of the stone and φ the coefficient of friction, the frictional resistance to motion is at any instant φP. The work against friction in a very short distance dx is $\varphi P dx$. Let dP be the resulting decrease in weight. Then it can be said that

$$- dP = c\varphi P dx \tag{1}$$

in which c is a constant of proportionality. Tne minus sign indicates that P decreases as x increases--that is, - dP goes with + dx. Integration yields

$$P = P_0 e^{-ax} \tag{2}$$

or

$$\log_{10} P = \log_{10} P_0 - ax \log_{10} e = \log_{10} P_0 - 0.434ax \tag{3}$$

with $c\varphi$ replaced by "a" and $\log_{10} e$ by 0.434. In this, the Sternberg abrasion law, P is the weight of a stone in pounds after traveling a distance of x miles downstream from the starting point where the initial weight was P_0 while e is the base of natural logarithms. The quantity "a" is called the coefficient of abrasion or wear of the bed-load material and represents the loss in weight of a stone weighing one pound after traveling one mile; the units of "a" are pounds per pound per mile or mile^{-1}. It might just as well be called the coefficient of weight decrease, a significance that will be recalled below.

Krumbein [2, p. 579] measured the average pebble-size along the beach at Little Sister Bay, Wisconsin, and found empirically that the size-variation with distance along the beach followed an exponential law like that in equation (2).

Since the bed-slope of a river and the size of bed-load material are known to decrease from source to mouth, it is not far-fetched to assume the slope proportional to the size of bed-load material. Mathematically expressed

$$S = kP_0 e^{-ax} \tag{4}$$

where S is the bed-slope and k is another constant of proportionality. At the starting point where x = 0, S = S_0, so that $kP_0 = S_0$ and

$$S = S_0 e^{-ax} \tag{5}$$

or

$$\log_{10} S = \log_{10} S_0 - 0.434ax \tag{6}$$

which is the equation of the slope of river profiles. A more detailed derivation of equations (2) and (5) will be found in reference [3].

$S = S_0 e^{-ax}$ is a rationally deduced formula, based on reasonable or at least plausible assumptions and not on measured data. There is no compulsion for a measured, actual bed-profile to conform to it. But if profiles can be shown to have an equation of this form, the inference must be that equation (5) is reliable and valid. Proof of this will follow below.

Application to practical problems has shown that a slight variation in the form of above slope-distance equation is convenient. It is desirable to let S_0 be the slope at a downstream initial point and to measure x positive upstream from S_0, where x = 0. Equation (5) then becomes

$$S = S_0 e^{ax} \qquad (7)$$

The simple mathematical transformation need not be given here. Figure 1 is a schematic representation of the significance of the variables for this equation and another to be derived later.

The above formulas are dimensionally correct, so that any consistent system of units may be used. In this paper the following will be the system of units: S in feet per miles, x in miles, and "a" in pounds per pound per mile or mile^{-1}.

Validity of $S = S_0 e^{ax}$--Equation (7) can be written

$$\log_{10}S = \log_{10}S_0 + ax \log_{10}e \qquad (8)$$

whence it is evident that $S = S_0 e^{ax}$ should plot as a straight line on semi-logarithmic paper, which is the clue to the proof of its reliability. If the data from an actual river yield a linear relation on semi-logarithmic paper, then $S = S_0 e^{ax}$ is justified.

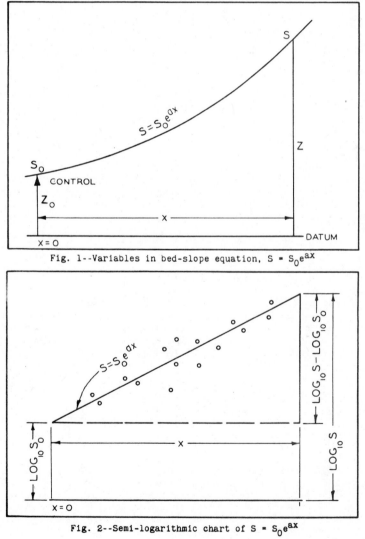

Fig. 1--Variables in bed-slope equation, $S = S_0 e^{ax}$

Fig. 2--Semi-logarithmic chart of $S = S_0 e^{ax}$

The proof has another important aspect. From (8) can be obtained

$$0.434a = (\log_{10}S - \log_{10}S_0)/x \tag{9}$$

But the right-hand side of the above is the slope of the straight line on semi-logarithmic paper, as Figure 2 shows; and the wear-coefficient, a, is then the slope of the line divided by 0.434 or

$$a = (\log_{10}S - \log_{10}S_0)/0.434x = [\log_{10}(S/S_c)]/0.434x \tag{10}$$

Accordingly, if the wear-coefficient so determined from the plotted data for an actual river corresponds to the kind of material of which the bed-load is known to consist, a second test of validity has been made.

By writing (10) thus

$$\log_{10}(S/S_0) = 0.434ax \tag{11}$$

it can be seen that the logarithm of the ratio of slopes is proportional to the loss in weight suffered by a one-pound stone in traveling x miles, the distance between S_0 and S, for a is the loss in weight of a one-pound stone in a distance of one mile.

The procedure is to break a given profile into a series of connected straight lines, determine the slope of each section and plot this slope against the distance of its midpoint from the starting place.

The Mississippi River was the first one selected to check the foregoing equations. The basic data were taken from the first page of reference [4]. Circumstances did not permit the calculation of an average line from the 1932 thalweg given there. It was initially assumed, for the purpose of this exploratory computation, that the profile made from the lowest low-water reading at each gage (regardless of time) would be an adequate approximation of the bed-profile. With the Fort Jackson, Louisiana, gage as x = 0, the slopes of the different reaches were plotted against the midpoint of the reach (Fig. 3). The calculations extended to Cairo, Illinois, 1,051 miles above Fort Jackson. The points for the main stretch of the river reveal an unmistakable trend, though not necessarily a clearly defined straight line. But, in view of the complexity of the problem, it must be admitted that the results in Figure 3 are really gratifying, for too much should not be expected in these initial efforts.

The evaluation of the overall wear-coefficient from the straight line put in by eye in Figure 3 is

$$a = [\log_{10}(S/S_0)]/0.434x = \log_{10}[(0.403/0.130)]/0.434(700) = 0.00162 \text{ pound per pound per mile} \tag{12}$$

A check was made by using the 1901 low-water profile of the Mississippi   , but no appreciable change in the magnitude of the coefficient resulted. Only the points for the main stretch of the river were used in this determination. The points below Baton Rouge are excluded because the 1901 low-water profile [4] shows that the Gulf backwater extends up to Baton Rouge; while the points above Cottonwood Point were also not considered as the river-slopes in this reach are known not to conform to Mississippi River experience, as Figure 3 shows strikingly.

The coefficient thus computed is really not representative of abrasion except in a very loose way; in fact, "abrasion" might be a misleading misnomer in this case. But it can be regarded as a coefficient of weight decrease that is derived from the actual profile, without any implication of the process by which the decrease occurs. In this light, the coefficient might be considered an overall characteristic representative of the morphologic behavior of river-profiles.

The value of 0.00162 mile^{-1} corresponds to a very tough material, slightly less wear-resistant than cast iron [1, p. 354]. Computed from actual profile-data, this coefficient includes the effects of the solids loads of the tributaries. Its smallness may be due to the fineness of the bed-load material and to travel in suspension. A remarkable practical check of this value of 0.00162 has been made by the prominent river engineer, Gerard H. Matthes. He found years ago that pebbles from the Mississippi River near Memphis would scratch the steel blade of his pocket-knife and quite recently, that a piece of gravel would scratch a razor-blade with ordinary hand pressure.

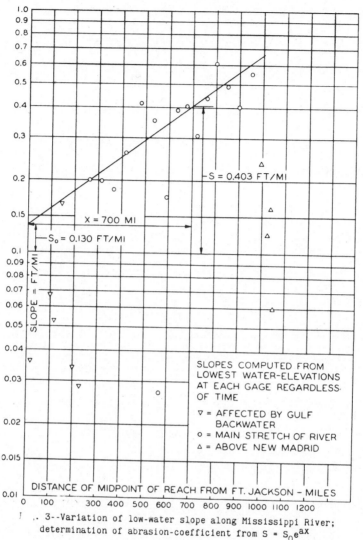

Fig. 3--Variation of low-water slope along Mississippi River;
determination of abrasion-coefficient from $S = S_0 e^{ax}$

.ver from Cairo, Illinois, to Pittsburgh, Pennsylvania, a distance of 980 miles,
was n   the same way. The profile-data were obtained from the lowest low-water
gag(s of time [6]. The plot of slope against distance is given in Figure 4,
wh.c.   exhibit.   raging trend and regularity. At Mile 748 solid rock is known to
exist, which may exp   e scattering of some of the data above this locality.

The value of 0.00293 mile^{-1} or pounds per pound per mile is obtained for the wear-
coefficient for the Ohio River from the slope of the straight line put in by eye in Figure 4.
This would be a material as resistant as a mineral somewhere between porphyry and silicious
snale [1, p. 354], which Mr. Matthes believes corresponds well with Ohio River material. This
means that Mississippi River gravel is about twice as tough as Ohio gravel, a fact borne out by
practical observation.

A slope-distance chart, like Figure 3 or 4, of the Colorado River from Boulder Dam to the
International boundary-line (about 350 miles) demonstrated a similar trend and yielded a value
of the wear-coefficient very close to that for quartz--which is what would be expected for the
material of the Colorado River.

With ᵈ   ven by Krumbein [2, p. 586] it was found that the slope of the surface of the
alluvial ᵢan aᵗ ᵗhe mouth of San Antonio Canyon (Cucamonga, California, topographic map) conforms

205

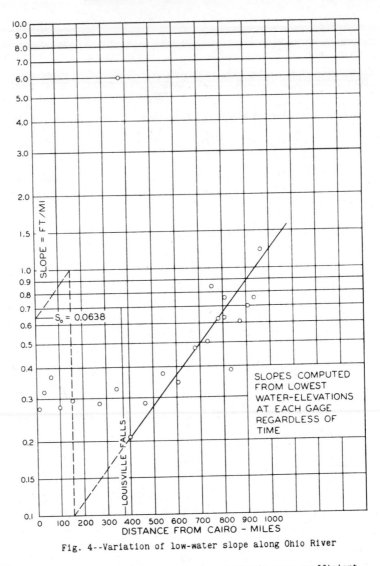

Fig. 4--Variation of low-water slope along Ohio River

to $S = S_0 e^{ax}$ very closely. No attempt was made to compute the wear-coefficient.

The conclusion is that the Mississippi, Ohio, and Colorado rivers and an alluvial fan offer corroborative evidence of the validity of the rational equation of $S = S_0 e^{ax}$ for the slopes of rivers: First, because the plot of the profile-data on a semi-logarithmic chart exhibits an overall linear trend well within the limits of accuracy of such morphologic data; and second, because the wear-coefficient derived from the profile agrees astonishingly well with the nature of the bed-load or bed-material of the rivers.

Another form of the profile-equation--A variation of the bed-profile equation, in terms of elevation and horizontal distance, can be derived from $S = S_0 e^{ax}$. Let z_0 be the elevation at $x = 0$ where the slope is S_0, and let z be the elevation at any point x where the slope is S (Fig. 1). If dz is the change in elevation in a very short horizontal distance dx, then the slope $S = dz/dx$ and equation (7) becomes

$$S = dz/dx = S_0 e^{ax} \tag{13}$$

or

$$dz = S_0 e^{ax}\, dx \tag{14}$$

which can be integrated to

$$z - z_0 = (S_0/a)(e^{ax} - 1) \tag{15}$$

If the elevation is taken through the origin, $z_0 = 0$ and equation (15) can be simplified to

$$z = (S_0/a)(e^{ax} - 1) \tag{16}$$

It must be remembered that equations (15) and (16) are merely derivations from $S = S_0 e^{ax}$ and not independent formulas. But they are more directly applicable to profiles and therefore more interesting to the river engineer. Their significance and utility will be discussed.

This different form of equation is not suited to an easy check of the basic principles, though a profile can be computed if the wear-coefficient, a, is known. However, Gandolfo [7, p. 60] tried equation (15) on the San Juan River in Argentina and found agreement of practical adequacy between actual and computed values of the river-profile in an 11.5-mile stretch of the river for which comparisons could be made. The coefficient was computed from the mechanical composition curves of the bed-material in a manner similar to that suggested by Schoklitsch [1, p. 357], which space requirements prevent from explaining here. Gandolfo's investigation is therefore another verification of the general method.

The profiles of the Middle Rhine (Mittelrhein), Maas, Mur, and Enns rivers in Europe also conform to equation (15) [8].

The semi-logarithmic slope-distance plots (Figs. 3 and 4), not being common engineering practice, are not very illuminating and the physical significance is not easily visualized. Furthermore, the scattering of the points on these diagrams might induce doubt and the fitting of a straight line to the data by inspection might be questioned. For this reason the elevation-distance equations (15) or (16) are quite reassuring in the diagrams they yield, for they show that the straight-line approximation and the resulting value of the wear-coefficient give good elevation-profiles. The gradient of the line on the slope-distance chart cannot be changed too much and still be sensibly acceptable; but the small possible shifts of the line would not alter the computed elevation-profile appreciably and the calculated profile is well within reasonable limits of accuracy. To illustrate this, the profiles of the Mississippi and Ohio rivers will be determined from equation (16).

For rivers all the variables in equation (16) are easily determinable except the wear-coefficient a. As explained elsewhere [1, 3, 9, 10], it is not a constant for a given rock or bed-load material: It increases with the one-fourth power of the particle-velocity, is proportional to the diameter of the material over which the particle rolls, and depends on the pebble-shape. That a should vary for different parts of a river is evident, the reduction in weight per pound per mile decreasing downstream in general. This difficulty is circumvented for river-engineering purposes by computing an overall coefficient for the entire stretch of river under consideration; the shorter the reach, the more representative the coefficient. Yet as will be seen presently, this method yields useful results even for a 1,000-mile continuous stretch of river.

Where it is not practicable to work from profile-data, a value of the wear-coefficient can be estimated for the type of mineral in the river from experimentally determined values [1, pp. 352-354].

The choice of S_0, the slope at the starting point, $x = 0$, is slightly troublesome. It is best to determine S_0 from the semi-logarithmic chart (Figs. 2, 3, and 4). The intersection with $x = 0$ of the straight line through the plotted points yields a good value of S_0 for the purpose.

With $a = 0.00162$ mile^{-1} from equation (12) and $S_0 = 0.130$ foot per mile from Figure 3, equation (16) gives for the elevation-profile of the Mississippi River

$$z = (0.130/0.00162)(e^{0.00162x} - 1) = 80.2(e^{0.00162x} - 1) \tag{17}$$

Values of e^{ax} can be secured from any handbook [11]. The profile given by equation (17) was computed and fitted by inspection to the 1901 low-water profile (Fig. 5). The calculations were made with $x = 0$ at Fort Jackson which is affected by Gulf backwater. The 1901 profile in reference [4] shows that the Gulf effect extends up to Baton Rouge, 209 miles from Fort Jackson. The best visual fit of equation (17) was found to be the portion of the calculated curve from $x = 203$ miles upward, if begun on the actual profile at Mile 230. The equation of the fitted profile would then be

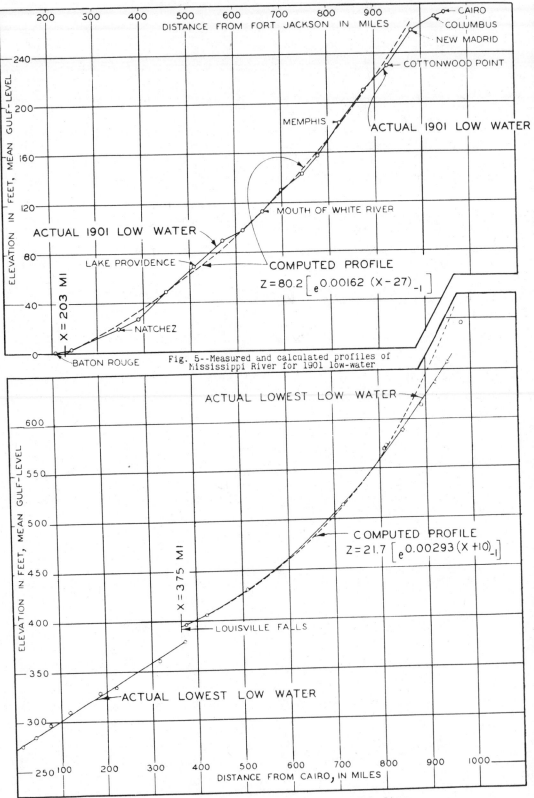

Fig. 5--Measured and calculated profiles of Mississippi River for 1901 low-water

$$Z = 80.2 \left[e^{0.00162 \, (X-27)} - 1 \right]$$

$$Z = 21.7 \left[e^{0.00293 \, (X+10)} - 1 \right]$$

Fig. 6--Measured and calculated profiles of Ohio River

$$z = 80.2 \ [e^{0.00162(x-27)} - 1] \qquad\qquad (18)$$

A closer fit might have been obtained by least-square methods. The maximum deviation of the computed profile from the 1901 Mississippi low-water line below Cottonwood Point is only about six feet. The rather marked divergence above Cottonwood Point is due to the fact that the portion of the river above it was not utilized in the determination of the wear-coefficient from Figure 3.

The satisfactoriness of the Mississippi River profiles in Figure 5 is no added proof of the basic tenets of this article. Figure 5 merely affords a better idea of the closeness of fit, of the utility of the method and of the effect of a variation in the wear-coefficient.

For the Ohio River, with $a = 0.00293$ mile^{-1} and $S_0 = 0.0638$ foot per mile from Figure 4, the derived profile is given by

$$z = 21.7 \ [e^{0.00293(x+10)} - 1] \qquad\qquad (19)$$

shown in Figure 6. At Mile 800 the Little Kanawa River enters the Ohio River, which may explain the divergence of the two lines above this point. Both Figures 4 and 6 depict strikingly the change in regimen at the Louisville Falls.

General remarks on applicability and limitations--The rather good results with the Mississippi and Ohio River profiles must not be judged too optimistically or too enthusiastically. Plots of other streams do not always show the regularity of these examples, but in many cases careful inspection of the stream gives a physical interpretation of seeming discrepancies: Rock outcrops, dams, flashy tributaries, debris-cones, local overloading of the stream-capacity for solids transport, etc., may disturb the wear-phenomena on which the ideas in this paper are predicated. In such instances the profile can sometimes be approximated by a series of lines calculated with locally varying coefficients. Steep headwaters in mountainous regions may not fit the framework since collision more than wear might be the predominating agent.

Conclusions--The Mississippi, Ohio, and San Juan rivers, several rivers in Europe, and an alluvial fan substantiate the premise of this paper, that wear-phenomena offer a rational approach to river-bed-profile morphology. The inference is that the bed-load plays a very important role in forming the river-channel.

Tho caution is indicated, the rational instrument offered here for the analysis of river-profiles gives a practical means for expressing the vertical shape of a river-bed so that the morphologic effect of man-made measures can be studied. The usefulness of $S = S_0 e^{ax}$ and $z = (S_0/a)(e^{ax} - 1)$ lies in the fact that they formulate the equilibrium-profile, that which will prevail ultimately or after complete morphologic development. Hence, if the regimen of a river is altered by regulation, a practical prediction of the final form can be ventured, with more rational basis for the estimate than has been the case hitherto.

A fanciful possibility is the establishment of a relation between an overall wear-coefficient like "a" and the watershed geology that would permit fluvial or physiographic predictions in a manner akin to the use of flood-formulas--certainly an accuracy equal to the dubious one of this common hydrologic tool should be attainable.

Acknowledgments--The author is grateful to General M. C. Tyler and Gerard H. Matthes for a critical perusal of the paper and many valuable suggestions. Bruno Rigoni assisted in the calculations and plotted the river-data.

References

[1] A. Schoklitsch, Über die Verkleinerung der Geschiebe in Flussläufen, Proc. Acad. Sci. Vienna, Math.-nat. sci. class, sect. IIa, v. 142, No. 8, pp. 343-366, 1933.

[2] W. C. Krumbein, Sediments and exponential curves, J. Geol., v. 45, No. 6, pp. 576-601, 1937.

[3] S. Shulits, Fluvial morphology in terms of slope, abrasion, and bed-load, Trans. Amer. Geophys. Union, pp. 440-444, 1936.

[4] Mississippi River Commission, Maps of the Mississippi River, Cairo, Illinois, to the Gulf of Mexico, Louisiana, 7th ed., revised January 1939.

[5] Mississippi River Commission, Highest and lowest annual stages of the Mississippi River and principal tributaries to 1937; 1939.

[6] Chief of Engineers, The Ohio River--charts, drawings and description of features affecting navigation, etc., pp. 323-324, 1935.

[7] J. S. Gandolfo, Estudio de la evolucion fluvial que determina el endicamiento del Rio San
    Juan, Publications of the Faculty of Physico-Mathematical Sciences, third series, v. 2,
    special publications, La Plata, Argentina, pp. 1-21, 1940.

[8] A. Schoklitsch, Hydraulic structures, Amer. Soc. Mech. Eng., v. 1, p. 153, 1937.

[9] A. Schoklitsch, Geschiebebewegung in Flüssen und an Stauwerken, Julius Springer, Vienna,
    pp. 3-7, 1936.

[10] A. Schoklitsch, Stauraumverlandung und Kolkabwehr, Julius Springer, Vienna, pp. 4-17, 1935.

[11] O. Eshbach, Handbook of Engineering Fundamentals, John Wiley and Sons, New York, pp. 1-103,
    1936.

War Department,
    U. S. Waterways Experiment Station,
        Vicksburg, Mississippi

10

ON THE LONGITUDINAL PROFILE OF THE GRADED RIVER

Eiju Yatsu

Abstract--After examining the longitudinal profiles and the grain-size distribution of fluviatile deposits of nine main rivers in central Japan, graded profile is concluded not to be an exponential curve which has been considered as the most adequate description up to the present. It is due to the discontinuity of wearing out of bed load, that is to say, the sediments of two to four mm in grain size are not easily produced and therefore comparatively of smaller quantity.

Introduction--Several decades ago, the conception of graded river was introduced into geomorphology and a great number of investigations and debates on the longitudinal profile of graded rivers have been made by civil engineers and geomorphologists. However, complete agreement has not been reached in these works, and therefore, the author has investigated the profiles of lower courses of main rivers in central Japan.

Data relating to the Joganji, Sho, Nagara, Kiso, Tenryu, Abe, Yahagi Rivers in the Chubu District and the Kinu and Watarase Rivers in the Kwanto District are given by the Department of Construction (see location map, Fig. 1). Various data concerning sediments of these rivers presented herein are collected for the most part through the author's effort and the grain-size distribution is expressed in ϕ scale.

Longitudinal profile of graded rivers--The conception of graded rivers was reviewed in detail by BAULIG [1925], KESSELI [1941], WOODFORD [1951], and Others. A river is at grade with the attainment of an equilibrium between energy of the water and resistance of the bed (after A. Surell and M. Dausse), or between the power and the load [after GILBERT, 1877, and his followers]. Exactly speaking, though the precise balance will not be unquestionably maintained as KESSELI [1941] asserts, the graded river has a smooth-curve profile and seems to be fairly stable as it approaches maturity in the cyclic development according to DAVIS [1902]. Thus the graded river is a system in equilibrium: its diagnostic characteristic is that any change in any of the controlling factors will cause displacement of the equilibrium in a direction that will tend to absorb the effect of the change as demonstrated by MACKIN [1948].

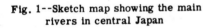

Fig. 1--Sketch map showing the main rivers in central Japan

What shape has the graded river? Taylor concluded a profile of equilibrium is parabola or hyperbola. JOHNES [1924] introduced a empirical logarithmic curve and GREEN [1934] simplified it. WOODFORD [1951] found Green right and followed his formula. Ordinarily, the exponential curve has been admitted to be most appropriate [STERNBERG, 1875; EXNER, 1922; FORCHHEIMER, 1930; SCHOKLITSCH, 1937; SHULITS, 1941; and AKI, 1941]. Recently STRAHLER [1952] showed it as an exponential function of two variables, the time and the distance from streamhead along the river course.

In order to scrutinize these theories, the writer selectively examines the profiles of main rivers in central Japan, whose lower courses have neither tributaries nor distributaries and so may be regarded as graded rivers.

Figures 2-10 show the mean lowwater levels or the water levels observed simultaneously in lieu of the former, and the lowest longitudinal profiles of the rivers drawn by connecting the deepest points of cross sections.

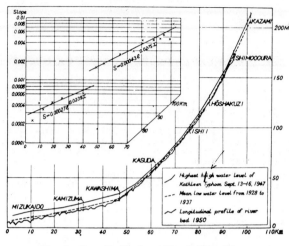
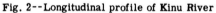

Fig. 2--Longitudinal profile of Kinu River

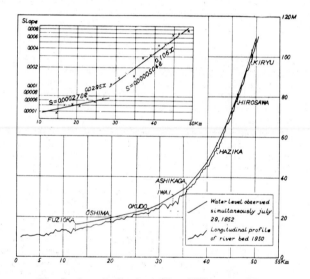
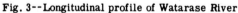

Fig. 3--Longitudinal profile of Watarase River

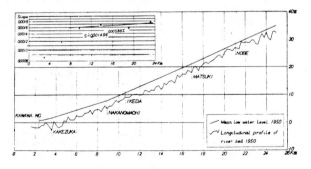
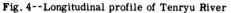

Fig. 4--Longitudinal profile of Tenryu River

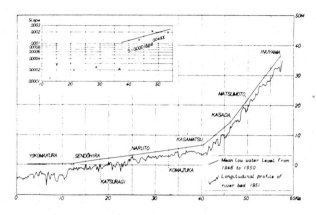

Fig. 5--Longitudinal profile of Kiso River

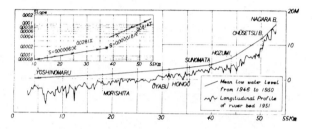

Fig. 6--Longitudinal profile of Nagara River

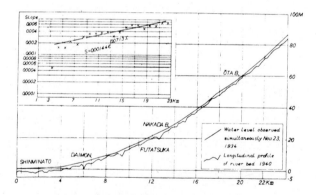

Fig. 7--Longitudinal profile of Sho River

As the Joganji River has neither data of mean water level nor simultaneous water level, the mean altitude of the river bed calculated from cross sections of the river course is expressed. River slopes given on the figures are computed by the method of least squares from the water level or mean altitude of each river bed. Table 1 gives slope data for these nine rivers.

The Yahagi and the Abe Rivers are both distinctly represented by one continuous exponential function of the distance from the river mouth. The other seven rivers, however, have slopes consisting of two exponential curves. If the river slope indicates one exponential curve the longitudinal profile of this river should be exponential because river profile is the integral of the river slope.

213

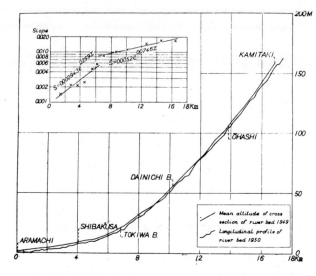

Fig. 8--Longitudinal profile of Joganji River

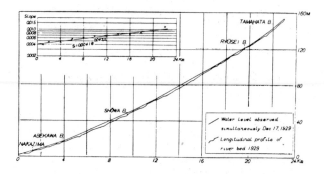

Fig. 9--Longitudinal profile of Abe River

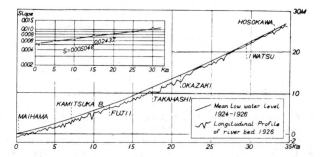

Fig. 10--Longitudinal profile of Yahagi River

Thus, the River Yahagi and the River Abe each coincide with Sternberg's theory but the other rivers do not. Is such discrepancy due to the fact that these seven rivers might not yet have attained maturely graded conditions?

Table 1--Data on nine rivers selected for this research

River	Reach[a]	Slope[b]	Locality of slope discontinuity
	km		km
Kinu	0-40 48-100	0.00027 exp 0.0239x 0.00043 exp 0.0275x	40-48
Watarase	13-27 29-50	0.000278 exp 0.0295x 0.0000504 exp 0.106x	27-29
Tenryu	10-24	0.00149 exp 0.00588x	8
Kiso	40-55	0.000168 exp 0.049x	40
Nagara	4-40 40-53	0.000060 exp 0.0281x 0.0000181 exp 0.0814x	40
Sho	4-24	0.00144 exp 0.0713	4
Joganji	0-6 6-17	0.00943 exp 0.269x 0.0052 exp 0.0746x	6
Abe	0-23	0.0041 exp 0.043x	none
Yahagi	0-35	0.00504 exp 0.0243x	none

[a]Distance from the river mouth or junction along the river course
[b]x is the distance above the mouth or junction

According to LOBECK (1939) the following observable characteristics of mature streams may be taken to indicate that a graded profile has been established: (a) flood plain, with natural levee, (b) meander, with cut-off and oxbow lakes, (c) width of valley equal to or greater than width of meander belt, (d) no rapids or falls, etc. Judging from these topological criteria, all of these nine rivers have already attained graded conditions. How is this contradiction to be solved?

Perhaps some geomorphologists may assert that these rivers do not show one exponential curve as they flow out over the fans and their bordering alluvial plains so that a discontinuous decrease of slope springs up at the boundaries between fans and alluvial plains. However, the suddenly decreasing points of river gradient do not coincide with the fan margins but distinctly advance farther forward than the latter. The Kiso River shows at least two km of such advance, and the Joganji River three km. Moreover such rivers on the alluvial fans do not intactly flow on them but sculpture them, especially in the vicinities of the apex of the fans, and deposition is always occurring at the margin of the alluvial fans, therefore the river gradients do not always agree with the topography of the fans. Furthermore, even in the case of the obscurity of fan topography, river slope discontinuity of the Kinu River and of the Watarase River is very distinct. That the remarkable border line of the fan margin exists is not the cause for the river slope discontinuity, but rather the slope discontinuity originating in the river seems to be the root for the former.

Nor does it seem correct to conclude that this discontinuous decrease of the river gradient is due to the eustatic movement of sea level or crustal movement and that this slope discontunuity should spring up on the former shore line at the early Holocene transgression. The reason for the above statement is that the points of the slope discontinuity of the Kinu River and of the Watarase River are far away from shell mounds, relics of the prehistoric Japanese Tribes, which indicate the inner limit of the transgression of the early Holocene.

The renovation depth of river deposits by flood is so great (for example, 2.0 m at Kitamatsuno on the Fuji River course [AKI, 1941] by the high flood water level of 8.5 m, and at Kawamata on the Tone River in Kwanto Plain, 1.5 m in depth by the high water level of 3.5 m [ITO, 1934]), that the river course will surely be reduced to a graded stream and that the river will fairly soon attain equilibrium on the unconsolidated material except where there is hard rock. For about a decade, the river bed of the Sho below Komaki Dam has been deepened. It attained stability in 15 years after construction of this dam [AKI, 1951]. This fact is not caused by the long gradual changes such as the crustal movement or changes of sea level.

What then is the reason for such discontinuous decrease of the river slope?

Critique on the theory of equilibrium and discussion of the discontinuity of grain size distribution of fluvial deposits--It is not adequate to enumerate the factors one by one and debate on them seperately, such as discharge, velocity, mass of the load, the form of the cross section, its caliber, etc. which determine the gradient of graded rivers like WOODFORD [1951] and other investigators have done. The most pertinent method is to deal with the balance between the bed load and the tractive shear force which is expressed as follows by P. du Boys in 1879.

$$\tau = \gamma H I$$

where γ is the density of water, H and I are hydraulic depth and slope of river respectively. The formula of KRAMER [1934] for critical shear force τ_0 is defined next as

$$\tau_0 = (100/6) (d_m/M) (\gamma_1 - \gamma)$$

where τ_0 is the critical shear force in grams per square meter, $(\gamma_1 - \gamma)$ is the effective density of the bed load in grams per cubic centimeter, d_m is a mean grain diameter in millimeters and M is defined as

$$M = \sum_{p = 0 \text{ pct}}^{p = 50 \text{ pct}} d \Delta p / \sum_{p = 50 \text{ pct}}^{p = 100 \text{ pct}} d \Delta p$$

AKI's [1951] formula is very similar to KRAMER's. Lately the mechanism of entrainment of particles was investigated by O'BRIEN [1934], KALINSKE [1947], and others.

In natural open channels, the fluvial deposit will agree with the tractive force, and in turn the latter will change itself so that it may agree with the debris. For instance, the tractive force in excess of τ_0 will transport debris, the river bed at this place will be deepened as compared with its lower course, and the river slope will gradually decrease as does the tractive force. Such process is termed degradation. Therefore the balance between tractive force and bed loads causes the longitudinal profile of the river to be steady and smooth.

The grain size of debris decreases downstream by attrition. STERNBERG [1875] dealt with a portion of the Rhein which receives relatively little water or bed load from its tributaries. He assumed the reduction in weight of a particle to be directly proportional to the work done overcoming friction in the distance traveled, and he introduced Sternberg's abrasion law which is defined as follows

$$p = p_0 e^{-c \int x}$$

where p is the weight, $\int$ the coefficient of friction, x the distance traveled, measured positive downstream, c the constant of proportion, and p is p_0 at x = 0.

Sternberg's law originated the thought that a graded river has an exponential profile. Assuming that the gradient of many rivers is directly proportional to the particle size, which decreases downstream according to Sternberg's law on a reach of the river receiving no water from tributaries, the exponential longitudinal profile is mathematically deduced. For example, SHULITS [1936, 1941] expressed it as

$$S = \sigma p_0 e^{-\alpha x}$$

where S is the slope and σ the constant. If x = 0, S = S_0, so that $\sigma p_0 = S_0$ and S = $S_0 e^{-\alpha x}$. Let Z be the elevation of any point on the profile, then S = dz/dx. Integration of this formula yields an exponential curve for longitudinal profile. The slope equation of PUTZINGER [1919] is of nearly the same form.

Does Sternberg's law leave no room for doubt? Sternberg investigated the deposits of the Rhein from Huningen to Mannheim and found them to consist mainly of gravel. Many works in Japan by MINO [1950], NAKAYAMA [1952], and OTSUKA and YATSU [1948] also recognized that Sternberg's law is legitimate so far as the diameter of grains is greater than the pebble size (four mm). In case of the Tama River, flowing to Tokyo Bay,

$$y = 95.4e^{-0.0192x}$$

in which y is the median diameter of deposits in millimeters and x the distance along the river from Ome in kilometers. And yet it is very noteworthy that the grain-size decrease of the debris from geschiebe to sand is discontinuous and does not obey the exponential equation. This fact was reported by the author [YATSU, 1951, 1952 ab]. In Figure 11 are shown the relations between the distance traveled and the median grain size of sediments of the main rivers in central Japan. On the reaches of the Yahagi and Abe Rivers decreases in the grain size showed an exponential curve because the deposits of the former are almost sandy particles and the median diameter of the deposits of the latter is gravel. When the river course in discussion consists of two parts in which the median diameter is gravelly and sandy respectively, the grain size decreases according to two exponential curves and thus the discontinuity from gravel to sand downstream is very striking as shown on the Figure 11.

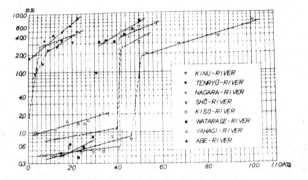

Fig. 11--Median diameter of fluvial deposits and the distance
from the river mouth or junction along the river course

In order to explain the cause of the discontinuity of the grain-size clearly, the writer will illustrate the grain-size distribution of fluvial deposits of these rivers. Figures 12-14 give a solution. Let us investigate the distribution of the particle size within an individual sample of deposits. The frequency curves are made graphically from cumulative curves [TWENHOFEL and TYLER, 1941]. While the deposits of sandy materials have only one maximum, the deposits which consist of sand and gravel ordinarily have two maxima and one minimum. This minimum always occurs at the particle size from two to four mm in diameter. Assuming the wearing out of the debris moving downstream to be exponential, the maximum of the frequency would be shifted regularly on the horizontal axis of ϕ -scale from left to right for the ϕ -scale is logarithmic (ϕ = log ξ in which ξ is the diameter of particles), and such a minimum would not be stagnant at the particle size 2-4 mm. The debris of such particle size seems to be produced rarely since the pebble has a tendency to be crushed into individual minerals. Thus the concept of discontinuity of wearing out of the debris from gravel to sand has, of course, to be admitted. Naturally, the difference of rocks, such as, in mineral size and hardness, seems to cause the discontunuity to vary to some degree. For example, a particle has a minimum of about eight mm if the deposits consist of the granitic debris as in the Yahagi River.

In such a manner, the quantity of granules is relatively small because of the discontinuous wearing of the debris. This is the cause for the fact that the seven rivers with the exception of the Yahagi and Abe Rivers have profiles represented not by one but by two segments. The Abe River transports gross materials to the river mouth, but the course of the Yahagi River under consideration is replete only with coarse sand. Therefore these two rivers indicate no discontinuous decrease of river gradient on the longitudinal profile. The Mississippi River from Baton Rouge to Cairo investigated by SHULITS [1941] has an exponential longitudinal profile, for, the writer thinks, this river course has deposits from coarse sand to silt [RUSSELL and TAYLOR, 1937].

Conclusion--If a river attains the graded state by degradation or aggradation, its longitudinal profile has a portion of discontinuous decrease of stream gradient and will be divided into two ex-

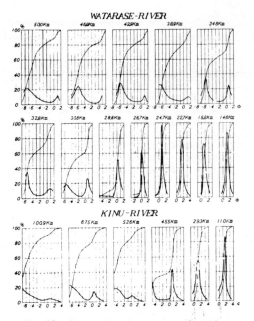

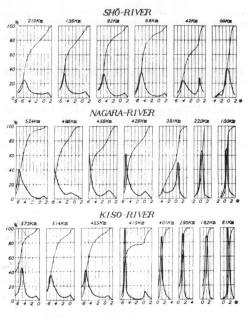

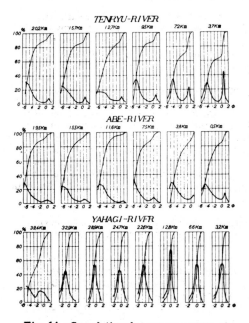

Fig. 12--Cumulative-frequency curves with class units in phi terms of the deposits of the Watarase and Kinu; y-axis expresses the weight percentage; Sampling localities are indicated on each graph by the distance along the river course from the river mouth or junction

Fig. 13--Cumulative-frequency curves of the deposit of the Sho, Nagara, and Kiso Rivers

ponential curves, because of the discontinuous collapse at the grain size from two to four mm which seems to occur in streams. Sternberg's law is correct on the river course, deposits of which are only gravelly or only sandy and silty.

The distinct boundary limits between fans and their bordering alluvial flat plains also seem to be due to the discontinuous collapse of the debris.

Acknowledgment--The author wishes to express his appreciation to late Yanosuke Otsuka, Fumio Tada, and Yokichi Ishikawa for their guidance and gratefully acknowledges the assistance and helpful suggestions made by Yoshimi Nakazima, engineer of the Department of Construction and many thanks are given to Tadashi Machida, Sadao Takematsu, Sakae Hiratsuka, Masao Inokuchi, and Isamu Komine who made a great deal of assistance in field surveys.

Fig. 14--Cumulative-frequency curves of the deposits of the Tenryu, Abe, and Yahagi

References

AKI, K., Potamology ('Kasoron' in Japanese), Iwanami, Tokyo, 1951.

BAULIG, M. H., La notion de profil d'équilibre; histoire et critique, Congrès Inter. Géog. C.-R., v. 3, pp. 51-63, 1925.

BROWN, C. B., Sediment transportation, Engineering Hydraulics, Proc. Fourth Hydraulics Conference, Iowa Institute of Hydraulic Research, 1949.

DAVIS, W. M., Base level, grade, and peneplain, J. Geol., v. 10, pp. 77-111, 1902.

EXNER, F. M., Zur physikalischen Auffassung der Gefallskurve von Fluessen, Sitzber. Akad. Wiss., Wien, math-naturw. Kl., pt. 2a, v. 131, pp. 147-153, 1922.

FORCHHEIMER, PH., Hydraulik, pp. 527-539, 1930.

GILBERT, G. K., Report on the geology of Henry Mountains, Washington: U. S. geographical and geological survey of Rocky Mountain region, 1877.

GREEN, J. F. N., and Others, The River Mole: its physiography and superfical deposits, Geol. Soc. Proc., v. 45, pp. 35-59, 1934

ITO, T., Hydrology on the River Tone, J. Civ. Eng. Soc. Japan, v. 20, pp. 1439-1450, 1934.

JOHNES, O. T., The upper Towy drainage system, Q. J. Geol. Soc. London, v. 80, pp. 568-609, 1924.

KALINSKE, A. A., Movement of sediment as bed load in river, Trans. Amer. Geophys. Union, v. 28, pp. 615-620, 1947.

KESSELI, J. E., The concept of the graded river, J. Geol. v. 49, pp. 561-588, 1941.

KRAMER, H., The practical application of the Du Boys tractive force theory, Trans. Amer. Geophys. Union, pt. 2, pp. 463-466, 1934.

LOBECK, A. K., Mature streams, Geomophology, McGraw-Hill, 1939.

MACKIN, J. H. Concept of the graded river, Bull. Geol. Soc. Amer., v. 59, pp. 463-511, 1948.

MINO, Y., On the gravel in Koromogawa, Akita Prefecture, Japan, Sci. Rep. Tokyo Bunrika Daigaku, Sec. C. 1950.

NAKAYAMA, M., The distribution of the size of fluvial gravel, Geog. Rev. Japan, v. 25, pp. 401-408, 1952.

O'BRIEN, M. P., and B. D. RINDLAUB, The transportation of bed-load by streams, Trans. Amer. Geophys. Union, pt. 2, pp. 593-603, 1934.

OTSUKA, Y. and E. YATSU, River deposits of the Tama. Jap. J. Geol. v. 54, pp. 40-43, 1948.

PUTZINGER, J., Das Ausgleichsgefalle geschiebefuehrender Wasserlaufe und Flusse. Zs. Öster. Ing. u. Arch.-Verein., no. 13, pp. 119-123, 1919.

RUSSELL, R. D., and R. E. TAYLOR, Roundness and shape of Mississippi River sand, J. Geol. v. 45, pp. 225-267, 1937.

SCHOKLITSCH, A., Der Wasserbau, p. 1, 1930.

SHULITS, S., Fluvial morphology in terms of shape, abrasion, and bed load, Trans. Amer. Geophys. Union, p. 2, pp. 440-444, 1936.

SHULITS, S., Rational equation of riverbed profile, Trans. Amer. Geophys. Union, v. 22, pp. 622-630, 1941.

STERNBERG, H., Untersuchungen über Längen-und Querprofil geschiebe-fürende Flüsse, Zs. Bauwesen, v. 25, pp. 483-506, 1875.

STRAHLER, A. N., Dynamic basis of geomorphology, Bull. Geol. Soc. Amer. v. 63, pp. 923-938, 1952.

TWENHOFEL, W. H., and S. A. TYLER, Method of study of sediment, p. 109, McGraw-Hill, 1941.

WOODFORD, A. D., Stream gradient and Monterey Sea valley, Bull. Geol. Soc. Amer., v. 62, pp. 799-852, 1951.

YATSU, E., Preliminary study on the fluvial deposits of main rivers in Kwanto plain, Geog. Rev. Japan, v. 24, pp. 144-147, 1951.

YATSU, E., On the fluvial deposits of main rivers in Boso peninsula, Geog. Essays in Commemoration of Prof. Kanichi Uchida's sixty-first birthday, pp. 397-403, 1952a.

YATSU, E., and Others, On the transporting material of the river Watarase, Geog. Rev. Japan, v. 25, pp. 182-192, 1952b.

Faculty of Technology,
   Chuo University, Tokyo, Japan

(Communicated manuscript received August 2, 1954;
open for formal discussion until January 1, 1956.)

Erratum:

The Woodford reference should read: "Woodford, A. O., . . ."

U.S. Geol. Survey Prof. Paper 294-B, 53-63.

11

Studies of Longitudinal Stream Profiles in Virginia and Maryland

JOHN T. HACK

FACTORS DETERMINING THE SLOPE OF THE STREAM CHANNEL

G. K. Gilbert stated as early as 1877 (p. 114) that declivity (or slope) is inversely proportional to quantity of water (discharge). Although some workers have followed Sternberg (see Woodford, 1951, p. 813) in the belief that the slope of the stream channel is related directly to the size of the bed load, it has been generally accepted since Gilbert's time that discharge is an important factor.

W. W. Rubey (1952, p. 132) has analyzed stream slopes using data obtained by Gilbert in an experimental flume (Gilbert, 1914). Rubey concludes that when the form ratio (or depth-width ratio) is constant, the graded slope decreases with decrease of load or particle size, or with increase in discharge. A stream may adjust, for example, to an increase in particle size either by an increase in depth (in relation to width) or by an increase in slope.

Rubey's conclusions are summarized by him in the formula:

$$S_G X_A = K \frac{L^b D^c}{Q^e} \qquad (1)$$

where

S_G = graded slope of a water surface measured after adjustment to load, discharge, and other controlling variables,

X_A = optimum form ratio, the proportions of adjusted cross section, or depth-width ratio, which gives to a stream its greatest capacity for traction,

L = the stream load, the quantity transported through any cross section in unit time,

D = average diameter of particles that make up the load,

Q = volume of water discharged through any cross section in unit time,

and K, a, b, c, e = constants.

In this formula, the channel slope S_G and the form ratio X_A are dependent variables, either or both of which may be adjusted to the conditions of load and discharge imposed from upstream. The data presented in this report permit an appraisal of some of the factors discussed by Rubey, and a similar, though less comprehensive, conclusion is reached independently in the present analysis.

In this discussion it is assumed that the slopes of the streams studied are determined by conditions imposed from upstream. As stated by Rubey (1952, p. 134), "The slopes at different points and the shape of the profile are controlled by duties imposed from upstream, but the elevation at each point and the actual position of the profile are determined by the base level downstream." The

220

measurements of the various factors studied are plotted on a series of scatter diagrams so that the relations among them can be assessed.

DISCHARGE AND DRAINAGE AREA

The quantity of water or discharge is one of the most important factors controlling slope but as a practical matter cannot be measured except where there are gaging stations that have been in operation for many years. There are only three of these on all the rivers studied for this report. One is on the Middle River a few miles above its mouth, and two are on the North River. However, a conservative relation exists in this region between drainage area and discharge; that is, enlargement of drainage area is accompanied by proportional increase in discharge.

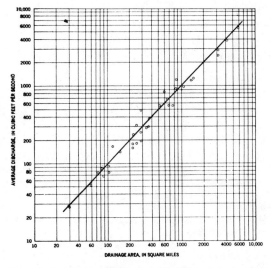

FIGURE 15.—Logarithmic graph showing the relations between drainage area and discharge at gaging stations in the Potomac River basin above Washington, D.C. Data from U. S. Geological Survey Water-Supply Paper 1111.

This is shown by the scatter diagram of figure 15, in which the average discharge determined at all the gaging stations in the Potomac River basin is plotted against the drainage area at these stations. The diagram shows that within narrow limits the average annual discharge in cubic feet per second equals the drainage area, measured in square miles. It must be kept in mind that the relation holds only for average annual discharge, which is probably not the most significant frequency of discharge controlling stream morphology. It must also be kept in mind that in detail, especially in small streams, there are significant departures from the conservative relation shown in figure

15. With these qualifications in mind, we may therefore substitute drainage area at a locality for discharge.

Drainage area has been plotted against channel slope for the localities in table 8, and the paired values are shown in the scatter diagram, figure 16. The graph shows that in a general way channel slope decreases as drainage area increases. The scatter of points in the graph is large. If, however, the localities where the paired measurements were made are classified according to the geology of the area in which they lie, the scatter is considerably reduced. The introduction of a geologic classification of the localities results in a grouping of points that strongly suggests geologic controls for the values of the stream slopes. The differences in values from one area to another are large, for in the Tye River channel slopes are 10 to 15 times as great as they are in the Martinsburg shale area of the Shenandoah Valley, at the same drainage area. Not only are the values of slopes different in different areas, but the rates of change of slope are distinctly different. Thus in Gillis Falls and in the limestone area the rate of decrease of slope as area increases is relatively low. In the alluvial terrace area of the North River, however, it is several times higher than in the other streams.

SIZE OF MATERIAL ON THE STREAM BED

At each locality the median grain size of the material resting on the stream bottom was measured during the period of low water between June 15 and October 15, 1953, by the method described on page 48. As the samples were taken from the surface of the stream bed, the figures for median size are representative of the surface material and not the material beneath, though there is, of course, a relation between the two. Study of all the data indicates that the size of the bed material may increase or decrease in a downstream direction, or remain constant, depending on the geologic nature of the drainage basin. The size of the bed material is one of the factors controlling slope in such a way that, for a given drainage area (or discharge), slope increases in proportion to a function of particle size.

General characteristics of stream-bed material.—General observations as to the nature of stream beds were made in the field, which bear upon the relation of slope to size. One of the most surprising observations so far as the writer is concerned is that the size of the material on the bed remains essentially constant for a fairly long reach of river and is not ordinarily affected by position in the channel with respect to pools and riffles. Several size analyses were made at localities close together in the Calfpasture River, and no variations were observed that had any discernible relation to local differences in channel width, depth, or slope. Table 1 shows figures for width, depth, local slope, and parameters describing size distribution at 3

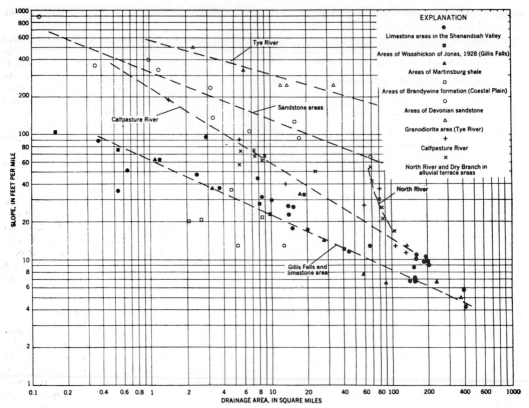

FIGURE 16.—Logarithmic scatter diagram showing the relation between channel slope and drainage area at the measurement localities (table 8).

localities within a reach 0.2 mile long. These localities are on the Calfpasture River, 24 miles from the head of the stream, where the average slope is 11.4 feet per mile.

TABLE 1.—*Measurements at locality 654, Calfpasture River, to show variations in size of bed material in a short reach*

	Riffle Upper locality	Pool Middle locality	Below pool Lower locality
Approximate river length (miles)	24.0	24.1	24.2
Width (feet)	82	99	120
Average depth (feet)	2.6	2.9	1.6
Local slope (feet per mile)	28	0	18
Median size of bed material (millimeters)	62	75	53
1st quartile (millimeters)	106	123	64
3rd quartile (millimeters)	50	50	32
Trask sorting coefficient	1.6	1.5	1.4

Many measurements of particle size, several of them very closely spaced, were made in the Middle River, in the limestone region. In this area the Middle River has a considerable flow even in the driest seasons and low-water depths are 4 feet or more in some pools. In this region size of bed material was rather closely correlated with its lithologic nature, but not with the position of pools and riffles. The only conspicuous changes in size within short reaches occur at the lower ends of some riffles, where, during low-water periods, sand is transported down the riffle and deposited in a small delta at the upper end of the pool.

In some small streams, particularly in the limestone region, plants such as water cress grow locally in profusion. The plants collect fine particles and form wide mud banks a few inches thick on top of the gravel. At other places, especially where there are steep banks of fine material, the banks may collapse at low-water periods and spread a layer of mud over the outer edge of the channel gravel. Such localities were avoided in selecting sites for size analyses.

Within a single reach of river, greater variations in size

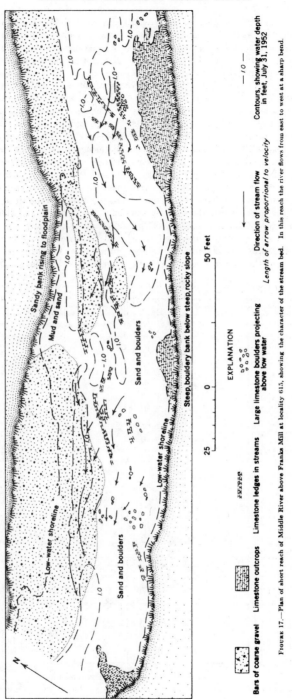

FIGURE 17.—Plan of short reach of Middle River above Franks Mill at locality 615, showing the character of the stream bed. In this reach the river flows from east to west at a sharp bend.

of material are observed in a cross section of the stream bottom than in a longitudinal section. These differences, however, were averaged out by the method of analysis that was used, because the grid by which the boulders and pebbles were selected always included the entire width of the bed. Few statistical data are available, therefore, on lateral variation in size. Bars of fine gravel are common, especially on the inner side of bends, and the coarsest boulders are in places concentrated in the deepest parts of the channel, though not necessarily where the low-water flow is the swiftest. Figure 17 is a plane-table sketch showing the depth of water and the position of rock outcrops, large boulders, and gravel bars at a typical riffle.

Probably the bed material of the rivers in this region is moved only at periods of high water. In low water, movement is restricted to fines that get into the river by the slumping of banks or in wash off the land surface. There is little deposition at low water and even the low flow is probably sufficient to carry away most of the fines. Rivers such as the upper part of the North River, East Dry Branch, and the Calfpasture River are dry most of the year. The bed material in these rivers shows no evidence of a coating of fines, such as might be expected if fines are dropped during the waning stages of a flood. Although downstream variations in size in a given reach seemed to be small, size analyses were most often made at the upstream end of riffles, in the interest of uniformity.

The sorting observed in the size analyses is good. Trask sorting coefficients generally range from 1.5 to 2.5 and average about 2.0. An exception to this generality occurs in the upper reaches of ephemeral streams that have gentle slopes, where the sorting coefficient becomes high, generally exceeding 4.0. This poor sorting is probably due to the fact that the amount of fine-grained soil material supplied to the flowing water greatly exceeds the coarse. As the flow is ephemeral and seldom attains high velocities, the material carried, and hence the material making up the bed, is predominantly fine and becomes mixed with the pebbles and boulders that are the product of infrequent flood flows. Measurements made at such localities, where

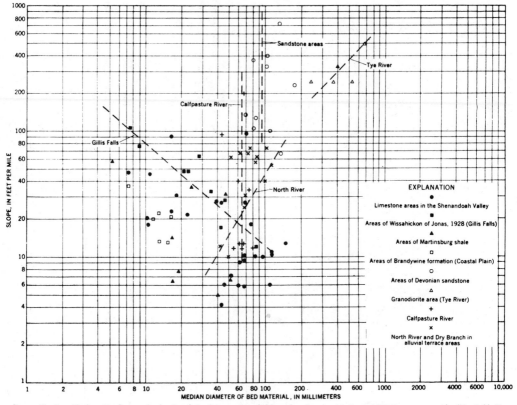

FIGURE 18.—Logarithmic scatter diagram showing the relation between channel slope and median size of bed material at the measurement localities (table 8).

sorting is poor, are not used in the analysis of slopes in this report (see p. 85). In steep, mountainous terrain, however, sorting coefficients remain low even in extremely small channels.

Relation of median particle size to slope.—Although local variations in bed material size are small, the overall change in a single stream may be great. In Gillis Falls, for example, discussed on page 69, the median size of bed material was observed to increase from 7 millimeters to 85 millimeters in a distance of 10 miles. The relation between size and slope for all the streams is shown on the scatter diagram, figure 18. The diagram demonstrates that there is no apparent direct correlation between size and slope if all the localities are considered. In streams whose bed load has a median size of 100 millimeters, for example, slopes may range from 6 feet per mile to over 1,000 feet per mile. In some individual streams, however, or in groups of streams classed according to the geology of their basins, there is a systematic relation

between the two variables. In Gillis Falls size increases as slope decreases. In the Calfpasture River and in the Devonian sandstone areas size seems to remain essentially constant, regardless of the slope.

The variations in the relation between size and slope are clarified if a third factor, drainage area, is taken into account. Figure 19 is a scatter diagram in which channel slope, S, is plotted against the ratio of the size of bed material to drainage area (M/A). The points in the diagram are clustered in a field about a line, drawn by inspection through the points. This line may be expressed by the equation

$$S = 18 \left(\frac{M}{A}\right)^{0.6} \tag{2}$$

where S is channel slope in feet per mile, M is median particle size of the bed material in millimeters, and A is drainage area in square miles. The constant, 18, is determined by the units of measurement used. This equa-

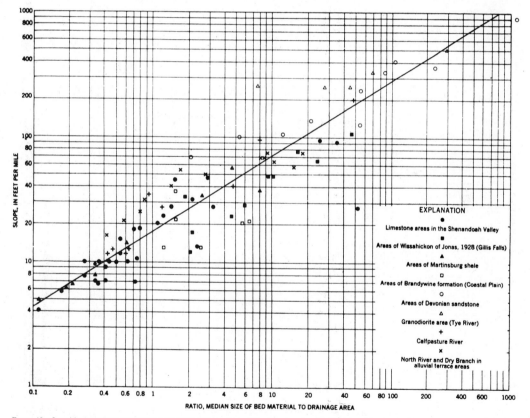

FIGURE 19.—Logarithmic graph showing the relation between channel slope and the ratio of median size of bed material to drainage area, at the measurement localities.

tion states simply that slope is directly proportional to the 0.6 power of the ratio of grain size to drainage area. In terms of the relation between the three individual variables, the equation states that for any given drainage area, slope is directly proportional to the 0.6 power of the size of bed material, and for any given size, slope is inversely proportional to the 0.6 power of the drainage area.

The correlation between slope and the ratio M/A is far better than the correlation between slope and either M or A plotted separately (figs. 16 and 18). Not only is the field of scatter greatly reduced, but the inclination of the lines drawn through localities along individual classes of streams (such as the Calfpasture River or the Devonian sandstone areas) are more nearly the same. In consideration of the data available and the difficulties involved in measurement, the correlation seems good. Furthermore, the variables considered in this graph are only three of several more, such as channel cross section and amount of load, that we know are involved in the problem. No one

individual stream except the Calfpasture River fits the equation exactly. Nevertheless equation 2 may be considered an empirical generalization that expresses the relations between the three independent variables: slope, drainage area, and size of bed material.

Another way to determine the relation between the three variables would be to plot on a graph the relation of slope to size for localities on different streams having the same drainage areas; in other words, to compare slope and size at a constant drainage area. The data obtained in the field are simply not adequate to determine quantitatively the relations between the variables by this means. It is shown by the graph of figure 20, however, that for streams within a certain range of drainage areas, slope increases directly as size of bed material increases. Two groups of localities were chosen, one at drainage areas of 1 to 10 square miles and the other at drainage areas of 50 to 100 square miles. Each of these groups encompasses a wide range in slope value.

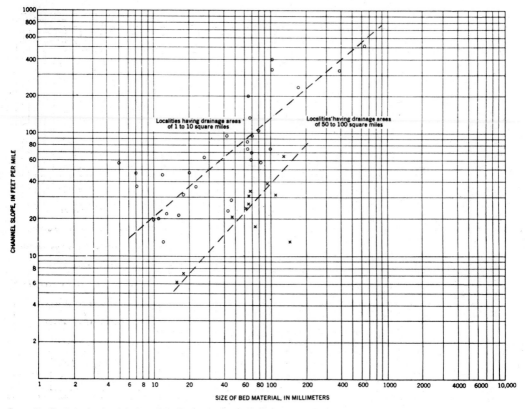

FIGURE 20.—Graph showing the relation between the slope and the size of the bed material at stream localities having drainage areas between 1 and 10 square miles and between 50 and 100 square miles.

226

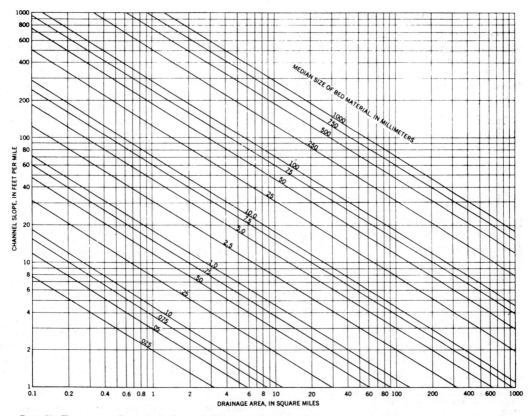

FIGURE 21.—Three-component diagram showing the general relation among channel slope, drainage area, and size of bed material, expressed by the equation
$$S = 18 \ (M/A)^{0.6}.$$

The general relation among the three variables based on equation 2 are shown in the three-component diagram, figure 21. The diagonal lines have a slope of −0.6. They represent lines of equal bed-material size and illustrate the effect of changes of size of bed material on changes in channel slope. Proceeding downstream (increasing discharge), for example, if bed-material size remains the same, the slope decreases as the 0.6 power of the drainage area increases. If bed-material size increases in a downstream direction, the slope will decrease less sharply in proportion to some power greater than the −0.6, such as −0.3. If the increase in grain size is very sharp, the slope may remain constant or even increase. On the other hand, if size decreases as area increases, the decrease in slope will be very sharp.

CHANNEL CROSS SECTION

Measurements of cross-sectional areas, widths, and computed mean depths were made at most of the localities and are included in table 8. Measurements of channel width and average depth are plotted with respect to drainage area in figure 22. They show, as Leopold and

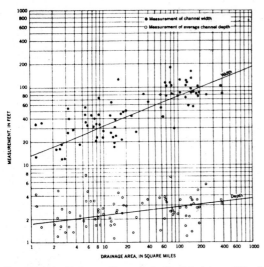

FIGURE 22.—Logarithmic scatter diagram showing the relation between width and drainage area (upper graph) and depth and drainage area (lower graph) at all the localities measured (table 8). The lines through the clusters of points are drawn by inspection and because of the large variation have no quantitative value.

Maddock (1953) found from data at stream gaging stations, that width increases in a downstream direction and suggest likewise that depth increases downstream. The rate of change of width as drainage area increases is greater than the rate of change of depth. As a consequence, the ratio of depth to width decreases downstream.

The ratio of depth to width is plotted on figure 23. In this diagram, as in several others, the localities are classified according to geologic criteria and lines are drawn through points on streams that show a rough correlation between the depth-width ratio and drainage area. Although variations in depth-width ratio are large and apparently unsystematic if all the localities are considered, variations in the ratio within areas having the same bedrock correlate well with drainage area. This suggests that the form of the cross section of the channel is in some way related to the rocks that enclose it. The shallowest cross sections are in the mountain areas, particularly in the Calfpasture River. The deepest cross sections are in the lowlands of the Shenandoah Valley, the piedmont of Maryland, and the coastal plain. Depth-width ratios for Dry Branch

and the North River in the alluvial terrace areas are high, but they decrease at anomalous rates.

The significance of the data bearing on depth-width ratio is not understood. The data are in accord with the statement of Rubey (1952, p. 133) that most natural streams probably become proportionately wider downstream, and with the theory that the depth-width ratio, like slope, is a dependent variable such that either this ratio, or channel slope, or both may adjust to changes in load or discharge. Several attempts have been made to relate, on scatter diagrams, ratios including slope, depth, and width on one axis to bed-load size and drainage area on the other. The data, however, do not seem to permit any refinement of the relation expressed by equation 2 that

$$S = 18 \left(\frac{M}{A} \right)^{0.6}$$

SUMMARY OF FACTORS CONTROLLING CHANNEL SLOPE

The data obtained at the measurement localities studied for this report indicate that the channel slope of rivers whose bed material is of the same size is inversely proportional to a function of drainage area (or discharge), and where drainage area is the same, it is directly proportional to a function of the size of the bed material. This generalization holds roughly for a stream with a drainage basin of only 0.12 square miles as well as a stream draining over 370 square miles, the largest river reach studied. Equation 2, which summarizes the generalization, is empirical. It does not indicate that either size of bed material or drainage area must be the principal direct determinant of slope, but it is a useful equation because it deals with size of bed material, a factor in stream equilibrium that must be a function of geologic conditions.

One of the most significant results of the analysis of the data is the finding that areas which have the same geology and drainage area are adjusted to load, slope, and channel cross section in the same way. Thus the classification of the localities according to a scheme that emphasizes the lithologic nature of the drainage basin results in a grouping of points much closer than the total grouping in many of the diagrams. For example, the localities in the Devonian sandstone area tend to have relatively steep slopes for equivalent drainage areas as compared with localities in other geologic regions (fig. 16). The bed material is nearly of the same size in the various localities in the sandstone area (fig. 17), and the depth-width ratios are distinctive (fig. 23). The same sort of generalization could be made about streams in other lithologic environments. Since drainage area is one of the variables in each of these diagrams we may conclude that streams within a single geologic unit that have equivalent drainage areas have also similar channel slopes, size of bed material, and, from figure 23, channel cross sections.

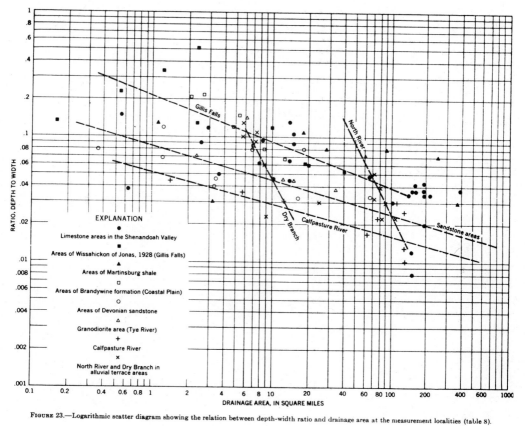

FIGURE 23.—Logarithmic scatter diagram showing the relation between depth-width ratio and drainage area at the measurement localities (table 8).

References

Gilbert, G. K., 1877, *Report of the Geology of the Henry Mountains:* U.S. Geographical and Geological Survey Rocky Mountain Region, 160 pp.
———, 1914, The transportation of debris by running water: U.S. Geological Survey Prof. Paper 86, 259 pp.
Leopold L. B. and Maddock, Thomas, Jr., 1953, The hydraulic geometry of stream channels and some physiographic implications: U.S. Geol. Survey Prof. Paper 252, 57 pp.
Rubey, W. W., 1952, Geology and mineral resources of the Hardin and Brussels quadrangles (in Illinois): U.S. Geol. Survey Prof. Paper 218, 175 pp.
Woodford, A. O., 1951, Stream gradients and Monterey Sea Valley: *Geol. Soc. America. Bull.,* V. 62, pp. 799-852

American Journal of Science, 1950, Volume 248, pp. 687–690

12

Equilibrium Theory of Erosional Slopes Approached by Frequency Distribution Analysis

A. N. STRAHLER

Relations of Slopes to Channel Gradients.—Davis (1909, p. 266-268) clearly stated the concept that the slopes of a mature landmass are graded, as are the streams. We may restate this principle by saying that slope profiles are in equilibrium with the channel profiles to which the slopes contribute their debris. For a given area free of systematic structural control, but subject to uniformly controlling factors of climate, vegetation, soil and stage of development, all morphological characteristics tend to approach a time-independent form. Ground and channel gradients, as well as drainage density achieve a form best adapted to maintaining a steady state in the removal of debris. This is simply an extension of Playfair's Law to include all form-aspects of the topography.

If the type of adjustment described above actually exists, one would expect the angle of slope of valley walls to vary systematically with gradient of channel at the slope base. Steep ground slopes would be expected to correspond with steep channel gradients; low ground slopes with low stream channel gradients. This relationship has been stated by R. E. Horton (1945, p. 285) who uses the definition

$$\text{slope ratio} = \frac{S_c}{S_g} \quad \begin{array}{l} \text{where } S_c = \text{channel slope} \\ \text{and} \quad S_g = \text{ground slope} \end{array}$$

Ground slope can be determined by the field methods previously described in this paper. For each slope reading the channel gradient at the base of the slope would need to be measured. This was not done in the field by the writer, but the general trend of the slope ratio was obtained from large-scale topographic maps, including two which were specially mapped for the present study. Figure 8 shows the means of ground slopes and channel slopes plotted on log-log paper. Each point represents means of a large number of measurements of ground slopes and channel slopes. Because samples were taken from maps and the correlation is believed to have wide inherent spread of values, a curve was fitted by inspection. We might say that, if these data are representative of general conditions, ground slope varies as somewhat less than the first power of channel slope, and that the slope ratio tends to range from 1/5 or 1/4 for low values of slopes, up to about 1/2 in the higher values.

There are several uncertain elements in the foregoing analysis. Data from a greater number of regions would be expected to modify the estimating equation considerably. Substitution

231

of careful field measurements for map measurements would increase the confidence in the data. It is further obvious that channel slope steepens rapidly toward the head of a valley, whereas ground slope tends to remain nearly constant along the sides of the valley, as the frequency distribution studies show. To minimize this variable, which can easily vitiate the results, readings were made along second-order stream basins, near the point where they are formed by the junction of two first-order streams (Horton, 1945, p. 281). This assures that all data come from the same relative position in the drainage system. Further standardization is desirable.

There is a suggestion from the data of figure 8 that climate has a profound influence on the slope ratio. Areas 7 and 9, which lie to the right of the line of the estimating equation, and area 8 which is on the line, have typical bare ground surfaces of badlands, or are lightly covered by chaparral, as in

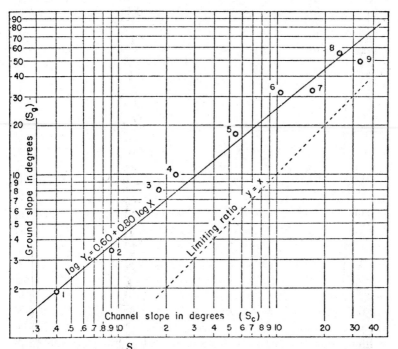

Fig. 8. Slope ratio, $\dfrac{S_c}{S_g}$, for nine maturely dissected regions. 1. and 2. Grant, La., 3. Rappahannock Academy, Va., 4. Belmont, Va., 5. Allen's Creek, Ind. 6. Hunter-Shandaken, N. Y. 7. Mt. Gleason, Calif. 8. Petrified Forest, Ariz. 9. Perth Amboy (clay fill), N. J. All data from U. S. G. S., A. M. S. or special field maps.

the Mt. Gleason area (7). Here one might expect a given slope of valley side to supply proportionately more detritus to the channel than a comparable slope in vegetation-clothed regions in the humid climates. The thinly vegetated areas would require relatively steeper channel gradients for the transportation of the greater quantity of detritus. In the two cases lying to the right of the line the channel slope is high in proportion to ground slope. While this could easily be merely the result of chance sampling, it is in agreement with the deduced behavior. On the other hand, well-vegetated slopes in the humid climate would tend to supply less detritus because of the increased surface resistivity and infiltration capacity, and would be associated with relatively lower channel slopes. As if to verify this deduction, points 3 through 6, representing humid regions, lie to the left of the line of the estimating equation. As this could readily be the result of chance, the observation merely makes more intriguing the prospect for a more adequate investigation of this phase of equilibrium relationships.

References

Davis, W. M., 1909, *Geographical Essays*, Ginn and Co., Boston.
Horton, R. E., 1945, Erosional development of streams and their drainage basins; hydrophysical approach to quantitative morphology: *Geol. Soc. Amer. Bull.*, V. 56, pp. 275–370.

Channel Patterns

VI

Why should a river follow anything but a straight course to the sea? That is, why do rivers meander? This question has attracted the attention of some of the best minds of the scientific world, including Albert Einstein (1926). The final answer will require a combination of hydraulic and geomorphic data and insight.

One way of approaching the problem is through model studies. Friedkin's paper is widely quoted and his photographs have been reproduced in many geology texts. The first part of his report is reproduced here because it is of major significance and because it is not readily available. Friedkin's concern is the behavior of rivers and the effect of altered hydrologic regimen on rivers such as the Mississippi. The second part of his report, which is not included, deals with the effects of bank stabilization on thalweg pattern and the stability of alternate bars. The footnote on page 8 deserves special consideration because it, in effect, states that thalweg meanders formed during experimentation rather than channel meanders.

The Leopold-Wolman paper is significant because the authors show that all patterns, braided, meandering, and straight, are part of a continuum of channel patterns that result from variations of discharge and slope. They describe experiments concerning the development of bars and braided patterns, and then they compare the experimental results with field observations. Selections from their paper emphasize these experiments and their efforts to show the interdependency of patterns. Much of their discussion of field sites, especially anastomosing channels in Wyoming, is not included.

A particularly interesting aspect of patterns is the relation between discharge and meander wavelength and the possibility that valley meanders reflect vastly greater Pleistocene discharges (Dury, 1964). For further discussions of river patterns, see Chitale (1966), Leopold and Wolman (1960); Speight (1967); and Ackers (1964).

WAR DEPARTMENT

CORPS OF ENGINEERS, U. S. ARMY
MISSISSIPPI RIVER COMMISSION

13

A LABORATORY STUDY

OF THE

MEANDERING OF ALLUVIAL RIVERS

CONDUCTED UNDER THE DIRECTION OF

BRIGADIER GENERAL MAX C. TYLER
PRESIDENT, MISSISSIPPI RIVER COMMISSION

BY

J. F. FRIEDKIN
CAPTAIN, CORPS OF ENGINEERS

U. S. WATERWAYS EXPERIMENT STATION
VICKSBURG, MISSISSIPPI

54—M.R.C.1M.7-45

1 MAY 1945

A LABORATORY STUDY

OF THE

MEANDERING OF ALLUVIAL RIVERS

INTRODUCTION

Authorization. This report presents the results of a laboratory study of the meandering of alluvial rivers conducted at the United States Waterways Experiment Station from 1942 to 1944 under authorization of the President of the Mississippi River Commission.

The problem. The meandering of alluvial rivers refers to the continually changing sinuous course developed by rivers flowing in erodible alluvial sediments. The problem was two-fold: first, to determine the basic principles of meandering; second, to determine the basic principles as to the changes brought about in the channel of a meandering river by stabilization of the caving banks.

Means of study. In the laboratory, small-scale rivers in erodible materials develop naturally a series of continually changing bends by eroding their concave banks and by building convex bars (plate 1). These laboratory rivers have all the general characteristics of meandering rivers. Bends migrate downstream as they develop, channels are relatively deep in bends and shallow in crossings between bends, and sand deposits in crossings during high flows and scours out during low flows. In the laboratory rivers, changes take place in a few hours which would normally take years in a natural river. The movement of sand along the bed can be observed and followed from its source to its location of deposition. The elements, discharge, bed material, axial slope, and bed load can be controlled so that many of the interfering conditions found in nature can be eliminated, and each of the elements can be at least partially isolated. Laboratory rivers of this type provide a means of rapidly reducing meandering to its simplest forms for analysis.

The small-scale rivers varied in size from one to five feet in width, and 50 to 150 ft in length, with depths of 0.05 to 0.30 ft. Several types of bed materials were used including river sands and silts. In all tests, flows and bed materials were such that erosion of banks and movement of sediment along the bed took place naturally. The tests were conducted in flumes of sufficient width to permit the streams to meander freely.

Scope. The first part of this report presents the results of study of the elements of meandering rivers—the basic principles. It sets forth the results of tests with analyses and discussions as to the causes of meandering; the development of a meandering course and the characteristic cross sections; the source, path of travel, and location of deposition of sand; the role of sand entering at the head of a meandering river, and of sand entering from the caving banks; the effects of discharge, slope and alignment on the size and shape of bends; the degree of sinuosity; the importance of the rate of bank erosion; the interrelationships between the variables; the limiting width and length of meanders; the formation of chutes; the causes of natural cut-offs; and the braiding of rivers. Finally, a general discussion is given to show how all of the major elements and other aspects work together in the meandering of the Lower Mississippi River as indicated by this study.

The second part presents the principles involved as to the effects of stabilizing the caving banks of a meandering river. First, it sets forth the results of stabilizing the banks of naturally formed meanders consisting of a series of nearly uniform bends; that is, the changes brought about in channel capacity, depths of cross sections, and alignment of the small-scale rivers. Second, it sets forth the results of stabilizing the caving banks of a small-scale meandering river which had the alignment of a section of the Lower Mississippi River. Also included in the second part are the results of tests to indicate whether stabilization of the banks of a river should progress upstream or downstream.

In the third part, the general testing methods, the materials used, and the measuring devices are described. Also included in this part is the technique which was developed toward making erodible-bank model studies.

NATURAL DEVELOPMENT OF LABORATORY MEANDERING RIVER

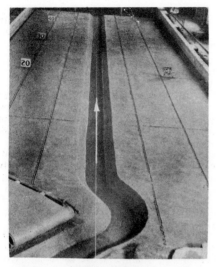

INITIAL CHANNEL

AFTER 3 HOURS

AFTER 4 HOURS

AFTER 6 HOURS

MISSISSIPPI RIVER COMMISSION
U. S. WATERWAYS EXPERIMENT STATION

LABORATORY STUDY OF THE MEANDERING OF ALLUVIAL RIVERS

PLATE 1

Part I

THE BASIC PRINCIPLES OF MEANDERING

This part sets forth the basic principles of the meandering of alluvial rivers, as shown by small-scale meandering rivers. It describes the natural mechanics of the phenomenon, the role of each of the elements, and their interrelationships.

Syllabus

Meandering results primarily from local bank erosion and consequent local over-loading and deposition by the river of the heavier sediments which move along the bed. Meandering is essentially a natural trading process of sediments from banks to bars. Sand entering at the head of an alluvial river travels only a short distance before it deposits on bars along the inside of bends and is replaced by sand eroding from concave banks. In turn the sand from the caving banks of a bend travels only a short distance before it deposits on bars and is replaced by sand from caving banks. The rate of trading depends upon the rate of bank caving. In uniform materials and on a uniform slope, a series of uniform bends will develop. The radii of bends increase with increase in discharge or slope for the same alignment of flow into the bends. For the same flow and slope, the size and shape of bends depend upon the alignment of the flow into the bends. Cross sections of a meandering river are deeper along the concave banks of bends because of the impingement of the flow against these banks. The depth of the channel of a meander-ing river depends upon the resistance of the banks to erosion. Resistant banks result in deep cross sections and easily eroded banks result in shallow cross sections. Every phase of meandering represents a changing relationship between three closely related variables: the flow and the hydraulic properties of the channel, the amount of sand moving along the bed, and the rate of bank erosion. These three variables constantly strive to reach a balance but never do even with a constant rate of flow. The bends of a meandering river have limiting widths and lengths. When a bend reaches this width, a chute forms and a new bend develops farther downstream. Distorted bends and natural cut-offs are caused by local changes in the character of bank materials.

Why Rivers Meander

Several hypotheses have been brought forward to explain meandering. Meandering has been attributed to the earth's rotation (9, 18, 48, 60)[1], to the excessive slope and energy of a river (17, 56), and to changes in stage (51). It is often considered that an irregularity in the bankline or a snag will disturb the flow and cause meandering. In an effort to ascertain the fundamental causes of meandering, a test was conducted in which a constant rate of flow was passed through a straight channel molded in uniform material. This stream developed a meandering course.

Test. On plate 2, the photograph on the left shows the initial straight channel molded in uniform sandy material, through which a constant rate of flow was passed which had a velocity sufficient to move sand along the bed and to erode the banks. These were the only prerequisites. No sand was fed at the entrance of the stream. Beginning with these initial conditions, the photographs show that the stream developed naturally the characteristic shifting sinuous channel of a meandering river. The scallops along the boundaries of the meander belt are the banklines of earlier courses. Throughout the duration of the test the stream was constantly shifting its path of flow in the mid and lower sections. It is noted in the photographs that the degree of meandering increased downstream. This was brought about by the fact that no sand was fed at the entrance.

---

[1] References, page 37.

DEVELOPMENT OF
MEANDERING CHANNEL FROM A STRAIGHT CHANNEL
IN UNIFORM MATERIAL

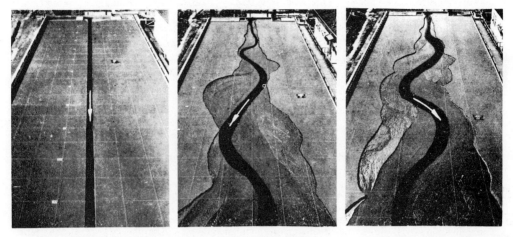

INITIAL STRAIGHT CHANNEL   CHANNEL AFTER 48 HRS OF FLOW   CHANNEL AFTER 72 HRS OF FLOW

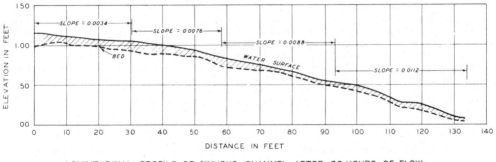

LONGITUDINAL PROFILE OF SINUOUS CHANNEL AFTER 72 HOURS OF FLOW
NO SAND WAS FED AT ENTRANCE

TEST DATA

BED MATERIAL .... MISSISSIPPI RIVER SAND (KINGS POINT)
DISCHARGE .... 0.30 CFS (CONSTANT)
VALLEY SLOPE 0.009
INITIAL CROSS SECTION

MISSISSIPPI RIVER COMMISSION
U. S. WATERWAYS EXPERIMENT STATION
LABORATORY STUDY OF THE
MEANDERING OF ALLUVIAL RIVERS

PLATE 2

In the upstream section, the stream deepened its channel and flattened its slope, as shown in the profile, until the flow no longer had the velocity to move material and erode the banks in this section.

Analysis and discussion. Observation of the behavior of this small-scale river as it began to meander showed that a local disturbance to the flow was created by a sand bar which resulted from bank erosion. Sand from caving banks overloaded the stream and deposition took place. This test indicated that aside from the changing conditions and irregular banklines found in nature, rivers which erode their banks will meander, simply because a flow of water has a limited capacity for carrying sand along its bed. The only requirement for meandering is bank erosion.

It should be added that a stream may erode the banks only temporarily. In several tests, streams began eroding their banks, but the channel cross sections became so wide and shallow, and velocities were so reduced that bank erosion and meandering stopped. This resulting condition is found in nature in wide-shoaled sections of rivers.

Development of Meander Pattern

Once the flow had been disturbed and a bend or lateral oscillation had been initiated, there was a marked tendency for the flow to develop a series of bends downstream. The following tests show that under ideal conditions of uniformity, an initial bend is perfectly transmitted downstream, thus resulting in a series of uniform bends.

Tests. On plate 3, the photograph on the left shows the initial channel of a laboratory stream which was straight except for an initiating bend. The bed and banks of this small-scale river were composed of uniform erodible material, the axial slope was uniform, and a constant rate of flow was passed through the channel. The center photograph on plate 3 shows the resulting uniform meanders. The photograph on the right shows the results of the check test which demonstrate that the results are capable of duplication. Also, it is noted that a series of practically identical bars formed on the inside of bends. The cross sections show the superelevation of the flow on the concave side of bends.

Analysis and discussion. The afore-described tests showed that when all outside disturbing influences were eliminated and the elements were reduced to their simplest forms, the development of a series of uniform bends from an initiating bend was positive and capable of duplication. Each bend developed as a result of impingement and deflection from the banks and as a result of deposition of sand on the inside of the bend. When the flow was directed against a bank, the water piled up and was superelevated along the concave banks even in these small streams. The natural process might be likened to the oscillatory course taken by a ball which has been started down a grooved incline so that it oscillates from side to side. However, water requires confinement in order to develop its erosive forces, and this was brought about naturally by the deposition of sand on the inside of bends which propagated their development.

Development of Meandering Channel, A Series of Deeps and Shoals

Characteristic of meandering rivers, the cross sections of the small-scale rivers were deep along the concave banks of bends and shallow in the tangents between bends so that the talweg profiles consisted of a series of deeps separated by shoals. Study of the development of these features confirmed the generally accepted cause—that rivers are deeper in bendways because of the greater turbulence and erosive power of the flow in bends as a result of impingement against the concave banks.

Tests. Plate 4 presents typical cross sections and the talweg profile of one of a number of streams which naturally developed a meandering pattern of flow from a straight channel except for an initiating bend. The photograph shows the naturally developed sinuous channel. In the bends, characteristic triangular-shaped cross sections developed with the deep section along the concave bank, and in the crossings characteristic wide-shallow cross sections developed. The talweg profile shows the characteristic deeps in the bends separated by shallow crossings.

242

DEVELOPMENT OF MEANDER PATTERN

INITIAL CHANNEL

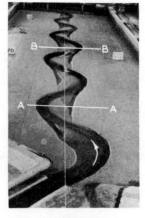
AFTER 3 HRS

(CHECK TEST)
AFTER 3 HRS

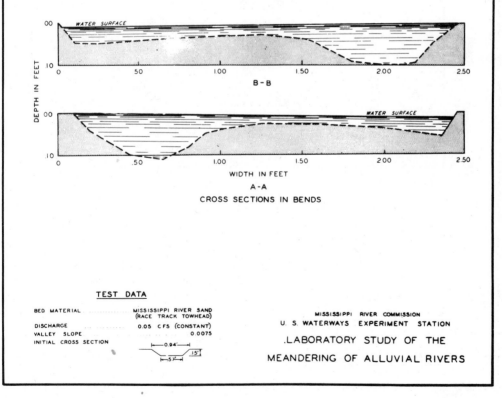

B - B

WIDTH IN FEET

A - A

CROSS SECTIONS IN BENDS

TEST DATA

BED MATERIAL	MISSISSIPPI RIVER SAND (RACE TRACK TOWHEAD)
DISCHARGE	0.05 CFS (CONSTANT)
VALLEY SLOPE	0.0075
INITIAL CROSS SECTION	

MISSISSIPPI RIVER COMMISSION
U. S. WATERWAYS EXPERIMENT STATION

.LABORATORY STUDY OF THE

MEANDERING OF ALLUVIAL RIVERS

PLATE 3

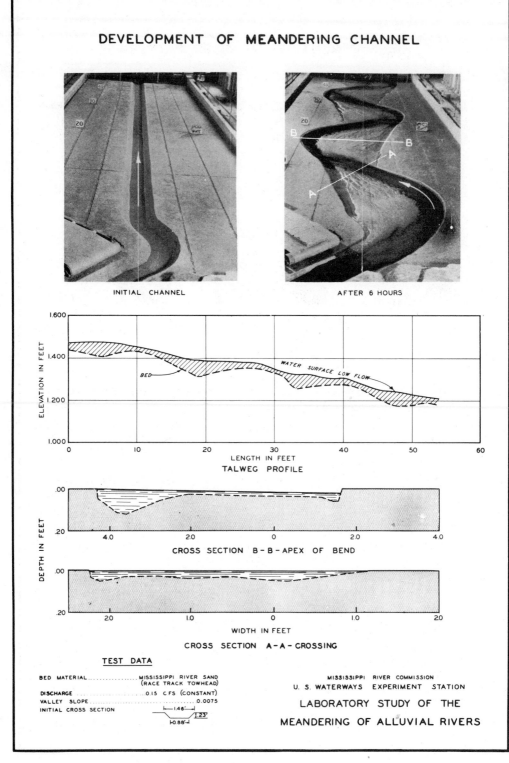

DEVELOPMENT OF MEANDERING CHANNEL

INITIAL CHANNEL

AFTER 6 HOURS

TALWEG PROFILE

CROSS SECTION B-B-APEX OF BEND

CROSS SECTION A-A-CROSSING

TEST DATA

BED MATERIAL...............MISSISSIPPI RIVER SAND
                          (RACE TRACK TOWHEAD)
DISCHARGE ....0.15 CFS (CONSTANT)
VALLEY SLOPE....................................0.0075
INITIAL CROSS SECTION

MISSISSIPPI RIVER COMMISSION
U. S. WATERWAYS EXPERIMENT STATION

LABORATORY STUDY OF THE
MEANDERING OF ALLUVIAL RIVERS

PLATE 4

244

DEVELOPMENT OF MEANDERING CHANNEL

INITIAL CHANNEL

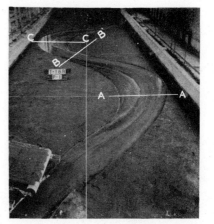

CHANNEL AFTER 12 HOURS

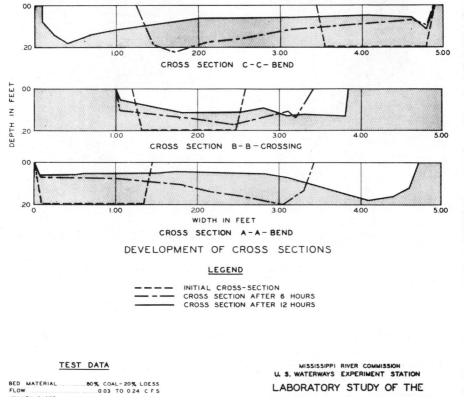

CROSS SECTION C-C- BEND

CROSS SECTION B-B-CROSSING

WIDTH IN FEET

CROSS SECTION A-A- BEND

DEPTH IN FEET

DEVELOPMENT OF CROSS SECTIONS

LEGEND

– – – – INITIAL CROSS-SECTION
— – — CROSS SECTION AFTER 6 HOURS
——— CROSS SECTION AFTER 12 HOURS

TEST DATA

BED MATERIAL ....80% COAL-20% LOESS
FLOW ....0.03 TO 0.24 C F S
VALLEY SLOPE............................0.003
INITIAL CHANNEL AS SHOWN

MISSISSIPPI RIVER COMMISSION
U. S. WATERWAYS EXPERIMENT STATION
LABORATORY STUDY OF THE
MEANDERING OF ALLUVIAL RIVERS

PLATE 5

SOURCE, PATH OF TRAVEL
AND LOCATION OF DEPOSITION
OF SAND IN A MEANDERING RIVER

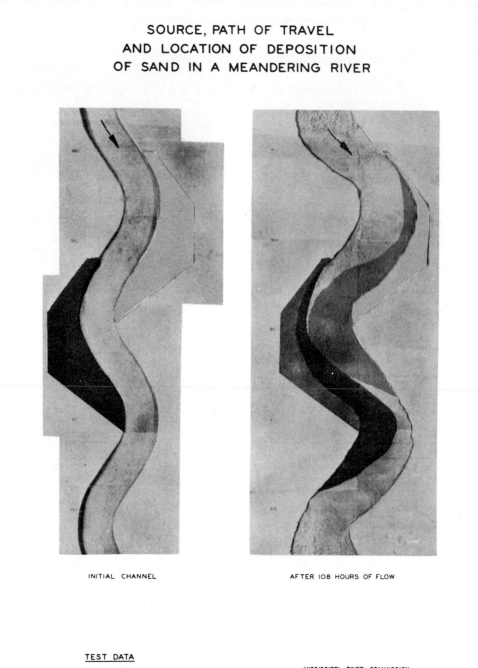

INITIAL CHANNEL   AFTER 108 HOURS OF FLOW

TEST DATA

BED MATERIAL................MISSISSIPPI RIVER SAND-80%
                                                       (KINGS POINT)
                                       MISSISSIPPI RIVER SILT-20%
                                                       (MILLIKEN BEND)
DISCHARGE ....0.025 TO 0.50 CFS
VALLEY SLOPE...0.0038

MISSISSIPPI RIVER COMMISSION
U. S. WATERWAYS EXPERIMENT STATION
LABORATORY STUDY OF THE
MEANDERING OF ALLUVIAL RIVERS

PLATE 6

To further prove the natural tendency of sinuous streams to develop these characteristic cross sections and profiles, a test was conducted which began with a sinuous pattern and with uniform trapezoidal cross sections throughout the length of channel (plate 5). The photographs and cross sections again show that the characteristic features developed.

Analysis and discussion. Observation of the flow patterns and movement of sand along the bed of these streams indicated clearly that the bendway cross sections are deeper than the crossings because of the impingement of flow against the concave banks. As a result of impingement the flow is more turbulent and has more erosive power in the bends than in the crossings. This cause must be supplemented by the repeated observations that the sand entering a bend is practically all on the convex side of the talweg, where all or part of the sand deposits and confines the flow.

Source, Travel, and Deposition of Sand in Meandering Rivers

This study showed that of the total sand and silt burden of a river, only the bed load or sand which moves along the bed and deposits on bars directly[1] affects the meandering of alluvial rivers. The study did not go into the mechanics of bed-load movement, which have been studied in detail at a number of laboratories (II)[2,3]. Rather, this study was concerned with the source, path of travel, and location of deposition of the sand. These studies showed that within a meandering river the source of the sand is the caving banks, and the sand travels only a short distance to the first convex bar downstream where velocities are low enough to permit deposition. Only minor amounts of sand from a caving bank cross the channel to the convex bar opposite. There is more or less continuous trading of sand along a river, deposition on bars and replacement from caving banks. The rate of trading varies, depending upon the rate of bank caving.

Tests. On plate 6, the photograph on the left shows the molded sinuous channel of a small-scale river in which the concave banks of two successive bends were composed of colored sand. The photograph on the right shows the resulting channel after 108 hours of flow. The green sand from the first concave bank travelled to and deposited on the convex bar immediately downstream on the same side of the river, and the red sand from the concave bank in the next bend travelled to and deposited on the next convex bar immediately downstream. Only minor amounts of sand eroded from a concave bank crossed the channel to the bar opposite. In this "perfect" meandering river in which the bends were all eroding at the same rate and at a rate equal to the sand-carrying capacity of the flow, there was a complete interchange of sand in each bend, deposition on the bar and replacement from the caving bank opposite. This was the case of rapidly and uniformly eroding banks.

On plate 7, the diagrammatic sketch on the left shows the source, path of travel, and location of deposition of sand under the conditions of rapidly eroding banks just described.

In some tests which began with sinuous channels, the banks did not erode at all, and the movement of sand under these conditions is shown diagrammatically in the sketch on the right of plate 7. Sand entering at the head of the river passed nearly continuously through the channel. The sand moved along the convex-bar side of the talweg in bends and crossed the talweg at the tangents between bends. This was the case of a sinuous channel having stable banks[4].

Between the two extremes of rapidly eroding banks and stable banks, there were some tests in which the banks eroded slowly (plate 7, center sketch). Under these conditions part of the sand entering each bend deposited on the convex bar, and part passed through

---

[1] Indirectly, the suspended load does influence meandering in that it deposits in abandoned channels which may later form resistant banks (57), and it has been indicated that the suspended load has some effect on the sand-carrying capacity of a river (33).

[2] References.

[3] Certain incidental findings as to the mechanics of bed-load movement are described in Part III. These findings, together with observations of the movement of bed load in the small-scale streams, emphasized that it is the velocities and turbulence of the filaments near the bed which motivate the movement of particles. It was indicated that formulas based on bulk flows, that is, formulas based on the slope and depths or on mean velocities, are not applicable to meandering sections of rivers, because of the turbulence set up by impingement of the flow against the banks and because of the continually changing cross sections and distribution of velocities. Depending upon local conditions, the velocity and turbulence of the filaments along the bed may or may not vary directly with the mass of flow.

[4] The tests with stable banks confirm the results of earlier laboratory studies on this subject (37, 38).

the bend. The sand which deposited on the bar was replaced by sand from the caving bank opposite. In this case there was a partial interchange of sand in each bend.

Analysis and discussion. The three cases presented, rapidly eroding banks, slowly eroding banks, and no bank erosion, cover the range of conditions believed to exist in meandering rivers[1]. The general rule is that within a river the source of the sand is the caving banks. The sand travels only a relatively short distance before it deposits on a bar, and the deposited sand is replaced by sand from caving banks. However, it seems clear that in meandering rivers the rate of trading must vary considerably, because no two bends are eroding their banks at the same rate, and in some sections little or no bank caving occurs. Therefore, no set rules can be laid down as to the source of the sand in each bend. Depending upon local conditions, the sand in a section of river may have come from the banks of the bend immediately upstream or from a bank several bends upstream. The varying rate of trading along the Lower Mississippi River is well indicated by the varying rate of bank caving shown on plate 8. This diagram is representative of the natural conditions of the river; only few of the banks had been revetted and no artificial cut-offs had been made.

It is particularly important to note that in practically all cases the bed load which enters a bend from upstream tends to travel along the convex bar side of the talweg[2] where it either deposits or passes through to the next bend. Generally, only the sand eroded from the adjacent concave bank moves along the talweg and along the concave side of the talweg. This consideration becomes of primary importance in analyzing the changes brought about in the cross sections by increasing the toughness of banks or by stabilizing the banks, which changes are discussed later in this report.

The diversion of sand from the talweg to the bar as it enters a bend is one of the most important phenomena of meandering rivers. It results in the building of convex bars in bends. Observations of this phenomenon showed that the sand diverted to the bar because the slow bottom currents which carry the sand tended to divert from the talweg to the bar[3].

In the bendway only minor amounts of the sand which were eroded from the adjacent bank crossed the talweg and deposited on the convex bar opposite. The sand which did cross the channel was eroded from the concave bank in the upstream part of the bend and deposited on the downstream part of the convex bar opposite, near the crossing. There was evidence of helicoidal flow in the bends (34) and consequently there was a tendency for particles eroded from a bank to cross the channel. However, the forces were not strong enough to carry the particles across the talweg before the downstream currents carried them to the crossing or bar below.

Changes in the Direction of Flow and
Movement of Sand with Changes in Stage

The preceding tests and discussions dealt with the movement of sand in general. Changes in stage brought about changes in the source, path of travel, and location of deposition of the sand in each bend as well as changes in the volume of sand moved.

Tests. On plate 9 there are shown two talweg profiles of the small-scale river shown in the photograph. One was taken during low flow and the other was taken during bankfull stage. These profiles show that during the higher flow the water-surface slope was nearly uniform, and deposition took place in the wide crossings. During low flow the slopes were flat in the pools and steep over the crossings, and as a result the bed of the crossings was scoured down.

The sketches on plate 9 show the changes in direction of flow and movement of sand with changes in stage, as indicated by the small-scale rivers. During low stage the movement of sand was largely confined to the crossings, where sand was scoured

[1] Generally this set of tests confirms the indications shown by an experiment on the Mississippi River itself, where 1000 tons of chat and 1000 tons of crushed coal were placed in two bends (32).
[2] Talweg is defined as the deepest part of the channel.
[3] The principle involved in this phenomenon appears to be related to the principles involved in the diversion of sediment at branching channels, references V.

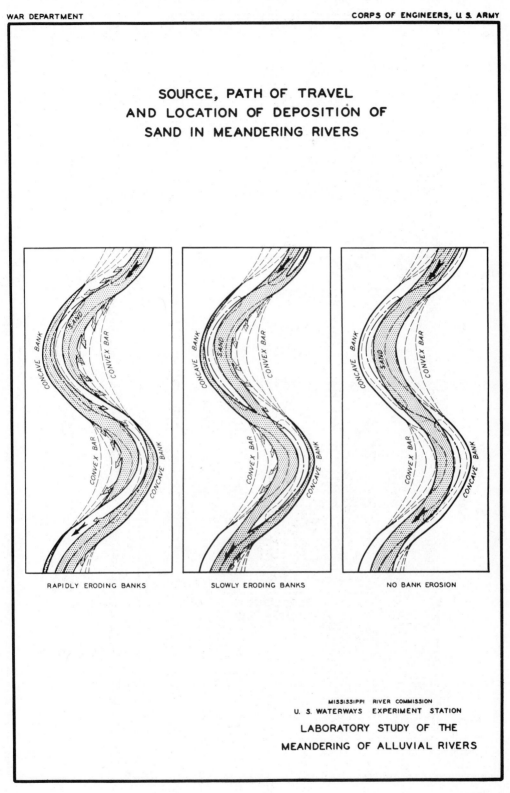

SOURCE, PATH OF TRAVEL
AND LOCATION OF DEPOSITION OF
SAND IN MEANDERING RIVERS

RAPIDLY ERODING BANKS

SLOWLY ERODING BANKS

NO BANK EROSION

MISSISSIPPI RIVER COMMISSION
U. S. WATERWAYS EXPERIMENT STATION

LABORATORY STUDY OF THE
MEANDERING OF ALLUVIAL RIVERS

PLATE 7

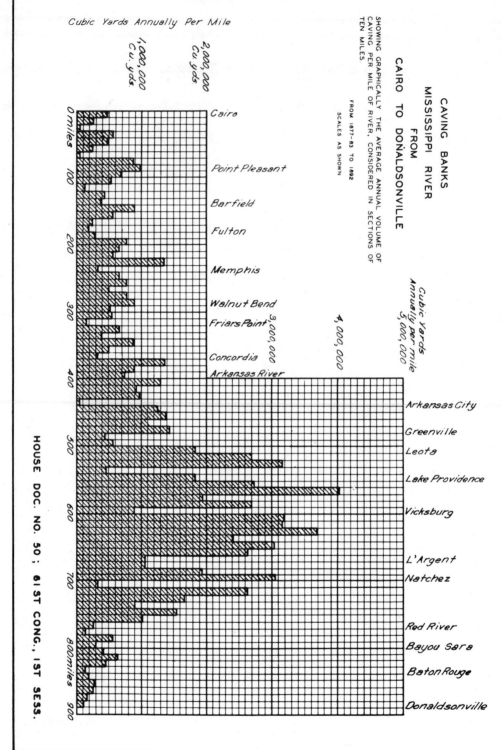

CAVING BANKS
MISSISSIPPI RIVER
FROM
CAIRO TO DONALDSONVILLE

SHOWING GRAPHICALLY THE AVERAGE ANNUAL VOLUME OF
CAVING PER MILE OF RIVER, CONSIDERED IN SECTIONS OF
TEN MILES.

FROM 1877-83 TO 1892
SCALES AS SHOWN

Cubic Yards Annually Per Mile

PLATE 8

HOUSE DOC. NO. 50 ; 61 ST CONG., 1ST SESS.

250

CHANGE IN SOURCE, PATH OF TRAVEL, AND DEPOSITION OF SAND WITH CHANGE IN STAGE

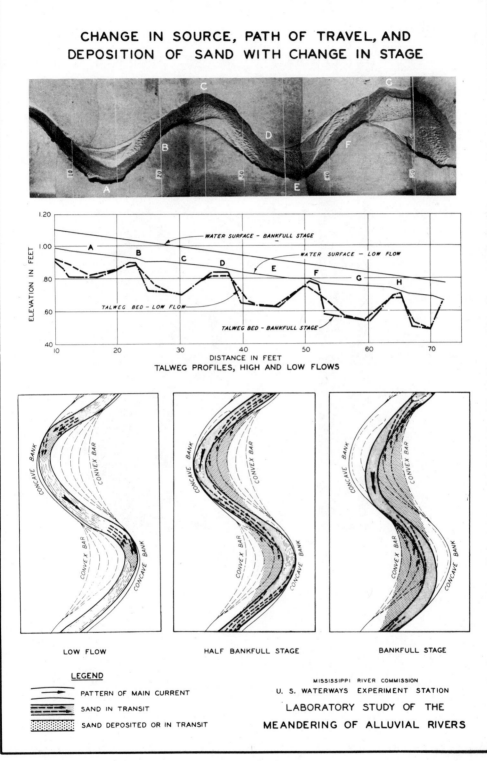

TALWEG PROFILES, HIGH AND LOW FLOWS

LOW FLOW   HALF BANKFULL STAGE   BANKFULL STAGE

LEGEND

→ PATTERN OF MAIN CURRENT

SAND IN TRANSIT

SAND DEPOSITED OR IN TRANSIT

MISSISSIPPI RIVER COMMISSION
U. S. WATERWAYS EXPERIMENT STATION

LABORATORY STUDY OF THE
MEANDERING OF ALLUVIAL RIVERS

PLATE 9

EFFECT OF
NOT FEEDING SAND AT THE ENTRANCE

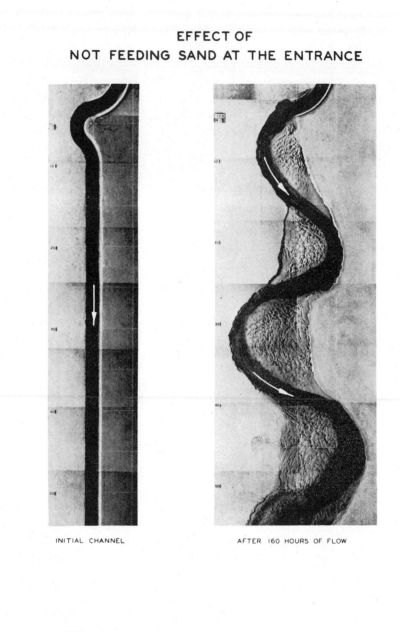

INITIAL CHANNEL　　　　　　　　　　　AFTER 160 HOURS OF FLOW

TEST DATA

BED MATERIAL　　　　　MISSISSIPPI RIVER SAND-80%
　　　　　　　　　　　　　　　　(KINGS POINT)
　　　　　　　　　　　MISSISSIPPI RIVER SILT-20%
　　　　　　　　　　　　　　　(MILLIKEN BEND)

VALLEY SLOPE.................................. 0.007
DISCHARGE ....0.05 TO 0.50 CFS
INITIAL CHANNEL

MISSISSIPPI RIVER COMMISSION
U. S. WATERWAYS EXPERIMENT STATION

LABORATORY STUDY OF THE
MEANDERING OF ALLUVIAL RIVERS

PLATE 10

252

out and deposited in the pools below. In many tests there was low-water bank attack in the upstream part of the bends, and the eroded sand deposited in the pools immediately downstream from the point of erosion. As the stage increased, the bank attack and erosion shifted downstream, and movement of sand began in the bendway. The sand which deposited in the talweg during low flows and the sand which eroded from the banks moved downstream and deposited along the edges of the bars. Some deposition took place in the crossings. At bankfull stage, the path of the main current in the bends was generally across the convex bars, and the attack and erosion of concave banks was along the downstream part of bends. The eroded sands deposited largely along the top of convex bars, and deposition also occurred in the crossings. During the high stages, there was a tendency for the sand on upstream parts of the convex bars to be swept downstream and to deposit in the crossings. During the highest stages there was little or no movement of sand in the talweg in the upstream part of the bends.

Analysis and discussion. The tests emphasized that the erosion of banks, path of sand movement, and the location of deposition changed markedly with changes in stage. This was because the path of the main current of the flow changed with changes in stage, as shown on plate 9. The reasons for the changes in the path of main current of the flow are discussed later in this report.

It is to be noted that in meandering rivers, the filling of the crossings during high flows and the scouring down of the crossings during low flows are contrary to the conditions found in straight restricted sections of channels with erodible beds, where the bed generally scours down during high flows and fills during low flows. In these meandering streams, the high flows tended to deteriorate the low-water channel. This tendency is clearly illustrated on plate 13, which will be discussed later.

Sand Entering at the Head of a Meandering River

Several tests were conducted in which no sand was fed at the entrance, in order to prove further that the source of sand within a meandering stream is the caving banks, and to learn the importance of the sand entering at the head of an alluvial stream.

Tests. On plate 10, the photograph on the left shows the initial channel of a test in which sand was not fed at the entrance. The bed and banks of the stream were composed of sandy material, and the bed was given a uniform axial slope sufficient to enable the flow to erode its banks and move sand along its bed. The photograph on the right shows the resulting sinuous channel after 160 hours of flow. The lack of sand entering the stream did not prevent meandering. The source of the sand which made up the bars was the caving banks along the stream, except for the upstream bar which was formed from material eroded from the bed immediately below the entrance.

However, it should be noted that the bends did not develop uniformly, but increased in size from the first to the second to the third bend. Plate 11 shows the comparative talweg traces and the profiles of the stream as it developed. In the upstream bend, bank erosion stopped after about 30 hours of flow, the channel deepened, and the slope became so flat that the flow no longer had the velocity to erode its banks. The second bend received the sand eroded from the banks and bed of the first bend and made a larger bend, but bank erosion in this bend stopped after about 100 hours of flow. The profiles show that deepening of the channel and flattening of the slope extended downstream from the first bend. The third bend received a larger amount of sand from the second bend and made a still larger bend. The third and fourth bends were about the same size and were slowly eroding their banks at the end of the test.

Analysis and discussion. Tests of this type[1] present further evidence that the source of sand within a meandering river is the caving banks. The immediate and direct effects of not adding sand at the entrance were only local, in the upstream section. However, the tests showed that the sand entering at the entrance is also of primary importance. The lack of sand entering the first bend resulted in deepening of the channel in the first bend and in flattening of the slope until the velocities became too low to erode the banks,

---

[1] A similar test without an initial angle of attack is shown on plate 2.

and this change slowly progressed downstream. The fundamental principle indicated by these tests is that the cross sections, slope, and meandering in each local section of river are dependent upon the sand entering that section. Just below the head of the laboratory rivers, it was the sand which was added at the entrance which maintained the cross sections and slopes, and deposited on the bars. Farther downstream, it was the sand from caving banks which maintained the slopes, cross sections, and meandering. As a result of the natural trading process, the sand entering at the head of the river was soon replaced by sand from caving banks.

The conditions of this test might be considered analogous to stopping the supply of sand at the head of a meandering river. It was indicated, for example, that if the sand entering the Lower Mississippi River at Cairo were stopped, the only immediate effect would be deepening and flattening of the slope in the section just below Cairo. Below this section, meandering would continue just as before. However, the deepening would slowly progress downstream, and as it progressed downstream the slopes would flatten, and meandering would slow down and finally stop in the deepened sections.

Laboratory flume studies with stable banks and sand beds (27, 29, 30) have shown conclusively that for a given flow which has the capacity to move sand, only one rate of sand feeding maintains the given cross sections and slope. With less than the required rate, deepening of the cross sections and flattening of the slope take place beginning at the upstream end, while excessive sand feeding causes aggradation of the channel and steepening of the slope. In natural rivers with stable banks, it has been found that after dams stopped the supply of sand, the channel below degraded for considerable distances downstream in spite of the reduction in maximum flows (VIII). This study and earlier meander studies (58) at the Experiment Station have shown that this principle also applies to the upstream section of meandering rivers.

Size of Bends—Effect of Discharge

It is common observation that a general relationship exists between the size of rivers and the size of bends in meandering rivers; little rivers make little bends, and big rivers make big bends. Compilations of data on a number of rivers (46, 54) showed that as the width of a river increases, the size of the bends increases, but the points plotted from the data were badly scattered. The recent geological study on the Lower Missisippi River (57) verified the general relationship between discharge and the size of bends. In the field it is not possible to make true comparisons between the size of bends and any one element of a river, because of the lack of parallelism of the other elements. In the laboratory each of the elements can be more closely isolated, and the effect of each on the size and shape of bends can be determined more closely. These studies showed that for the same bank material and the same initiating angle of attack, the size of bends becomes greater with increase in discharge and slope. The following tests show that an increase in discharge results in increasing the size of bends.

Tests. To determine the effect of discharge on the size of bends, three tests were conducted in which all conditions were similar except the discharge. The results are shown by the photographs[1] on plate 12. Each of these small-scale rivers began with a straight channel except for an initiating bend (see initial channel, plate 1). The bed and bank material, valley slope, initial angle of attack, and duration were the same. The initial cross sections were geometrically similar. For each flow the proper amount of sand to be fed at the entrance was determined by several preliminary trial and error tests as the amount necessary to prevent filling or scouring of the channel just below the entrance. The photographs show that as the discharge increased, the size of bends increased both in length and width; that is, an increase in discharge resulted in an increase in radii of bends. The curves on plate 12 show the correlation between discharge, and the length and width of bends.

The results of an interesting and important test regarding the changes in the meander pattern brought about by changes in discharge are shown on plate 13. In this test a meander pattern was first developed by relatively low flows. Then, each of the flows

[1] Practically all photographs were taken at extremely low flow so as to define the pattern of the stream.

EFFECT OF
NOT FEEDING SAND AT THE ENTRANCE

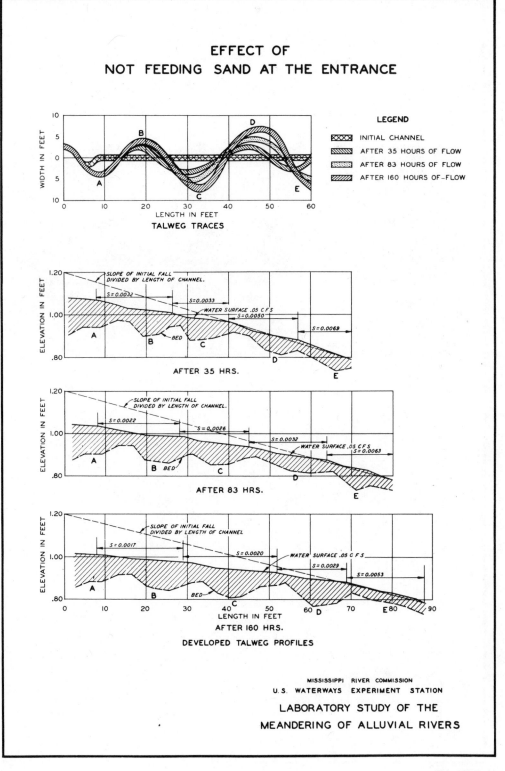

LEGEND

INITIAL CHANNEL
AFTER 35 HOURS OF FLOW
AFTER 83 HOURS OF FLOW
AFTER 160 HOURS OF-FLOW

TALWEG TRACES

AFTER 35 HRS.

AFTER 83 HRS.

AFTER 160 HRS.

DEVELOPED TALWEG PROFILES

MISSISSIPPI RIVER COMMISSION
U.S. WATERWAYS EXPERIMENT STATION

LABORATORY STUDY OF THE
MEANDERING OF ALLUVIAL RIVERS

PLATE 11

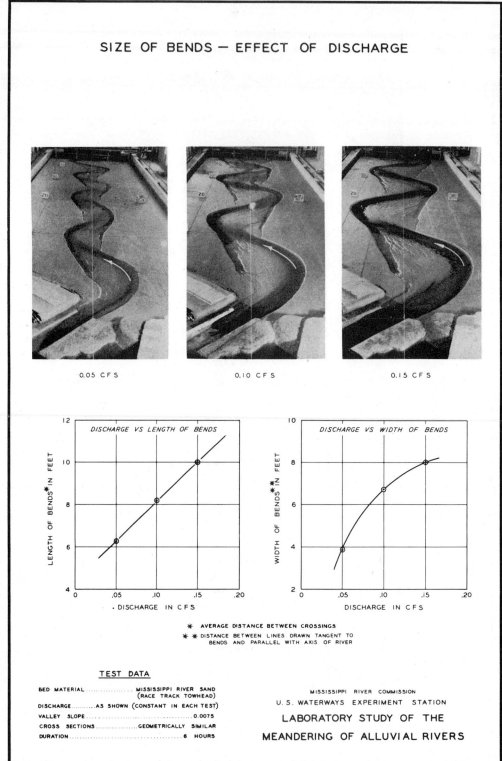

SIZE OF BENDS — EFFECT OF DISCHARGE

0.05 CFS   0.10 CFS   0.15 CFS

DISCHARGE VS LENGTH OF BENDS

DISCHARGE VS WIDTH OF BENDS

LENGTH OF BENDS* IN FEET

WIDTH OF BENDS** IN FEET

DISCHARGE IN CFS

DISCHARGE IN CFS

✳   AVERAGE DISTANCE BETWEEN CROSSINGS

✳✳ DISTANCE BETWEEN LINES DRAWN TANGENT TO
       BENDS AND PARALLEL WITH AXIS OF RIVER

TEST DATA

BED MATERIAL................. MISSISSIPPI RIVER SAND
                                          (RACE TRACK TOWHEAD)
DISCHARGE...........AS SHOWN (CONSTANT IN EACH TEST)
VALLEY SLOPE..................................0.0075
CROSS SECTIONS.................GEOMETRICALLY SIMILAR
DURATION...6 HOURS

MISSISSIPPI RIVER COMMISSION
U.S. WATERWAYS EXPERIMENT STATION

LABORATORY STUDY OF THE
MEANDERING OF ALLUVIAL RIVERS

PLATE 12

SIZE OF BENDS – EFFECT OF DOUBLING THE DISCHARGE
ON MEANDER PATTERN

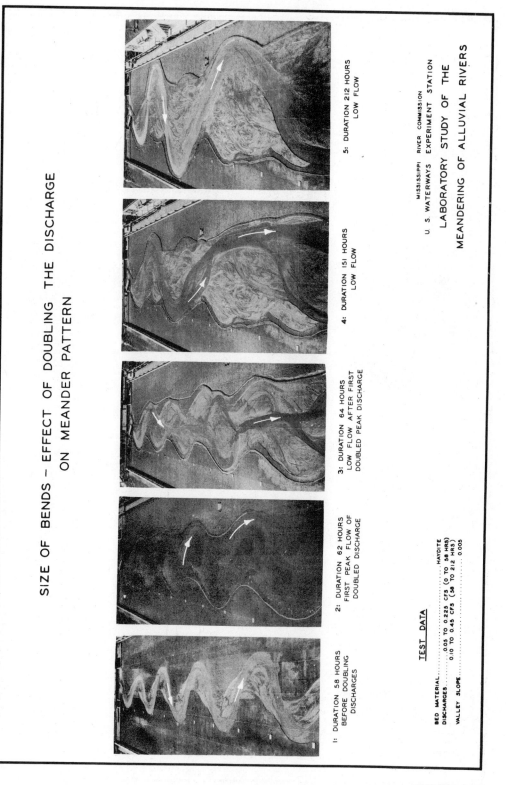

1: DURATION 58 HOURS
BEFORE DOUBLING
DISCHARGES

2: DURATION 62 HOURS
FIRST PEAK FLOW OF
DOUBLED DISCHARGE

3: DURATION 64 HOURS
LOW FLOW AFTER FIRST
DOUBLED PEAK DISCHARGE

4: DURATION 151 HOURS
LOW FLOW

5: DURATION 212 HOURS
LOW FLOW

TEST DATA

BED MATERIAL........................HAYDITE
DISCHARGES.........0.05 TO 0.225 CFS (0 TO 58 HRS)
                    0.10 TO 0.45 CFS (58 TO 212 HRS)
VALLEY SLOPE.......................0.005

MISSISSIPPI RIVER COMMISSION
U. S. WATERWAYS EXPERIMENT STATION
LABORATORY STUDY OF THE
MEANDERING OF ALLUVIAL RIVERS

257

PLATE 13

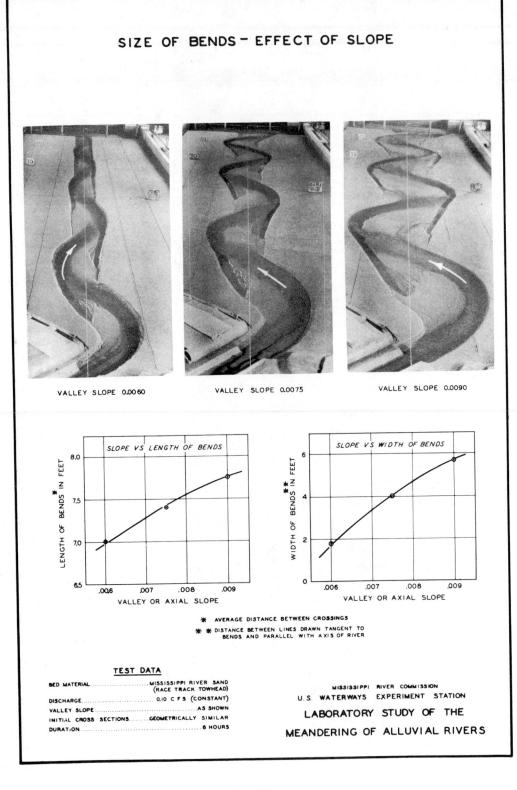

SIZE OF BENDS – EFFECT OF SLOPE

VALLEY SLOPE 0.0060

VALLEY SLOPE 0.0075

VALLEY SLOPE 0.0090

SLOPE VS LENGTH OF BENDS

SLOPE VS WIDTH OF BENDS

* AVERAGE DISTANCE BETWEEN CROSSINGS
** DISTANCE BETWEEN LINES DRAWN TANGENT TO BENDS AND PARALLEL WITH AXIS OF RIVER

TEST DATA

BED MATERIAL................MISSISSIPPI RIVER SAND (RACE TRACK TOWHEAD)
DISCHARGE........................0.10 C F S (CONSTANT)
VALLEY SLOPE...............................AS SHOWN
INITIAL CROSS SECTIONS........GEOMETRICALLY SIMILAR
DURATION..8 HOURS

MISSISSIPPI RIVER COMMISSION
U. S. WATERWAYS EXPERIMENT STATION

LABORATORY STUDY OF THE
MEANDERING OF ALLUVIAL RIVERS

which made this meander pattern was doubled, and a series of the doubled hydographs was passed through the channel. Photograph 1 of plate 13 shows the channel developed by the relatively low flows. After this photograph was taken levees were placed along the banks and the same pattern of flows was repeated except that each flow was doubled. Photograph 2 shows the first peak flow of the doubled-discharge hydrograph. Photograph 3 shows the confused and braided channel at low flow after the first new peak discharge. Each of the former convex bars was swept downstream and the former pattern was completely destroyed. Photograph 4, taken after several hydrographs of doubled discharges, shows that the stream was shaping a new meander pattern. Photograph 5, taken at the end of the test, shows that the stream completely established a new pattern of bends which were over twice as wide and long as the bends in the former meander pattern. It is to be noted that even though the bends increased in size, the total length of channel became less. It should also be added that doubling the discharges did not cause deepening of the channel.

Analysis and discussion. The important point brought out by these tests is that each rate of flow has a meander pattern of its own, and the higher the discharge the bigger are the bends. This finding bears out the general relationship observed in nature between small rivers and large rivers. In a single meandering river it explains the changes in direction of flow and the downstream shifting of the attack against the concave banks with rises in stage as shown on plate 9. The low flows tend to make short-radius bends, and the high flows tend to make long-radius bends. The greater masses of flow during high stages simply cannot make as sharp turns as the low flows. There is a natural divergence between the paths of travel of low and high flows which cannot be avoided, and the shorter the radii of bends, the greater is the divergence. This is important in planning for the improvement of rivers wherein it is desirable that the paths of low flow and high flow coincide as nearly as possible.

Size of Bends—Effect of Slope

The following tests show that for the same angle of attack an increase in axial slope also resulted in increasing the size of bends.

Tests. Plate 14 shows three streams in which all conditions were similar except the valley or axial slopes. Each of these small-scale rivers began with a straight channel except for an initial-attack angle. The bed and bank material, discharge, initial angle of attack, and duration were the same, and the initial cross sections were geometrically similar. The proper amount of sand to be fed at the entrance was determined by preliminary tests. The photographs show that as the slope increased the size of bends increased both in length and width, and the curves show the correlation between slope and the length and width of bends.

Analysis and discussion. The tendency for an increase in discharge or slope to cause an increase in the size of bends is logical, since both discharge and slope are functions of the energy of a stream, its mass and velocity. However, it should be noted that the initial angle of attack in these tests was the same.

The reason why an increase in slope resulted in bigger bends is the same as for an increase in discharge. For a given mass or discharge the higher the slope and velocity, the less able is the flow to make sharp turns. This explains the tendency of rivers to cut across the points of convex bars of bends after a cut-off has been made immediately below. Before the cut-off, the river made a bend to fit the existing conditions. After the cut-off, velocities are increased and the flow is not able to make as sharp a turn as before. The flow tends to pile up, so to speak, against the bank, and the main current is forced to take an inside path over the bar.

The velocity and energy of flows depend upon the hydraulic radius or depth of cross sections as well as the slope. The increase in slope also resulted in marked changes in the cross sections. These changes are described later in this report.

259

Size of Bends—Effect of Angle of Attack

In the preceding tests to learn the effects of changes in discharge and changes in slope on the size of bends, the initial angle of attack or the alignment of the flow into the channel was the same. However, this too is an important factor in determining the size and shape of bends, and the rate of bank erosion.

Tests. On plate 15 are shown the results of three tests that began with a straight channel except for the initiating angle of attack which was increased from 30° to 45° to 60°. All other conditions were the same. The photographs and curves show that as the degree of initial attack increased, the length of bends decreased and the width of bends increased; that is, the greater the angle of attack, the shorter were the radii of bends.

Analysis and discussion. These tests, together with the two preceding sets of tests, indicated that the size and shape of bends depend upon the discharge, the slope, and the angle of attack or alignment of the flow into the bends. In each meandering river it is the direction of flow into each bend which largely determines its size and shape. It is to be noted that in the small-scale rivers with uniform bed and bank material, the initial angle of attack affected the size and shape of the bends throughout the length of the streams. This, of course, is not true in natural rivers where local changes in the bank materials often change the angle of attack from one bend to another, but it illustrates the principle that a change in alignment in one bend tends to change the alignment for a considerable distance downstream. In this discussion it should be pointed out that when the angle of attack of a flow against a bank approached 90°, the flow did not deflect from the banks such that a bend developed farther downstream on the opposite bank. It was noted that when the attack was directly against a bank, the lateral oscillatory motion appeared to be destroyed by the excessive piling up and turbulence.

Degree of Sinuosity

The degree of sinuosity of meandering rivers refers to the ratio of the talweg length to the airline distance. It has been considered that meandering was a river's means of increasing its length and reducing its gradient because of excess energy (17, 56), and the more energy a river had the more sinuous it should be. Tests showed that this tendency was present only under certain conditions.

Tests. The curves on plate 16 show: first, the maximum sinuosity versus discharge; and second, the maximum sinuosity versus valley slope, as indicated by the results of the tests shown on plates 12 and 14. For the same initial angle of attack, the curves show an increase in sinuosity or length of channel with increase in discharge or slope. Also plotted on these graphs are the maximum sinuosities found in the tests in which the initial-attack angle was changed (plate 15). The three streams which had the same discharge and slope but different angles of attack did not attain the same length. Some tests were conducted without an initial-attack angle, and no sinuosity developed; the channels became so wide and shallow that bank erosion stopped.

Analysis and discussion. These tests showed that the sinuosity depends upon the initial angle of attack or direction of flow into bends as well as the discharge and slope. The tests, because of the stable entrances, did not bring out that the angle of attack often depends upon the velocity of the flow. A sand bar or other obstruction which will turn and direct a flow of low velocity into a bank may be swept downstream by a flow of high velocity, as in the test shown on plate 13. That is, as velocities increase, the flow may take a straighter course, and thereby decrease the angle of attack against the banks. In nature it is common to find rivulets running straight down a steep hillside, parallel to their banks. In summary, it was indicated that a river does tend to decrease its bank-eroding power as the slope or discharge increases, but depending upon local conditions, increasing its length is only one of the natural methods of decreasing its bank-eroding power, straightening and decreasing the angle of bank attack is another, and shoaling its channel is another.

SIZE OF BENDS—EFFECT OF ANGLE OF ATTACK

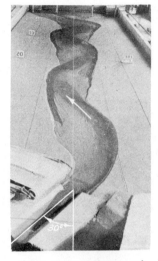

INITIAL ANGLE OF ATTACK - 30°

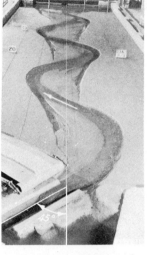

INITIAL ANGLE OF ATTACK - 45°

INITIAL ANGLE OF ATTACK - 60°

ANGLE OF ATTACK VS LENGTH OF BENDS

LENGTH OF BENDS ✱ IN FEET

INITIAL ANGLE OF ATTACK - DEGREES

ANGLE OF ATTACK VS WIDTH OF BENDS

WIDTH OF BENDS ✱✱ IN FEET

INITIAL ANGLE OF ATTACK - DEGREES

✱   AVERAGE DISTANCE BETWEEN CROSSINGS
✱✱   DISTANCE BETWEEN LINES DRAWN TANGENT TO
      BENDS AND PARALLEL WITH AXIS OF RIVER

TEST DATA

BED MATERIAL................MISSISSIPPI RIVER SAND
DISCHARGE.................0.10 C.F.S. (CONSTANT)
VALLEY SLOPE.............................0.0075
DURATION.................................6 HOURS
INITIAL CROSS SECTIONS

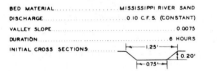

MISSISSIPPI RIVER COMMISSION
U. S. WATERWAYS EXPERIMENT STATION

LABORATORY STUDY OF THE
MEANDERING OF ALLUVIAL RIVERS

PLATE 15

DEGREE OF SINUOSITY

RATIO OF TALWEG DISTANCE TO AIRLINE DISTANCE

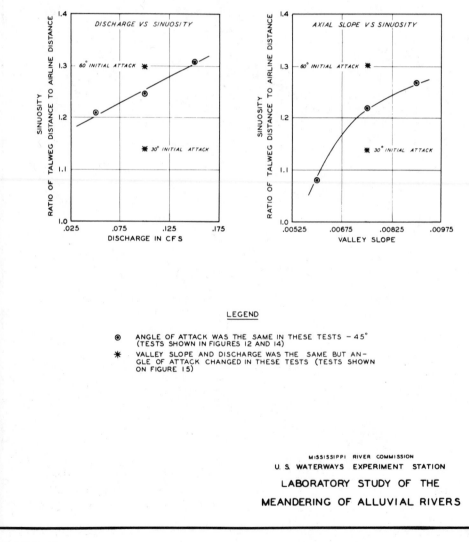

LEGEND

◉   ANGLE OF ATTACK WAS THE SAME IN THESE TESTS – 45°
       (TESTS SHOWN IN FIGURES 12 AND 14)

✳   VALLEY SLOPE AND DISCHARGE WAS THE SAME BUT AN-
       GLE OF ATTACK CHANGED IN THESE TESTS (TESTS SHOWN
       ON FIGURE 15)

MISSISSIPPI RIVER COMMISSION
U. S. WATERWAYS EXPERIMENT STATION

LABORATORY STUDY OF THE

MEANDERING OF ALLUVIAL RIVERS

PLATE 16

Sand Entering from Caving Banks
Rate of Bank Erosion—Effect on Cross Sections

The foregoing tests showed that within a meandering river the source of the sand is the caving banks. The rate at which sand enters a meandering river from caving banks, that is, the rate of bank erosion, is important not only in determining the rate of meandering, but also in determining the depth and width of the cross sections of a meandering river. It is evident that the more slowly the banks erode the slower will be the rate of meandering. The following tests also show that the more resistant the banks are to erosion the deeper are the cross sections.

Tests. On plate 17 the photographs show two naturally developed laboratory meandering rivers which began with slightly sinuous channels. In these two tests the flow, initial cross sections, valley slopes, and time of operation were the same, but the bank materials were different. In the stream shown on the left photograph, the bank material consisted largely of tough silt which was slowly eroded, whereas in the stream shown on the right photograph, the bank material consisted mainly of cohesionless sand which was relatively easily eroded. The stream in the easily eroded material, of course, meandered to a greater degree. The two cross sections shown on plate 17 represent two similarly located cross sections in the apex of bends in the two streams. In the tough material a relatively narrow and deep cross section developed, whereas in the easily eroded bed material a wide and shallow cross section developed.

The rate of bank erosion depends upon the force of the water against the banks as well as on the toughness of the banks. Plate 18 shows the results of three tests in which the bank material and all other conditions except slope were the same; that is, the bank material was the same, but the force of water against the banks was different. Under these conditions, the degree of meandering and rate of bank erosion increased with increase in slope, and again marked changes took place in the cross sections. On the lowest slope the stream practically maintained its initial depth, but as the slope and rate of bank erosion increased, the cross sections became more shallow.

Analysis and discussion. These tests showed that the rate of bank erosion determines the shape of the cross sections of a meandering river. Rapidly eroding banks result in wide shallow cross sections, and slowly eroding banks result in deep narrow cross sections. The tests brought out that for the same alignment, the depth of the cross sections along the concave banks is determined by the relationship between the rate of bank erosion and the rate at which the eroded sand is carried downstream. These two variables constantly work toward a balance. In these tests when the rate of bank erosion exceeded the rate of movement along the talweg, the channel shoaled and the height of bank became less, so that the amount of sand which entered the cross section became less per unit of bank recession. The shallowing of the talweg and consequent decrease in height of bank were simply natural adjustments toward reaching a balance between the sand entering and leaving the talweg. It should be particularly noted that it is the rate of sand feed from the adjacent eroding bank which determines the depth of the talweg. The sand which enters a bend from upstream is generally along the convex bar side of the talweg as shown on plate 7.

In preceding tests and discussions, it was shown that the cross sections and slope of a section of a meandering river depend upon the rate of sand entering that section of river. These tests go one step further and show that the shape of cross sections depends upon the location in the cross sections at which the sand enters. Probably the most important conception of a meandering river is that over each square foot of the bed, shoaling or deepening takes place depending upon the relationship between the sand entering that area and the ability of the flow over that area to carry sand. Predominance of either or a change in either without a corresponding change in the other will cause deposition or scour.

These tests bring out the possible fallacy of considering that increasing the slope or discharge in the channel proper of an alluvial river will increase velocities and cause deepening. The increased velocities may also cause increased bank erosion which may widen and shallow the channel instead of deepening it, depending upon the character of the banks and the angle of impingement of the flow against the banks.

In this discussion, the well-recognized fact should be added that in the case of resistant banks, the depth of the talweg along concave banks depends upon the degree of impingement of the flow against the banks. That is, when the banks are composed of rock or tough clays, or when the banks are stabilized by revetment, the depth along the concave bank increases with increase in the angle of impingement of the flow against the banks.

This study emphasized that the rate of bank erosion and the rate of movement of sand along the bed are not directly related; an increase in the rate of bank erosion does not mean an equal increase in the rate of sand movement along the bed. The force required to erode the banks is only that required to dislodge the particles which may be greater or may be less than that required to carry the particles downstream. As to the mechanics of bank erosion, the tests indicated that turbulence along the banks is the dominant eroding agency. In several tests which began with sinuous channels, erosion of the banks was slow, so long as the banks were smooth; however, as soon as a pocket formed or the banks became ragged, the rate of bank erosion increased.

Sand Entering from Caving Banks
Rate of Bank Erosion—Effect on Slopes

The rate of bank erosion affects the slopes of a river as well as the rate of meandering and the depth of cross sections. This effect has to do with the lowering or raising of tne bed and is separate and apart from the changes in gradient brought about by the increased length of a river as a result of meandering. The preceding tests showed that the more resistant the banks are to erosion the deeper are the cross sections, and the following tests show that general deepening of the cross sections is accompanied by flattening of the slopes.

Tests. In the preceding tests to learn the effect of the rate of bank erosion on cross sections, the tailwater levels were adjusted so as to maintain the initial axial slope. In these tests the initial tailwater levels were held constant throughout each test in order to allow the streams to adjust their slopes naturally. To illustrate clearly the effect of changes in the rate of bank erosion on the slopes as well as on cross sections, the results of two tests in which extreme changes took place are shown on plate 19. In these tests all conditions were the same except that the bed and bank material in one contained a small per cent of cement. The photograph on the left of plate 19 shows the initial channel used in both tests, and the center and right photographs show the resulting channels with and without cement, respectively. In the material with cement the stream was unable to erode its banks, and a miniature canyon developed even though the bed was composed of the same material as the banks. In the material without cement the banks eroded and a relatively shallow meandering river developed. The profiles on plate 19 show the changes which took place in the slopes of the bed of the channels. In the resistant-bank material the bed scoured considerably and the slope was reduced to less than half the initial slope. In the easily eroded material the stream shoaled its channel and increased its initial slope in spite of the fact that the stream meandered and increased its length.

To illustrate this principle further, there are shown on plate 20 the results of two tests which began with the alignment of a section of the Lower Mississippi River. The photograph on the left shows the channel at the beginning of both tests, in which all conditions were the same except that the bank material in one contained a small percentage of cement. The cross sections show that only slight bank erosion took place in the stream with tough banks, and the channel deepened. In the second, the banks eroded rapidly and the channel shoaled. The talweg profiles show that the slope flattened in the resistant material and steepened in the easily eroded material.

Analysis and discussion. It follows that as the bed of a river lowers or raises, the water-surface slopes also change. The adjustments in slope together with the adjustments in cross sections comprise the natural channel changes brought about by changes in the rate of bank erosion. These are the natural adjustments toward bringing about a balance between the rate of bank erosion and the rate of movement of sand along the talweg. The tests indicated the natural limits of over-all deepening or shoaling of a

EFFECT OF RATE OF BANK EROSION
ON CROSS SECTIONS

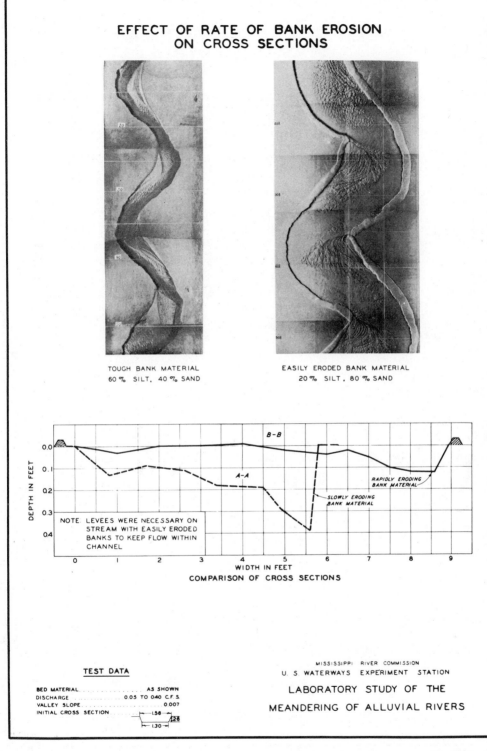

TOUGH BANK MATERIAL
60 % SILT, 40 % SAND

EASILY ERODED BANK MATERIAL
20 % SILT , 80 % SAND

NOTE: LEVEES WERE NECESSARY ON
STREAM WITH EASILY ERODED
BANKS TO KEEP FLOW WITHIN
CHANNEL

COMPARISON OF CROSS SECTIONS

TEST DATA

BED MATERIAL................ AS SHOWN
DISCHARGE .... 0.05 TO 0.40 C.F.S.
VALLEY SLOPE................... 0.007
INITIAL CROSS SECTION

MISSISSIPPI RIVER COMMISSION
U. S. WATERWAYS EXPERIMENT STATION

LABORATORY STUDY OF THE

MEANDERING OF ALLUVIAL RIVERS

PLATE 17

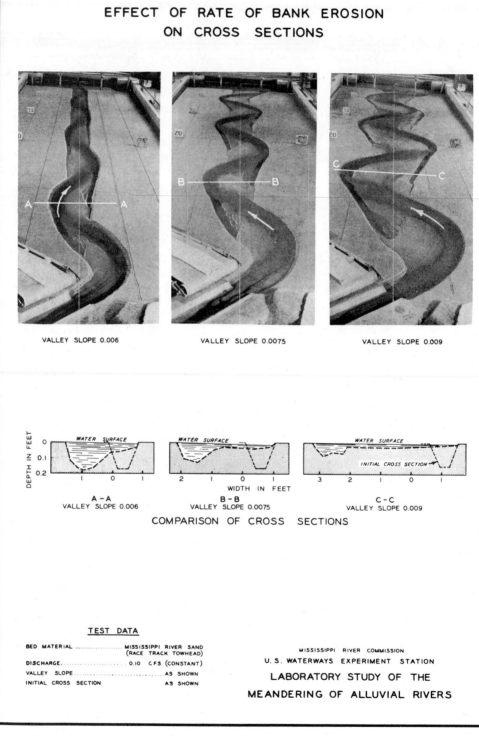

EFFECT OF RATE OF BANK EROSION
ON CROSS SECTIONS

VALLEY SLOPE 0.006

VALLEY SLOPE 0.0075

VALLEY SLOPE 0.009

A - A
VALLEY SLOPE 0.006

B - B
VALLEY SLOPE 0.0075

C - C
VALLEY SLOPE 0.009

COMPARISON OF CROSS SECTIONS

TEST DATA

BED MATERIAL .... MISSISSIPPI RIVER SAND
(RACE TRACK TOWHEAD)
DISCHARGE .... 0.10 CFS (CONSTANT)
VALLEY SLOPE .... AS SHOWN
INITIAL CROSS SECTION   AS SHOWN

MISSISSIPPI RIVER COMMISSION
U. S. WATERWAYS EXPERIMENT STATION
LABORATORY STUDY OF THE
MEANDERING OF ALLUVIAL RIVERS

PLATE 18

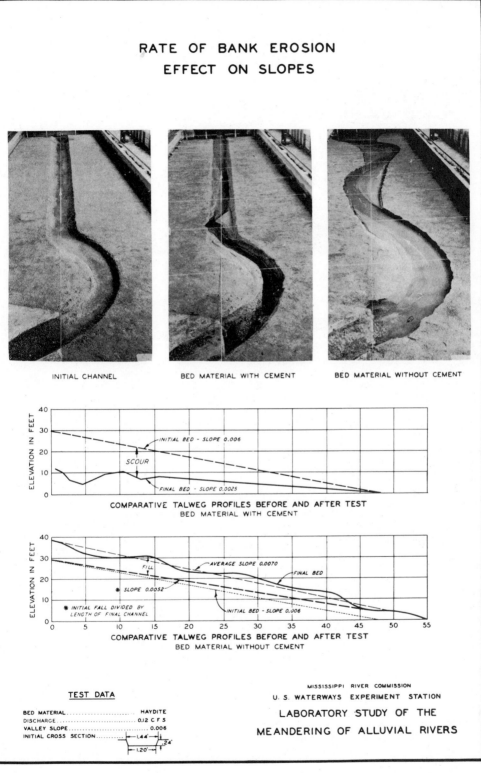

RATE OF BANK EROSION
EFFECT ON SLOPES

INITIAL CHANNEL

BED MATERIAL WITH CEMENT

BED MATERIAL WITHOUT CEMENT

COMPARATIVE TALWEG PROFILES BEFORE AND AFTER TEST
BED MATERIAL WITH CEMENT

COMPARATIVE TALWEG PROFILES BEFORE AND AFTER TEST
BED MATERIAL WITHOUT CEMENT

TEST DATA

BED MATERIAL................... HAYDITE
DISCHARGE...................... 0.12 C F S
VALLEY SLOPE.................. 0.006
INITIAL CROSS SECTION..........

MISSISSIPPI RIVER COMMISSION
U. S. WATERWAYS EXPERIMENT STATION
LABORATORY STUDY OF THE
MEANDERING OF ALLUVIAL RIVERS

PLATE 19

RATE OF BANK EROSION
EFFECT ON SLOPES

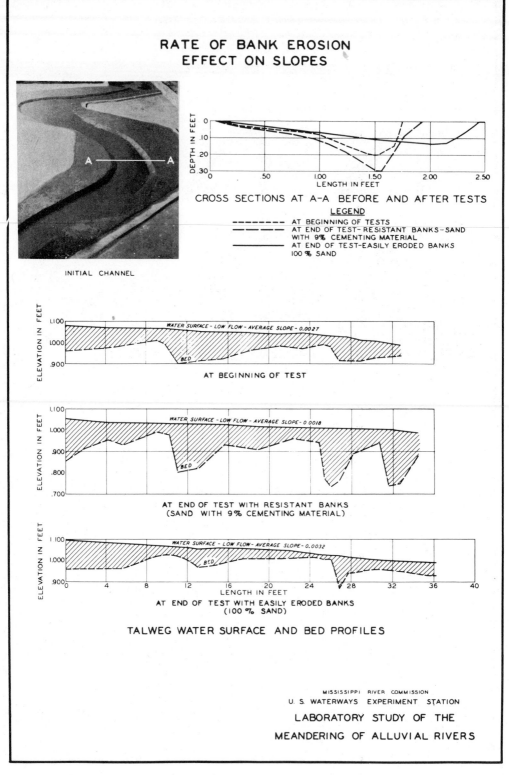

CROSS SECTIONS AT A-A BEFORE AND AFTER TESTS

LEGEND

-------- AT BEGINNING OF TESTS

- - - - AT END OF TEST-RESISTANT BANKS-SAND
WITH 9% CEMENTING MATERIAL

———— AT END OF TEST-EASILY ERODED BANKS
100 % SAND

INITIAL CHANNEL

WATER SURFACE - LOW FLOW - AVERAGE SLOPE - 0.0027

BED

AT BEGINNING OF TEST

WATER SURFACE - LOW FLOW - AVERAGE SLOPE - 0.0018

BED

AT END OF TEST WITH RESISTANT BANKS
(SAND WITH 9% CEMENTING MATERIAL)

WATER SURFACE - LOW FLOW - AVERAGE SLOPE - 0.0032

BED

AT END OF TEST WITH EASILY ERODED BANKS
(100 % SAND)

TALWEG WATER SURFACE AND BED PROFILES

MISSISSIPPI RIVER COMMISSION
U. S. WATERWAYS EXPERIMENT STATION

LABORATORY STUDY OF THE

MEANDERING OF ALLUVIAL RIVERS

PLATE 20

268

meandering channel. With resistant banks the channel deepens, and the slope flattens until the flow no longer has the velocity to scour the bed. With easily eroded banks the channel shoals, the height of banks becomes less, and the slope steepens until the rate of movement along the talweg equals the rate of bank erosion.

The cross sections and slopes found in meandering rivers are the results of the afore-described adjustments. The radical adjustments which took place in these small-scale rivers were caused by the fact that the initial cross sections and slopes were not the proper elements for the given bank material to result in the generally stable cross sections and slopes found in meandering rivers like the Lower Mississippi. However, the tests clearly brought out the changes in the slopes and cross sections brought about by differences in the rate of bank erosion. These tests indicate part of the reason why the Lower Mississippi River developed a deep channel with flat slopes in its lower sections and a relatively shallow channel with steep slopes in the upper sections.

Initial Cross Sections

During these tests it was considered that the depth and width of the initial cross sections might be an important factor. Tests showed that within reasonable limits the initial cross sections had little to do with the behavior of the streams—they soon made their own characteristic cross sections.

Tests. The photographs on plate 21 show the initial channels and resulting meander-ing channels of two streams after three hours of flow in which all conditions were the same except the initial cross sections. In the stream on the left, the initial cross section was narrow and deep, while in the stream on the right the initial cross section was wider and shallower. The photographs show that the resulting meander patterns were nearly identical, and resulting similarly located cross sections, also shown on plate 21, were practically the same.

Analysis and discussion. In these tests the initially deeper channel shoaled more rapidly and attained practically the same cross section as the initially wider and shallower channel. The tests present proof that in erodible materials a river will shape its cross sections in accordance with its flow, slope, bank materials, and alignment, irrespective of its initial cross sections, provided the initial cross sections are not so wide and shallow that the flow does not have sufficient velocities to move sand along the bed and erode the banks. Of practical importance, these tests showed that in erodible sediments there is no advantage in digging a new channel for a river deeper than is normally found under similar conditions.

These tests confirm the findings of afore-described tests in that the cross sections of an alluvial river deepen or shoal toward reaching a balance between the rate of sand entering the cross sections from the adjacent banks and the rate at which the sand is carried downstream. With this understanding, it is logical that these two streams should have attained practically the same cross sections.

The Variables and Their Interrelationships

These tests showed that every phase of a meandering river depends upon the relation-ship between three closely related variables: first, the discharge and the hydraulic properties of the channel which determine its sand-carrying capacity and eroding power; second, the amount of sand to be transported; and third, the rate of bank erosion. The ability of an alluvial river to move sand and erode its banks depends upon the discharge and velocity, which in turn depend upon the slope and depth of the cross sections. But, the tests showed that the slope and depth of the cross sections depend upon the rate of bank erosion and the amount of sand to be moved. The variables form a circle of dependency. These tests showed that a change in either discharge, slope, amount of sand entering a bend, or rate of bank erosion tends to bring about definite changes in the channel cross sections and pattern of a meandering river. However, the extent of these changes is often impossible to determine, because changes in one variable are opposed and limited by

269

changes in another variable. This is the complex side of meandering which prevents set rules or formulas. However, knowledge of the tendencies and counter tendencies brought about by changes in each of the variables provides a qualitative understanding of meandering.

Size of bends. This study showed, for example, that increasing the velocities by increasing the slope resulted in increasing the size of bends and increasing the rate of bank erosion. It was also shown that the more rapid the rate of bank erosion, the shallower were the cross sections. Thus, the tendency to increase velocities by increasing the slope was opposed by the decrease in hydraulic radius which tended to reduce velocities. The effects of shallowing of cross sections with increase in discharge or slope are indicated by the flattening of the curves showing relationship between discharge and slope, and width of bends (plates 12 and 14). The end point of this tendency and counter tendency is an extremely wide and shallow stream which does not erode its banks and does not meander. This resulting condition occurred in several tests and is found in natural rivers in wide shoaled reaches and in braided rivers.

Movement of sand, deposition, and scour. The tests emphasized that deposition or scour over each small area of the bed depends upon the relationship between the amount of sand entering that area and the sand-carrying capacity of the flow over that area. If the amount of sand entering an area just equals the sand-carrying capacity of the flow, of course, neither deposition nor scour takes place. An increase in the amount of sand or a decrease in velocity causes deposition, and conversely, a decrease in the amount of sand or an increase in velocity results in scour. Deposition or scour may be viewed simply as the natural adjustments of the bed toward reaching a balance between the sand entering and leaving an area of the bed. Deposition tends to decrease the cross-sectional area and increase the slope and velocity. Scour tends to increase the cross-sectional area and decrease the slope and velocity. The only reason why an alluvial river with an erodible bed does not deepen its channel is that sufficient sand enters the channel to use up its sand-moving capacity.

Bar building and bank caving. The development of each bend of a meandering river is the result of both of the natural processes just described, deposition on the convex-bar side and erosion along the concave bank. For analysis, consider a bendway cross section as divided into three parts: the convex bar side, the talweg, and the concave bank. The tests (plates 6 and 7) showed that the sand entering a bend tends to divert from the talweg and move toward the bar where deposition generally takes place. This deposition tends to reduce the cross-sectional area, confine the flow, and increase velocities. On the concave side the turbulent flow erodes the banks in an effort to increase the area of the channel. Here, again, there are two opposing interdependent tendencies— bar building tending to reduce the area, and bank erosion tending to increase the area. A change in either affects the other. The sand eroded from the concave banks feeds the talweg, which deepens or shoals depending upon the rate of erosion of the adjacent banks, as is shown on plate 17. Deepening of the talweg, without bank erosion, also tends to increase the cross-sectional area and often resulted in bar building in the small-scale rivers.

Limiting Width and Length of Meanders
Formation of Chutes

Aerial photographs of meandering rivers show that in each river there is a general limiting width to the lateral development of bends. Accompanying this limiting width there is an approximate limiting length of rivers. However, meandering rivers do not stop caving their banks when bends reach this limiting width and length. The flow short-cuts over the convex bars of bends, chute channels[1] form, and a new bend develops a little farther downstream. Tests provided examples of this natural phenomenon.

Tests. The photograph on the left in the upper half of plate 22 shows a meandering channel as it approached its limiting width after six hours of flow. This meandering

---

[1] A chute channel is defined as a channel across a bar or a pointway channel. It differs from a cut-off, wherein a river cuts through a narrow neck which has been developed between the upper and lower arms of a bend.

INITIAL CROSS SECTIONS

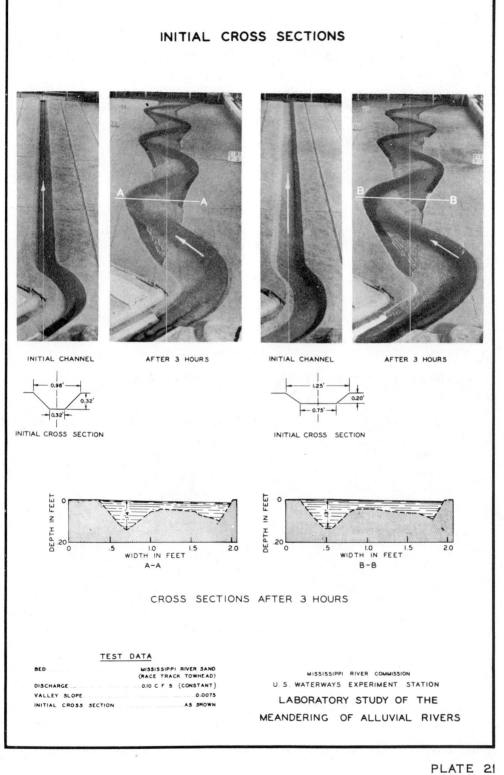

INITIAL CHANNEL   AFTER 3 HOURS   INITIAL CHANNEL   AFTER 3 HOURS

INITIAL CROSS SECTION   INITIAL CROSS SECTION

CROSS SECTIONS AFTER 3 HOURS

TEST DATA

BED .... MISSISSIPPI RIVER SAND
                                (RACE TRACK TOWHEAD)
DISCHARGE .... 0.10 C F S (CONSTANT)
VALLEY SLOPE 0.0075
INITIAL CROSS SECTION .... AS SHOWN

MISSISSIPPI RIVER COMMISSION
U. S. WATERWAYS EXPERIMENT STATION
LABORATORY STUDY OF THE
MEANDERING OF ALLUVIAL RIVERS

PLATE 21

271

LIMITING WIDTH OF MEANDERS
FORMATION OF CHUTES

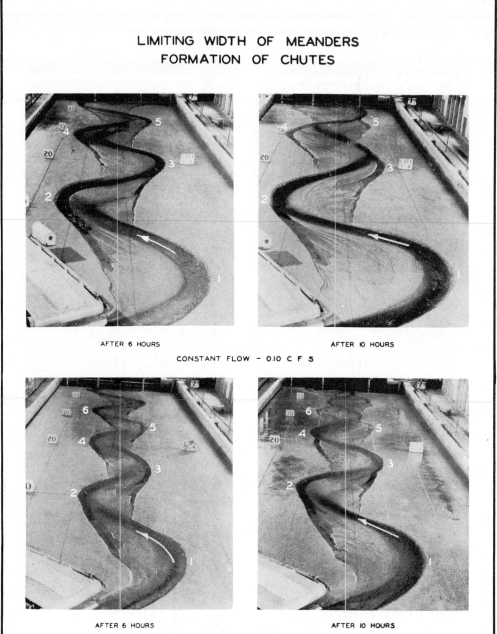

AFTER 6 HOURS   AFTER 10 HOURS

CONSTANT FLOW – 0.10 C F S

AFTER 6 HOURS   AFTER 10 HOURS

CONSTANT FLOW – 0.05 C F S

TEST DATA

BED MATERIAL	MISSISSIPPI RIVER SAND
	(RACETRACK TOWHEAD)
DISCHARGE	AS SHOWN
VALLEY SLOPE	0.0075

MISSISSIPPI RIVER COMMISSION
U. S. WATERWAYS EXPERIMENT STATION

LABORATORY STUDY OF THE
MEANDERING OF ALLUVIAL RIVERS

PLATE 22

272

LIMITING WIDTH AND LENGTH OF MEANDERING RIVERS
FORMATION OF CHUTES

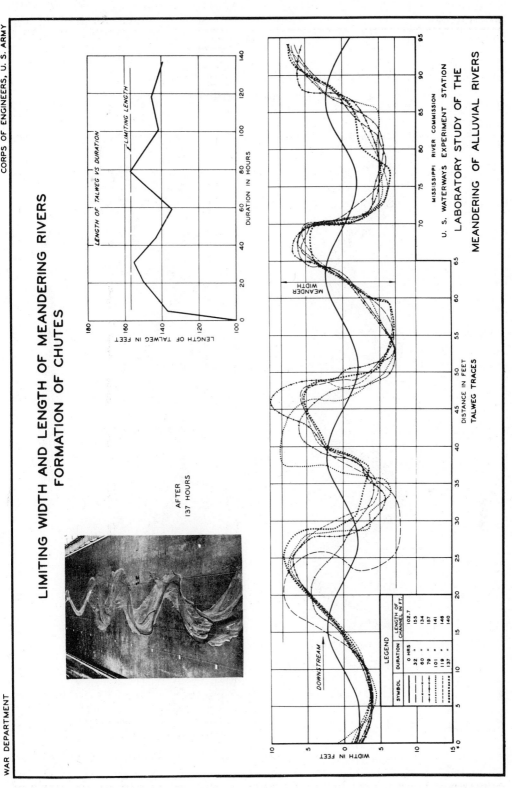

AFTER
137 HOURS

MISSISSIPPI RIVER COMMISSION
U. S. WATERWAYS EXPERIMENT STATION
LABORATORY STUDY OF THE
MEANDERING OF ALLUVIAL RIVERS

PLATE 23

273

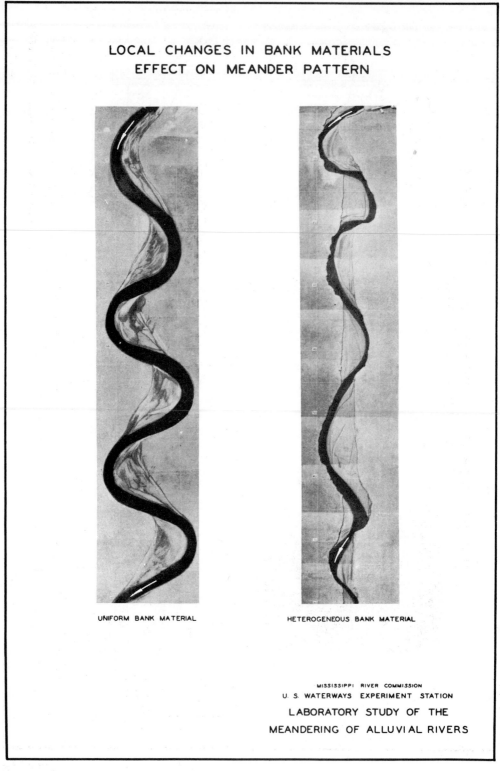

LOCAL CHANGES IN BANK MATERIALS
EFFECT ON MEANDER PATTERN

UNIFORM BANK MATERIAL

HETEROGENEOUS BANK MATERIAL

MISSISSIPPI RIVER COMMISSION
U. S. WATERWAYS EXPERIMENT STATION
LABORATORY STUDY OF THE
MEANDERING OF ALLUVIAL RIVERS

PLATE 24

channel was developed by a constant flow of 0.10 cfs. It is to be noted in the fourth bend that the flow was beginning to short-cut over the bar. The photograph on the right shows that after 10 hours of flow the stream completely abandoned its former channel in the fourth bend and was beginning to develop a new bend farther downstream. It is also to be noted that the stream developed a chute in the third bend and abandoned the former channel in this bend. This stream, beginning with a length of 48 ft, reached a maximum length of 65 ft before it shortened its channel.

The photograph on the left in the lower half of plate 22 shows a meandering channel developed by a flow of 0.05 cfs after six hours. At this time the stream was approaching its limiting width, and length of 63 ft. The photograph on the right taken after 10 hours of flow shows that the stream abandoned the upper part of the fourth bend and made a new bend farther downstream. The fifth bend was also completely abandoned. It is noted that the limiting width of bends with 0.05 cfs was less than with 0.10 cfs.

The photograph on plate 23 shows a small-scale river after a relatively long period of natural meandering. The talweg traces show the various channels occupied by the stream, and the graph shows the varying length of the talweg traces. It is to be noted that throughout the meandering of this stream, the bends did not develop laterally beyond nearly fixed limits. The curve of the length of talweg versus duration of time shows that the river reached a maximum length of about 155 ft, shortened its length because of chute development, again attained approximately the same length, and again shortened.

Analysis and discussion. It is important to note that even with a constant rate of flow, the small-scale rivers did not reach a stable condition when they attained their maximum width and length. As the bends elongated laterally, bank erosion did become less; however, before bank erosion stopped, the bends reached their limiting length and curvature, and chutes developed. The tests showed that the greater the flow, the greater was the lateral extent of bends before chutes developed. It appeared that the maximum width of a bend is attained and a chute develops when the bend increases its length and curvature to the extent that resistance to flow is less over the bar than through the bend. It was observed in some tests that the increased resistance to flow, because of the development of a sharp bend, often caused a chute to form, even though the bend did not reach the general maximum width of bends.

There is another and probably more common cause for the formation of chutes. Changes in the alignment upstream, such that the flow is directed across the bar of a bend, will cause chutes to form. Frequently, it is difficult to determine which of these causes predominates in the formation of a chute.

Local Changes in Bank Materials
Effect on Meander Pattern

Uniform bank materials were used in practically all laboratory streams in order to reduce the phenomenon to its simplest terms, and nearly uniform bends developed. In nature the bends of a meandering river are quite dissimilar in shape. It seems clear that this difference is brought about by local variations in the bank materials and this deduction is verified by the following tests.

Tests. Plate 24 shows a typical laboratory stream in uniform bank material and a typical laboratory stream in heterogeneous material. In the stream on the left, the bank material was uniform and easily eroded. In the stream on the right, the bank material contained a small per cent of cement which was not evenly distributed through the banks. The results are evident. In the uniform material perfectly uniform meanders developed, and in the heterogeneous material there was a wide dissimilarity between bends. Some bends were long with easy curvature, and some were sharp.

Analysis and discussion. The laboratory rivers with uniform bank material showed that there was a marked tendency for an initial bend to result in a series of uniform bends downstream. No such tendency was found in the stream in which the bank material was not uniform. The shape of each bend and the direction of flow into the bend below

275

was determined by the rate of erosion in each bend. Therefore, while there is a tendency for the changes in one bend to affect the alignment of several bends downstream, the extent of this tendency depends upon local differences in the bank material.

Further evidence of the effect of tough banks on the channel cross sections was given by these two streams. In the easily eroded bank material, a relatively wide shallow channel developed, while in the cemented material, the channel was deeper and had less width.

Cause of Natural Cut-Offs

Natural cut-offs occur when a meandering river develops and finally erodes through a narrow neck between the upper and lower arms of a bend. A sketch of a typical cut-off is shown on plate 25. In over 50 laboratory streams in uniform materials not a single cut-off of this type developed. This fact indicates that natural cut-offs result from local differences in the erodibility of bank materials.

Test. The development of a typical laboratory meandering river in uniform materials is shown on the left on plate 25. It is to be noted that as the bends developed laterally, they also migrated downstream at practically the same rate. It is also to be noted that there was no tendency for the stream to erode its banks so that the flow was directed back up the valley, as occurs in some natural cut-offs. After the last survey was taken, after 10 hours of flow, the stream shortened by making chutes, but no neck cut-offs occurred. This meander pattern was developed by a constant bankfull flow; however, plate 13 shows a stream in which the discharges were doubled and considerable overbank flow occurred. The overbank flows developed chutes through practically all bends, but no cut-offs occurred.

Analysis and discussion. With all bends in a meandering river migrating down the valley at the same rate, a cut-off cannot possibly develop. The upper arm of a bend never catches up with the lower arm. For a natural cut-off to develop, erosion on the downstream bank of the lower arm of a bend must be slower than along the upper arm. Generally, when a cut-off develops, erosion in the bend proper has taken place so that the flow in the lower arm of the bend has become directed up-valley as shown in the sketch, and a narrow neck has developed. It is, therefore, indicated that it is the local differences in erodibility of the bank materials in natural rivers which cause narrow necks to form and cut-offs to develop.

Braided Rivers

Rivers are described as braided when the channel is extremely wide and shallow and the flow passes through a number of small interlaced channels separated by bars. There is little or no erosion of the main banks. The channel as a whole does not meander, although local meandering in minor channels generally occurs. The following test showed that braiding results when the banks of a channel are extremely easily eroded.

Test. The braided river shown on plate 26 is the downstream part of a laboratory river which started from a straight channel except for an initiating bend. This stream at first developed a series of bends, but erosion of banks was so rapid that the channel in the bendway became as shallow as the bars. The flow overran the bars and dispersed through the channel, as shown in the photograph. No sand was fed at the entrance of this stream; braiding resulted solely from excessive bank erosion. As the channel shoaled and the bed of the river raised, the slope became steeper.

Analysis and discussion. Braided rivers are often termed "overloaded rivers" and are often associated with steep slopes. This was verified by these tests, but primarily because the banks were extremely easily eroded and a wide shallow channel resulted. Whether or not a flow becomes overloaded with bed load depends upon the velocity as well as on the amount of bed load entering a section of river. The velocity in turn depends upon the slope and shape of the cross sections. In resistant banks, a deep narrow channel with low slopes can develop the same velocity and carry as much bed load as a wide shallow channel on a steep slope. This test may not be considered a valid example

276

CAUSE OF NATURAL CUT-OFFS

DEVELOPMENT OF
NATURAL CUT-OFF

DEVELOPMENT OF LABORATORY
MEANDERING RIVER IN UNIFORM BANK MATERIALS

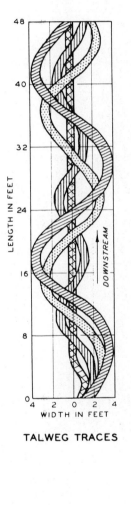

SKETCH OF CONDITIONS
JUST PRIOR TO NATURAL CUT-OFF

TALWEG TRACES

LEGEND

INITIAL CHANNEL
AFTER 3 HOURS OF FLOW
AFTER 6 HOURS OF FLOW
AFTER 10 HOURS OF FLOW

MISSISSIPPI RIVER COMMISSION
U. S. WATERWAYS EXPERIMENT STATION

LABORATORY STUDY OF THE

MEANDERING OF ALLUVIAL RIVERS

PLATE 25

BRAIDED RIVER

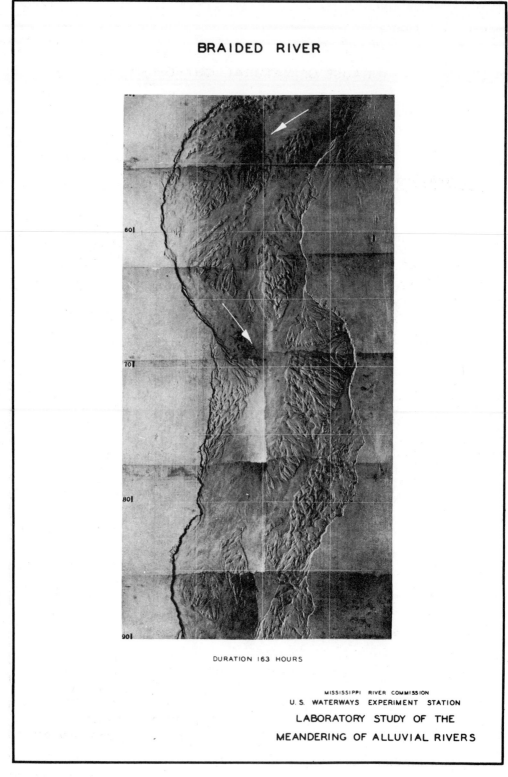

DURATION 163 HOURS

MISSISSIPPI RIVER COMMISSION
U. S. WATERWAYS EXPERIMENT STATION

LABORATORY STUDY OF THE
MEANDERING OF ALLUVIAL RIVERS

PLATE 26

of a braided river because no sand was entering at the head of the laboratory river; however, for this same reason, this test clearly illustrates that a braided channel results when the banks are extremely easily eroded.

Reference is made to the test shown on plate 2, where the flow developed a sinuous course from a straight channel. Actually the channel in this test was on the border line between a meandering and braided channel.

Reaches

Between meandering channels and braided channels there is an intermediate type of channel in which the alignment is nearly straight and the flow is divided by only a few bars or islands. This type of channel is termed a reach and is commonly found between meandering sections of a river. On the Lower Mississippi River from Cairo to Baton Rouge at least 20 per cent of the river's length is made up of reaches. This type of channel seems to develop and persist for two closely related reasons: first, the flow lacks a positive angle of attack against a bank; and second, the channel is wide and shoaled because of the ease with which the banks erode. The lack of a positive attack against a bank results in a wide shoaled channel, and a wide shoaled channel keeps the flow dispersed and prevents the formation of a positive attack against a bank.

Resume of Types of Channels and Erodibility of Banks

The results of this entire study stress the importance of the rate of bank erosion on the type of channel developed by alluvial rivers. In the first type, where the banks were entirely resistant to erosion, a deep narrow channel developed with extremely flat slopes. In the second type, where the banks eroded slowly, a slowly meandering relatively deep channel with fairly flat slopes developed. In the third type, which had easily eroded banks, a wide shallow meandering channel developed with fairly steep slopes. In the fourth type, with extremely erodible banks, a braided type of river resulted with extremely steep slopes. Between the third and fourth types there is the reach type of channel in which the cross sections are wide and shallow, and the flow is divided by only a few bars or islands.

Combination of Principles and Other Aspects

In order to tie together all the individual principles and other aspects as shown by these tests, the following paragraphs describe their application to the general meandering characteristics of the Lower Mississippi River, and are believed to apply generally to every meandering river in alluvium.

To obtain an understanding of the general meandering characteristics, it is necessary to begin with the alluviation of the valley[1]. At that time the flow with its sediment from the watershed entered a basin in which the slopes were too flat for the flow to carry its sediment to the sea. Deposition took place in the basin until a slope was built up which enabled the flow to carry its load. In the upstream part of the alluvial valley the coarser sediments deposited, the fine sediments were carried downstream to the mid-part of the valley, and finer sediments were deposited in the lower part of the valley. The alluvial sediments which then make up the banks of the river consist generally of coarse sediments which have little cohesion in the upper part of the valley, fairly fine sediments which have some cohesion in the mid-part, and finer sediments which have considerable cohesion in the lower part.

In the upper part of the valley, in the easily eroded sediments, the flow developed relatively wide and shallow cross sections and a relatively steep valley slope. This is the valley slope which was required for the flow to develop velocities sufficient to carry its sediment without further over-all aggradation in the wide and shallow cross sections. In the mid-part of the valley, where the banks have more cohesion, deeper cross sections and somewhat flatter valley slopes developed. In the lower part of the valley in the very

---

[1] The general conditions of valley alluviation were taken from "Geological Investigation of the Alluvial Valley of the Lower Mississippi River," by Harold N. Fisk, Ph. D., 1 December 1944.

cohesive material, the cross sections became still deeper, and even flatter valley slopes developed. There is another reason why the slopes became flatter downstream. As the sediments which make up the banks of the river become finer in size, the load also becomes finer because of bank caving and trading of sediments. Therefore, less slope and less velocity are required to carry the finer load in the lower parts of the valley. The present general picture is a river flowing in sediments which are generally increasing in their cohesive properties downstream, through cross sections which are comparatively wide and shallow in the upstream sections and become narrower and deeper downstream, and on valley slopes which gradually decrease downstream.

With the resulting slopes and velocities, the flow has the power to erode and cave its banks. This results in meandering. The flow develops a series of continually changing bends in which it deposits sand on the bars and picks up sand from caving banks. The channel is deep in the bends because of the impingement and turbulence set up along the concave banks and because of confinement of the flow by the bars. For the given discharges and slopes, the shape of each bend depends upon the alignment of the flow into the bends. The nearly uniform bends found in laboratory rivers do not develop. Local differences in erodibility of the bank materials change the shape of bends, and the alignment into and shape of bends downstream. The result is that no two bends are alike. The sand which enters the channel at Cairo and from tributaries travels but a short distance before it deposits on bars and is replaced by sand from caving banks. In turn, the sand from caving banks travels but a short distance before it deposits on bars and is replaced by sand from other caving banks. This process continues throughout the river. However, the rate of trading of sediments is generally irregular because of the varying alignment and varying rate of bank erosion. The river forms chutes when the bends become too long or when the alignment into a bend changes so that the flow is directed across the convex bar. Cut-offs occur when local resistant banks prevent the normal downstream migration of a bend, and a narrow neck forms between the upper and lower arms. The river does not consist of a continuous series of bends; reaches often occur where the channel is wide and shallow.

In the upper part of the valley where the sediments are comparatively easily eroded and the slope is steeper, meandering is not more rapid than farther downstream (see plate 8); the easily eroded materials and steeper slopes are counterbalanced by the wider and shallower cross sections which tend to reduce the velocities and eroding power of the flow. Reaches, where the flow is often divided by islands, occur frequently in the upper part of the river because of the wide shallow cross sections and the lack of a positive attack against banks. In the mid-part of the valley where banks are more resistant to erosion and slopes are somewhat flatter, bank erosion and meandering are more rapid than in the upstream part, because the flow is more confined. Reach sections are less frequent in this part. In the lower part of the valley, the meandering and trading of sediments are slow because of the extreme resistance of bank materials to erosion. The maximum width of bends does not differ materially in the upper and lower parts of the river. The lack of slope in the lower parts is compensated for by the increased depth and efficiency of cross sections. Throughout the river some bends are elongating, others are developing chutes, and occasionally natural cut-offs occur, so that on the whole the length of river fluctuates within fairly narrow limits.

For simplicity, flow has been discussed as if it were a single discharge. Actually, each flow during the rise and fall plays an important part in the river's behavior. The low flows scour the crossings and often attack the concave banks in the upstream parts of bends. The intermediate flows tend to make longer bends, attack the concave banks in the mid-parts of bends, and deposit sand along the edges of bars. The highest flows tend to make even longer bends, attack the concave banks along the downstream parts of bends, and deposit sand along the tops of bars.

Throughout its length the river is continually changing its meander pattern because bank erosion never stops. The meandering is augmented by changes in stage, by local changes in bank materials, and accompanying changes in alignment. Locally the channel is very unstable because of the different rates of bank erosion and the varying relationship between the flow and its burden of sand. However, over long sections of river the average cross sections maintain about the same area, and the average slopes remain about the same.

References

2   Fargue, M., 1868, Etude sur la corrélation entre la configuration du lit et la profondeur d'eau dans les rivieres a fond mobile: *Annales Ponts et Chausseés, Memoires et Documents.*

9   Lacey, J. M., 1922-1923, Some problems connected with rivers and canals in southern India: *Inst. Civil Eng. Proc.*, V. 216.

11 Teubert, Oskar, 1932, *Binnenschiffahrt,* , Leipzig, Engelmann.

17 Schoklitsch, A., 1937, *Hydraulic Structures,* translated by Samuel Shulits, translation reviewed by L. G. Straub, Amer. Soc. Mech. Eng.

18 Chatley, Herbert, 1938, Hydraulics of large rivers: *Civil Eng. Public Works Rev.*, Feb. 1938.

27 Gilbert, G. K., 1914, Transportation of debris by running water: U. S. Geol. Survey Prof. Paper 86.

29 U. S. Waterways Exp. Station, 1935, Studies of river materials and their movement with special reference to the lower Mississippi River, Paper 17, Mississippi River Comm., Vicksburg.

30 Johnson, J. W., 1943, Laboratory investigations of bed load transportation and bed roughness: Soil Conservation Service Tech. Pub. 50.

32 Corps of Engineers, 1932, Unpublished report, Experimental investigation of movement of material in Merriwether and Tamm Bend with coal and chat: U.S. Engineer Office, Memphis, Tenn.

33 Wright, C. A., 1936, Experimental study of the scour of a sandy river bed by clear and muddy water: *J. Res. Nat. Bur. Standards*, V. 17, pp. 193-206.

34 Thomsen, James, 1876, *Royal Society Land Proc.*, Mar. 1876.

37 Engels, H., 1926, Movement of sedimentary materials in river bends, in *Hydraulic Laboratory Practice* (J. R. Freeman, ed.), Amer. Soc. Mech. Eng., p. 105.

38 Engels, H., and Kramer, Hans, 1932, Large scale experiments in river hydraulics: *Civil Eng.*, V. 2, Nov. 1932.

46 Jefferson, M. S., 1902, Limiting width of meander belts: *Nat. Geogr. Mag.*, V. 13, pp. 373–384.

48 Eakin, H. M., 1911, the influence of the Earth's rotation upon lateral erosion of streams: *J. Geol.*, V. 18, pp. 435–437.

51 Russell, R. J., 1936, Physiography of lower Mississippi Delta, Reports Geology of Plaquemines and St. Bernard Parishes: *La. Geol. Survey Bull. 8.*

54 Bates, R. E., 1939, Geomorphic history of Kickapoo region, Wisconsin: *Geol. Soc. Amer. Bull.* V. 50, pp. 819–880.

56 von Engeln, O. D., 1942, *Geomorphology*, McGraw-Hill, New York.

57 Fisk, H. N., 1945, Geological investigation of the alluvial valley of the lower Mississippi River: Miss. River Comm., Vicksburg.

58 Tiffany, J. B., and Nelson, G. A., 1939, Studies of meandering of model streams, *Amer. Geophys. Union Trans.*, 1939, part 4, pp. 644–649.

60 Quraishy, M. S., 1943, River meandering and the Earth's rotation: *Current Sci.*, Oct. 1943.

281

River Channel Patterns: Braided, Meandering and Straight

By LUNA B. LEOPOLD *and* M. GORDON WOLMAN

14

PHYSIOGRAPHIC AND HYDRAULIC STUDIES OF RIVERS

GEOLOGICAL SURVEY PROFESSIONAL PAPER 282-B

UNITED STATES GOVERNMENT PRINTING OFFICE, WASHINGTON : 1957

From the consistency with which rivers of all sizes increase in size downstream, it can be inferred that the physical laws governing the formation of the channel of a great river are the same as those operating in a small one. One step toward understanding the mechanisms by which these laws operate in a river is to describe many rivers of various kinds.

This study is primarily concerned with channel pattern; that is, with the plan view of a channel as seen from an airplane. In such a discussion some consideration must also be given to channel shape. Shape, as we shall use it, refers to the shape of the river cross section and the changes in shape which are observed as one proceeds along the stream, both headward to the ultimate rills and downstream to the master rivers. Because the shape of the cross section of flowing water varies, depending upon whether the river is in flood or flowing at low flow, shape must take into consideration the characteristics of river action at various stages of flow.

The channel pattern refers to limited reaches of the river that can be defined as straight, sinuous, meandering, or braided. Channel patterns do not fall easily into well-defined categories for, as will be discussed, there is a gradual merging of one pattern into another. The difference between a sinuous course and a meandering one is a matter of degree and a question of how symmetrical are the successive bends. Similarly, there is a gradation between the occurrence of scattered islands and a truly braided pattern.

The interrelationship between channels of different patterns is the subject of this study. Because neither braided channels nor straight channels have received the attention in the literature that meanders have, our observations of these patterns precede the discussion of the interrelations between channels of different patterns.

STAGES IN THE DEVELOPMENT OF A BRAID

These observations suggest a sequence of events in the development of a braided reach. In an originally single or undivided channel, a short, submerged central bar is deposited during a high flow. The head of the new gravel bar is composed of the coarse fraction of the bed load which is moving down the center of the channel bed. Because of some local condition not all the coarse particles are transported through this particular reach and some accumulate in the center of the channel. Most of the smaller particles move over and past the incipient bar, but part of the finer fraction is trapped by the coarser material and so deposited. Though the depth is gradually reduced, velocity over the growing bar tends to remain undiminished or even to increase so that some particles moving along the

bar near the center of the channel roll along the length of the new bar and are deposited beyond the lower end where a marked increase in depth is associated with a decrease in velocity. Thus the bar grows by successive addition at its downstream end, and presumably by some addition along the margins. The downstream growth is suggested by the fact that willows became established at the upstream tip while the downstream portions were still bare. A similar gradation in age of vegetation exists in many other islands studied.

The growth of the gravel bar at first does not affect the width of the stream, but when the bar gets large enough, the channels along its sides are insufficient in width to remain stable. Widening then occurs by trimming the edges of the central bar and by cutting laterally against the original sides of the channel until a stable width has been attained. At the same time, some deepening of the flanking channels may occur and the bar emerges as an island. The bar gradually becomes stabilized by vegetation. At some stage lateral cutting against the bar to provide increased channel width becomes just as difficult as against the banks of the original channel, and so the bar is not eliminated. The hydraulic properties of the channel during this process of island formation will be discussed in a later section.

After the island has been formed, the new channels in the divided reach may become subdivided in the same manner. As successive division occurs, the amount of water carried by an individual channel tends to diminish so that in some of these, vegetation prevents further erosion and, by screening action, promotes deposition.

CHANGES ASSOCIATED WITH CHANNEL DIVISION

FLUME EXPERIMENTS

Experimental work in a flume at California Institute of Technology allowed us to test the hypothesis of bar deposition just outlined. The observations made in the laboratory provide some insight into not only the sequence of events leading to braiding but also into the hydraulic relations between the divided and undivided reaches of channel. First, the progressive development of braids in the flume will be discussed and compared with field examples. Second, the interrelations of hydraulic factors in both the laboratory and natural rivers will be analyzed.

The 60-foot flume had a width of about 3 feet and was filled to a depth of about 5 inches with a poorly sorted medium sand (identical to run 1, app. A).

It is important to emphasize the fact that the channel developed in the flume was not a model river but was the prototype of a small stream. The flume-river adjusted not only its slope, but also its depth and width.

The first example showing the development of a braided reach is a set of runs (6a, b and 8) in which the initial channel cut by the template was 15 inches wide and 1½ inches deep. For these runs the flume was set at a slope of 0.0114. The discharge was 0.085 cfs, and load was introduced at the rate of 120 g per minute or a sediment concentration, C_s, of 830 ppm by weight. Customarily, the initial width of channel increased very rapidly through the action of the flowing water and

attained a minimum value which was stable for the given discharge. In the river being discussed, the average stable width for a discharge of 0.085 cfs was 1.1 feet, The template channel being 1.25 feet (15 inches). slightly larger than the minimum stable value, there was no rapid adjustment. During 22 hours of flow (interrupted for purposes of measurement) a series of bars and islands developed in a 12-foot reach between stations 10–22. The lower end of the entrance box was

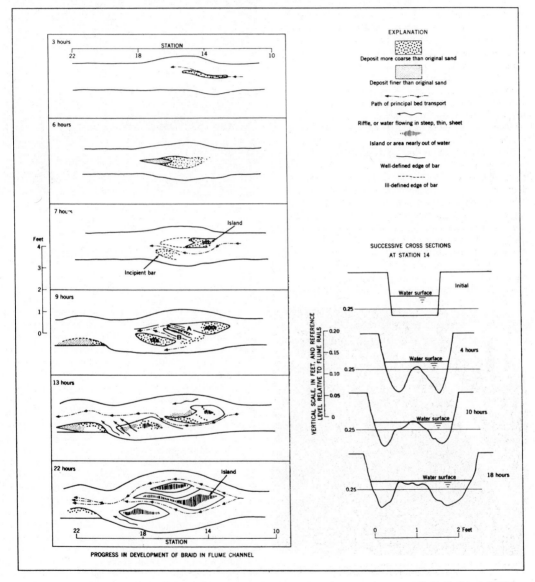

FIGURE 34.—Sketches and cross sections showing progress in development of braid in flume-river (February 16–22, 1954, runs 6–8.)   (Profiles shown in fig. 38.)

285

at station 3, which means that the head of the braided reach was 7 feet downstream from the entrance.

The sequence of stages in the development of this braided reach is shown in figure 34, which includes sketches made of the pattern at various stages and detailed cross sections at one position or station along the flume. A photograph of this braid looking upstream is shown in figure 35. At the end of 3 hours of flow the development of a central submerged bar had proceeded so far that its lower end had caused some deflection of the flow toward the right bank. This resulted in a small arcuate reentrant in the formerly straight bank. The head of the submerged bar had similarly caused some cutting on the left bank. The cross sections shown at the right of figure 34 were taken by means of the point gage on the traveling carriage after the load and water were temporarily stopped. The stopping and starting had little effect on the configuration of the bed.

The cross section at station 14 after 4 hours of flow shows the pronounced central ridge or submerged bar. It should be noted, however, that in the upper left diagram showing the plan view at 3 hours, the band of principal bed transport lies *on top of the submerged central bar*. The grain movement in the deeper parts of the channel adjacent to the central bar was usually negligible in the early stage of island development. The central bar continued to build closer to the water surface yet the principal zone of movement remained for a time along the top of the building bar. It was there that some of the larger particles stopped, trapping

FIGURE 36.—Island formed in a braided reach of the flume-river (April 8, 1954, 7:15 a. m., run 30, stations 6-9.)

smaller particles in the building bar. These smaller grains could have been moved by the existing flow had they not become protected or blocked by larger grains.

The central bar in the flume-river was caused by local sorting, the larger particles being deposited in the center of the stream at some place where local competence was insufficient to move them. But, as explained, bar building by sorting does not imply that the deposit is composed only of grains too large to be moved further (see app. B). The sketches of the developing braided reach show an irregular distribution of well-sorted fine material, usually deposited near the toe or downstream edge of the bar where progressive bar development consisted of foreset beds as in a delta. The continual shifting of the channels, then, builds a heterogeneous bar consisting of patches of materials of different size and different degrees of sorting.

By the end of 7 hours of flow the central bar had been built so high that individual grains rolling along its ridge actually "broke" the water surface. Leopold and Miller had noted previously (1956, p. 6) that in arroyos, many large pebbles and cobbles were observed to roll in flows of depth only half the diameter of the rolling stone. By such a process a true island cannot be formed in uniform discharge. However, the deflection of the water by the central bar usually caused local scour in some part of the channels separated by the

FIGURE 35.—Braided channel developed in flume (February 19, 1954, runs 6-8, 2 p. m.) Note similarity to Horse Creek, figure 30.

central bar, and this scour caused a lowering of the water surface which left the bar sticking out of the water as a real island. Such scour was observed in many of the runs and the islands which are indicated in the sketches in figure 34 emerged as a result of this process. This condition is also shown in figure 36, a photograph of a developing island.

The area designated as "incipient bar" in figure 34 at hour 7 had enlarged and emerged as an island by hour 9. Furthermore, after hour 9 of flow a linear bar had developed in the channel area between the two islands, bisecting the flow into two parts, marked A and B. By hour 13, continued bar building in channel A and subsequent lowering of the channel B diverted most of the water out of the old channel A and the primary zone of transport over the bar area was restricted to channel B.

Similar sequences continued to change the configuration of the braided reach, moving the principal zones of transport from one place to another, and at hour 22 there were three island areas. It should be understood that in the flume-river the constant discharge did not permit the islands to receive any increment of deposition after emergence so that an "island" actually represented merely the highest knob of a bar most of which remains submerged. The cross section of station 14 at hour 18 (bottom diagram, right side, fig. 34) illustrates this feature.

Nearly all observers who have recorded notes on the action of a braided stream have remarked on the shifting of bars and the caving of banks. Once a bar is deposited it does not necessarily remain fixed in form, contour, or position. This can be seen in the successive cross sections of four stations made during the run pictured in figure 37. Time changes at a particular position are arranged side by side and the downstream variation at a particular time can be seen in the vertical groups. A reference level is given for each section so that the changes of water surface elevation can be compared. The sections grouped on the uppermost horizontal line are at station 6. Comparing the sections from left to right it can be seen that station 6 underwent continued aggradation and the shape of the cross section changed radically, much more than did the area of the cross section.

The horizontally arranged group of sketches at station 10 illustrate the varying elevation of water surface which rose between hours 1½ and 4, fell from hours 4 to 6, and rose again from hours 6 to 11. The fall of water surface elevation is clearly due to the scour of the right-hand channel between hours 4 and 6.

The initial linear nature of the central bar is best illustrated at 6 hours where a central ridge is present through an 11-foot reach between stations 6 and 17.

This is shown on the sketch of the plan view in the lower right part of figure 37 and on the cross sections for that time arranged vertically on the figure.

The growth and subsequent erosion of a central bar is also illustrated at station 10 (fig. 37). On the left-hand diagram of station 10 the shape of the initial channel molded by template is shown as a dashed line. After 1½ hours this shape had been altered by the building of a central bar and by slight degradation of the channels beside the bar. By the end of 4 hours the combination of lateral building and deposition on the bar surface had widended the bar and made a double crest. Bar building resulted in a diversion of most of the water into the right channel at station 10 which caused local scouring.

DIVIDED AND UNDIVIDED REACHES IN THE FLUME AND IN NATURAL RIVERS

In both natural streams and the flume-river the slope of the divided reach proved to be greater than that of the undivided reach. The steepening of the divided reach in the flume is very marked. Figure 38 shows the water surface profile data associated with runs 6a and b and 8, February 16–22, 1954. The measurements presented in the left part of the figure are interpreted diagrammatically on the right half of the figure. When considering the measurements it must be recalled that the elevation of the water surface was measured relative to a sloping datum. Thus, water surface profiles which rise downstream relative to the datum mean that the water surface became adjusted to a slope less than that of the flume rails. This can be seen by reference to the diagrammatic profiles on the right of figure 38 where the initial profile, shown as a heavy line, represents the slope of the water surface when the run began and the water started to flow down a channel parallel to the sloping rails. By the end of 9 hours, aggradation had taken place in the reach between station 6 and station 12, and also downstream from station 35. Degradation of the initial channel had occurred between stations 15 and 35 with the establishment of a steep reach in the divided or braided section.

Between hours 9 and 20 of flow, continued aggradation took place in the divided reach but, in general, the steep slope was maintained approximately parallel to that which existed at the end of hour 9. Similarly, the aggrading reach downstream from station 20 maintained nearly the same average slope as that which existed at hour 9, this slope being much flatter than that of the divided or braided reach. A similar sequence can be observed in the profiles presented in the lower left-hand part of figure 37 (associated with run 17, March 11–12). In figure 37 it can be seen that between hours 1½ and 4, the reach from station 10 to

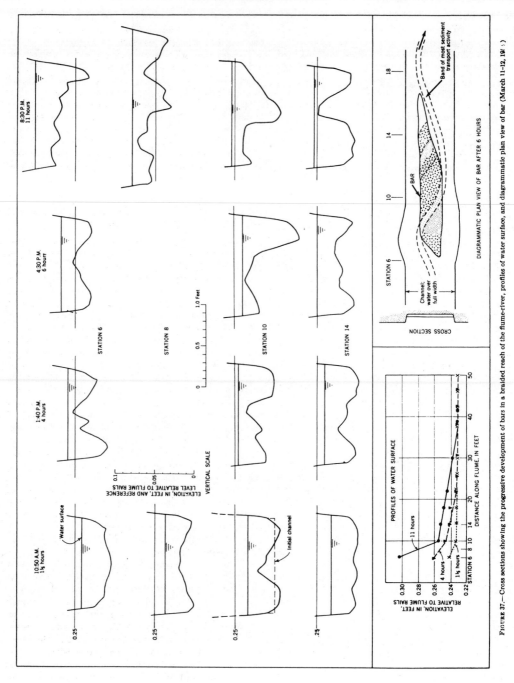

FIGURE 37.—Cross sections showing the progressive development of bars in a braided reach of the flume-river, profiles of water surface, and diagrammatic plan view of bar (March 11–12, 19).

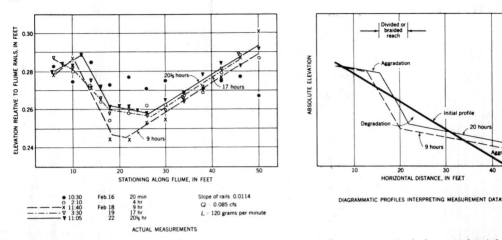

ACTUAL MEASUREMENTS

● 10:30	Feb. 16	20 min	Slope of rails 0.0114
○ 2:10		4 hr	
——×—— 11:40	Feb 18	9 hr	Q 0.085 cfs
——▽—— 3:30	19	17 hr	L = 120 grams per minute
——▼—— 11:05	22	20½ hr	

DIAGRAMMATIC PROFILES INTERPRETING MEASUREMENT DATA

FIGURE 38.—Measured and diagrammatic profiles of flume-river during run of February 16–22, 1954. (Plan view and cross sections for these runs are shown in fig. 34.)

station 22 steepened markedly, but from hours 4 to 11 aggradation occurred at approximately the same slope which existed in this downstream reach at hour 4. In the braided reach upstream from station 10, however, continued aggradation was accompanied by continued steepening between hours 4 and 11.

It is important to note in these runs that *aggradation could take place at a constant slope* without braiding even when the total load exceeded the capacity of the channel for transport. Braiding is developed by sorting as the stream leaves behind those sizes of the load which it is incompetent to handle. If such sorting results in progressive coarsening of the bed material then the slope increases progressively If the stream is competent to move all sizes comprising the load but is unable to move the total quantity provided to it, then aggradation may take place without braiding. Hence, contrary to the assumption often made, the action in the flume river suggests that braiding is not a consequence of aggradation alone. This is brought out in flume runs 30a to 35 which are discussed later in relation to the adjustment of slope in natural channels.

Although the steepening of slope in the divided reach is one of the more obvious of the observed changes in the channel associated with division around an island, nearly all other hydraulic parameters are also affected. Detailed comparisons of an undivided channel and a channel divided around an island, or a potential island, are available for three river reaches and four runs in the flume-river. These comparisons are presented in table 1. (Complete data are tabulated in app. D). Comparisons are shown as ratios of the measurements in the divided reach to similar measurements in the undivided one. The width in a reach containing an

TABLE 1.—*Ratio of hydraulic factors of divided to undivided reaches of braided streams (natural rivers and flume-river)*

	Green River near Daniel. Wyo.	New Fork River near Pinedale, Wyo.		Flume at California Institute of Technology			
		Reach 1 (1953)	Reach 2 (1954)	Feb. 15 Sta. 10 and 14	Feb. 16 Sta. 14 and 22	Feb. 18 Sta. 10 and 14	Mar. 5 Sta. 12 and 38
Area	1.3	1.03	1.6	0.94	1.08	0.78	1.07
Width	1.56	1.83	2.0	1.05	1.34	1.48	1.70
Depth	.88	.56	.79	.90	.80	.52	.63
Velocity	.77	.97		1.06	.93	1.27	.93
Slope	5.7	2.3	1.4	1.3	1.4	1.9	1.7
Darcy-Weisbach resistance factor	10.5	1.3		1.1	1.3	.63	1.25

island is the width of flowing water. The width of the undivided reach is the width of the water surface upstream or downstream from the island or where there is but a single channel.

All examples show that channel division is associated with increased width of water surface, increased slope, and with decreased depth. In the three comparisons from our measurements of natural rivers the sum of the widths of the divided channels ranges from 1.6 to 2.0 times that of the undivided one. In the four comparisons made in the flume the ratios vary from 1.05 to 1.70.

This increase in water surface width caused by development of a bar or an island is accompanied by a decrease in mean depth. The mean depth of the divided reach was computed by dividing the cross-sectional area of flowing water by the total width of water surface in the two channels. The ratio of depths in the divided reach to depth in the undivided reach varied from 0.6 to 0.9 in natural rivers and from 0.5 to 0.9 in the flume-river.

289

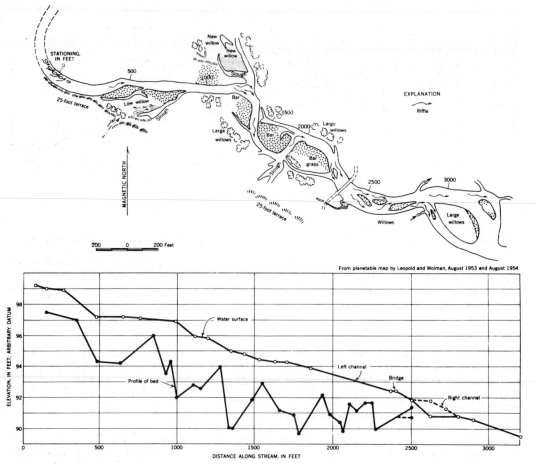

FIGURE 40.—Plan and profile of a braided reach of the New Fork River, 3.4 miles below Pinedale, Wyo.   (American Gothic reach.)

SUMMARY: THE BRAIDED RIVER

A braided river is one which flows in two or more anastomosing channels around alluvial islands. This study indicates that braided reaches taken as a whole are steeper, wider, and shallower than undivided reaches carrying the same flow. A mode of formation of a braided channel was demonstrated by a small stream in the laboratory. The braided pattern developed after deposition of an initial central bar. The bar consisted of coarse particles, which could not be transported under local conditions existing in that reach, and of finer material trapped among these coarser particles. This coarse fraction became the nucleus of the bar which subsequently grew into an island. Both in the laboratory-river and in its natural counterpart, Horse Creek near Daniel, Wyo., gradual formation of a central bar deflected the main current against the channel banks causing them to erode.

The braided pattern is one among many possible conditions which a river might establish for itself as a result of the adjustment of a number of variables to a set of independent controls. The requirements of channel adjustment may be met by a variety of possible combinations of velocity, cross-sectional area, and roughness. Braiding represents a particular combination, albeit a striking combination, of a set of variables in the continuum of river shapes and patterns.

Braiding is not necessarily an indication of excessive total load. A braided pattern once established, may be maintained with only slow modifications. The stability of the features in the braided reaches of Horse Creek suggests that rivers with braided patterns may be as close to quasi-equilibrium as are rivers possessing meandering or other patterns.

STRAIGHT CHANNELS

In the field it is relatively easy to find illustrations of either meandering or braided channels. The same cannot be said of straight channels. In our experience truly straight channels are so rare among natural rivers as to be almost nonexistent. Extremely short segments or reaches of the channel may be straight, but it can be stated as a generalization that reaches which are straight for distances exceeding ten times the channel width are rare.

THE WANDERING THALWEG

Figure 41 shows in plan and profile a reach of Valley Creek near Downingtown, Pa. For 500 feet this channel is straight in a reach where the alluvium of the valley is 30 feet thick. Its sinuosity (ratio of thalweg length to valley length) is practically 1.0.

The thalweg, or line of maximum depth, is indicated by a dashed line in the upper portion of figure 41. Though the channel itself is straight, the thalweg wanders back and forth from positions near one bank and then the other. This is typical of a number of nearly straight reaches which we have studied. The wandering thalweg is easier to see in the sketch shown in the lower part of figure 41 in which the position of the thalweg relative to a channel of uniform width is plotted.

Along with the wandering thalweg it is not uncommon to find deposits of mud adjacent to the banks of straight channels. These commonly occur in alternating (as opposed to "opposite") positions. A similar observation has been made by Schaffernak (1950, p. 45). The alternating mud "bars" are related to a thalweg which also moves alternately from bank to bank. In an idealized sense, this plan view of straight channels appears to bear a remarkable resemblance to a meander.

In a straight flume Quraishy (1944) observed that a series of alternating shoals formed in the channel. These he referred to as "skew shoals" (p. 36). Similarly, Brooks (1955, p. 668–8) called the condition in which low channel bars formed alternately adjacent to the left and right walls of his straight flume a "meander" condition.

POOLS AND RIFFLES

Another characteristic of natural streams even in straight reaches is the occurrence of pools and riffles. This has been noted by Pettis (1927), Dittbrenner (1954), and Wolman (1955). Figures 40, 42, and 43, respectively, the New Fork River near Pinedale, Wyo., the Middle River near Staunton, Va., and the Popo Agie near Hudson, Wyo., present plans and profiles for a braided reach, a straight reach, and a meandering reach. Profiles of these three examples are compared

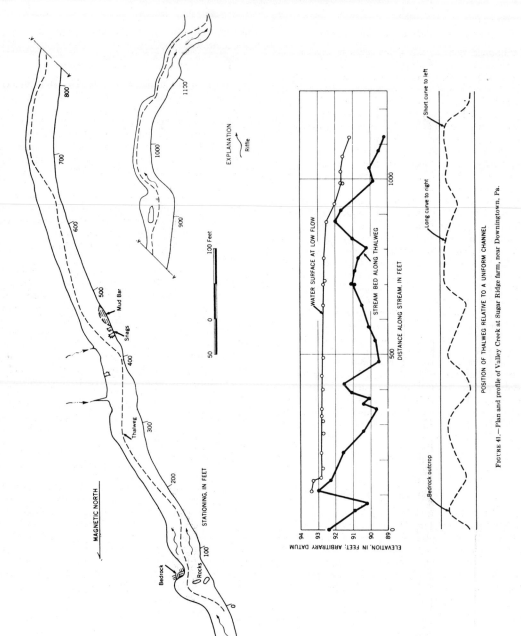

FIGURE 41.—Plan and profile of Valley Creek at Sugar Ridge farm, near Downingtown, Pa.

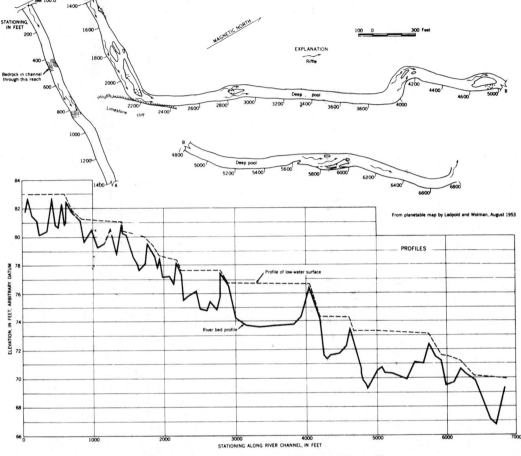

FIGURE 42.—Plan and profile of a reach of the Middle River near Staunton, Va.

in figure 44 which reveals a similarity in the profiles of streams possessed of very dissimilar patterns. Thus, *a straight channel implies neither a uniform stream bed nor a straight thalweg.*

As demonstrated first by Inglis (1949, p. 147), the wavelength of a meander is proportional to the square root of the "dominant discharge." One wavelength (a complete sine curve or 2π radians) encompasses twice the distance between successive points of inflection of the meander wave. It is well known that meandering channels characteristically are deep at the bend and shallow at the crossover or point of inflection. Thus, twice the distance between successive riffles in a straight reach appears analogous to the wavelength of a meander and should also be proportional to $Q^{0.5}$. As an initial test of this hypothesis, bankfull discharge, which we consider equivalent to "dominant discharge" of the Indian literature, has been plotted in figure 45A against wavelength of meanders. The figure includes data from straight reaches for which "wavelength" is twice the distance between successive riffles.

The data in figure 45, tabulated in appendix E, include measurements of rivers in India from Inglis (1949), our own field measurements, and some flume data from Friedkin (1945) and Brooks (1955 and personal communication). The wavelengths in Brooks' data obtained in a fixed-wall flume (no. 259, appendix E) represent, as in the nonmeandering natural channels, twice the distance between the "riffles," or low bars, which he observed.

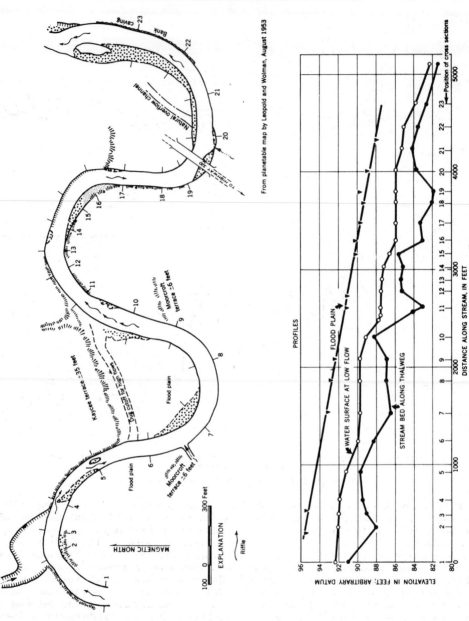

FIGURE 43.—Plan and profile of a meandering reach of the Popo Agie River near Hudson, Wyo.

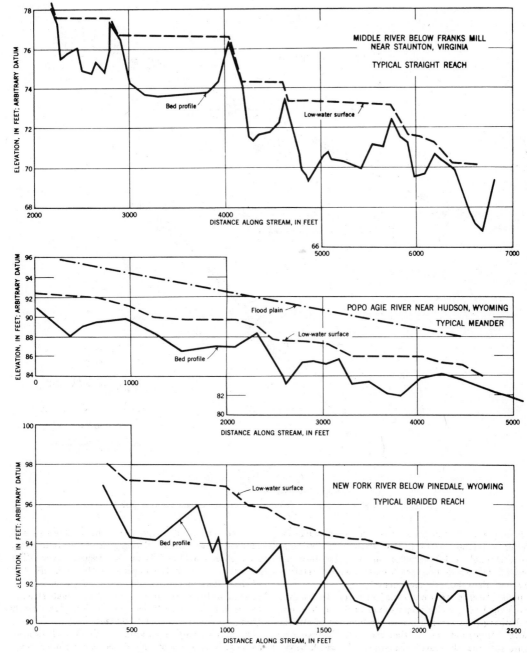

FIGURE 44.—Profiles of three rivers including straight, meandering, and braided reaches.

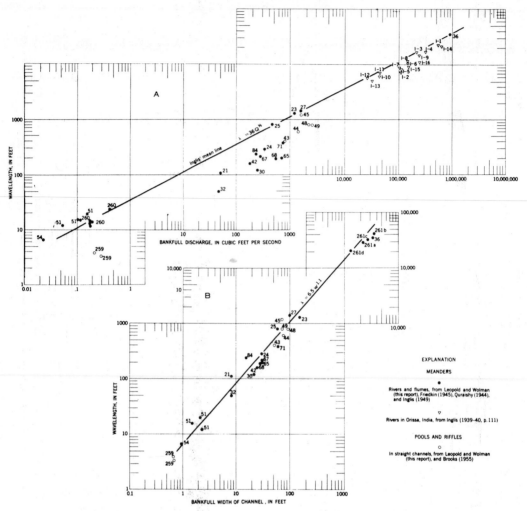

FIGURE 45.—Wavelength of meanders and of riffles as functions of bankfull discharge and channel width.

Figure 45A demonstrates that, with considerable scatter, a relation between wavelength and discharge exists through a 10^8 variation in Q. The data for straight channels do not vary from the average relation any more than those for meanders.

Inglis (1949, p. 144) had called attention to the fact that since width is also proportional to the square root of discharge, wavelength is a linear function of stream width. Inglis did not mention the fact, illustrated in figure 45B, that the scatter of points in the width-wavelength relation is less than that in the discharge wavelength relation. The relation in figure 45B is quite consistent though it includes straight channels as well as meanders, and the widths range from less than 1 foot in the flume to 1 mile in the Mississippi River. The line drawn through the plotted points in figure 45B indicates that in general, the ratio of wavelength to bankfull width varies from about 7 for small streams having widths of 1 to 10 feet, up to 15 for large rivers having widths in excess of 1,000 feet.

Dr. T. M. Prus-Chacinski has told us that European engineers have a rule-of-thumb that the meander wavelength is 15 times the channel width. That our ratio is 1:15 only for large rivers may possibly be influenced by the fact that our data show bankfull width rather than width at some lower stage. Our data indicate that the relation is not a constant ratio but a power function having an exponent slightly larger than 1.0, specifically $\lambda = 6.5w^{1.1}$

Comparison of figures 45A and 45B leads us to postulate that in terms of the mechanical principles governing meander formation and the formation of pools and riffles, the wavelength is more directly dependent on width than on discharge. It is argued later in this paper that in general, at a constant slope, channel width follows from discharge as a dependent variable. We suggest, therefore, that wavelength is dependent on width and thus depends only indirectly on discharge. That this relation describes both the distance between riffles in straight channels and the wavelength of meanders leads us to conclude that the processes which may lead to meanders are operative in straight channels.

SUMMARY: STRAIGHT CHANNELS

The observations discussed lead us to three tentative conclusions. First, pools and riffles are a fundamental characteristic of nearly all natural channels and are not confined to meanders. Second, river curves all tend to have a wavelength that is a function of stream width

and thus indirectly a function of discharge. Third, even straight channels exhibit some tendency for the flow to follow a sinuous path within the confines of their straight banks.

THE CONTINUUM OF CHANNELS OF DIFFERENT PATTERNS

The physical characteristics of the three specific channel patterns discussed in the preceding section suggest that all natural channel patterns intergrade. Braids and meanders are strikingly different but they actually represent extremes in an uninterrupted range of channel pattern. If we assume that the pattern of a stream is controlled by the mutual interaction of a number of variables, and the range of these variables in nature is continuous, then we should expect to find a complete range of channel patterns. A given reach of river may exhibit both braiding and meandering. In fact, Russell (1954) points out that the Meander River in Turkey, which gave us the term "meandering," has both braided and straight reaches.

This conception of transition in pattern or interrelation of channels of diverse pattern is supported by the data in figure 46 in which the average channel slope is plotted as a function of bankfull discharge (data tabu-

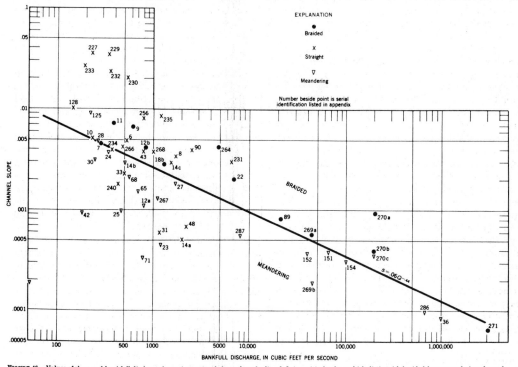

FIGURE 46.—Values of slope and bankfull discharge for various natural channels and a line defining critical values which distinguish braided from meandering channels.

297

lated in app. F). Meandering, braided, and straight channels are designated by different symbols. The reaches which have been called meanders are those in which the sinuosity, the ratio of thalweg length to valley length, is equal to or greater than 1.5. This value is an arbitrary one but in our experience where the sinuosity is 1.5 or greater, one would readily agree that the stream is a true meander. Many channels which appear to the eye to be very tortuous actually have rather low sinuosity ratings. The reader may be helped in visualizing these values by inspecting the map of the Popo Agie River near Hudson, Wyo. (fig. 43). This meander on the Popo Agie, the most symmetrical that we have seen in the field, has a sinuosity of 1.73.

The term "braid" is applied here to those reaches in which there are relatively stable alluvial islands, and hence two or more separate channels.

The data in figure 46 indicate .that in the rivers studied the braided channels are separated from the meanders by a line described by the equation

$$s = 0.06 \ Q^{-.44} \qquad (1)$$

For a given discharge, meanders, as one would expect, will occur on the smaller slopes. At the same slope a braided channel will have a higher discharge than a meandering one. The figure shows, moreover, that straight channels, those with sinuosities less than 1.5, occur throughout the range of slopes. This supports the view that the separation of a true meander from a straight channel is arbitrary. Study of the sinuosities of these channels does not reveal an increasing sinuosity with decreasing slope; that is, greater tortuosity is not necessarily associated with decreasing slope. A diagram similar to the one in figure 43 has been plotted by Nuguid.[1] His designation of meanders was not based upon a particular sinuosity but was apparently an arbitrary designation based upon the plan or map of the channel. Nuguid indicated that what he calls normal, or straight, channels have a smaller value of slope than meanders for any given discharge. The present data do not demonstrate such a distinction.

In considering figure 46 it is important to keep in mind that these data describe certain natural channels. In natural channels specific variables often occur in association. For example, steep slopes are associated with coarse material. In a system which contains, as we have pointed out, a minimum of seven variables, a diagram such as figure 46 which treats only two of these cannot be expected to describe either the mechanism of adjustment or all theoretically possible conditions. Because it is drawn from nature, however, it does

[1] Nuguid, C. P. 1950, A study of stream meanders: Iowa State Univ., master's thesis.

describe a set of conditions which are to be expected in many natural channels.

Two ideas that will be explored more fully are inherent in figure 46. First, at a given discharge various slopes are associated with varying channel shapes and patterns. Second, in considering an individual bifurcating channel, we are concerned with a division of discharge comparable to the comparison of a downstream point with an upstream point in a river channel system.

Cottonwood Creek near Daniel, Wyo., is a striking illustration of an abrupt change from one stream pattern to another (fig. 47). Above the gaging station, Cottonwood Creek is a very sinuous meander. Immediately below the gage it becomes a braid. The character of the channel where braiding begins is shown by the photograph in figure 48. As the profile in figure 47 shows, the meander reach has a slope of 0.0011, while the braided section occurs on a slope of 0.004. The difference in slope is accompanied by a change in the median grain size from 0.049 foot in the meander to 0.060 foot in the braided reach.

Data for this reach are plotted in figure 46. At a discharge of 800 cfs points 12a and 12b represent, respectively, the meandering and the braided parts of the reach of Cottonwood Creek pictured in figure 47. In changing from a meander to a braid at a constant discharge we should expect the two conditions on Cottonwood Creek to be represented by points on different sides of the line of figure 46, and indeed this expectation is fulfilled.

It is clear that through the short reach of Cottonwood Creek discharge is the same in both meandering and braided parts, for no tributaries enter. The load carried is the same in both meandering and braided parts. There is no indication of rapid aggradation or degradation, and to the extent that this is true, if the meandering reach is assumed to be in quasi-equilibrium, then the braided reach is also. The braided pattern here is not due to excessive load but appears to be a channel adjustment caused by the fortuitous occurrence of a patch of coarser gravel deposited locally in the valley alluvium, the bulk of which was probably laid down in late Pleistocene time.

The relation of channel pattern to slope and discharge is of particular interest in connection with the reconstruction of the alluvial landscape from profiles of terrace remnants and from alluvial fills. Changes of climate such as occurred in the Pleistocene might be accompanied by changes in precipitation and runoff. Such variations in streamflow might produce changes in the stream pattern without any accompanying change in the quantity or caliber of the load. An increase of flow could result in a meander becoming a braid; a decrease in discharge could make a braided channel

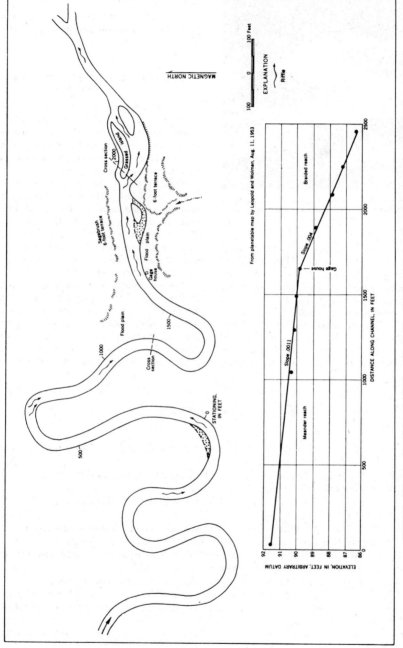

FIGURE 47.—Plan and profile of Cottonwood Creek near Daniel, Wyo. In this reach the river changes its pattern from meander to braid.

FIGURE 48.—Views upstream of the braided part of Cottonwood Creek near Daniel, Wyo. *A* indicates gaging station house where pattern changes from meander to braid. At *B* the first meander bend upstream can be seen.

a meandering one. Yet, a change in the character of the load, such as an increase in caliber which the presence of a valley glacier might provide, could result in an increase in slope and a change from meandering to braiding without any change in the precipitation or discharge. The presence, then, of material of different sizes in successive valley fills suggests that at different periods in its history the river which occupied the valley may have had several distinctive patterns. As the pattern of major rivers in an area is a significant

feature of the landscape, the application of such principles to historical geology may prove of some help in reconstructing the past.

SUMMARY: THE CONTINUUM OF CHANNEL PATTERNS

The observations described above demonstrate the transitional nature of stream patterns. A braided stream can change into a meandering one in a relatively short reach. Individual channels of a braided stream may meander. A tributary may meander to its junction with a braided master stream.

When streams of different patterns are considered in terms of hydraulic variables, braided patterns seem to be differentiated from meandering ones by certain combinations of slope, discharge, and width-to-depth ratio. Straight channels, however, have less diagnostic combinations of these variables. The regular spacing and alternation of shallows and deeps is characteristic, however, of all three patterns.

This continuum of channel types emphasizes the similarity in physical principles which determine the nature of an individual channel. The next section discusses some aspects of these principles. Although our understanding of them is far from complete, the analysis does indicate the complex nature of the mechanisms controlling diverse natural channels.

References

Brooks, N. H., 1955, Mechanics of streams with movable beds of fine sand: *Amer. Soc. Civil Eng. Proc.*, V. 81, paper 668, 28 pp.

Dittbrenner, E. F., 1954, Discussion of river-bed scour during floods: *Amer. Soc. Civil Eng. Proc.*, V. 80, Paper 479, 16 pp.

Freidkin, J. F., 1945, A laboratory study of the meandering of alluvial rivers: U. S. Waterways Exp. Station, Vicksburg, 40 pp.

Inglis, C. C., 1949, The behavior and control of rivers and canals: Central Waterpower Irrigation and Navigation Research Station, Poona, India, V. 13, pt. 1, 283 pp.

Leopold, L. B., and Miller, J. P. 1956, Ephemeral streams—hydraulic factors and their relation to the drainage net: U. S. Geol. Survey Prof. Paper 282-A.

Pettis, C. R., 1927, A new theory of river flood flow: privately printed, 68 pp.

Quraishy, M. S., 1944, The origin of curves in rivers: *Current Sci.*, V. 13, pp. 36–39.

Russell, R. J., 1954, Alluvial morphology of Anatolian rivers: *Ass. Amer. Geogr. Ann.*, V. 44, pp. 363–391.

Schaffernak, F., 1950, *Grundriss der Flussmorphologie und des Flussbaues*: Springer-Verlag, Wien, 115 pp.

Wolman, M. G., 1955, The natural channel of Brandywine Creek, Pa.: U. S. Geol. Survey Prof. Paper 271.

Bed Form, Scour and Deposition

VII

In this section the movement of sediment in open channels and its eventual deposition are considered in three papers.

Lane and Borland's paper demonstrates, as does a later paper by Colby (1964), that in unconstricted channels scour during floods may be small. Nevertheless, it is known that at high discharges river channels frequently contain more water than their cross-sectional areas alone would indicate. Although a geomorphologist should be interested in all aspects of the morphology of the air-water-earth interface, the fact that the patterns of sediment distribution on the floor of an alluvial channel change with discharge may not excite him. Nevertheless, it should, and for this reason the paper by Simons, Richardson, and Nordin is included. Recent studies reveal that a change of bed forms may decrease channel roughness and increase flow velocity during floods. For example, at high discharge a change from dunes to plane bed permits the channel to accommodate a considerably greater discharge at flood peaks (Simons and Richardson, 1963). If this were not so, flood damages would be greater and channels of major rivers might be considerably larger than they are at present. The significance of details of channel and sediment character is clearly demonstrated by the experiences of those attempting to estimate the total scour expected to occur after construction of the Fort Randall Dam on the Missouri River. At least 20 feet of scour was anticipated but only 6 feet occurred as an armor of pebbles formed on the channel floor. This insignificant percentage of coarse sediment in the alluvium became critical when, during degradation, it was not transported, but instead it formed a lag gravel thereby preventing further scour (Livesey, 1965).

Finally, a selection from a much longer report on valley deposition, mostly man induced, in several small valleys near Oxford, Mississippi, will conclude this section. Happ, Rittenhouse, and Dobson developed a descriptive classification of fluvial deposits. Modern alluvial rivers are flowing in and on such deposits, and variations in channel width and pattern can frequently be attributed to variations in the alluvium through which a river is flowing (Fisk, 1957).

301

AMERICAN SOCIETY OF CIVIL ENGINEERS

Founded November 5, 1852

TRANSACTIONS

Paper No. 2712

RIVER-BED SCOUR DURING FLOODS

By E. W. Lane,[1] M. ASCE, and
W. M. Borland,[2] A.M. ASCE

15

With Discussions by Messrs. E. E. Dittbrenner; Emmett M. Laursen
and Arthur Toch; and E. W. Lane and W. M. Borland

Synopsis

Scour in wide, steep rivers during floods is not general throughout the flooded reach since deposition occurs at wide sections. The measurements of river action are almost always made at narrow sections, causing a misconception that is not supported by studies of the transported sediment. In the design of a project for the protection and rehabilitation of the middle Rio Grande Valley in New Mexico, the question of the depth of scour of the river beds during floods assumed unusual importance. A study was made, therefore, to determine this depth. The study, its results, and revised theories based on it are explained in this paper.

Conditions in the Middle Rio Grande Valley

Before the intense agrarian use of the area by white settlers, the middle Rio Grande Valley had probably reached a sedimentation status approaching equilibrium, in which the sediment carried out of the valley nearly equaled the sediment brought into it by the Rio Grande and its tributaries. In recent years, however, a large portion of the upstream runoff has been used for irrigation, thus decreasing the flow downstream in the valley. In addition, overgrazing of the watershed has increased the sediment load brought into the main stream by tributaries. Evidence suggests that a secular change of climate may also be responsible. Thus, the load of sediment brought into the valley has increased, and the flow available to carry it out has decreased, with the result that the valley is filling at a rate that the latest measurements (1952) indicate to

Note.—Published, essentially as printed here, in August, 1953, as *Proceedings-Separate No. 254.* Positions and titles given are those in effect when the paper or discussion was received for publication.

[1] Cons. Hydr. Engr., Bureau of Reclamation, U. S. Dept. of the Interior, Denver, Colo.

[2] Head, Sedimentation Section, Hydrology Branch, Bureau of Reclamation, U. S. Dept. of the Interior, Denver, Colo.

be about ½ in. per year.   The river bed at Albuquerque, N. Mex. (the principal city of the valley), had risen above the level of the streets by 1952.

This condition not only increases the danger of floods but also tends to raise the ground-water level on the agricultural land of the valley—threatening it with waterlogging.   In addition, water-loving plants have grown up in the abandoned areas.   This vegetation absorbs the available water to an extent that seriously decreases the water supply.   The rise of the river bottom is thus threatening the future prosperity of the valley.

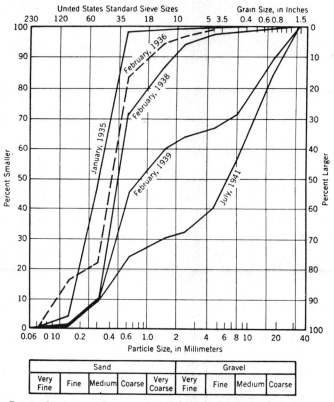

FIG. 1.—INCREASE IN COARSENESS OF BED MATERIAL BELOW LAKE MEAD, LOWER COLORADO RIVER

To remedy this condition, a plan of improvement, developed jointly by the Bureau of Reclamation, United States Department of the Interior (USBR), and the Corps of Engineers, United States Department of the Army, was approved by the 80th Congress in 1948.[3]   The plan consists principally of the construction of (1) two dams for the storage of sediment and temporary reten- tion of flood flows, and (2) control works whereby the channel scours out—and thus lowers—its bed.   The storage of sediment in the basins and the release of the clarified water into the river channel is expected to make possible a

---

[3] "Flood Control Act of 1948," *Public Law No. 858*, 80th Cong., U. S. Govt. Printing Office, Washing- ton, D. C., 1948.

lowering of the river bed through the picking up of the bed material by the clarified water. Considerable degradation of the stream below Lake Mead on the lower Colorado River has resulted from the release of clarified water. As will be shown, the rate of degradation in the Rio Grande Valley is related to the depth to which the river bed of this stream scours during floods. A study of the phenomenon was important for this reason.

Observations made at Lake Mead indicate that, when the clarified water is released from the dams on the Rio Grande, the flow will carry away from the bed more fine particles than coarse particles. As a result, the average particle size of the bed material will gradually become larger. For example, Fig. 1 shows the increase in size of the bed material a short distance below Hoover Dam on the lower Colorado River. Since a specified flow cannot carry so large a volume of coarse as of fine material, this increase in bed coarseness will cause a slow decrease in scour volume. Thus, the rate of degradation will be reduced gradually, and the rate of lowering of the bed will become negligible. The rate at which the fine sand is removed and the length of time before the degradation rate becomes negligible depend on the depth to which the river bed is scoured during high flows, since the volume of fine material that can be removed by the river depends on the volume of this material that comes in contact with the flowing water. If the depth of scour is small, little fine material can be carried away before the bed becomes covered with coarse material; however, if the depth of scour is great, much fine material will be carried away before the average size becomes large. The removal of the small quantity with small depth of scour will lower the bed much less than the removal of the large amount if the depth of scour is great. It was necessary, therefore, to know the scour depth.

The middle Rio Grande is a steep stream having a slope of 4.5 ft per mile in the vicinity of Albuquerque, and it carries a heavy sediment load averaging at San Marcial (New Mexico) approximately 1.18% by weight. The river is generally wide, shallow, and relatively straight. The channel contains many islands that give it a "braided" pattern, similar to many others in the western United States.

The Commonly Accepted Concept of Depth of Scour

Since the early 1900's, the discharges of the Rio Grande and other similar rivers in the western states have been measured thousands of times under widely varying flow conditions. In each of these observations, the cross section was determined by frequent soundings across the stream bed. As the flow of water in the stream increases, the increase in the average depth of the flowing water usually is found to exceed the rise in water-surface elevation. This indicates that the bottom of the stream has been scoured out. It is not uncommon for the bottom to recede as much as the water surface rises. When the flood crest is passed and the flow decreases, the bottom begins to fill, and when the flood has passed, the bottom has risen nearly to the level that existed before the flood. This is indicated by Fig. 2, which shows the changes in the river bed at the San Marcial gaging station on the Rio Grande during 1929.

Similar changes in the Rio Grande and other western rivers have been observed so frequently that it is the general impression of many experienced engineers that such action is normal for streams of this type. It is believed that, when a flood occurs, the bed of the stream (for the greater part of its length and width) scours materially and refills as the flood recedes. This opinion is widely held by men who have gaged the Rio Grande and is sub-

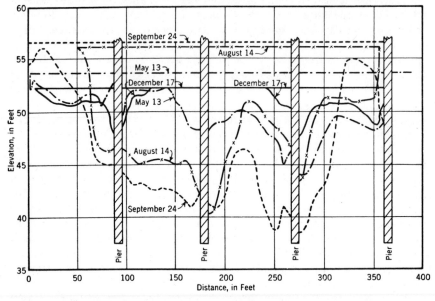

FIG. 2.—CHANGES IN CROSS SECTION OF THE RIO GRANDE AT SAN MARCIAL,
NEW MEXICO, 1929

stantiated by observations of the effect that the floods exert on pilings driven for bank-protection work. These pilings are observed to rise suddenly in the water and float away, despite the fact that they are 40 ft long—with most of this length below the stream bottom. Bridges supported by 60-ft pilings have been washed out during such floods. If such deep scour occurs over the entire stream bottom during floods, the volume of river-bed material from which the finer particles can be drawn is great; a long time will elapse before the clear water from the proposed sediment-control reservoirs will stop the degradation of the stream bed by increasing the coarseness of the grain sizes.

THE CONFLICT BETWEEN THEORETICAL AND ACTUAL SEDIMENTATION

The belief of many experienced observers—that the entire bed of the Rio Grande scours deeply during floods—seems to be based on quite conclusive evidence; but a quantitative examination proves even more conclusively that such deep general scour has not occurred during floods in recent years. If the Rio Grande scours downward several feet throughout its width and length, it must transport a large quantity of material down the river. Nearly all the material transported in the section of stream under study is deposited in the Elephant Butte Reservoir (New Mexico). The volume of sediment being

306

deposited in this basin has been measured frequently, and the amount is known within a reasonable degree of accuracy. Comparison of this volume with that which would have to be moved into the reservoir with even so small an average depth of scour as 1.5 ft shows that the sediment actually deposited is decidedly less than would occur with this scour. Thus occurs the apparently conflicting evidence of the scour unquestionably observed by the stream gagers and the equally unquestionable lack of a corresponding volume of material deposited in the reservoir.

In quantitative terms, this difference may be shown by an example. The section of the Rio Grande from Cochiti (New Mexico) to San Marcial has a length of 160 miles and an average width of 1,170 ft, giving it a surface area of 22,700 acres. For each foot of average depth of scour below the elevation of the bed at the start of the flood, a volume of 22,700 acre-ft would, therefore, be carried into the lake. The average yearly volume of material carried into the lake is 18,276 acre-ft, of which only 1,800 acre-ft are composed of sand and larger sizes, such as would be scoured out of the stream bottom. Since floods sufficient to scour the river bed occur almost every year, it is evident that the average depth of scour during floods, even if all the deposited coarse material is assumed to be moved out of the bed, is of the order of magnitude of 0.08 ft.

Another proof of the nonexistence of large depths of scour over nearly the entire stream-bed area is that the measurements of sediment concentration made in the river do not show the presence of sufficiently large volumes of sand to account for a deep scouring of the channel bed. For a flood to scour an average of 5 ft of depth from the bed of the Rio Grande would require that it move 113,500 acre-ft of sediment, almost all sand, from the river bed. The concentrations in the Rio Grande below the mouth of the Rio Puerco sometimes become as great as 20% resulting mainly from flash floods from the Rio Puerco, which is probably the carrier of the highest sediment concentration of any stream in the United States (and possibly the world), 68% concentration by weight having been observed in it.[4] Above the mouth of the Rio Puerco, concentrations in the Rio Grande rarely reach above 5%. These high concentrations are of short duration and only a small part of them is composed of sand particles. Although the sand loads are great, no flows have been observed at the lower end of the river with sufficient volume of discharge and concentration of sand sizes to account for the 113,500 acre-ft of loss of material necessary to deepen the river bed an average of 5 ft.

Since the river bed refills as a flood recedes, an inflow of 113,500 acre-ft of sand would be required to provide this material, but no such flows have been observed. If this scouring action took place, there would be a high concentration of sand at the lower end of the valley during the first part of the flood, but a large flow with low concentration during the latter part of the flood. A high sediment concentration during the early part of the flood is commonly observed; the concentration differences between rising and falling floods, however, are insufficient to account for an extensive general scour.

---

[4] "Sedimentation Studies at Conchas Reservoir in New Mexico," by D. C. Bondurant, *Transactions*, ASCE, Vol. 116, 1951, p. 1283.

L. G. Straub, M. ASCE, has made extensive studies of the changes of river-bed level resulting from contractions, including both model studies and observations on the Missouri River.[5, 6] He reached the conclusion that the scour observed at contracted sections was not general throughout the length of the river.

A General Study of Scour

Since the data available on depth of scour in the Rio Grande were so conflicting that no satisfactory quantitative values could be obtained, the available literature bearing on this subject was studied with a view to obtaining more information on this subject. The principal information thus gleaned is summarized here.

Few measurements for the primary purpose of determining general bed scour have been made (1953). Most of the available data have been secured from measurements made primarily for other purposes, such as the determination of stream discharge or surveys to determine depths available for navigation. Observations of local scour (such as those made at bridge piers or abutments) are of no value in determining the general bed scour. The available data seem to deal with two general classes of rivers: (1) Large rivers of small or moderate slope, like the Mississippi and Missouri rivers, and (2) smaller rivers of steep slope, such as are often found in the western United States. The situation in these two types of streams differs somewhat. The larger rivers, if they flow in alluvial beds, generally consist of a series of bends between which are fairly straight reaches. In these straight reaches, the main channel of the river usually shifts from one side of the river to the other at places called "crossings." At ordinary stages the bends are usually deep and relatively narrow, and the crossings are wider and shallower.[7]

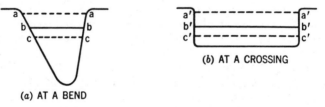

(a) AT A BEND

(b) AT A CROSSING

Fig. 3.—Typical Cross Sections of a Large River

In Fig. 3 are shown diagrammatically a cross section typical of a large river at a bend and a typical cross section at a crossing. The water level at medium stages is represented by the lines bb and b'b', and at high and low discharges by aa and a'a' and by cc and c'c', respectively. At medium stages, the cross-sectional area of flow is almost the same in both cases; consequently the velocity of flow also is nearly the same. During floods, the water level rises to aa and a'a'—a rise of approximately the same height above bb and b'b'. Because the

---

[5] "Effect of Channel-Contraction Works upon Regimen of Movable Bed-Streams," by L. G. Straub, *Transactions*, Am. Geophysical Union, 1934, Pt. II, p. 454.

[6] *House Document No. 238*, by L. F. Straub, 73rd Congress, 2d Session, U. S. Govt. Printing Office, Washington, D. C., Appendix XV, p. 1150.

[7] "A Laboratory Study of the Meandering of Alluvial Rivers," by J. F. Friedkin, U. S. Waterways Experiment Station, Vicksburg, Miss., 1945, Plate V.

width at the crossing is considerably greater than that at the bend, the rise in water level increases the cross section at the crossing more than at the bend; therefore, the total cross-sectional area at the crossing becomes greater than that at the bend. This difference causes a lower velocity at the crossing than at the bend; hence the flow tends to produce less scour in the crossing than in the bend. At the low-water stage the opposite action occurs. The areas at the bends become larger than at the crossings, and more scour results at the crossings. At high-water stages, therefore, the pools usually scour out and deposition occurs at the crossings; whereas during low-water stages, the crossings scour out and the bends fill.

The Rio Grande is a relatively straight river and does not have the bends and crossings that characterize the large alluvial rivers, but it does have a series of alternately narrow and wide sections. If the river has approximately the same area in both types of sections at normal flows, during floods it should have larger areas at the wide sections and smaller areas at the narrow ones, producing deposit at the wide sections and scour at the narrow ones—the same action as that in large alluvial streams.

The fact that the bed of the Rio Grande is lowered during the period of floods (at least at certain places) is indicated by the cross sections shown in Fig. 2. These cross sections represent the bed of the river under the Santa Fe Railroad bridge at San Marcial in 1929. Some of the measurements were taken during the large flood of that year. At this place, the stream is contracted somewhat at high flows, and the presence of bridge piers doubtlessly increases the scour. The tendency of the bed to be deeper near the piers is evident at these sections. The piers are set at an angle with the direction of flow, which also increases the scouring effect.

Discharge measurements have been made in the Colorado River at Yuma, Ariz., since 1878. The great depths of stream-bed lowering that have been measured at this station during floods have received wide publicity and have been partly responsible for the belief that the bottoms of such streams are scoured deeply at flood stage. Some of the flow cross sections for the years 1912, 1916, and 1929 are shown in Fig. 4. The maximum increase in depth at the section is usually twice the rise in the water surface. These measurements were made from a cableway at a narrow section of the river where one or both banks are of scour-resistant material, and where the bed material is fine sand. Backwater curve studies made to determine levee grades below Yuma indicate that this degradation effect continues along a narrow reach of the river extending approximately 12 miles below Yuma.

In contrast with the deep stream-bed degradation at the Yuma station was the condition at the site of the Imperial Dam. A cable station was operated at this site for a short period before the dam was constructed. During this period the flow reached a maximum of 65,000 cu ft per sec. Although the bottom shifted considerably (being higher first on one side and then on the other), there was no appreciable change of the mean bottom level.

During the excavation for Hoover Dam, a sawed and planed 2-in. by 6-in. wooden plank was found in the river-bed material 50 ft below low-water surface and 40 ft below the bottom of the river channel. This discovery indi-

309

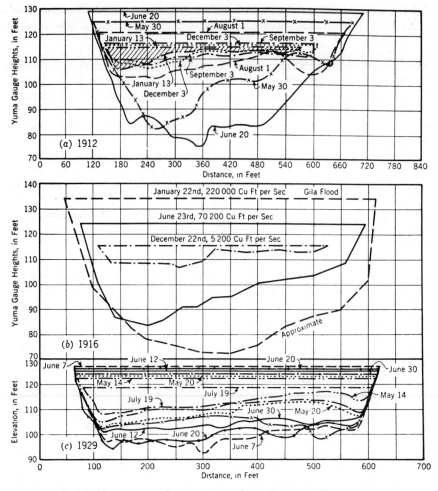

FIG. 4.—CHANGES OF A COLORADO RIVER CROSS SECTION AT YUMA, ARIZ.

cated that at some comparatively recent time, the river in this canyon had scoured out the bed to the depth of this plank.

Fig. 5 shows the cross sections at two stations on the Yellow River in China as described by J. R. Freeman.[8] These sections indicate the degradation of the bed of this stream during a flood. The cross sections were determined at gaging stations where the river was probably narrow. At one of them, rock was exposed nearby on one bank. For the shaded area in Fig. 5 (b), the gaging station is several hundred feet upstream from bedrock. At two other stations for which sections were not given, a similar degradation was observed. Mr. Freeman apparently believed that the degradation was continuous along the part of the river that he studied. Cross sections of the Verde River near

<hr />

[8] "Flood Problems in China," by J. R. Freeman, *Transactions*, ASCE, Vol. 85, 1922, p. 1436.

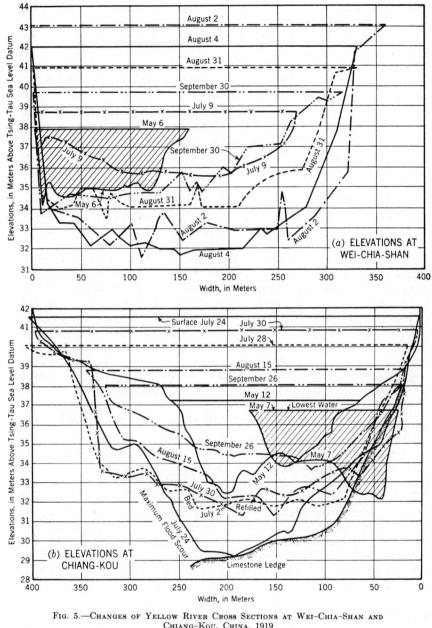

FIG. 5.—CHANGES OF YELLOW RIVER CROSS SECTIONS AT WEI–CHIA–SHAN AND
CHIANG–KOU, CHINA, 1919
(1 METER = 3.28083 FT)

Fort McDowell, in Arizona, which indicate a considerable degradation of
this stream at high flows, are provided by F. N. Holmquist.[9] This gaging

[9] "Behavior of Debris-Carrying Rivers in Flood," by F. N. Holmquist, *Engineering News-Record*, Vol.
94, 1925, pp. 362–365.

station is situated where the river runs between rock banks and is confined to a comparatively limited width.

An examination of the foregoing data shows that, at most of the gaging stations mentioned, the bottom recedes considerably at high flows. All the cases in which the bottom receded were (1) at bridges, where the presence of piers would induce scour, (2) at stations where the river was narrow, or (3) at places where the stream was probably narrow—since measuring stations are usually so situated. The only place where a stream has been measured from a cableway at a section that was not contracted is on the lower Colorado River at the site of Imperial Dam. There, no stream-bed deepening was observed. The quantity of material carried into the Elephant Butte Reservoir also proves that no great average depth of material is scoured from the Rio Grande bed in floods and is carried into the reservoir. Similarly conclusive is the fact that the concentration of sediment carried in most streams during floods is insufficient to account for the amounts excavated or refilled if the degradations indicated by measurements at most gaging stations are typical of the entire length and width of the river.

The Holmquist Hypothesis

An explanation consistent with all the observed data, except those taken at the site of the Imperial Dam, is that the river behaves as described by Mr. Holmquist.[9] It is his theory that wide, steep rivers at flood stage, excavate a deep channel over only a portion of their width, depositing the excavated material in the shallower parts of the channel a short distance downstream. He believes that this deep channel tends to approach the outside of the bends; thus it may cross from one side of the river channel to the other. The constant shift of the channel position usually results from side erosion, but occasionally the shift may be by avulsion (a complete and sudden abandonment of a part of the river's former course and an adoption of a new channel).

Observations During the 1948 Flood in the Rio Grande

After the foregoing studies were completed, both ground and air observations were made of the conditions during the flood in the middle Rio Grande at the end of May, 1948, at which time the flow at Albuquerque reached 13,000 cu ft per sec.

There was a special effort during these observations to determine the existence of a narrow, deep channel, such as that described by Mr. Holmquist; but no evidence of such a phenomenon was found. However, the fact that most of the bridges and gaging stations were at narrow sections of the river was definitely observed. The observations that these narrow sections scour during floods agreed with the visual evidence, which also strongly indicated that the removed material was deposited at the next wide section downstream and not carried on down the river. These observations agree with all the other observed data on the middle Rio Grande, a fact which tends to confirm the accuracy of these observations.

This explanation also agrees with another observed condition—that the greatest danger to the levees along the middle Rio Grande is from the cutting of the banks, and that this cutting seems to be most active in the falling stages of a flood. It is believed that, during the height of the flood, deposits occur in the wide, shallow sections. Because of the shallow depth, a channel may be largely filled by a deposit of moderate depth, the volume of which is within the capacity of the stream to transport and lay down. Similarly, a bar may be formed to a height that equals a considerable percentage of the depth of the flow. When the flood recedes, the bottom topography may differ considerably from that which existed at the start of the flood because of these deposits; the former channel may be sufficiently blocked to force the stream to follow a new channel. If this channel impinges on the bank when the flow decreases, a new and unexpected scour occurs which under particularly unfavorable conditions may have serious consequences.

This is a different action from that which occurs on large alluvial rivers where the greatest bank cutting also accompanies a falling stage of the flood. In the case of the large river, this action is caused principally by (1) softening of the bank and the outward pressure at the bottom of the banks resulting from the return of the seepage water to the river, and (2) the sloughing of the high banks of saturated material exposed as the water recedes. This action is not important on the Rio Grande because the rise of the water during a flood is not large.

Conclusions

As a result of the studies described, it was concluded that during floods the bed of the Rio Grande (in general) scours at the narrow sections, and that most of the material thus removed is deposited in the next wide section downstream. This action causes the wide section to fill up somewhat and occasionally promotes channel changes in the wide sections which may cause the stream to attack the bank. It is believed that this action is typical of rivers in this category which includes most of the Great Plains rivers. It was also concluded that the common opinion that there is a general lowering of the bed of such streams during floods is unsound. The belief arises because the bottoms at gaging stations usually scour out; but such stations are in the great majority of cases situated at bridges or cableways where the rivers are narrow, and are not typical of the greater part of the length of the river. The unsoundness of the concept of a general lowering is proved by (1) the observation that the volume of deposit in the Elephant Butte Reservoir is less than that which would result from such scour, and (2) the lack of sufficient concentrations in the flowing water to carry such excavation during the rising flood or to deposit it as the flood recedes.

Although these general studies did not lead to a quantitative evaluation of the average depth of scour of the Rio Grande bed during flood, they proved that the scour was much less than it was generally believed to be by experienced hydrologists.

Acknowledgments

The writers wish to acknowledge the helpfulness of the suggestions of Thomas Maddock, Jr., in the preparation of this paper.

SEDIMENTARY STRUCTURES GENERATED BY FLOW IN ALLUVIAL CHANNELS

BY

D. B. SIMONS, E. V. RICHARDSON, AND C. F. NORDIN, JR.

Reprinted from
Primary Sedimentary Structures and their Hydrodynamic Interpretation
A Publication of the Society of Economic Paleontologists and Mineralogists
A Division of
The American Association of Petroleum Geologists
Special Publication No. 12

314

SEDIMENTARY STRUCTURES GENERATED BY FLOW IN ALLUVIAL CHANNELS

D. B. SIMONS[1], E. V. RICHARDSON[2], and C. F. NORDIN, JR.[2]

Fort Collins, Colorado

ABSTRACT

Several geometric forms or bed configurations are molded from the bed material by the flow in alluvial channels. These forms are broadly classified by their shape and effect on flow resistance and by the mode of bed-load transport. The most common bed forms include ripples, dunes, a transition form as the dunes change to a plane or flat bed, plane bed, standing waves, and antidunes. The bed forms change from ripples to dunes and ultimately to antidunes as the tractive force is increased.

Important interrelated variables likely to affect bed forms include: characteristics of bed material such as physical size and sorting; the temperature or fluid viscosity; the concentration of very fine sediment; and the depth as well as velocity and slope. Methods of predicting bed forms from known characteristics of the flow and sediment are inexact, but as a first approximation, the bed form is related to stream power and median fall diameter of bed material.

Different types of cross bedding are associated with the various bed forms established under equilibrium flow conditions in recirculating flumes. The tendency for all flows to meander, even in straight channels, complicates both the bed forms and the types of cross bedding. This tendency to meander is reinforced by the large bars (depositional structures) which exist adjacent first to one bank and then to the other on the beds of alluvial channels. These bars may be of such small amplitude as to go almost unnoticed in a given system, particularly when small width-depth ratios exist. However, if by reducing depth or by widening the channel, the width-depth ratio is increased, these large bars may develop to almost the full depth of the channel. The regular forms of bed roughness are in general superposed on these large bars, but the bed forms change dramatically as the depth, local slope, and direction of flow change over the bar as deposition and development of the bars progress.

INTRODUCTION

Many significant aspects of flow in open channels, after nearly two centuries of study, are still only vaguely understood. The principal reasons for this lack of progress are the complex and interrelated nature of the variables and the lack of any concerted, sustained study since that of Darcy and Bazin in 1865.

An alluvial boundary is formed in cohesive or non-cohesive materials that have been and can be transported by a stream. At some discharges the material forming the boundary may not move, and the alluvial channel behaves as a rigid channel. However, once general movement of the bed material commences, the alluvial boundary can be molded into many bed configurations by the flow, as shown by the classical experiments of Gilbert (1914). In addition, the fluid properties and turbulent characteristics of the flow are changed by the moving sediment (Vanoni, 1946; Bagnold, 1956; Elata and Ippen, 1961; Simons and others, 1963). The movable alluvial boundary thus adds another dimension to flow problems, increasing their complexity, because in addition to the fluid, flow, and boundary characteristics, it is necessary to include the sediment characteristics in the study of alluvial channels.

A systematic study was initiated in 1956 at Colorado State University by the U. S. Geological Survey to determine resistance to flow and bed material transport in alluvial channels. Thus far (1964) the study has been limited mostly to steady equilibrium flow in flumes over sand bed material, although some qualitative preliminary studies have been made for the unsteady case (Simons and Richardson, 1962b), and some special studies have been made on the effect of changes in viscosity, either real or apparent, and of the effect of the sorting of the bed material on the bed configuration, resistance to flow and bed material transport.

This report describes the bed configurations generated by flow in alluvial channels, the stratification formed by these bed configurations, and the corresponding resistance to flow as measured by the Chézy coefficient.[3] The bed configurations are used to classify flow into two flow regimes with a transition between. The variables that influence the form of the bed configuration, sediment transport, and resistance to flow are discussed, and a method for predicting the bed-form is presented that appears to have merit.

Only a brief description of the sand sizes, equipment and procedure used in the collection of data is given. A more detailed description of the procedure is given by Simons and Richard-

[1] Colorado State University.
[2] U. S. Geological Survey. Publication of this paper authorized by the Director, U. S. Geological Survey.

[3] For definition of the Chézy coefficient, see paper by Briggs and Middleton and glossary.

son (1964b), and complete documentation and description of all of the basic data collected from 1956–1962 by the Geological Survey at Colorado State University will be included in a data report which is presently (1964) in preparation.

EXPERIMENTAL EQUIPMENT AND DATA COLLECTION

The basic study was conducted in a tilting recirculating flume 150 feet long, 8 feet wide and 2 feet deep. Slope in this flume could be varied from 0 to 0.013 feet per feet and discharge from 2 cfs to 22 cfs. In addition, a smaller tilting recirculating flume 60 feet long, 2 feet wide and 2.5 feet deep was used for special studies. Slope in this flume could be varied from 0 to 0.025 feet per feet and discharge from 0.5 cfs to 8 cfs. The special studies in the 2-foot wide flume were made to determine the importance of viscosity (Simons an others, 1963; Hubbell and Ali 1961), density of the bed material (Haushild and Fahnestock, personal communication) and sorting of the bed material (Daranandana, 1962) on flow in alluvial channels.

The size distributions of the bed material used in the 8-foot flume study are given in figure 1. Those for the 2-foot flume are given in figure 2. The size distributions are in terms of the fall diameter (Colby and Christenson, 1956) unless specified otherwise, and are based upon the analyses of a large number of samples taken at random preceeding, during, and after the study. A more detailed description of the sands is given by Simons and Richardson (1964b, p. 32).

The general procedure for each run was to recirculate a given discharge of the water-sediment mixture until equilibrium flow conditions were established. Equilibrium flow is defined as flow which has established a bed configuration and slope consistent with the fluid flow and bed material characteristics over the entire length of

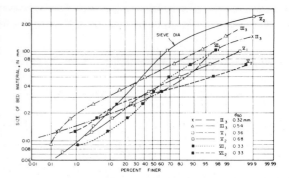

FIG. 2.—Size-distribution curves for the sands used in the 2-ft. flume.

the flume neglecting entrance and exit affected reaches; that is, the time-average water surface slope of the flow is constant and parallel to the time-average bed surface; and the time-average concentration of the bed material discharge is constant. Equilibrium flow should not be confused with steady uniform flow because with equilibrium flow the velocity may vary at a point, and from point to point. Steady uniform flow as classically defined ($\partial v/\partial t = 0$, $\partial v/\partial x = 0$) does not exist in an alluvial channel unless the bed is plane.

After equilibrium flow was established, water surface slope, S; discharge of the water-sediment mixture, Q; water temperature, T; depth, D; velocity distribution in the vertical V_y; total sediment concentration, C_T; suspended sediment concentration, C_s; and the geometry of bed configuration (length, L; height, h; and shape) were determined. Also, photographs were taken of the bed and water surface for all runs with a still camera and normal and time-lapse sequences of the flow of water and sediment were photographed with a 16 mm movie camera. Many of the flow phenomena which were observed are recorded and documented in the Geological Survey film entitled "Flow in Alluvial Channels" which the Survey staff with assistance from Bandelier Films, Albuquerque, New Mexico filmed in the laboratory at Colorado State University and in the field on the Rio Grande near Albuquerque, New Mexicc

REGIMES OF FLOW IN ALLUVIAL CHANNELS

The flow in alluvial channels can be classified into lower flow regime and upper flow regime, with a transition between. This classification is based on form of the bed configuration, mode of sediment transport, process of energy dissipation, and phase relation between the bed and water surface (table 1).

The typical forms of bed roughness are illus-

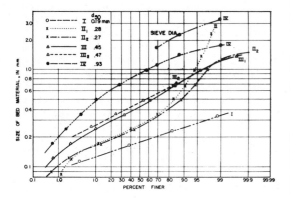

FIG. 1.—Size-distribution curves for the sands used in the 8-ft. flume.

TABLE 1.—*Classification of Flow Regime*

Flow regime	Bed form	Bed Material concentrations (ppm)	Mode of sediment transport	Type of roughness	Phase relation between bed and water surface
Lower regime	Ripples	10–200	Discrete steps	Form roughness predominates	Out of phase
Lower regime	Ripples on dunes	100–1,200	Discrete steps	Form roughness predominates	Out of phase
Lower regime	Dunes	200–2,000	Discrete steps	Form roughness predominates	Out of phase
Transition	Washed out dunes	1,000–3,000		Variable	
Upper regime	Plane beds	2,000–6,000	Continuous	Grain roughness predominates	In phase
Upper regime	Antidunes	2,000→	Continuous	Grain roughness predominates	In phase
Upper regime	Chutes and pools	2,000→	Continuous	Grain roughness predominates	In phase

trated in figure 3. This subdivision into flow regimes is quite general. There is probably an infinite number of different bed forms and patterns within any single subdivision such as ripples, ripples on dunes, or dunes. But, since within any one of these suggested categories the shape and spacing of the elements, the resistance to flow, and sediment transport are similar and also quite different from those in other categories, the proposed subdivision of bed forms is a convenient way to describe form roughness and hence resistance to flow in a general way. Detailed differences between the various bed forms are given in the section "Forms of Bed Roughness and Flow Phenomena."

Lower Flow Regime

In the lower flow regime resistance to flow is large and sediment transport relatively small. The bed form is either ripples or dunes or some

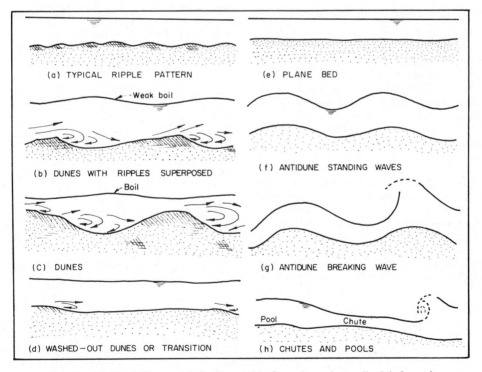

FIG. 3.—Idealized diagram of the forms of bed roughness is an alluvial channel.

combination of ripples and dunes all of which are triangular shape elements of irregular shape. The water surface undulations are out of phase with the bed surface, and there exists a relatively large separation zone downstream from the crest of each ripple and dune. Total resistance to flow is the result of grain roughness and form roughness with the latter dominant. The most common mode of bed material transport is for the individual grains to move up the back of the ripple or dune and avalanche down its face. After coming to rest on the downstream face of the ripple or dune, the particles remain there until exposed by the downstream movement of the dunes, whereupon the cycle of moving up the back of the dune, avalanching and storage is repeated. Thus, the movement of most of the bed material particles is in steps that are as long as the ripple or dune, with a time between steps dependent on the velocity and amplitude of the ripple or dune. The velocity of the downstream movement of the ripple or dune depends on their height and the velocity of the grains moving up their back. In small flume studies the ripple bed configuration is the usual one studied within the lower flow regime, whereas, in natural streams and rivers, dunes with ripples superimposed on dunes are the dominant bed forms in the lower flow regime.

Upper Flow Regime

In the upper flow regime resistance to flow is small and sediment transport is large. The usual bed forms are plane bed or antidunes. The water surface is in phase with the bed surface except when an antidune breaks, and normally there is no separation between the fluid and the boundary. A small separation zone may exist downstream from the crest of an antidune prior to breaking. Resistance to flow is the result of grain roughness with the grains moving, of wave formation and subsidence, and of energy dissipation when the antidunes break. The mode of sediment transport is for the individual grains to roll almost continuously downstream in sheets a few diameters thick. When antidunes break, much bed material is briefly suspended, then movement of water and sediment very nearly stops temporarily, the suspended material falls toward and onto the bed and there is some storage of the particles that reach the bed prior to reestablishment of flow.

Transition

The bed configuration in the transition from the dunes of the lower flow regime to the plane bed and standing waves of the upper flow regime is erratic. In the transition between the two flow regimes, the bed configuration may range from that typical of the lower flow regime to that typical of the upper flow regime, depending primarily on antecedent conditions. If the bed configuration is dunes, the depth or slope can be increased to values more consistent with the upper flow regime without changing the bed form; or conversely if the bed is plane, depth and slope can be decreased to values more consistent with dunes without a change in the bed form. Often in the transition from the lower to the upper flow regimes, the dunes will decrease in amplitude and increase in length before the bed becomes plane (sheared-out dunes). Needless to say, resistance to flow and sediment transport have all the variability of the bed configuration.

FORMS OF BED ROUGHNESS AND FLOW PHENOMENA

The order of occurrence of the forms of bed roughness with increasing stream power ($V\tau_0$ where V is the mean velocity, $\tau_0 = \gamma DS$ is the shear stress and γ is the specific weight of the fluid) starting from plane bed without movement, is ripples, ripples on dunes, dunes, transition, plane bed, antidunes and chutes and pools for bed material finer than 0.6 mm. For material coarser than 0.6 mm, dunes form after beginning of motion at small values of stream power instead of ripples. In the following sections these bed configurations and the associated flow phenomena are described in the order of their occurrence with increasing stream power.

Bed Configuration Without Sediment Movement

If the bed material of a stream moves at one discharge, but does not move at a smaller discharge, the bed configuration at the lower discharge will be a residual of the bed configuration formed when sediment was moving. The problem in this case is knowing when beginning of motion of the bed material occurs (Kramer, 1935; Shields, 1936; and White, 1940) and the bed form that may develop. The bed configuration after the beginning of motion can be any of the preceding ones depending on flow and bed material.

Plane bed without movement was studied to determine the shear stress for the beginning of motion and the bed configuration that would form after beginning of motion. A plane bed was obtained by screeding the bed. Within the accuracy of visual observation, Shields' relation for the beginning of motion is adequate. After beginning of motion, the plane bed changed to ripples for the sand sizes smaller than 0.5 mm and to dunes for the 0.93 mm sand. This was contrary

FIG. 4—Ripple bed configuration, initial development, 8 ft. flume. Bed material was sand No. II, slope = 0.00018, depth = 0.91 ft., discharge = 6.1 cfs, $C/\sqrt{g} = 11.6$.

to Liu's (1957) findings, who reported a plane bed for a range of shear stresses after beginning of motion. Knoroz (1959) reported that a plane bed did not persist after the beginning of motion and that ripples do not form for the coarser sand sizes. Resistance to flow for a plane bed without sediment movement is small. In the flumes, values of $C/\sqrt{g}$, where C is the Chézy coefficient, range from 15 to 20.

Ripples

Ripples are small triangular-shaped elements with gentle upstream slopes and steep downstream slopes. They are less than about 1 ft. in length from crest to crest, and 0.02 ft. to 0.2 ft. in height, and have rather small width normal to the direction of flow. When initially formed, ripples are quite uniform in shape and spacing (fig. 4), but with continued flow, the spacing becomes more irregular (fig. 5) and the ripples may be considered of uniform size and shape only in a statistical sense. Between upstream and downstream slopes, a significant segregation of bed material occurs (figs. 4 and 5). Resistance to flow is large, $C/\sqrt{g}$ ranging from 7 to 12. There is a relative roughness effect with resistance decreasing with increasing depth. The amplitude of the ripple is independent of flow depth, the ripple shape is independent of sand size, and the effect of grain roughness is small relative to the form roughness. The separation zone downstream from a ripple causes very little, if any, disturbance on the water surface and the flow contains little suspended sediment. The water is clear enough that the bed configuration can be photographed through the running water. The concentration of total bed material discharge is

relatively small, ranging from 10 to 200 parts per million (ppm) by weight.

Dunes

If by one means or another one gradually increases the boundary shear stress and stream power associated with ripples or the plane bed in the case of coarse sand bed materials, a rate of bed material transport, a magnitude of velocity and a degree of turbulence are soon achieved that cause larger sand waves called dunes to form. With the smaller shear stress values, the dunes have ripples superimposed on their backs, (see fig. 6). These ripples will tend to disappear at larger shear values particularly with the coarser sand ($d_{50} > 0.4$ mm).

Viewed in elevation, the dunes are large triangular-shaped elements similar to ripples. Their lengths range from 2 ft. to many feet and height from 0.2 ft. to many feet depending on the scale of the flow system. In the large flume, the dunes range from 2 ft. to 10 ft. in length and from 0.2 ft. to 1 ft. in height, whereas Carey and Keller (1957) gave lengths of dunes for the Mississippi River of several hundred feet and heights as large as 40 feet. The maximum amplitude to which the dunes can develop is approximately average depth. Hence, in contrast with ripples, the amplitude of the dunes can increase with increasing depth so that the relative roughness can remain essentially constant or even increase with increasing depth of flow. The width of dunes is quite variable. In narrow flumes or channels they may extend unbroken across the bed of the channel, but the most usual field condition is similar to that illustrated in figure 6.

Field observations by the writers indicate that

FIG. 5.—Upstream view of ripple bed configuration after sustained flow, 8 ft. flume. Bed material was sand No. II, slope = 0.00065, depth = 0.94 ft., discharge = 12. 2 cfs, $C/\sqrt{g} = 11.6$.

dunes will form in any channel irrespective of the size of bed material if the stream power is sufficiently large to cause general transport of the bed material without exceeding a Froude number of unity. Furthermore, the length and shape of the dunes are a function of the fall velocity of the bed material although dune height did not appear to be in the flume experiments. The length of the dunes increased and the angle of the upstream face and downstream face decreased with a decrease in fall velocity. That is, with fine sand the length of the dunes is greater, and their shape is less angular than for the coarser sands.

Resistance to flow with dunes is large, although in the flumes with the finer sands and limited depths resistance to flow for ripples was larger than for dunes because of relative roughness effects. The discharge coefficient, $C/\sqrt{g}$, varies from 8 to 12. With changes in depth and fall velocity, resistance to flow increased with depth for coarser sands and decreased with depth with the finer sands. Also when dune lengths were longer than 10 times dune height, the grain roughness on the back of the dunes had a relatively larger effect than with ripples. Similarly, Knoroz (1959) observed that downstream from the separation zone resistance to flow depended on the grain roughness.

The dunes cause quite a disturbance in the flow and the separation zone is very large causing large boils on the surface of the stream. The flow contains relatively large concentrations of suspended sediment and the concentration of the total bed material discharge ranged from 200 to 2,000 ppm. Measurements of velocities within the zone of separation showed that upstream velocities existed that were one-half to two-thirds average stream velocity and the boundary shear sometimes was sufficient to form ripples oriented opposite to the direction of the primary flow in the channel. As with any flow phenomena that occurs in the tranquil flow regime the water surface is always out of phase with the bed configuration. The flow accelerates over the crests and decelerates over the troughs thereby contracting the flow over the crest and expanding it over the trough.

Some investigators do not agree that there is difference between ripple and dune bed configurations. Vanoni and Kennedy (1963) saw little reason for distinguishing between ripples and dunes since the mechanism by which they are formed and by which they move are similar. However, in addition to the scale difference, there is an opposite effect on resistance of flow with a change in depth (with ripples there is a relative roughness effect and with dunes there is not); ripples do not form when the median diam-

FIG. 6.—Upstream view of dune bed configuration, 8 ft. flume. Bed material was sand No. II, slope $=0.00167$, depth$=0.94$ ft., discharge$=15.7$ cfs, $C/\sqrt{g}=9.3$.

eter of bed material is coarser than 0.6 mm; resistance to flow with ripples is independent of the grain size whereas with dunes it is dependent on the grain size; and ripples move essentially in one horizontal plane with uniform amplitude while dunes move in many planes with many amplitudes. All of these observations indicate that there is a substantial difference between the two bed configurations. This question might appear academic were it not for the fact that in most flume investigations the ripple bed dominates, whereas in the field, dunes dominate. As Taylor and Brooks (1962) pointed out, if there is a fundamental difference between ripples and dunes, the problem of roughness analysis and modeling of alluvial channel cannot be resolved by small scale laboratory studies.

Considering the various forms of bed roughness observed in alluvial channels, perhaps the significance of ripples has been over stated. It is the simplest form of bed roughness to study in the laboratory and there is usually evidence of ripples in most sedimentary deposits, but it is rarely a significant form of bed roughness in alluvial channels. Ripples usually develop on the backs of dunes, in the troughs of dunes and at the end of runoff events when stream power diminishes sufficiently to form ripples. In essence, ripples occur under such conditions that there is usually evidence of their existence in sedimentary structures, but they may not be significantly related to the major factors which had to do with the formation of sedimentary deposits. It has been shown by Harms and Fahnestock (this volume) that ripples form only a veneer, based upon stratigraphic sections, at Vinton and Mesilla on the Rio Grande.

FIG. 7—Plane bed configuration, 8 ft. flume. Bed material was sand No. II, slope $=0.00167$, depth $=0.74$ ft., discharge $=21.8$ cfs, $C/\sqrt{g}=18.4$.

Plane Bed with Sediment Movement

A plane bed is a bed without elevations or depressions larger than the maximum size of the bed material (fig. 7). The resistance to flow with the plane bed is relatively small, resulting largely from grain roughness which is related to size of bed material, and $C/\sqrt{g}$ is large, ranging from 14 to 23. However, it is not the usual type of grain roughness. Now the grains are rolling, hopping and sliding along the bed, and the resistance coefficient is slightly less than for the static plane bed. The difference in resistance to flow between the plane bed with sediment moving and a static plane bed has been observed by many experimenters, and was attributed by Vanoni and Nomicos (1960) to dampening of the turbulence by the suspended sediment, whereas Elata and Ippen (1961) indicated that the structure of the turbulence was not damped by the suspended sediment, but that its structure was changed by the movement of the sediment at the boundary. A large part of the transported bed material is confined to a relatively thin layer near the bed, and the total bed material transport concentration ranged approximately from 2,000 to 6,000 ppm.

The Froude number (F_r) is commonly used to differentiate between subcritical and supercritical flow in rigid channels. However, it is not particularly useful for classifying flow and bed forms in alluvial channels. The magnitude of the stream power $\tau_0 V$ at which the dunes or transition roughness changed to the plane bed depended primarily on the fall velocity of the bed material. With the fine sands (low fall velocity) the dunes washed out at relatively low stream power in comparison to the coarser sands. Conse-

quently, in the flume experiments where the depths were shallow (0.5 to 1.0 ft.); the plane bed occurred in the finer sands at smaller slopes resulting in smaller velocities and Froude numbers than with the coarser sands. With the fine sands the plane bed occurred at slopes such that the Froude number based on average depth and average velocity, was as small as 0.3 and persisted until the Froude number was increased to about 0.8. With the coarse sands the larger slopes required to change from transition to the plane bed resulted in larger velocities and Froude numbers. Hence, in the flume with fine sand the plane bed after the transition is very common and exists over a relatively large range of Froude numbers (0.3 to 0.8). On the other hand, with coarse sand and shallow depths the transition may not terminate until the Froude number is so large that the subsequent bed form may not be a plane bed, but instead antidunes. In natural streams because of their larger depths the change from transition to plane bed may occur at much lower Froude numbers than in the flume experiments because of the larger stream power (large depth).

Antidunes

Antidunes are the bed forms in alluvial channels that occur in trains and that are in phase with and strongly interact with water-surface gravity waves (see figs. 8 and 9). The height and length of these waves depends on the scale of the flow system and the characteristics of the fluid and bed material. In the 8-ft. flume, the heights of the sand waves from the bottom of the trough to the crest ranged from 0.03 ft. to 0.5 ft. and the water waves were 1.5 to 2 times the height of the sand waves. The length of the waves from crest to crest or trough to trough range from 5 to 10

FIG. 8.—Downstream view of antidune flow. Bed material was sand No. II, slope $=0.00813$, depth $=0.55$ ft., discharge $=21.7$ cfs, $C/\sqrt{g}=13.0$.

feet. In natural streams, much larger antidunes form. In the Rio Grande, surface waves from 2 to 3 ft. in height and 10 to 20 ft. from crest to crest have been observed (Nordin, 1964a).

Antidunes do not exist as a continuous train of waves that never change, but trains of waves gradually build up with time from a plane bed and plane water surface. The water-surface waves may grow in height until they become unstable and break as the sea surf or they may gradually subside. The former have been called breaking antidunes or antidunes and the latter, standing waves. As the antidunes form and increase in height they may move upstream, downstream or remain stationary. Their upstream movement is the reason Gilbert (1914) named them antidunes.

Resistance to flow for antidunes in a reach of a stream or in the flume depends on how often the antidunes form, the area of the reach that they occupy, and the violence and frequency of the breaking of accompanying water-surface waves. When breaking waves do not occur with antidune flow, resistance to flow is about the same as for a plane bed. $C/\sqrt{g}$ ranges from 14 to 23. The acceleration and deceleration of the flow through the non-breaking waves (frequently called standing waves) increases slightly the resistance to flow above that for a plane bed. When antidune flow occurs with considerable breaking of surface waves, the waves dissipate a considerable amount of energy. With breaking waves $C/\sqrt{g}$ may range from 10 to 20. The magnitude of $C/\sqrt{g}$ depends on the magnitude and frequency of the breaking waves in the reach of the stream or length of flume under study.

When antidunes break, bed material is thrown into the flow (see fig. 9) and a large part of the total sediment discharge moves in suspension. When antidunes do not break, the concentration of the bed material discharge is only slightly higher than for the plane bed. With little fine sediment in the flow, concentrations of bed material ranged from approximately 3,000 to 40,000 ppm. In flows containing appreciable amounts of fine sediments, much higher concentrations of bed material have been recorded for antidune flows, and extreme concentrations of over 600,000 ppm with up to 450,000 ppm in sand sizes have been observed in several Southwestern streams, where the ephemeral flows often are characterized by violently breaking antidunes (Nordin, 1963). These extreme concentrations grade into mud flows, and there is perhaps some upper limiting concentration beyond which antidunes do not form, but available data are inadequate to establish the limit.

With antidune flow the in-phase water and

FIG. 9.—Side view of the antidune flow illustrated in figure 8 (scale in feet and tenths of feet).

bed surface is a positive indication that the flow is in rapid flow regime ($F_r \approx 1$). With dunes, the water surface is out of phase with the bed surface and is a positive indication that the flow is in the tranquil flow regime ($F_r < 1$). In both cases, the Froude number, which is based on the ratio of the mean velocity of the flow to the velocity of a gravity wave, c, must take into account the wave length, L. That is $c^2 = (gL/2\pi) \tanh 2\pi D/L$ and cannot be approximated by $c^2 = gD$ as often is done in open channel flow. Also the mean velocity must be that of the flow in the section of the stream where the antidunes are occurring and not for the entire cross section of the stream.

Chutes and Pools

At very large slopes, alluvial channel flow changes to what has been called chutes and pools. In the large 8-ft. flume this type of flow only occurred with the 0.19 mm sand. The coarser sands required a steeper slope to form chutes and pools than could be obtained. This type of flow consists of a long reach (10 to 30 ft.) where the flow rapidly accelerated. At the end of this chute there was a hydraulic jump followed by a long pool (10 to 30 feet in length) where the flow was tranquil, but was accelerating (figs. 10 and 11). These chutes and pools moved upstream at velocities of about 1 to 2 ft. per minute. As illustrated in figures 10 and 11, the elevation of the sand bed varied within wide limits, although at no time was the flume floor exposed. Resistance to flow with this type of flow phenomenon was large with $C/\sqrt{g}$ ranging from 9 to 16. Chutes and pools rarely are observed in the field because the stream power, turbulence, and sediment supply required are so large that the banks of a stream would be rapidly attacked, widening

FIG. 10.—Downstream view of chute and pool flow. The pool is in the foreground with the breaking wave in the background at the downstream end of the chute. Bed material was sand No. I, slope=0.0095, depth =0.65 ft., discharge=21.8 cfs, $C/\sqrt{g}$=9.2.

the channel, decreasing the velocity, and changing the flow from chutes and pools to some more common flow condition such as antidunes or plane bed.

Bars

The common types of bars which occur in alluvial streams include alternate bars, middle bars and point bars. These are large depositional features, which, with the exception of the point bars that develop on the convex side of bends, change position and form with time, and flow conditions. The bed forms discussed above are superposed on bars in irregular arrays depending on the flow conditions. Bar origin in straight reaches is related to and amplifies the tendency of a thread of current to meander.

When very large width-depth ratios were investigated in the flume by keeping depth of flow small, the main flow current meandered from side to side, as in natural streams, and bars of small amplitude and large area, on which the bed forms of figure 3 are superimposed, develop in an alternating pattern adjacent to the walls. In contrast to ripples or dunes, which may be small in relation to the channel width, the alternate bars extend across the channel one-half to two-thirds the full channel width and average in length three to five channel widths. Figure 12 shows a plan view of the alternate bars developed in the 8-ft. flume when the width-depth ratio was about 22, the slope was 0.0020, the discharge was 4 cubic feet per second, and the bed material had a median diameter of 0.19 mm.

STRATIFICATION

Although the flume investigations were ori-

ented toward the problems of flow resistance and sediment transport, some attention was given to the stratification of the various sedimentary structures comprising the elements of bed roughness. The most obvious features, of course, were the segregation accompanying the bed configurations of low regime flows, and the distinctive cross bedding, foreset, topset, and bottomset beds associated with dunes.

With ripples, the coarser fractions of the bed material segregate in the troughs, and the finer fractions accumulate on the crests (see fig. 5), a distinctive feature of water-generated ripples which differentiates them nicely from wind ripples, where the reverse is true (Bagnold, 1941, p. 152). With dunes, the bedding planes formed by the avalanching of material over the crests are more articulate than for ripples, and the stratification into bottom set, foreset, and topset beds is usually well defined. Figure 13 shows typical bottom set and foreset beds. With the passage of one dune over another, the deposit consists of foreset, bottom set, then foreset beds, as indicated in figure 13, with little or no evidence of a topset bed.

A peculiar segregation in the dune bed formations of the 0.93 mm median diameter bed material, not found in the finer sands, was observed. The coarser fractions of the bed material separated from the finer fractions over parts of the bed, and dunes composed entirely of the coarser fractions (greater than 1 mm) were sustained and propagated in the direction of flow for an appreciable time before remixing with the finer bed material. This phenomenon, which is not related to the mechanics of gravel bar formations described by Leopold and Wolman (1957, p. 47), may account for the small isolated bars of pea

FIG. 11.—Side view of the breaking antidune illustrated in figure 10. Note the large quantity of bed material in suspension.

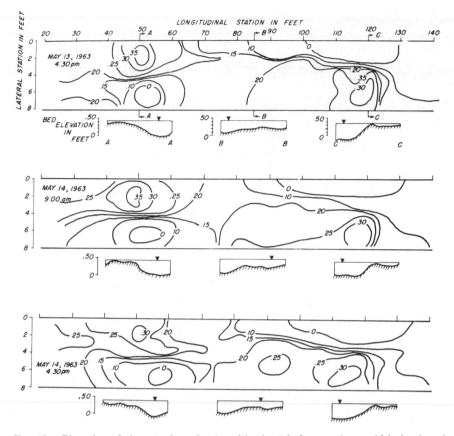

FIG. 12.—Plan view of alternate bars developed in the 8-ft flume at large width-depth ratios (contours are the bed elevation, in feet, above on arbitrary datum).

gravel observed by the writers in the upper Rio Grande in New Mexico. Similar segregation of granule patches have been observed in wind dune areas (Bagnold, 1941, p. 154), but it has not been verified that the sorting process is the same for both wind and water transport.

With ripples, the separation zone in the flow extended about two-thirds the distance from crest to crest and created only minor disturbances in the flow and bed roughness pattern, but with dunes, velocities of the reverse flow in the separation zone downstream from the crests were as great as one-half the mean flow velocity. The greater the velocity of reverse flow, the greater was the angle of the dune face, and in the extreme, the angle of the dune face was as much as four degrees steeper than the angle of repose of the bed material. Regressive ripples, the asymmetric ripples oriented in the direction opposite to the general direction of flow, described in detail by Jopling (1961), were observed to form in the troughs of the dunes for most of the dune runs. Generally, these ripples were destroyed by the avalanching of material down the dune faces,

and the vestiges of the ripples covered by the foreset beds as the dunes advanced were unrecognizable or at least modified to the extent that orientation of the ripples could not be established. However, sand with a heavy mineral

FIG. 13.—Stratification in dunes. This is a side view of the dune bed configuration illustrated in figure 6. Note the bottomset and foreset layering of the sand.

content which will effectively mark stratification sometimes allows one to see that the ripples migrated toward the avalanche face.

It is particularly significant that ripples move in essentially a single plane while dunes move in many planes; thus equilibrium flow over a dune bed may create, modify or obliterate structural features below the mean bed elevation to a depth equal at least to the mean flow depth.

As stream power and sediment transport increase for flow over a dune bed, the dunes become longer and the avalanching of material down the faces of the dunes is replaced by an almost continuous sheet flow of sediment. The dune bed appears to stretch longitudinally until dune height becomes very small and dune spacing very large and in the limit the bed becomes plane. The bedding planes parallel to the water surface form a crust ranging from a few grain diameters to a few inches thick, which is relatively firm compared to the surfaces of the dunes or ripples, and the truncated dunes and filled troughs showed plainly through the observation walls of the flume.

The symmetric sand waves in phase with the water-surface waves during the antidune flow do not produce obvious residual bed features; when the standing waves died without breaking, the bed again became plane, and when the waves broke, the bed was disturbed to a considerable depth. For chutes and pools, the bed was disturbed to a depth approximately equal to the mean flow depth.

Perhaps the most significant feature of the upper regime flow, so far as stratification is concerned, was the fact that the size distribution of the transported material was the size distribution of the bed material and that appreciable segregation did not occur. For the bed forms associated with lower regime flow, sorting or segregation of some kind was always observed, and the median diameter and sorting coefficient of the transported material were generally less than the median diameter and sorting coefficient of the bed material.

The development and movement of the large alternate bars that form at small width-depth ratios, and that have been observed both in the flume and in the field, present especially interesting complications in the structure of bed features. As these bars form and migrate downstream, the velocity, depth, and direction of flow change with time and with distance along the bar. Smaller bed features, the ripples, dunes, and plane bed, may all be present simultaneously on the bar, and on the downstream part of the bar where deposition is occurring the depositional sequence gives a reasonable. indication of the

flow regime associated with the deposition. However, as the direction of flow over the bars changes, so does the orientation of the smaller bed forms, and in any given depositional sequence, a variety of orientations present themselves, perhaps none of which indicate a direction of flow parallel to the main current of the stream. This was clearly illustrated in a study by Harms and others (1963, p. 512–574).

The development and subsequent erosion of large alternate bars relates significantly to (1) channel geometry including width, depth, bed forms and alignment (2) the sorting process by which sand size decrease downstream (3) scour phenomena and (4) the features of sedimentary deposit. Further study of the mechanics of the formation, migration, elimination and effects of these large bars warrants detailed consideration, both in straight reaches and in streams of various alignments.

Within the straight reaches these large bars develop in an alternate pattern—one on one side of the channel, the next on the other side—such that the main current meanders around them. These large bars move and are affected by changes in the geometry of the channel. When they reach a bend they are radically modified or destroyed by the secondary circulation and within the bend a point bar is formed which is attached to the convex bank. These point bars have shapes dictated by the geometry of the bend, flow parameters and bed material load. In very wide channels with large width to depth ratios, large bars may form within the channel away from the banks. In some cases these bars may be reinforced on their upstream point by vegetation or by coarse material in such a way that with subsequent scour and changes in the geometry of the stream they become semi-permanent islands.

COMPARISON OF FLUME AND FIELD CONDITIONS

The same types of roughness elements observed in the laboratory flume have been observed in natural streams. In natural channels however, there are usually additional complicating factors. The major differences between flume and field conditions are: (1) In the usual flumes only a limited range of depths and discharges can be investigated, but slope and velocity can be varied between wide limits. (2) In the field a larger range of depth and discharge is common, but slope of a particular channel reach is relatively constant. (3) Referring to 1 and 2, the variation in the shear stress and stream power is principally the result of slope variation in the flume studies, and depth variation in a particular stream. (4) The banks of the flume are non-erodible and hence the width is constant, whereas for most alluvial channels their width depends on flow and bank conditions. (5) In the laboratory flume, larger Froude numbers ($V/\sqrt{gD}$) can be achieved because in the field, as the Froude number increases, the distance between banks is increased by erosion. Rarely does a Froude number, based upon average velocity and depth, exceed unity for any extended time period in a stream with erodible banks. (6) In the field where the slope of the energy grade line is constant, the Froude number is also constant unless there is a change in the resistance to flow ($F_r = (C/\sqrt{g})\sqrt{S}$). (7) The flow is more two-dimensional in flumes; however, the main current meanders from side to side of a large flume as in the field, and at large width-depth ratios the alternate bars described above invariably will form. (8) In the field, the writers have observed that it is even more obvious that the flow meanders between the parallel banks of a straight channel and that this pattern of flow is closely related to the alternate bars which form opposite the apex of the meanders (Simons and Richardson, 1964b). As in the flume, the alternate bars increase in amplitude until they are close to the water surface. In fact, adjacent local scour in the main current may drop the water surface, slightly exposing the tops of these large bars. This has also been observed in the Rio Grande (Fahnestock, personal communication) and in other natural channels. In the field where the banks are not stable, the banks erode where the high velocity impinges and opposite these regions of local scour, deposition occurs. The ultimate development is a meandering stream if other factors such as slope, discharge, and size of bed material are compat-

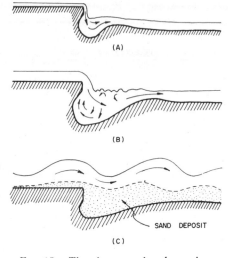

Fig. 15.—The plunge pool under various flow conditions.

ible. (9) In most natural channels, nonuniform velocity and depth result in multiple bed forms across a section or along a reach, whereas in the laboratory for the equilibrium flows, the bed configuration was established throughout the length of the flume. In the Rio Grande in New Mexico, as in many shallow streams, it is not uncommon to see violently breaking antidunes in the central part of the channel, bordered by a plane bed, with dunes and ripples in the lower velocities near the banks. (10) The influence of fine sediment on fluid and flow properties has been investigated in the laboratory (Simons and others, 1963), but the sedimentary structures formed in streams with cohesive beds or banks, such as the armored clay balls shown in figure 14, have not been subjected to intensive laboratory studies. The mechanics of the development of tractional sedimentary structures in streams with cohesive beds presents an important area for future research. (11) Finally, changes in the bed elevation of a natural stream, the result of either local scour and deposition or of changes in local base level, may complicate or completely modify the stratigraphic features of previous bed forms. For example, figure 15 is a schematic diagram of flow conditions over the headcut and plunge pool in the channel of the Rio Puerco which exposed the deposit of armored clay balls shown above (Nordin, 1964b). Both the depth of scour at the plunge pool which destroyed previous stratification, and the rate of advance of the headcut depended mostly on discharge, being a maximum at intermediate flows (fig. 15b) and a minimum at low flows, when there was insufficient energy to undercut the lip of the plunge pool (fig. 15a), and at high flows, when the cut

Fig. 14.—Deposit of clay balls, Rio Puerco near Bernardo, New Mexico.

channel became filled with sand (fig. 15c). In this case, the bed features generated by the flow and the stratification downstream from the headcut depended not only on the characteristics of the flow and fluid, but also on (1) downstream conditions, that is, the bed elevation of the Rio Grande which controlled the local base level; (2) upstream conditions, which determined the discharge and the availability of transported sand; and (3) antecedent conditions, which dictated the thickness of the armored clay layer forming the lip of the headcut.

In short, nature provides infinite variety, and the simpler sedimentary structures observed in the flume and in the field can serve only as rough guides in interpreting or reconstructing complex natural processes.

PRINCIPAL VARIABLES

The forms of bed roughness and the resistance to flow in alluvial channels are complicated by the large number of variables and by the interdependency, either real or apparent, of the variables. In addition, some variables may be altered or even determined by the flow, and changes in flow conditions may change the role of a dependent variable into that of an independent one. It is difficult, especially in field studies, to select the independent and dependent variables from the possible candidates.

In a recent study, Simons and Richardson (1964b) give a comprehensive analysis of the variables affecting bed configuration and flow resistance, their dependency and independency, the conditions whereby a dependent variable may become an independent one, and which variables may be eliminated as a first approximation. A detailed discussion is beyond the scope of this paper, but it is appropriate to list the variables affecting the bed forms and to discuss, in general terms, the effect or importance of the different variables. The variables that fix the form of bed roughness in alluvial channels are

$$\text{form of bed roughness} = \phi[D, S, d, \sigma, \rho, g, w, S_c, f_s] \quad (1)$$

where

$$w = \phi[d, \rho_s, \rho, g, S_p, \mu] \quad (2)$$

and in which $D=$ depth, $S=$ slope of the energy grade line, $d=$ median diameter of the bed material, $\sigma=$ measure of the size distribution of the bed material, $\rho=$ density of the water-sediment mixture, $g=$ acceleration due to gravity, $w=$ fall velocity of the bed material, $S_c=$ shape factor of the cross section, $f_s=$ seepage force in the bed of the stream, $\rho_s=$ density of the sediment, S_p = shape factor of the particles, $\mu=$ apparent dynamic viscosity of the water-sediment mixture.

The velocity of flow and the concentration of bed material transport, which some investigators have suggested are variables, have been omitted from equation (1) because under the constraint of equilibrium flow, both are dependent variables. If flow is not in equilibrium, that is, if the concentration of bed material entering a flume or reach is larger or smaller than the concentration leaving, the concentration would then be an independent variable and should be included in equation (1). The effect of bed material concentration on fluid properties is accounted for by using apparent viscosity and computed mass density of the water-sediment mixture for the viscosity and density terms in equation (1) (Simons and others, 1963). The influence of sediment concentration on the turbulent structure and velocity distribution of the flow is not considered in equation (1), but the effects are generally small for volume concentrations up to 20 percent (Elata and Ippen, 1961) and can be ignored for a first approximation.

The effects of fine sediment on the apparent viscosity of the water-sediment mixture are considered included in the viscosity term. Fine sediments do not appear to influence the turbulence structure or velocity distribution (Nordin, 1964b).

In a natural stream the energy losses and non-uniformity of flow caused by the bends and non-uniformity of the banks can have an important influence on the sedimentary structures generated by the flow, and a shape factor for the reach should be included in equation (1). For straight flumes with parallel walls and without large bars the shape factor of the reach is a constant and can be disregarded. Also, the shape factor for the cross section, S_c, can be disregarded unless exceedingly shallow flows in a very wide flume are studied or data from flumes of different widths are compared. Flow phenomena, bed configuration and resistance to flow will vary with the width of the flume.

Simons, Richardson and Haushild (1963) noted that (1) ripples observed in the 8-ft. wide flume did not occur with the same sand in the 2-ft. wide flume; (2) the dune fronts in the 8-ft. flume rarely were continuous from one wall to the other, whereas in the 2-ft. flume they always were, and (3) the antidunes in the 8-ft. flume could be two or three-dimensional and could occupy only a small part of the flume or could extend from wall to wall. Hence, the bed configurations were different in the two sizes of flumes for the same conditions (depth, slope, fall velocity, etc.). Vanoni and Brooks (1957, p. 5) also commented that there was a difference in results for their 10.5 inch and 33.3 inch flumes which could not be accounted for by sidewall correction.

Both the shape of the reach and of the cross

section are partially responsible for the fact that two or more bed configurations can occur side by side in natural streams.

The seepage force f_s is another variable which can be eliminated from equation (1) for the flume case. However, as Simons and Richardson (1962b) pointed out, in alluvial channels there is usually either inflow or outflow from the channel through the banks and bed material that causes seepage forces in the bed. If there is inflow, the seepage force acts to reduce the effective weight of the sand; and consequently, the stability of the bed material. If there is outflow from a channel, the seepage force acts in the direction of gravity and increases the effective weight of the sand and stability of the bed material. As a direct result of changing the effective weight, the seepage forces can influence the form of bed roughness and the resistance to flow for a given channel slope, channel shape, bed material, and discharge.

With the above simplifications and considering the acceleration due to gravity a constant, equation (1) becomes

form of bed roughness $= \phi(S, D, d, w, \sigma, \rho)$ (3)

The relation of the variables in equation (3) to the bed configuration will be discussed in the following paragraphs. The variables were not grouped into dimensionless parameters for discussion purposes to avoid masking the essential role of any one of them.

Depth and Slope

Slope enters as a factor in equation (1) primarily through its role in the shear stress, γDS, as the driving force responsible for particle motion; and, at steep slopes, through its contribution to a gravity component of the submerged weight of the sediment in the direction of flow (Bagnold, 1956). With changes in stream power or shear stress, the sedimentary structures generated at the bed by the flow change. To develop a given form of bed configuration in alluvial channels that have the same bed material, the slope will be large if depth is small, and the slope must be small if the depth is large.

Depth also enters the shear stress, and the combination of depth and slope in the shear term, γDS, and its relation to particle size has been investigated by Shields (1936), Bagnold (1956), Brooks (1958) and many others. However, depth is also important as a scale factor which limits the ultimate size of the bed features, it relates significantly to the relative roughness, and perhaps it is a factor which influences the turbulent energy spectrum. In addition, depth plays an important role in the bed material transport (Colby, 1961).

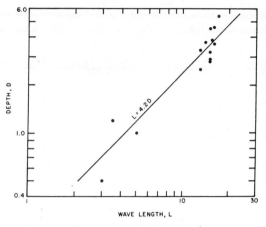

FIG. 16.—Relation of depth to wave length of standing waves (units are feet).

The sequence of bed forms which develop with increasing slope, holding depth constant, depends on both depth and fall velocity of the bed material. With shallow depth, the bed configuration may change from ripples to a plane bed with increasing shear stress because the shallow depths inhibit dune formation, while for greater depths, the same increase in shear stress will change the ripples to dunes. For bed material with a fall velocity greater than 0.22 ft/sec., ripples have not been observed for any combination of depth and slope. (Simons and Richardson, 1964b).

In natural channels, where slope is approximately constant, the same sequence of bed forms observed in the laboratory may result from changes in depth, and as in the laboratory, depth plays an important role as a scale factor. For example, the flow depth determines the height of the large alternate bars which form at high width-depth ratios, as well as the scale of any superposed features. Another example of depth effect is given by Nordin (1964a), where for the Rio Grande and tributaries, the wave length of standing waves was roughly related to measured flow depth in the vicinity of the waves (fig. 16).

The effects of the physical size of the bed material in the formation of the bed configurations are (1) its influence on the fall velocity which is a measure of the interaction of the fluid and the particle, (2) its effect as grain roughness, and (3) its influence on the turbulent structure and the velocity field of the flow.

The physical size of the bed material, as measured by fall diameter (Colby and Christensen, 1956) or by sieve-diameter, is a primary factor in determining fall velocity, although it is only important as it is related to the other variables in equation (2). Fall diameter has the advantage over the sieve-diameter of including the role of

TABLE 2.—*Comparison of the various characteristics of ripples and dunes with fall velocity of the bed material.*

	Sand		Ripples				Dunes			
No.	d_{50} (mm)	Fell velocity (ft./sec.)	Depth (ft.)	$C/\sqrt{g}$	L (ft.)	h (ft.)	Depth (ft.)	$C/\sqrt{g}$	L (ft.)	h (ft.)
I	.19	.064–.073	1.01	13.1	0.63	0.04	.91	12.0	8.4	.30
II	.27	.10 –.12	.96	11.1	.95	.04	.93	10.6	7.6	.30
III	.46	.20 –.22	.81	11.2	1.13	.10	.81	9.6	5.9	.30
IV	.93	.48 –.49	—	—	—	—	1.02	10.8	4.7	.21

the shape factor and density of the particle as variables. Knowing only the fall diameter, the fall velocity of the particle in any fluid at any temperature can be computed, whereas, with the sieve diameter knowledge of the shape factor and density of the particle are also needed.

The physical size of the bed material is the dominant factor in determining the friction factor for the plane bed condition and for anti-dunes when they are not actively breaking. With antidunes there is the additional dissipation of energy by the formation and breaking of the waves which increases with an increase in energy input or a decrease in the fall velocity of the bed material.

With dunes, the physical size of the bed material also has an effect on resistance to flow. The flow of fluid over the backs of the dunes is affected by the grain roughness, although the dissipation of energy by the form roughness of the dunes is the major factor. The form of the dunes is related to the fall velocity of the bed material (table 2).

Fall Velocity

Fall velocity is the primary variable that determines the interaction between the bed material and the fluid. For a given depth and slope, it determines the bed form that will occur, the actual dimensions of the bed form (table 2) and, except for the contribution of the grain roughness, the resistance to flow.

To illustrate the significance of fall velocity of the bed material on the spacing or length of dunes for various sizes of bed material at essentially constant depth, refer to figure 17. The dunes are not only shorter in length, but they are also much more angular (upstream and downstream faces are steeper) when the fall velocity of the bed material is relatively large. The magnitude of shear stress for the beginning of motion, which indicates when a plane bed without motion changes to ripples or dunes, and the magnitude of the shear stress where a dune bed is replaced with a plane bed with motion or antidunes depend primarily on the fall velocity. An increase in fall velocity requires an increase in the shear stress for the change from static plane bed to ripples or dunes or the change from dunes to plane bed and antidunes.

Fall velocity determines (1) whether ripples or dunes will form after the beginning of motion, (2) the magnitude of the shear stress where a plane bed without movement will begin to move and ripples or dunes form, and (3) the magnitude of the shear stress where ripples will change to dunes. Ripples will not form in material with a fall diameter larger than 0.6 mm or with a fall velocity larger than about 0.22 ft/sec., although there is some evidence that the physical size of the bed material also is important in determining whether ripples form. The magnitude of the shear stress required for the formation of ripples increases with an increase in fall velocity.

With dunes, the smaller the median fall velocity of the bed material, the less angular the dunes are and the greater their wave length, crest to crest, for similar depths of flow (table 2). Also, the smaller the median fall velocity the smaller the range of shear stress or of stream power within which a plane bed occurs.

For bed material with median fall velocity equal to or larger than 0.2 ft/sec., the range of stream power within which dunes occur is large

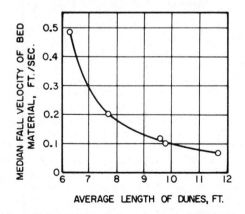

FIG. 17.—Approximate relation of length of dunes to median fall velocity of bed material, at constant depth.

and the range of stream power within which plane bed occurs is small. In fact, whether or not a plane bed occurs at all between dunes and standing waves is intimately related to fall velocity and depth. With shallow depths and bed material with relatively large fall velocity, the bed configuration may change from transition to standing waves without the development of plane bed.

With antidunes, the magnitude of the shear required for them to form and the amount of antidune activity (formation and breaking of the antidunes) for a given shear stress depends on the fall velocity. With a decrease in fall velocity there is a corresponding decrease in the magnitude of the shear required for the formation of the antidunes and for an increase in antidune activity.

The changes in bed form discussed in the preceding paragraphs were primarily the result of changes in the fall velocity and were independent of whether the fall velocity was varied by changing the viscosity of the water-sediment mixture or by varying the density of the bed material (Simons and Richardson, 1964b). Viscosity was varied by changing the temperature or the concentration of fine sediment of the water-sediment mixture. With a change in fall velocity and other factors held constant, the bed configuration and resistance to flow changed (Hubbell and Ali, 1961; Simons and others, 1963) and in the extreme case, by decreasing fall velocity, a dune bed could be changed to a plane bed, or a plane bed into antidunes.

In addition to the flume experiments, observations on natural streams have verified that the bed configuration and resistance to flow will

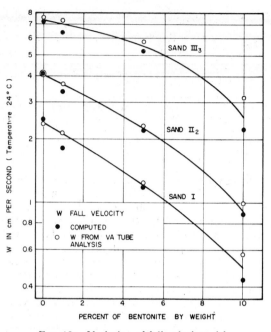

FIG. 19.—Variation of fall velocity with percent of bentonite in water.

change with changes in fall velocity when the discharge and bed material are constant (Hubbell and others, 1956). For example, the Loup River near Dunning, Nebraska, has dunes as the bed roughness in the summer when the stream fluid is warm and less viscous; but the bed is essentially plane during the cold winter months. Similarly, data collected by Fahnestock (personal communication) on a stable reach of the Río Grande show that at similar discharges, when the water was cold the bed of the stream was plane, but when the water was warm, the bed form was dunes.

Apparent Viscosity and Density

The effect of the various factors given in equation (2) on fall velocity are well known. However, the effects of fine sediment in suspension on fluid viscosity and fall velocity are less well known (Simons and others, 1963). In figure 18, the effect of fine sediment (bentonite) on the apparent kinematic viscosity of the mixture is illustrated. The magnitude of the effect of fine sediment on viscosity is large and depends on the chemical makeup of the fine sediment. The changes in the fall velocity of the median fall diameter as a result of the changes in the viscosity and the fluid density can be noted in figure 19.

In addition to changing the viscosity, fine sediment suspended in water increases the mass density, ρ, and the specific weight, γ, of the mix-

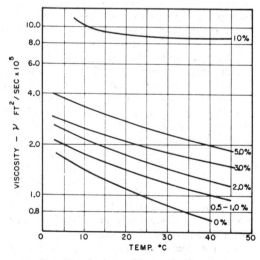

FIG. 18.—Apparent kinematic viscosity of water-bentonite dispersions.

ture. The specific weight, γ, of a sediment-water mixture can be computed from the relation:

$$\gamma = \gamma_w \gamma_s / [\gamma_s - C(\gamma_s - \gamma_w)] \qquad (4)$$

where γ_w is the specific weight of the water (about 62.4 lb. per cu. ft.), γ_s is the specific weight of the sediment (about 164.5 lb. per cu. ft. for sand), C_s is the concentration (in percent by weight) of the suspended sediment (Simons and others, 1963). A sediment-water mixture, where $C_s = 10$ percent, has a specific weight, γ, of about 70 lb. per cu. ft. and any change in γ affects the boundary shear stress and the stream power.

Sorting of Bed Material

The effect of sorting of the bed material on flow in alluvial channels, holding depth constant, was investigated in the 2-ft. wide 60-ft. flume using two quartz sands with the same d_{50} (the number VI sands in fig. 2 with $d_{50} = 0.33$ mm). The VI$_1$ sand was uniform with a sorting coefficient, σ, of 1.27 and the VI$_2$ sand was nonuniform with $\sigma = 2.07$ where

$$\sigma = \frac{1}{2}\left(\frac{d_{50}}{d_{16}} + \frac{d_{84}}{d_{50}}\right) \qquad (5)$$

The variation of the bed configuration, resistance to flow and sediment transport were observed and measured (Daranandana, 1962; Simons and Richardson, 1964a, 1964b).

The effect of the sorting of the bed material on bed form and resistance to flow is illustrated qualitatively in figure 20. With a plane bed without sand motion, the resistance to flow was slightly larger for the uniform sand, whereas for the plane bed with motion, resistance to flow was greater for the poorly sorted sand. With the ripple, dune and antidune bed configuration, resistance to flow was considerably larger for the uniform sand. The transition from a dune bed to a plane bed occurred over a narrower range of shear values for the uniform sand, whereas with the poorly sorted sands the transition occurred over a large range of shear values.

The average height and length of ripples with uniform sand were larger than for the poorly sorted sand and dunes in the uniform sand had ripples superposed on them, whereas dunes in the poorly sorted sand did not. Although the dunes in the uniform sand were smaller, the effect of the ripples on their back increased resistance to flow. Dune length and height were 3.33 ft. and 0.095 ft., respectively in the uniform sand and 4.00 ft. and 0.14 ft. in the poorly sorted sand. With antidunes, average lengths and heights of the sand waves were larger for the uniform sands; 5.05 ft. and 0.15 ft., respectively, com-

pared to 4.3 ft. and 0.085 ft. for the poorly sorted sand.

In general, bed features of the uniform sand were more angular than were the features of the poorly sorted sand.

Although quantitative relationships were not defined, the investigations definitely prove that there is an effect of sorting on the bed forms and emphasize that natural river sands should be used in flume experiments if their results are to be extrapolated to the field.

PREDICTION OF FORM OF BED ROUGHNESS

Knowledge of what the bed form is or may be under a given fluid, flow and sediment conditions has important engineering applications to stable channel design, to determining the stage-discharge relations for natural channels, and to estimating the water and sediment discharge of a stream. Similarly, in geologic studies, given a particular sediment and sedimentary structure it is often desirable to determine the flow condition or depositional environment which generated the structural features. A completely satisfactory method of predicting form of bed roughness has not been developed, but the relatively simple relation presented by Simons and Richardson (1964a), which relates stream power, median fall velocity of bed material, and form roughness has proved useful in both engineering and geologic applications. This relation, figure 21, gives an indication of the form of bed roughness one can anticipate given the depth, slope, velocity, and fall diameter of bed material. Both flume and field data were utilized to establish the boundaries separating the various bed forms (Simons and Richardson, 1964b).

Figure 21 was developed for the bed forms observed in alluvial channels, and therefore it is not applicable to such sedimentary structures as form in deltas, tidal estuaries, or lakes. However, it can be used to determine flow conditions (stream power) for ancient channels where the median fall diameter and sedimentary structures are determined. Furthermore, if an estimate of the slope of the ancient channel can be obtained from the slope of the deposit under consideration, the unit discharge of the channel can be roughly estimated.

SUMMARY

Based upon flume and field studies, the bed configurations generated on the bed of alluvial channels by the flow are ripples, ripples on dunes, dunes, plane bed, antidunes, and chutes and pools. The forms of bed roughness change with increasing tractive force from ripples to dunes and ultimately to antidunes or chutes and pools.

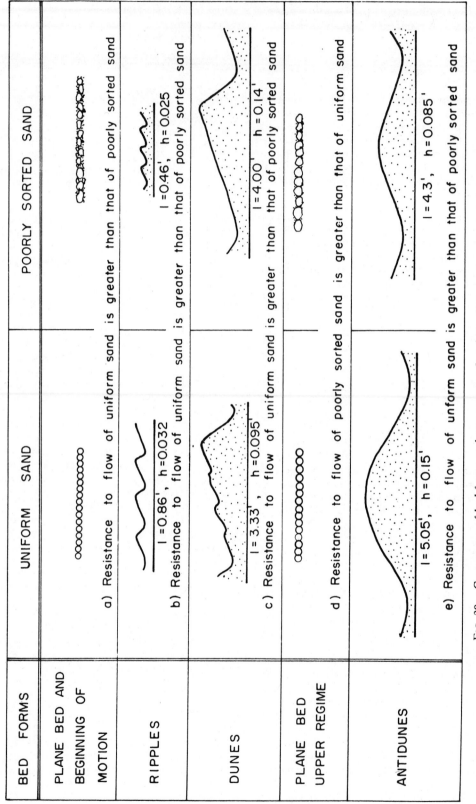

FIG. 20.—Comparison of bed forms and resistance to flow for uniform and poorly sorted sand.

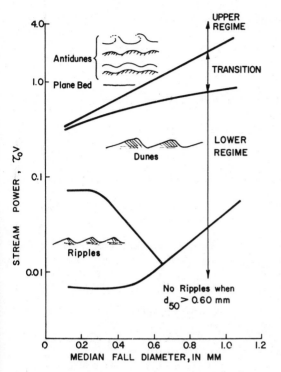

FIG. 21.—Relation of stream power and median fall diameter to form of bed roughness.

The flow generating the bed forms is classified into a lower flow regime and an upper flow regime. With lower flow regime, the bed forms are ripples or dunes or a combination of ripples and dunes; the flow resistance is high; the bed material transport rate is low; the water surface undulations are out of phase with the bed undulations, and considerable segregation of bed material occurs. With upper flow regime, the bed forms are plane bed, antidunes, or chutes and pools, or some combination of these; the bed material transport rate is high; segregation of the bed material is negligible; water surface and bed undulations are in phase; and flow resistance is low (excepting the chutes and pools or violent antidunes).

In addition to the above bed configurations, large bars, upon which the smaller bed features are superposed, will form in channels with large width-depth ratios. The orientation of the superposed features changes as flow over the bars varies. These bars may be alternate bars which form adjacent to the banks, bars detached from the banks, particularly when width-depth ratios are large, and point bars which are attached to the convex bank of the channel in bends.

The flume studies showed that regressive ripples form under equilibrium conditions, that ripples move in a single plane while dunes move in many planes, and that appreciable segregation occurs with lower flow regime, but not with upper flow regime.

For a given shear stress, the fall velocity of the bed material, which determines the interaction of fluid and particles, and the flow depth, which limits the ultimate size of the bed features, are the most important variables influencing the type and dimension of bed forms. The shape of the cross section and reach, seepage forces, the size distribution of the bed material, and the presence of fine cohesive material either in the fluid, or in the bed and banks of the channel, are also shown to be important.

Finally, a relation of bed form, stream power, and median fall diameter of bed material is presented which has some practical application to channel design or to interpreting depositional environments.

References

Bagnold, R. A., 1936, The movement of the desert sand: *Proc. Roy. Soc., Ser A.*, V. 157, pp. 594–620.

Bagnold, R. A., 1941, *The Physics of Blown Sands and Desert Dunes*. Methuen and Co., London, 165 pp. Reprinted 1954.

Bagnold, R. A., 1956, The flow of cohesionless grains in fluids: *Roy. Soc. London, Phil. Trans., Ser. A*, V. 249, pp. 235–297.

Brooks, N. H., 1958, Mechanics of streams with movable beds of fine sand: *Amer. Soc. Civil Eng. Trans.*, V. 123, pp. 526–549., Discussion, pp. 550–594.

Carey, W. C., and Keller, M. D., 1957, Systematic changes in the beds of alluvial rivers: *Amer. Soc. Civil Eng. Proc.*, V. 83, no. HY4, pp. 1–24.

Colby, B. C., and Christensen, R. P., 1956, Visual accumulation tube for size analysis of sand: *Amer. Soc. Civil Eng. J.*, V. 82, no. HY3, pp. 1–17.

Colby, B. R., 1961, Effect of depth of flow on discharge of bed material: U. S. Geol. Survey, Water-Supply Paper 1498-D, pp. 1–12.

Darandandana, Niwat, 1962, A preliminary study of the effect of gradation of bed material on flow phenomena in alluvial channels: Ph.D. Thesis, Colorado State University, 189 pp.

Elata, C., and Ippen, A. T., 1961, The dynamics of open channel flow with suspensions of neutrally buoyant particles: Mass. Inst. Tech., Dep. Civil Sanitary Eng. Tech. Rep. 45, 69 pp.

Gilbert, G. K., 1914, The transportation of debris by running water: U. S. Geol. Survey, Prof. Paper 86, 263 pp.

Harms, J. C., MacKenzie, D. B., and McCubbin, D. G., 1963, Stratification in modern sands of the Red River, Louisiana: *J. Geol.*, V. 71, pp. 566–580.

Hubbell, D. W., and All, K. A.-S., 1961, Qualitative effects of temperature on flow phenomena in alluvial channels: U. S. Geol. Survey, Prof. Paper 424-D, Art. 301, pp. 21–23.

Hubbell, D. W., *et al.*, 1956, Investigations of some sedimentation characteristics of a sand bed stream: U. S. Geol. Survey open-file report, Lincoln, Nebraska.

Jopling, A. V., 1961, Origin of regressive ripples explained in terms of fluid-mechanic processes: U. S. Geol. Survey Prof. Paper 424-D pp. 15–17.

Knoroz, V. S., 1959, The effect of the channel macro-roughness on its hydraulic resistance: *Inst. Gidrotekaniki*, V. 62, pp. 75–96 (in Russian). Translated by Ivan Mittin, U. S. Geol. Survey, Denver, Colo.

Kramer, H., 1935, Sand mixtures and sand movement in fluvial models: *Amer. Soc. Civil. Eng. Trans.*, V. 100, pp. 798–878.

Leopold, L. B., and Wolman, M. E., 1957, River channel patterns: braided, meandering, and straight: U. S. Geol. Survey, Prof. Paper 262-B, 85 pp.

Liu, H. K., 1957, Mechanics of sediment-ripple formation: *Amer. Soc. Civil Eng. Proc.*, V. 83, no. HY2, 23 pp.

Nordin, C. F., Jr., 1963, A preliminary study of sediment transport parameters, Rio Puerco, near Bernardo, New Mexico: U. S. Geol. Survey, Prof. Paper 462-C, 21 pp.

Nordin, C. F., Jr., 1964a, Studies of flow in alluvial channels. Aspects of flow resistance and sediment transport, Rio Grande near Bernalillo, New Mexico: U. S. Geol. Survey, Water-Supply Paper 1498-H, 41 pp.

Nordin, C. F., Jr., 1964b, A study of sediment transport and channel erosion: *Amer. Soc. Civil Eng. Proc.*, V. 90, no. HY-4, pp. 173–192.

Shields, A., 1936, Anwendung der Ahnlichkeitsmechanik und der Turbulenzforschung auf die Geschiebebewegung: Mitteilungen der Preuss. Versuch anst. f. Wasserbau u. Schiffbau, Berlin, Heft 26, 26 pp. See also translation by W. P. Ott and J. C. van Uchelen, U. S. Dep. Agriculture, Soil Conservation Service Coop Lab., Calif. Inst. Tech.

Simons, D. B., and Richardson, E. V., 1962b, Studies of flow in alluvial channels. The effect of bed roughness on depth-discharge relations in alluvial channels: U. S. Geol. Survey, Water-Supply Paper 1498-E, 26 pp.

Simons, D. B., and Richardson, E. V., 1964a, A study of variables affecting flow characteristics and sediment transport in alluvial channels; U. S. Dept. Agriculture Miscellaneous Publication 970, p. 193–207.

Simons, D. B., and Richardson, E. V., 1964b, Resistance to flow in alluvial channels: Colorado State University, Civil Eng. Rep. CER64DBS-EVR, 176 pp.

Simons, D. B., Richardson, E. V., and Hauschild, W. L., 1963, Some effects of fine sediment on flow phenomena: U. S. Geol. Survey, Water-Supply Paper 1498-G, 46 pp.

Taylor, R. H., Jr., and Brooks, N. H., 1962, Discussion of resistance to flow in alluvial channels: *Amer. Ass. Civil Eng. Trans.*, V. 127, pp. 982–992.

Vanoni, V. A., 1946, Transportation of suspended sediment by water: *Amer. Ass. Civil Eng. Trans.*, V. 111, pp. 67–102.

Vanoni, V. A., and Brooks, N. H., 1957, Laboratory studies of the roughness and suspended load of alluvial streams: Calif. Inst. Tech. Sedimentation Lab. Rep. No. E-68, 121 pp.

Vanoni, V. A., and Kennedy, J. F., 1963, Discussion of forms of bed roughness in alluvial channels: *Amer. Soc. Civil Eng. Trans.*, V. 128, pp. 311–317.

Vanoni, V. A., and Nomicos, G. N., 1960, Resistance properties of sediment-laden streams: *Amer. Soc. Civil Eng. Trans.*, V. 125, pp. 1140–1175.

White, C. M., 1940, The equilibrium of grains on the bed of a stream: *Proc. Roy. Soc., Ser. A.*, V. 174, pp. 322–338.

U. S. Dept. Agriculuture Tech Bull., 1940, 695, p. 22-31.

17

Some Principles of Accelerated Stream and Valley Sedimentation

S. C. HAPP,
GORDON RITTENHOUSE,
and G. C. DOBSON

Practically all the modern sediments in Tobitubby and Hurricane Valleys belong to one or another of four distinct genetic types of deposits, and at least two other genetic types are present in minor amounts. These six types are:

Channel-fill deposits.
Vertical accretion deposits.
Flood-plain splays.
Colluvial deposits.
Lateral accretion deposits.
Channel lag deposits.

Of these, the last two types are of little importance among the modern deposits, but they may have been more important under premodern conditions. There are practically no lacustrine deposits, for such ponding as occurs on the flood plains produces swamps rather than lakes, and the swamp deposits are usually indistinguishable from other vertical accretion deposits.

These genetic types of deposits occur in what may be called four distinct associations, as follows:

Normal flood-plain, or valley-flat, association.
Alluvial-fan, or alluvial-cone, association.
Valley-plug association.
Delta association.

CHANNEL-FILL DEPOSITS

The channel-fill deposits have accumulated in the stream channels where the transporting capacity has been insufficient to remove the sand as rapidly as it has been delivered. The process has not been a simple sorting out and deposition of the coarsest material, but a net accumulation from alternate scouring during rising flood stages and deposition during the falling stages. As the average amount of scour has been less than the average amount of deposition, the net result has been aggradation of the channel bed.

The process of channel filling has proceeded rapidly in the upper parts of both Tobitubby and Hurricane Valleys, in many places, or perhaps in most, in connection with the development of valley-plug deposits (described on pp. 29–31). The present stream beds are usually higher than the buried premodern flood-plain surface, and in some places they are higher than the present flood-plain surface on either side. At range T–2 [4] (fig. 8), for example, the channel bottom is more than 4 feet higher than the flood-plain surface 400 feet away and 11 feet higher than the lowest part of the buried premodern flood-plain surface. The extreme channel aggradation is partly due to thick growths of willows and other vegetation along the stream banks, which stabilize and promote upbuilding of the natural levees. Occasional channel training and cleaning operations by the landowners also tend to keep the channel confined to the same position on the flood plain. Eventually, however, the channel shifts to a new course during a flood. In places the abandoned aggraded channels may be recognized as low sandy ridges, upon which there is only a meager growth of vegetation. Such an abandoned channel is shown on the topographic map of part of East Goose Valley (fig. 5). Channel-fill deposits comprise only a small part of the total modern sediments,

---

[4] T, H, WG, EG, and G refer to Tobitubby, Hurricane, West Goose, East Goose, and Goose Valleys, respectively.

337

but they have been of great importance in causing increased over-bank flooding and, consequently, increased flood-plain deposition and sanding of parts of the valley bottom.

The available evidence indicates that such rapid channel aggradation was not in progress before the area was settled. Dark soil horizons, ferruginous concretions, and extensive bleaching in parts of the pre-modern deposits and the fact that the buried dark-soil horizons occur over large areas at uniform elevation suggest that the flood-plain surface was comparatively stable, and hence that the channels were probably aggrading very slowly, if at all. Old flood-plain silts prevailingly overlie what appear to be channel sand deposits, and the thickness of the finer old sediment is generally fairly uniform. This relation also suggests that either the channels were aggrading slowly, if at all, or that lateral migration was more important than at present, so that the channel shifted from side to side and left a layer of channel sands at about the same elevation all the way across the valley, to be covered later by flood-plain deposits of vertical accretion.

VERTICAL ACCRETION DEPOSITS

In times of flood the stream channels have insufficient capacity to carry all the water delivered to them as surface run-off. The excess water overflows the banks and spreads widely over the adjacent flood plain. Because of greater frictional resistance, this spreading results in marked reduction in velocity and even greater reduction in trans-porting capacity. Part of the sediment carried in suspension while the water was confined to the channel is therefore deposited on the flood plain. As the velocity decreases the coarser material is dropped first and builds up the characteristically sandy natural levees that border the channels. Finer sediment is carried farther from the channel and deposited as a thinner layer over the entire flood-plain surface. This is the process of vertical accretion (25), and the deposits are composed almost entirely of sediment that was carried to the place of deposition as suspended load. In this respect they differ from the channel deposits, which are largely composed of bed-load sediment.

FLOOD-PLAIN SPLAYS

The regularity of flood-plain deposition is interrupted in those places where excess water leaves the channel through restricted low sections or breaks in the natural levees. In such places the velocity of the escaping water may be sufficient to carry along an appreciable quantity of relatively coarse sediment, which is carried farther from the channel than would otherwise be the case. The sandy sediment is commonly spread outward onto a fan-shaped area of the flood plain, across which it is moved forward at least partly as bed load. These deposits are here designated as flood-plain splays. They are essentially similar in origin to deposits spread out upon the flood plain when a crevasse develops in an artificial levee. Glenn (29, pp. 39–40) has described what probably is a form of splay as "fans of sand and cobbles * * * spread over the once fertile surface" at the ends of short, shallow distributaries leading from an overloaded small Appalachian stream.

Splays occur along many streams that are bordered by well-developed flood plains, but in Tobitubby and Hurricane Valleys their number and size have been greatly increased during the modern period. Although individually of small areal extent (pl. 4, *A*), in the aggregate they cover a large area and cause most of the harmful sanding of the bottom lands.

COLLUVIAL DEPOSITS

Accelerated colluvial deposits have accumulated in considerable quantity on the flood plain at the base of most slopes bordering Tobitubby and Hurricane Valleys, and perhaps in even larger quantities above the flood plains on the lower parts of the longer slopes. They have caused little damage, however, and have not produced any significant modification of the valley forms. These deposits are composed chiefly of the debris from sheet erosion deposited by unconcentrated surface run-off or slope wash, together with talus and other mass-movement accumulations. In Tobitubby and Hurricane Valleys they are dominantly of fine texture, reach maximum thicknesses of only a few feet, and rarely extend more than 100 feet across the valley bottoms from the base of the bordering slopes. They are most prominent in the narrow headwater sections of the valleys, where flood-plain deposition has been minimized as a result of valley trenching.

LATERAL ACCRETION DEPOSITS

The deposits of lateral flood-plain accretion are formed along the sides of channels, where bed-load material is moved by traction toward the inner sides of channel bends. Normally such deposits of lateral accretion are later covered by finer material of vertical accretion, as the channel shifts farther away by lateral bank cutting so that the slip-off slope on the inside of the bend is overflowed less frequently and with less velocity. The deposits of lateral accretion are coarser than those of vertical accretion, but they are finer, on the average, than the channel-fill or channel lag deposits because of a greater admixture of material deposited from suspension in the shallow water on the slip-off slope of the channel side. They may be composed largely of material eroded from the outside bank of the bend that has been moved diagonally down and across the channel bed by the currents associated with helical flow (*21*) and deposited on the opposite, or inner, bank of the same stream bend, or the next bend downstream.

In Tobitubby and Hurricane Valleys it is notable that the channel aggradation has been accompanied by little lateral migration of the channel by bank cutting, and, consequently, modern deposits of lateral accretion are of insignificant amount. The banks are generally well protected by vegetation and are fairly stable except where they have been artificially cleared. Several channel changes by avulsion [5] were in various stages of completion at the time of investigation, however, and this type of change is apparently more important than channel migration by lateral cutting.

CHANNEL LAG DEPOSITS

Channel lag deposits are composed of the relatively coarser materials that have been sorted out and left as a residual accumulation in the normal process of stream action. They are prominently developed in the beds of most streams but do not indicate channel aggradation,

---

[5] Abandonment of one channel and development of another in a new location on the flood plain, as contrasted with migration of channels by progressive bank cutting on the outside of bends and filling on the inside of the bends.

as do the channel-fill deposits. These lag sediments also tend to be mixed with the deposits of lateral accretion, but in many places there is a considerable residual accumulation of the coarsest sediment in the deeper parts of the main channel and in parts of the stream where lateral accretion is not active. Such residual accumulations are genetically distinct and often can be recognized texturally where exposed in cut banks after burial and reexcavation. They are typically found at the base of the vertical flood-plain sequence; although in an aggrading valley, lag deposits may be found in old buried channels at any vertical position in the valley alluvium below the latest surface cover of vertical accretion.

NORMAL FLOOD-PLAIN, OR VALLEY-FLAT, ASSOCIATION

The various types of deposits are usually found in characteristic association with each other, composing together the sedimentary accumulation within the valley. In what may be considered the normal flood-plain, or valley-flat, association of genetic types, deposits of vertical accretion occur as a cover over older coarser deposits of lateral accretion and perhaps also of channel fill. This flood-plain cover derived from vertical accretion forms a layer of fairly uniform thickness, whose surface slopes gently and smoothly down valley and somewhat less gently away from the channel banks toward the valley sides. The modern deposits of vertical accretion usually lie upon older deposits of similar origin, which in turn are typically underlain by sandy channel deposits that were accumulated when the channel occupied other positions than at present. These older channel sands may represent lateral accretion on the inside of gradually shifting channel bends, or they may represent filling of former channels abandoned by avulsions. More recent deposits of lateral accretion, in generally crescentic shapes along the inside of stream bends, may still be exposed at the surface but are typically lower than the surface of the adjacent older flood plain, which has been covered by deposits of vertical accretion. The deposits of vertical accretion form most of the fertile bottom-land soils in these valleys as well as in most others in the United States.

Modern channel-fill deposits occur in the present stream channels and in narrow linear strips winding through the flood plain along the courses of abandoned channels. So far as is known, they always extend downward at least to the top of older, premodern channel sand deposits. Lag deposits may occur in the bed of the present stream channel as well as in association with the older channel fill and with deposits of lateral accretion in old abandoned channels in various places throughout the alluvial fill, but they never overlie the uppermost stratum of vertical accretion deposits. There may also be various forms of transitory bars in the channel. The sand splays are, of course, immediately alongside the present or former channels, from which they extend outward and interfinger with or overlie the flood-plain deposits of vertical accretion. The colluvial deposits occur only along the immediate base of the valley sides, where they extend outward into the valley and interfinger with the deposits of vertical accretion. There is characteristically a low area between the natural levees bordering the streams and the colluvial slopes bordering the valley sides. This is the back-swamp part of the flood plain.

The characteristics of the different types of deposits in the normal flood-plain association are summarized in table 4, and their typical location in the valley accumulation is shown in figure 6.

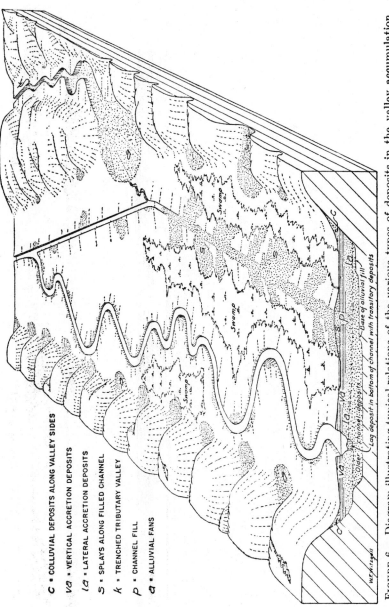

C = COLLUVIAL DEPOSITS ALONG VALLEY SIDES
va = VERTICAL ACCRETION DEPOSITS
la = LATERAL ACCRETION DEPOSITS
s = SPLAYS ALONG FILLED CHANNEL
k = TRENCHED TRIBUTARY VALLEY
p = CHANNEL FILL
a = ALLUVIAL FANS

FIGURE 6.—Diagram illustrating typical relations of the various types of deposits in the valley accumulation. (Drawn by W. F. Witzgall.)

341

TABLE 4.—*Characteristics of genetic types of valley deposits*

Basis of comparison	Colluvial	Type of deposit				
		Fluvial				
		Vertical accretion	Splay	Lateral accretion	Channel lag	Channel fill
Dominant methods of emplacement.	Concentration by slope wash and mass movements.	Deposition of suspended load.	Deposition of bed load.	Deposition of bed load always prominent, but suspended load may be dominant.	Deposition of bed load.	Deposition of bed load and suspended load.
Usual place of deposit	At junction of flood plain and valley sides.	On entire flood-plain surface.	On flood-plain surface adjacent to the stream channel.	Along side of channel, especially on the inside of bends.	On channel bottom.	Within the channel.
Dominant texture	Varies from silty clay to boulders.	Dominantly silt; often sandy, especially near channel; often much clay.	Usually sand; may be gravel or boulders.	Sand or gravel; may include silt or boulders.	Sand, gravel, and boulders.	Usually sand, silt, and gravel. May include clay or boulders.
Relative distribution in the valley fill.	Interfinger with the fluvial deposits, along outer margins of flood plain.	Overlie deposits of lateral accretion and channel deposits; overlain by or interbedded with splay and colluvial deposits; usually cover most of flood-plain surface.	Form scattered lenticular deposits overlying or interbedded with vertical accretion deposits adjacent to present or former channels.	Usually overlain by vertical accretion deposits; often underlain by channel lag or channel-fill deposits. May extend across entire flood-plain width.	Underlie channel-fill, or lateral or vertical accretion deposits; either as a nearly horizontal stratum, a veneer lying on the bed-rock floor, or in linear channel beds.	Usually form elongate deposits of relatively small cross section, winding through flood plain; may overlie lag deposits and underlie vertical accretion deposits.

342

ALLUVIAL-FAN, OR ALLUVIAL-CONE, ASSOCIATION

In addition to the characteristic positions of the various types of deposits, as listed above, there are three other common groupings or associations that produce characteristic surface forms, always occur in similar locations relative to the surrounding topography, and result from certain definite associations of causes. These groupings are alluvial-fan, or alluvial-cone, deposits, accumulations here designated "valley-plug deposits," and delta deposits.

Alluvial fans are well-known geomorphic phenomena, although they are better known by the surface form than by the nature of the deposits. Such fan, or cone, deposits are typically formed where the gradient of a stream is abruptly lessened as the stream enters a relatively low area of gentler slope, such as the valley of a larger stream. Alluvial fans are found at the mouths of most gullies and larger tributaries entering Tobitubby and Hurricane Valleys. Channel filling, vertical and lateral accretion, and splays are the chief genetic types represented among the alluvial-fan deposits, but they are usually so intimately intermixed that there is little systematic surface or areal distinction between them. Most of the larger fans appear to have originated before modern time, but they have been considerably aggraded and extended outward by accelerated sedimentation. In a few places the reverse has been true, and the old fans have been trenched by deepened erosional channels, and have therefore been aggraded only slightly or not at all in modern time. Many of the smaller fans apparently originated, or at least first attained significant size, during the modern period, usually as a result of accumulation of debris derived from gullies.

Large parts of the present alluvial-fan surfaces are excessively sandy and therefore of little value for cropping. The fans are inherently unstable and are subject to frequent overflow, because the channels that determine the location and growth of the fans are typically subject to aggradational filling and to rapid lateral migration by bank cutting.

VALLEY-PLUG ASSOCIATION

The valley-plug deposits are always associated with filling of the stream channel. When the channel has been completely filled at one place the locus of deposition progresses upstream by backfilling. At the same time all the water flowing in the channel is forced overbank, where it drains down valley through the back-swamp areas until it again collects into definite channels and eventually returns to the main channel below the zone of complete channel filling. This process causes greatly increased development of sand splays and, to a somewhat lesser extent, increases the rate of vertical accretion from the water forced overbank. Channel-fill, sand-splay, and vertical accretion deposits are thus all represented in the valley-plug associations, but all in greater amounts than in the normal flood-plain association. The surface form of a valley plug is somewhat similar to that of an alluvial fan, but it is more elongated than most fans, occurs in different topographic relations, and results from different causes.

In contrast to alluvial fans, which characteristically occur where the gradient is markedly decreased, valley plugs occur where the stream gradient is uniform or normal. There now are slight irregularities in the longitudinal profiles of Tobitubby and Hurricane Creeks (fig. 7) at ranges H–1, H–5, T–2, T–8, and WG–6, which cross valley plugs, but these irregularities appear to result from the aggradation of the channels caused by the plugging.

In general, the plugs are caused by decrease in the capacity of the stream channel downstream. In some places the decreased channel

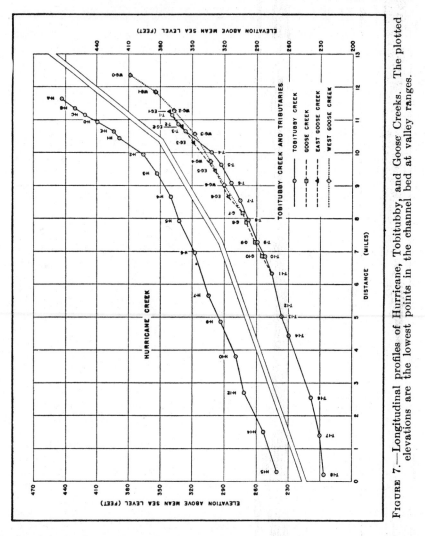

FIGURE 7.—Longitudinal profiles of Hurricane, Tobitubby, and Goose Creeks. The plotted elevations are the lowest points in the channel bed at valley ranges.

capacity results from artificial channel modification, as at the lower end of the Goose Creek drainage ditch, which emptied into a natural winding channel of smaller capacity than the ditch. In other places, as on Hurricane Creek below range H–5, the cause has apparently been delivery of sediment from a tributary in such quantities as to choke completely the main stream channel. The nature of the original channel obstruction is usually not evident, but at some plugs, jams of driftwood were probably a primary locus for sand accumulation in the channel.   In this respect the process may be analogous to that by which the famous "rafts" of driftwood and sediment formerly choked the channel of the Red River in Louisiana.   The development of plugs may also be similar to the kind of intermittent valley filling that McGee (*51, pp. 261–273*) described as part of the process that he called varigradation.

DELTA ASSOCIATION

Wherever the velocity of a sediment-carrying stream is checked as it enters a body of comparatively quiet water, deposition occurs and a delta forms.   Deltas have long been recognized as characteristic sedimentary associations, and Twenhofel (*77, pp. 836–850*) has given a detailed summary of delta conditions and deposits.   A typical delta is composed of bottom-set, fore-set, and top-set beds.   The top-set beds include both subaqueous and subaerial deposits.   The subaerial top-set beds are composed of the several types of fluvial sediments intermixed with lacustrine, paludal, and lagoonal deposits and merge upstream with the valley flood-plain sediments, from which they may be indistinguishable.   Since most of the subaqueous top-set beds, as well as the fore-set and bottom-set beds, are formed below the level of the quiet water, they are not properly classified as fluvial deposits.   A delta may, however, be built into a river (*77, p. 837*) or into a lake on the flood plain, and such delta accumulations become a part of the valley deposits.   The deltas formed in valley lakes or stream channels, and the subaerial top-set beds of other deltas, are included in the present classification as a distinctive valley association.   Thus deltas, although formed under characteristic genetic conditions and composed of a distinctive association of types of deposits, may be classed among lacustrine, marine, or valley associations, depending on their location.

The subaerial deltaic surfaces are similar to valley-plug areas, and the characteristic association of genetic types of sediments in the subaerial top-set beds is likewise very much like that in the valley-plug association, except that complete channel filling is less important.   The fore-set and bottom-set delta beds are the peculiarly distinctive features that justify recognition of the delta complex as a separate type of association.   The present valley studies have not yet afforded an opportunity for detailed attention to delta deposits, however, and a more complete discussion and description of the delta association will not be attempted at this time.

Deltas appear to have been unimportant in modern sedimentation in Tobitubby and Hurricane Valleys except as they have formed the initial obstruction in some of the channels that have been plugged. The evidence in these places is inferential in large part, for the sediment in both the delta and the channel fill is sand, and the beds are not exposed for detailed study.   No important delta deposits are known to have formed in the shallow ponds on the flood plains.   In other parts of the United States, however, deltas may be of much greater importance in valley sedimentation.

References

21 Eakin, H. M., 1935, Diversity of current-direction and load-distribution on stream bends: *Amer. Geophys. Union Trans.*, V. 16, pt. 2, pp. 467–472.

25 Fenneman, N. M., 1906, Flood plains produced without floods: *Amer. Geogr. Soc. Bull.*, V. 38, pp. 89–91.

29 Glenn, L. C., 1911, Denudation and erosion in the southern Appalachian region and the Monongahela basin: U. S. Geol. Survey Prof. Paper 72, 137pp.

51 McGee, W. J., The Pleistocene history of northeastern Iowa: U. S. Geol. Survey Ann. Rep. 11, pp. 189–577.

77 Twenhofel, W. H., et al., 1926, *Treatise on Sedimentation*, 2nd ed., Williams & Wilkins Co., Baltimore, 926 pp.

Geologic Perspective

VIII

In this final section, Fisk's paper is selected to show the importance of straightforward geologic studies on an understanding of river morphology. This short paper reviews the monumental effort that Fisk and his colleagues performed in the collection and analysis of vast amounts of data obtained by the U. S. Army Corp of Engineers and petroleum companies in the Mississippi River valley. Fisk's work demonstrates that many aspects of a river system cannot be understood without some conception of its Quaternary history.

Finally, an attempt to summarize and to indicate the direction of future research into the morphology and behavior of rivers seems necessary. The final selection, therefore, is based on two lectures presented at an Institute on River Mechanics held at Colorado State University in June of 1970. The Institute was designed to acquaint working engineers with recent advances in their field. The organizers of the Institute considered that there should be a geomorphic input and so two chapters were written in order to acquaint the engineers with recent geomorphic studies of rivers and, especially, to demonstrate how the geologic perspective could be of aid in river control.

It should be clear to the reader by now that the geologists' historical view of rivers can provide new insight into river control problems, whereas the quantitive results of engineering research can aid in the solution of traditional geologic-geomorphic problems.

AMERICAN SOCIETY OF CIVIL ENGINEERS

Founded November 5, 1852

TRANSACTIONS

Paper No. 2511

18

MISSISSIPPI RIVER VALLEY GEOLOGY RELATION TO RIVER REGIME

By Harold N. Fisk[1]

Synopsis

The Mississippi River alluvial valley developed concurrently with the advance and retreat of the final stage of continental glaciation. Sea level dropped as the ice accumulated, and the Mississippi River system eroded a deeply entrenched valley system. A rise in sea level when the ice melted reduced stream gradient, the river was forced to drop its load, and the valley system became filled with a gradational sequence of alluvium. Characteristics of the alluvial deposits show that the river was an overloaded braided stream most of the time that sea level was rising and that the river did not take on its meandering habit throughout the entire length of the valley until sea level reached a stand about 5,000 years ago. The river has developed and abandoned several courses, the positions of which are still visible in traces of river migration or well-defined zones of meander belts. Each ancient course is marked by an alluvial ridge along its meander belt and by a characteristic pattern of distributary streams in its delta area.

Remaining alluvial features show that the river has maintained a close adjustment between its load, slope, and the bed and bank materials. The river is said to be poised because it has shown no tendency either to aggrade or degrade its channel. The adjustment to bed and bank materials is shown by the local and regional characteristics of the channel and by its rate of migration. A broad, shallow, shifting channel is developed in sandy bed and bank materials, whereas a narrow, deep, slowly-migrating channel takes shape in fine-grained deposits. Each of several course diversions has left a clear record of slow and orderly development. The modern Atchafalaya River-Mississippi River relationship suggests an early stage in course diversion.

Note.—Published in July, 1951, as *Proceedings-Separate No. 80*. Positions and titles given are those in effect when the paper or discussion was received for publication.

[1] Chf., Geologic Research Section, Humble Oil and Refining Co., Houston, Tex.

349

INTRODUCTION

A great deal of information concerning the surface and subsurface features of the alluvial valley of the lower Mississippi River was collected and analyzed in connection with a geological investigation of the region conducted for the Mississippi River Commission. The project was undertaken to determine the origin and development of the alluvial valley and, from the geological relationships, to evaluate the factors controlling Mississippi River behavior. Results have been published in two reports,[2,3] and those points which demonstrate the relationship between geological features and the river's regimen are briefly summarized in this paper.

THE ALLUVIAL VALLEY

The alluvial valley of the lower Mississippi, a broad lowland varying in width from 25 miles to 125 miles, extends for more than 600 miles across the Gulf coastal plain from Cape Girardeau, Mo., to the Gulf of Mexico (Fig. 1) and covers an area of approximately 50,000 sq miles. This valley is primarily a region of alluviation which has developed as a result of long-continued depositional action of the Mississippi River and its tributaries. Throughout almost the entire length of the valley, the lowland surface, or alluvial plain, is bordered by abrupt walls which gradually lose elevation in a southward direction and disappear where the upland surface slopes beneath the coastal marshlands of Louisiana. The valley walls are breached where the flat-surfaced alluvial plains of tributary valleys merge with the surface of the Mississippi valley.

The continuity of the plain is broken by two ridges: (1) Crowleys Ridge, centrally located in the northern part of the valley, rises 200 ft above the plain and extends for 200 miles south of Commerce, Mo.; and (2) Macon Ridge rises to a maximum of 40 ft above the valley lowlands and extends from Eudora, Ark., to Sicily Island, La., a distance of approximately 100 miles. The plain has an elevation of more than 300 ft at the north end of the valley and has a very low regional slope to the Gulf of Mexico. The slope gradually decreases southward and is practically nonexistent south of central Louisiana.

GENERAL GEOLOGIC FEATURES

Data from thousands of scattered borings, supplemented by detailed information from several trans-valley lines of close interval borings, show the surface of the alluvial valley to be underlain by a thick mass of alluvial deposits that grade upward from a substratum of sands and gravels into a top stratum of silty sands and silty clays (Fig. 2). The substratum comprises most of the mass at the north end of the valley, where it almost reaches the surface, but near the Gulf of Mexico the substratum is deeply buried beneath the top stratum (Fig. 3). The alluvium buries a rugged valley system in which trenches of the major tributaries extend inland from their junctions with the master trench. The valley walls are the surface manifestations of the margins

---

[2] "Geological Investigation of the Alluvial Valley of the Lower Mississippi River," by Harold N. Fisk, Mississippi River Comm., Vicksburg, Miss., December, 1944.

[3] "Fine-Grained Alluvial Deposits and Their Effect on Mississippi River Activity," by Harold N. Fisk, Waterways Experiment Station, Vicksburg, Miss., July, 1947.

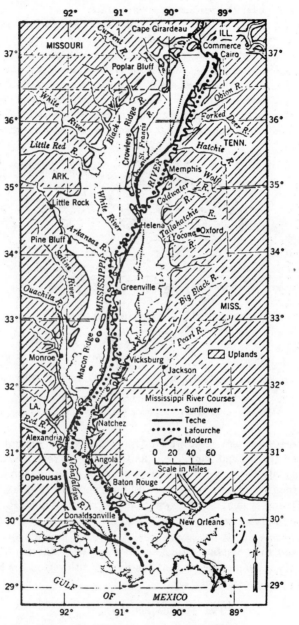

Fig. 1.—The Mississippi River Alluvial Valley

of the main stream trenches. Crowleys Ridge marks the divide between the upper Mississippi and Ohio river trenches, and Macon Ridge marks the divide between the Arkansas and lower Mississippi river trenches. Divides between minor tributary valleys are all buried beneath the alluvial mass, although they lie near the surface in several areas.

The alluvial valley is actually a valley-in-valley feature reflecting the cyclical events that occurred during the latest epoch of geologic time. The entrenched valley system was eroded during the last glacial stage (late Wisconsin) during the time the sea was being lowered 450 ft as water was withdrawn to form huge glacial ice masses. These ice masses reached their climax of growth about 30,000 years ago. When the glaciers began to disappear, the waters from their melting returned to the oceans and caused the sea to reach its present level approximately 5,000 years ago. Stream gradients were

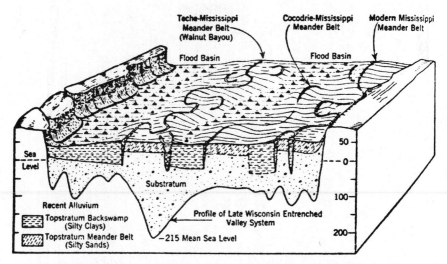

Fig. 2.—Block Diagram of Mississippi Alluvial Valley in Latitude of Natchez, Miss.

relatively steep when sea level was low, and sands and gravels were transported beyond the present shoreline. As the sea level rose, stream gradients were progressively decreased, and a great wave of alluvium spread upstream, resulting in the deposition of progressively finer particles (Fig. 3).

The sedimentary mass laid down near the shore of the Gulf of Mexico during and subsequent to the rise in sea level is much thicker than any that could result from a 450-ft rise in sea level. Both top stratum and substratum are present and their combined thickness is more than 600 ft. The excessive thickness of the section indicates that the river mouth region has been sinking during the period of sedimentation.

The Mississippi River

The lower Mississippi River starts at Cairo, Ill., at the junction of the upper Mississippi-Missouri rivers and the Ohio River and follows a crooked

1,000-mile path to reach the Gulf of Mexico. Its course lies close to the eastern wall of the alluvial valley except in the central part of the region, south of Memphis, Tenn., where it swings far to the west of Greenville, Miss. Its flow is divided near Angola, La., where the principal · distributary, the Atchafalaya River, starts a relatively short course to the Gulf of Mexico. The main Mississippi River flow continues past New Orleans, La., and then separates into several minor distributaries (or passes) which form the river mouth delta. The master stream is joined on the western side of the valley near Greenville by waters of the Arkansas and White river systems, and near Angola by those of the Red and Ouachita river systems (Fig. 1). Tributaries from the eastern side of the valley are all small, the Yazoo River—which joins the Mississippi near Vicksburg, Miss.—being the largest.

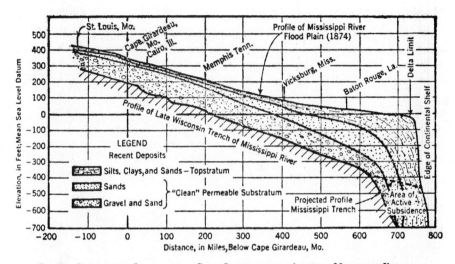

FIG. 3.—GENERALIZED LONGITUDINAL CROSS SECTION OF THE ALLUVIAL MISSISSIPPI VALLEY

An outstanding feature of the Mississippi River is the active migration of its channel. Bank surveys dating from 1765 show that the channel has migrated rapidly and over wide areas in the northern part of the valley. Below Donaldsonville, La., its migration has been very slow, and the shift in river position has been slight. Inequalities in the erosional and depositional activity of the flowing water mass are directly responsible for channel migration. The highest water velocities and deepest channel are at points of bend (bendways) where the thalweg lies close to the concave river bank. Bendways are separated by "crossings" in which the channel is comparatively broad and shallow and the velocities highly variable. Scouring is most intense in the thalweg of bendways, and bank retreat occurs when the concave bank becomes over-steepened and caves into the river. Coarse sediments derived from river bank caving are transported downstream and deposited on sand bars in the shallow slackwater areas along the convex bank of the downstream bend. Thus, the retreat of the concave bank is accompanied by concurrent advance of the convex bank as a result of accretion. Irregularities in the retreat of the concave river bank are caused by normal changes in channel alinement, resulting from variation in river stage and by local resistance to bank caving. The advance of the convex bank is also irregular and is marked by a succession of sand bar ridges and intervening swales. A bend enlarges as the bank-caving and bar-building processes continue, and the channel may eventually form a meander loop. The history of development of the loop is faithfully recorded in the arrangement of point bar ridges and swales (the accretion topography) within the loop.

Shortening of the river is accomplished by a neck "cutoff" when the up-stream and downstream arms of the loop intersect. The ends of the cutoff

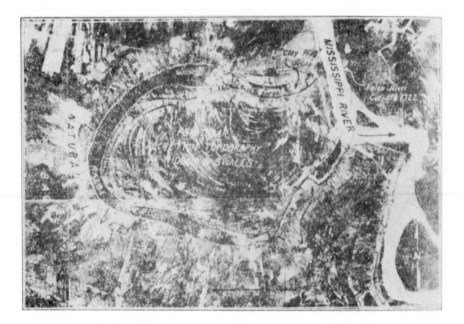

FIG. 4.—AERIAL PHOTOGRAPH OF FALSE RIVER, LA.

channel become plugged with sediment, and the remaining portion of the channel forms an oxbow lake which eventually becomes filled with a "clay plug" of silts and other fine-grained alluvial materials. Shortening of the channel is also brought about by "chute" cutoffs which follow a short channel (or chute) across the point bar. Such channels are originally established in swale lowlands between sand bar ridges and gradually enlarge to carry the main river flow. This type of cutoff is more common above Memphis, where it gives rise to a number of large islands.

Channel migration occurs within wide zones called meander belts, the limits of which can be accurately established from aerial photographs and topographic maps. Within such a zone channel migration is indicated by abandoned channels, accretion topography, oxbow lakes, and similar phenomena. Many cutoff meander loops line the channel north of Donaldsonville, and their associated accretion topography provides an excellent tool for interpreting the history of river migration. One of the larger meander loops, False River, La., which was cut off in 1722, is shown in Fig. 4, the aerial photograph mosaic.

The river experienced wide variations in level and under natural conditions frequently overflowed its banks. When the river topped its bank, sediments were piled up in natural levees (wedge-like ridges extending landward from the river bank). These levees are better drained than other flood-plain features and form a large part of the cultivated lands in the valley. A typical one borders the cutoff meander loop occupied by False River. Natural levees line the entire course of the river and, as a result, the stream flows within an alluvial ridge which rises a few feet above the lowland surface.

South of Donaldsonville the ridge is a simple feature made up of broad continuous landward-sloping levees on either side of the channel. To the north, however, it is a complex feature made up of a large number of natural levee elements which border abandoned channel segments within the meander belt, as well as the active channel.

The Alluvial Plain

The surface of the alluvial valley is a wide plain of very low relief that has been constructed through depositional activity of the Mississippi River and its tributaries. The nature and distribution of drainage lines and of such topographic features as natural levees, bar accretions, and old channels provide evidence of long-continued stream action and demonstrate that each of the rivers has occupied and abandoned several courses while the plain has been under construction. Most prominent of the depositional features are the meander belt ridges marking ancient courses of the Mississippi River. Each ridge now holds traces of river activity comparable to that of the modern Mississippi, and each course branches near the coast into a pattern similar to that formed by the Mississippi distributaries. The generalized position of the axial lines of three of the old Mississippi courses is shown in Fig. 1. Although ancient meander belts of the Red, Arkansas, and White rivers, and other large tributaries are minor features, they are well defined and easily traceable on aerial photographs.

The various alluvial ridges formed by the Mississippi River separate the valley into flood-basin lowlands called backswamps (Fig. 2). Typical of these is the Yazoo River Basin (or "delta") in which floodwaters are impounded between the eastern valley wall and the Mississippi meander belt ridge between Memphis and Vicksburg. Low alluvial ridges, such as the one marking the ancient Mississippi-Sunflower course separate the basin into minor lowland elements. The extensive Atchafalaya Basin in southern Louisiana lies between the alluvial ridges of the ancient Teche-Mississippi course and the modern river. It is separated into minor basins by the alluvial ridge of the Lafourche-Mississippi course and by a ridge along the Atchafalaya River. The heavily forested flood basins hold a complicated network of drainage lines which serve both to introduce floodwaters and to release ponded waters as a flood subsides. Near the coast the basins merge with grass-covered marshlands and are connected with the Gulf of Mexico through a series of minor bayous and lakes.

The three main sections distinguishable in the alluvial plain are shown in Fig. 5, together with the sedimentary deposits which underlie them. In Fig. 5, the meander belt deposits include bar accretions, channel fillings, and natural levees. The alluvial fan deposits are locally overlain with thin backswamp deposits. Included in these backswamp deposits are fresh water sediments laid down in flood basins. The deltaic plain deposits consist of backswamp, marsh, and marine deposits. The flood plain is the most extensive of these sections and covers a total area of 22,000 sq miles. This flood plain includes all the meander belt ridges and flood-basin lowlands in the valley that were subject to flooding under natural conditions. The deltaic plain is the most continuous section of the valley. It includes the near sea level lands, south of the head of the Atchafalaya River, which bear traces of river distributaries marking the deltas of the several courses of the river. The deltaic plain embraces an area of 13,000 sq miles and merges with the flood plain around its northern margin. The alluvial fan section lies in the northwestern and northern parts of the valley and rises slightly above normal flood level. This section consists of approximately 15,000 sq miles of slightly dissected lands that bear traces of braided stream courses and are the remnants of the old alluvial fans which were built into the valley surface while sea level was rising.

The Top Stratum Alluvium

The distribution and lithology of the top stratum are closely related to environments within the valley. The deltaic plain, flood basins, alluvial fans, and several units in the meander belts, all receive deposits of fine-grained sediments and have developed in the course of valley aggradation.

Viewed as a longitudinal unit extending along the valley through its principal environments of deposition, the top stratum is a wedge that thickens in a seaward direction, composed of relatively impermeable deposits grading from thin silty sands at the north end of the valley into a thick, predominantly silty clay mass near the Gulf of Mexico. This wedge is evident in Fig. 3. The top stratum materials everywhere grade downward into the "clean" sands and gravels of the substratum, reflecting the gradual changes which occurred in each of the environments as sea level rose. Along the Mississippi meander belts, where the river scours into the substratum over much of its course, scouring action and river migration have eroded the original top stratum and replaced it with meander belt deposits in which the top stratum element is less widespread and generally much thinner. As a result of meander belt development, the top stratum over much of the valley is divided into a series of long, thick prisms with intervening thinner and less regular masses, as shown in Fig. 2, the cross section of the narrow part of the valley near Natchez, Miss. Thicknesses of the regional top stratum wedge have been measured at several points where this wedge forms the river bank at the edge of the modern meander belt. The elevation of the base of the top stratum at these points is shown by

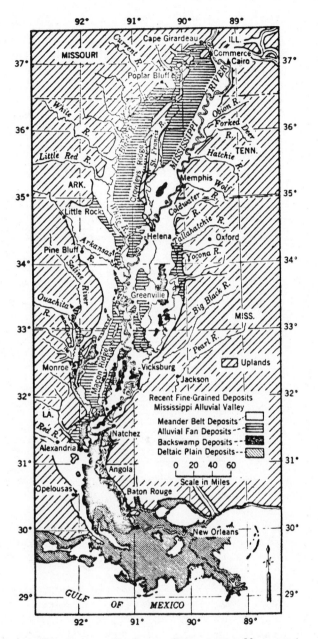

FIG. 5.—GENERALIZED DISTRIBUTION OF TOP STRATUM DEPOSITS IN THE MISSISSIPPI ALLUVIAL VALLEY

the line marked "top of clean sand" on the diagram (Fig. 6), demonstrating the seaward thickening of the mass.

The top stratum is most widespread and thickest beneath the deltaic plain, where it reaches a maximum thickness of over 300 ft (Fig. 3). Here it consists of materials laid down in several brackish water and marine environments, such as marshes, lakes, bays, beaches, and the gulf bottom. Near its margins the top stratum also includes fresh water deposits laid down in flood basins.

The backswamp deposits are made up of silts and clays carried in suspension by floodwater and dropped in the flood basins. The slow and long-continued accumulation of these beds is reflected in the characteristic sequence of homogeneous silt and clay layers that hold successive layers of logs and roots of

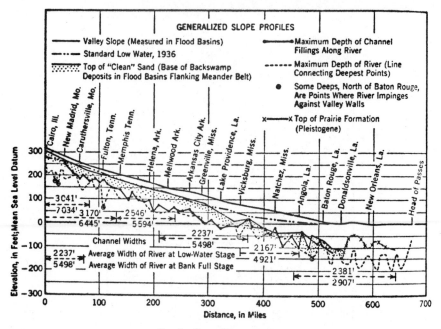

FIG. 6.—SLOPE RELATIONSHIPS

trees in several places. The backswamp deposits form only a thin mantle in the latitude of Memphis where they locally overlie the top stratum of the alluvial fan deposits, but these deposits gradually thicken southward to more than 100 ft in the latitude of Baton Rouge, La.

The top stratum of the alluvial fan deposits is a widespread mantle laid down during the period sea level was rising and the streams had steeper gradients. It is relatively coarse and consists primarily of silty sands with local channel fillings of silty clay. The entire mass is thin, generally not more than 20 ft thick.

Most complicated of the top stratum materials are those laid down in natural levees, point bar accretions, and abandoned channel fillings of meander belts. In the southern part of the valley natural levees are composed mainly of silty clays and reach a maximum thickness of 25 ft. At the north end of the valley the natural levees are composed of silty sands, and few are more than 15 ft thick. The point bar accretions are blanketed with an irregular thickness of silty sands and silty clays, sand bar ridges are overlain with silty sands, and swales are underlain by somewhat thicker silty clays.

The abandoned channel fillings (or clay plugs) are thicker than any other meander belt top stratum deposit. They are thickest in the position of the channel thalweg in bendways and in the area across the ends of the channel arms in which a deep scour pool forms when the cutoff is accomplished. Fig. 7 indicates generalized thicknesses of the top stratum within the channel and

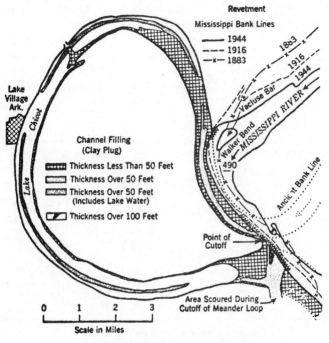

FIG. 7.—LAKE CHICOT CUTOFF MEANDER

over the scour pool of the abandoned Lake Chicot meander, in which the clay plug filling has been adequately tested by borings. The clay plugs have been mapped within the modern meander belt throughout the valley and their thickness, as determined from borings, is shown in Fig. 6. The maximum thickness of the plugs conforms to the maximum depths of abandoned channels and the thickness increases from an average of 60 ft in the north end of the valley to over 120 ft near Donaldsonville.

CONTROL OF RIVER BEHAVIOR BY ALLUVIUM

The characteristics of the Mississippi River reflect the adjustment of its load and great volume of flow to the valley slope and to the bed and bank materials in which its channel is scoured. The river everywhere scours into the alluvial mass, and its adjustment to the bed and bank materials is well shown by both the local and regional characteristics of the channel and by the rate of stream migration.

The relationship between high stage and low stage channel widths and bed and bank materials is summarized in the profiles of Fig. 6. The channel is wide and shallow at the north end of the valley above Memphis, where the slope is relatively steep and substratum sands and gravels form most of the bed and bank materials below the low waterline. The channel gradually narrows and deepens in a southward direction on the intermediate valley slopes between Memphis and Donaldsonville. These channel changes can be correlated with the gradual increase in thickness of the top stratum throughout this section that extends below the low waterline. Where the river scours into the substratum, its rate of migration has been relatively rapid and has resulted in the development of a wide meander belt. South of Donaldsonville, where the valley slope is low and the river is confined to a thick mass of fine-grained alluvium and valley-floor deposits, the channel is deep and comparatively narrow. The extremely slow rate of channel migration in this section is reflected in the comparative straightness of the stream course.

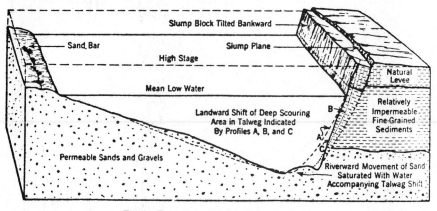

FIG. 8.—BANK RECESSION THROUGH SLUMPING

Top stratum materials effectively hinder local as well as regional channel migration. Thick channel fillings have long been known to form "hard points" that resist bank caving, and thereby alter the shape of the channel cross section and that of river bends, and bring about changes in the river alinement. The greater resistance offered to bank caving by the top stratum as compared to the resistance of sandy bed and bank materials reflects the physical properties of its mass. Inasmuch as fine-grained silty and clayey beds are more cohesive than sands and are relatively impermeable, they are not greatly influenced by fluctuations in hydrostatic pressure resulting from changes in river stage. The top stratum reacts as a unit when the bank caves. Large masses, called slump blocks, slip into the river, rotate, and are tilted bankward (Fig. 8). The resultant indentations give a scalloped bank line. Conversely, bank lines in sandy sediments are smooth because sands behave as a collection of individual particles and sandy banks continually retreat under river attack through a gradual process called sloughing.

The primary cause of bank caving is known to be scouring in the thalweg of bendways. This has been proved by dredging operations. In order to correct river alinement in some bendways, the Corps of Engineers, United States Army, have dredged in the thalweg and forced bank recession of the concave bank. The principle has also been proved experimentally through careful studies with large models.[4]

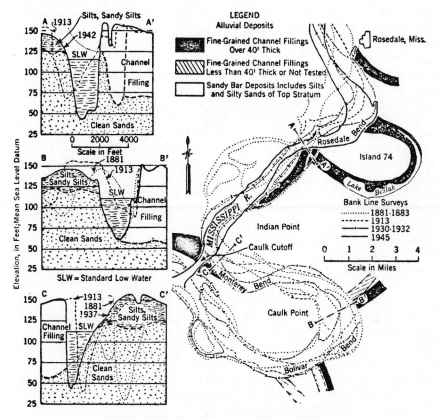

FIG. 9.—CLAY PLUGS ALONG THE MISSISSIPPI RIVER

The general conditions under which slumping occurs are shown in Fig. 8. The position of maximum scouring in the thalweg gradually shifts bankward and destroys conditions of equilibrium that tend to exist between the mass of river water and the water-charged substratum sands. Adjustment is effected by riverward movement of the river bed sands to the point of scouring and results in an undermining of the bank. Riverward movement of sands is possible because the sands are saturated with water that may be under a higher hydrostatic stress than the water in the river. The difference in hydro-

[4] "A Laboratory Study of the Meandering of Alluvial Rivers." by Joseph F. Friedkin, Mississippi River Comm., Vicksburg, Miss., 1945.

static stress may be caused by a falling river stage, a high ground-water level, turbulence in the river, or a combination of these factors.   If the bank consists primarily of sandy materials, adjustment is translated upward through the grains, and sloughing occurs immediately.   If the bank is formed of the cohesive substratum, however, scouring may proceed until the channel is greatly overdeepened, and the withdrawal of the material from beneath the top stratum causes the bank to collapse and to slump.

Many areas illustrate the control exerted on river migration by thick top stratum materials in local bank areas.   An excellent example is afforded by Walker Bend (river mile 490 below Cairo) that lies approximately 5 miles downstream from Greenville.   Here the western bank of the river is developed against a thick "clay plug," filling the arms and cutoff scour pool of the ancient Lake Chicot meander.   Surveys dating back to 1883 show that local channel migration has been slight and local river alinement has remained constant.   A slight eastward bulge in the bank line has formed in the vicinity of the thickest part of the clay plug which fills a scour pool over 100 ft deep.

The effect of widely spaced clay plugs on river alinement is illustrated in Fig. 9, showing selected bank line positions between Rosedale (Miss.) and Caulk Cutoff, dating from 1881.   The thin abandoned channel filling of the upstream arm of the Lake Beulah meander loop has retreated more rapidly than the thicker clay plug in the downstream arm.   As a result of this differential resistance, the channel has changed its alinement and has shifted westward below the Lake Beulah meander.   Similar effects of clay plugs on channel migration have occurred downstream along Bolivar Bend, an active section of the river's course prior to the artificially developed Caulk Cutoff.   The cross sections of Fig. 9 show the influence exerted by channel fillings on both the shape of channel cross sections and the rate of migration of bends.

VALLEY FLOOR DEPOSITS AND RIVER BEHAVIOR

Valley floor and wall materials are all better indurated than the alluvium and are more effective in hindering channel migration and in controlling river alinement.   At each point where the river impinges against the valley wall there is an abnormally deep scour hole in the river.   (See points on Fig. 6.) South of Donaldsonville the river is actually scouring its channel in tough soils of the Prairie formation buried beneath the top stratum, and several abnormally deep scour holes have developed in the bendways.

LONG-TERM STABILITY OF THE RIVER

The geological history of the alluvial region indicates that the character of the Mississippi gradually changed until the time when sea level reached its stand.   After that, the stream became adjusted to its constant base level, and it has now remained relatively stable for a long time.   This stable river is said to be poised[5] since it shows no tendency either to aggrade or degrade its channel.   The absence of appreciable quantities of silt and clay in the substratum and the presence of many lentils of well-sorted gravels indicate that

---

[5] "Basic Aspects of Stream Meanders," by Gerard H. Matthes, *Transactions*, Amer. Geophysical Union, Vol. 22, 1941, p. 632.

the Mississippi River was a comparatively fast-flowing, overloaded stream that occupied many shallow channels as sea level rose. At that time the behavior of the river on the steep valley slope was in all probability similar to that of modern braided streams such as the Platte River. The braided character of abandoned channel scars of Mississippi origin may still be seen on the surface of the alluvial fans at the north end of the valley west of Cairo (Fig. 5). The river did not begin to meander until the sea had almost reached its present level. The meandering habit started on the relatively low slope of the valley near the river mouth and gradually developed upstream as valley aggradation progressed and the upstream slope was lowered. Eventually sea level reached its stand, and a permanent adjustment was reached between slope, volume of flow, and load introduced by tributaries. After that the meandering channel of the lower Mississippi developed throughout the entire length of the valley.

River Diversions

Each time the Mississippi was diverted from a long-occupied course, traces of river activity were left in the various meander belts, and the cause of each diversion can be interpreted from flood-plain features. New courses became established in flood basins and developed because their shorter paths to the sea provided a gradient advantage. They appear to have developed slowly and in an orderly manner.

Most of the ancient diversions occurred when an actively migrating Mississippi meander loop reached an adjacent flood basin and intersected a tributary stream that had a channel sufficiently deep and open to carry low-stage flow from the river. Typical of such changes was the shift from the Teche-Mississippi to the modern course near Vicksburg when a migrating meander loop extended to the channel of the Yazoo River. Somewhat different conditions led to the development of the Atchafalaya River that carries a large volume of water from the Mississippi. Mississippi waters enter the Atchafalaya by way of Old River, a short stream which follows a lower arm of an ancient meander loop of the Mississippi. The Red River enters the upstream arm of the same loop and originally joined the Mississippi at the head of Old River. When the meander loop was breached, waters from both the Red River and Old (Mississippi) River flowed seaward through a network drainage channel within the Atchafalaya Basin. It is probable that the original enlargement of the Atchafalaya was accomplished primarily by the scouring action of the Red River rather than by that of the Mississippi. As the channel enlarged, an increasing quantity of Mississippi water passed through it.

Ancient courses of the Mississippi, such as the Teche, Lafourche, or Sunflower (Fig. 1), all present excellent evidence of diminishing flow prior to complete abandonment. The full-flow course may be seen outlined on photographs by natural levees and other distinctive features, but, in addition, the channel itself is filled with narrow accretion ridges. These depositional features have caused a narrowing and local straightening of the channel with a few abnormally sharp bends. Because there is no evidence of channel migration accompanying the filling of the channel, it is clear that the stream flow must have been greatly decreased before deterioration set in.

No record of the widening of the new channel is preserved, but the increase in flow is recorded in progressive course lengthening across the deltaic plain. The course grows seaward only after the Gulf bottom has been built to sea level and low natural levees can confine the flow. Many distributaries develop as sedimentation continues, but only those with favored alinements continue to carry water from the river. The final pattern of streams in the delta area is composed of a few large distributaries branching from a main channel near the coast with traces of many abandoned distributaries forking from the channel farther inland. Some evidence exists in this stream pattern that the oldest distributaries had narrow channels and were abandoned in the initial stages of course development during the time the river was carrying less volume.

Judging from ancient diversions, the Atchafalaya-Mississippi relationship illustrates an early stage in course diversion. The Atchafalaya is known to be actively enlarging its channel, and its course is being lengthened seaward. No channel deterioration effects, such as those which mark older courses, are as yet visible downstream in the Mississippi, and it is probable that they will not develop until the main low water flow follows the Atchafalaya.

ACKNOWLEDGMENT

The geological work in this paper was done under the direction of the writer. It was initiated in May, 1941, by Maj.-Gen. M. C. Tyler, M. ASCE, President of the Mississippi River Commission (Vicksburg, Miss.), and was under the general supervision of Gerard H. Matthes, Hon. M. ASCE. The work was continued during the administration of Maj.-Gen. R. W. Crawford during which time it was supervised by Charles Senour, M. ASCE. The project was concluded in July, 1948.

Water Resources Publication, 1971, Fort Collins, Colorado, Chapters 4 and 5

19

Fluvial Geomorphology in River Mechanics

H. W. Shen, Editor

S. A. SCHUMM

Chapter 4

FLUVIAL GEOMORPHOLOGY:

THE HISTORICAL PERSPECTIVE

by

S. A. Schumm, Professor of Geology,
        Colorado State University, Fort Collins, Colorado

Chapter 4

FLUVIAL GEOMORPHOLOGY:

THE HISTORICAL PERSPECTIVE

4.1 INTRODUCTION

Fluvial geomorphology is the cumbersome title applied to the geologic speciality that treats the morphology of rivers and river systems. However, it is more than the form behavior and mechanics of rivers that interests the geomorphologist. As geology is concerned with the history of Earth through billions of years, the geomorphologist views the fluvial landscape in a historical perspective. He utilizes the concept of unlimited time during which the landscape evolved to its present configuration. The engineer may question the relevance of the historical approach to river mechanics. Thus, one objective of this chapter is to demonstrate that it should not be ignored; that the investigation of river response to the climatic changes and diastrophic events of Earth's evolution provides information and insight into long-term river adjustment to altered hydrologic conditions.

Geologists, of course, are vitally concerned with modern river morphology and mechanics, because this information makes possible the interpretation of ancient river deposits. These interpretations are of considerable economic importance as the following three examples demonstrate: 1) Petroleum is now being found in sediments of river systems of late Paleozoic and Mesozoic ages (about 250 to 70 million years ago) in the United States and Canada (Martin, 1966). In most cases, these are valley-fill deposits composed of a complex of channel deposits rather than a single channel. 2) Uranium deposits of the Colorado Plateau are located in paleochannels that were functioning about 100 million years ago (Craig, and others, 1955).
3) The rich gold deposits of the Witwatersrand basin of South Africa are ancient placers (older than 1/2 billion years), complex river deposits laid down on an alluvial plain (Brock and Pretorius, 1964; Haughton, 1969, pp. 69-117). This gold is being mined at great depths, and any improvement of our understanding of the depositional environment of the Witwatersrand sediments could significantly reduce the costs involved in exploiting these mineral deposits.

Much of the geological effort is descriptive in order to establish the chronology of events in the history of a river system (for example, Hunt, 1969). Nevertheless, the insight gained into the long-term response of rivers to major climatic change or to movements of Earth's crust has bearing on problems of modern river regulation and control. Geological contributions are reviewed in standard geomorphology textbooks (Thornbury, 1969; Morisawa, 1968; Leopold and others, 1964; also pertinent articles in Fairbridge, 1969). Some works familiar to both

4-1

engineers and geologists are the classic papers of Gilbert (1914, 1917), Rubey (1952), Mackin (1948), and Lane (1955, 1957).

4.2 VARIABLES INFLUENCING RIVER CHANNELS AND RIVER SYSTEMS

River channels comprise only a small part of the total landscape, yet their significance far outweighs their areal extent. A river channel at any single location reflects the geology, geomorphology, biology, climate, and hydrology of a drainage basin that may extend for hundreds of miles upstream. Geomorphologists group these variables into three categories: process, structure, and stage. All landforms, including rivers, are the result of the interaction of these groups of variables (Davis, 1899).

Process. In the usual sense of the word, process includes all of the processes acting to form a landscape. As a river channel is primarily the result of flowing water, a detailed discussion of process would not appear to be necessary. However, the magnitude and frequency of runoff events can be a major factor determining the character of a river channel. For example, river channels characterized by high peak discharge can be very different from those characterized by a relatively uniform flow, although both rivers may have the same mean discharge. (see Fig. 5-3).

All effects of climatic differences and climate change, therefore, should be reflected in changes of erosional and depositional processes and ultimately the landscape. For example, morphoclimatic regions have been identified wherein the climate determines to a significant extent both the efficiency and type of erosion process as well as the landforms that result (Stoddart, 1969). There appears to be no quantitative description of these supposed differences for rivers. However, the effects of the greatly different flow regimes experienced throughout the world (Parde, 1964; Beckinsale, 1969) and the different types of sediments provided by tropical as compared to semiarid, arctic, and arid rock weathering should be detectable.

A comparison of the hydraulic geometry of perennial streams of humid and subhumid regions with that of ephemeral streams of semiarid regions demonstrates that significant differences can exist between climatic regions. For example, in contrast to perennial streams, depth increases less rapidly and gradient decreases less rapidly in a downstream direction in ephemeral streams. This probably is due to the high water loss in ephemeral stream channels and increase in suspended sediment concentration in a downstream direction (Leopold and others, 1964, Table 7-5).

In addition to the erosional forces acting on the surface of Earth, there are internal forces which cause displacement of Earth's surface. These forces generally act very slowly, yet if progressive uplift or downwarping of the crust occurs, this can be detected by changes in river behavior. The average rate of

4-2

367

uplift is estimated to be about 25 feet per 1000 years (Schumm, 1963). This is a very slow rate of deformation (0.3 inch per year), but sufficient to modify significantly the gradient of streams over several decades. It is not suggested that modern problems associated with rivers and canals in the United States can be attributed to slow up or downwarping of the crust, but examples can be cited where progressive tilting of Earth's surface has significantly modified the gradient of rivers. For example, Lake Victoria is drained by the Victoria Nile which flows north to Lake Kyoga (Fig. 4-1). Lake Kyoga and Lake Kwania appear to be artificial, formed perhaps by dam construction on the Victoria Nile. However, these lakes are, in fact, formed by uplift and eastward tilting of western Uganda. Flow in the Kafu River has been reversed, and water draining from Lake Victoria has found a new course to the north where it flows over Murchison Falls and into Lake Albert. The geologically relatively recent derangement of these drainage systems is the result of uplift that is apparently continuing at the present time (Holmes, 1965, p. 1057).

Another example of tectonic effects is found in Iraq where both the character of ancient irrigation systems and the Diyala River, a tributary of the Tigrus near Baghdad, have been altered

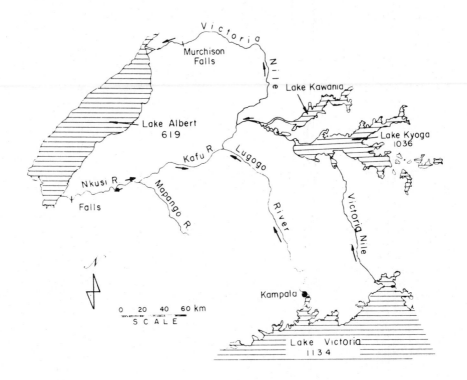

Fig. 4-1. Map of Lake Kyoga region, Uganda.
Arrows show direction of flow in rivers.

4-3

368

due to upwarping. Uplift during the last 1000 years caused incision of the Diyala River into its alluvial plain and abandonment of irrigation canal systems (Adams, 1965). Modern flood and river control problems in East Pakistan apparently are also enhanced by upwarping which has caused displacement of the Brahmaputra River to the west (Coleman, 1969).

In addition, the North American continent north of a line between Milwaukee, Cleveland and New York has been uplifted as a result of the isostatic response of the crust to the removal of the Pleistocene continental glaciers. Maximum uplift is in the Hudson Bay area and amounts to 302 m (Farrand, 1962; Embleton and King, 1968, p. 128), decreasing to zero at the Milwaukee-Cleveland-New York hinge line. No evidence is available concerning the influence of this uplift on rivers, but tilting will increase the gradient of rivers flowing south, decrease the gradient of rivers flowing north, and cause rivers flowing east and west to erode their south banks. The fact that such effects have not been described may be because of the derangement of the drainage patterns by Pleistocene continental glaciation.

   Structure. The term structure, as used in geomorphology, implies not only the effects of the various kinds of rocks but also the differential erosional character of the rocks, the influence of fractures (joints and faults) and other geologic structures, and their distribution in a drainage basin. Rivers draining from areas that differ greatly in the physical character of their rocks should themselves be significantly different, as the hydrologic character of the system and type and quantity of sediment load moved from the basin will differ. On a regional basis, the drainage pattern itself reflects these controls. For example, drainage density will be high for a region of weak impermeable material and low for resistant or highly permeable material. Further, spatial arrangement of channels frequently show a pronounced structural control (Fig. 4-2; Howard, 1967). These effects on river channels will be for the most part obvious and of little concern to the river engineer except as the sediment load derived from diverse geologic areas influences river channel morphology.

   Stage. The passage of time and the change of landform character through time is referred to as the stage of development of a landform or landscape. In the ideal case, a period of rapid uplift of a region is followed by dissection and the erosional evolution of the landforms. Through time there should be a progressive removal of earth materials by erosion, and eventually rugged landscape will be reduced to a relatively flat erosional surface, a peneplain, or pediplain (Thornbury, 1969). However, this ideal scheme of landform evolution, as proposed by Davis (1899), rarely occurs without interruptions by renewed uplift, climatic change, and changes of sealevel. For example, the past million or so years of Earth history (Quaternary Period) have been dominated by major climatic changes which have caused significant hydrologic and landform changes. In addition, ice   4-4

369

sheets advanced from the north. We see the effect of these
great glaciers north of the Missouri and Ohio Rivers, the
courses of which were established along the southern boundaries
of the ice. The quantity of water held in the glaciers of the
world during the major ice advances was sufficient to lower
sealevel 130 m (Milliman and Emery, 1968). The lower courses of
all river systems were profoundly influenced by this event. It
is not known how far upstream the effect of sealevel lowering
extended, but for many rivers it caused major deepening and
enlargement of the valley for long distances.

The progression of erosion in a given region is also
frequently marked by "competition" between river systems for
drainage area. The most aggressive river, with the steepest
gradient or greatest discharge or an advantage of lower altitude,
may capture the drainage area of another river system, thereby
decreasing the discharge delivered to the beheaded river and
increasing the discharge of the captor. Evidence of this is
clearcut when a small channel occupies a large valley that in
the past carried greater flows of water.

A striking example of river capture is that which resulted
in a transfer of water from the Indus River system into the
Ganges River system. Fig. 4-3A shows the reconstructed drainage
patterns in this area at about 2000 B.C. Between 500 B.C. and
1100 A.D. the river systems were as shown in Fig. 4-3B; the
Jumna captured the headwaters of the Chautang, thereby diverting
this flow into the Ganges River system, and a tributary of the
Beas captured the headwaters of the Sutlej. By 1400 A.D.
(Fig. 4-3C) the Sutlej had reoccupied part of its old channel,
and the drainage pattern was like that of the present with the
paleochannels of a major abandoned river system occupying the
alluvial plain between the Jumna and Sutlej Rivers.

Consider the following: "In physical systems events are,
in general, determined by the momentary conditions only. For
example, for a falling body it does not matter how it has
arrived at its momentary position, for a chemical reaction it
does not matter in what way the reacting compounds were produced. The past is, so to speak, effaced in physical systems.
In contrast to this, organisms appear to be historical beings."
(Von Bertalanffy, 1952, p. 109). The geomorphologist would
conclude that whole rivers are physical systems that can be
studied for the informatinn they afford during the present
moment of geologic time. They also are analogous to organisms
because they are systems influenced by history.

4.3 VARIABLES INFLUENCING RIVER MORPHOLOGY

In order to continue a discussion of river morphology beyond the purely descriptive stage, it is necessary to inquire
more closely into cause and effect relations. That is, just
what are the independent variables that in a given reach influence river morphology and behavior? It is at this point that
geologists and engineers may go their separate ways, with the

4-5

Fig. 4-2. Basic drainage patterns (from Howard, 1967, p.2248).
A. Dendritic occurs on rocks of uniform resistance
    to erosion and on gentle regional slopes.
B. Parallel occurs on steep regional slopes.
C. Trellis occurs in areas of folded rocks with ma-
    jor divides formed along outcrops of resistant
    rocks and valleys on easily eroded rocks.
D. Rectangular occurs in areas where joints and
    faults intersect at right angle.
E. Radial occurs on flanks of domes and volcanoes
    where there is no effect of differing rock
    resistance.
F. Annular occurs on eroded structural domes and
    basins, where resistant outcrops form major di-
    vides and weak rocks form valleys (a concentric
    type of trellis pattern).
G. Multi-basinal occurs in areas where the original
    drainage pattern has been disrupted by glacia-
    tion, recent volcanism, limestone solution, or
    permafrost.
H. Contorted occurs in areas of complex geology
    where dikes veins, faults or metamorphic rocks
    control the pattern.
    The fishhook pattern of the main stream might
    also result from capture of a northeast flowing
    stream by the southward flowing main stream.

4-6

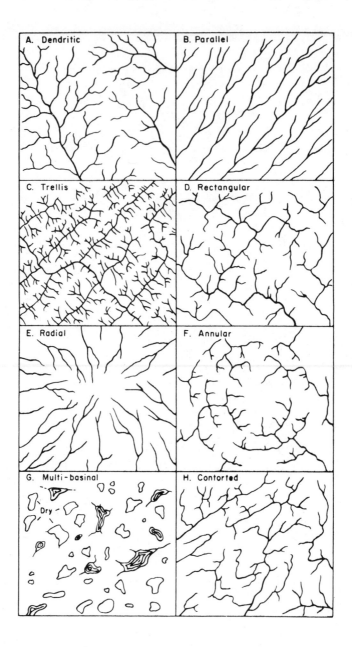

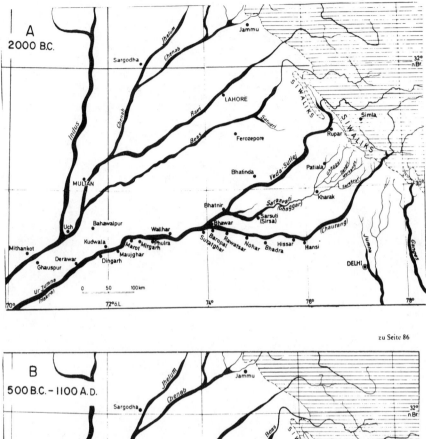

A
2000 B.C.

zu Seite 86

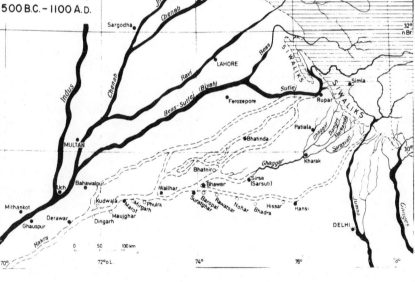

B
500 B.C. – 1100 A.D.

4-8

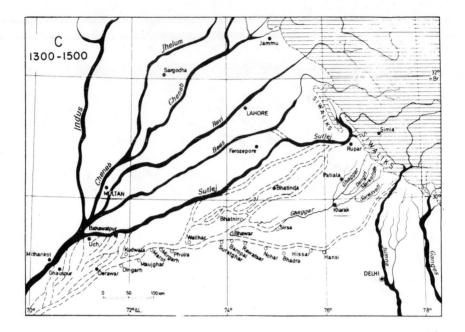

Fig. 4-3. Drainage changes in headwaters of Indus and Ganges
Rivers between 2000 B.C. and 1300-1500 A.D.
(from Wilhelmy, 1969).
A. 2000 A.D.
B. 500 B.C. - 1100 A.D.
C. 1300-1500 A.D.

geomorphologist concerning himself with the long-term response
of the river to Quaternary climate and tectonic influences and
the engineer with effects of man-induced changes of hydrology,
storm events, and the influence of modern channel morphology
(width, depth, slope) on flow characteristics and sediment
transport. To the geologist, time (stage) is an important variable, but to the engineer it need not be.
     There can be little doubt that there is an erosional
development of landforms through time, but as indicated previously, the erosion cycle of Davis is an idealized conceptual model
that over simplifies a complex erosional history (Davis, 1954,
p. 279). Nevertheless, it is possible to think of a river
during several million years of geologic time when it should be
slowly decreasing its gradient in response to the denudational
lowering of the sediment source area. Thus, during "geologic
time" a river is continually adjusting to the slow erosional
modification of the entire drainage system. However, both the
geologist and engineer recognize graded or stable rivers and
canals that adjust during a short time to changes of discharge,

4-9

374

but that over a decade or a century are essentially unchanged. These rivers are open systems in dynamic equilibrium during what may be referred to as "graded time." Finally, over a very brief span of time, a channel may be an open system in a steady state, as water and sediment move through the channel, but no change of channel characteristics occurs. The consideration of geologic time spans is wholly the concern of the geologist, whereas the events of graded time are of concern to both the geomorphologist and civil engineer. "Steady time" is of most interest to the hydraulic engineer. For a full understanding of the variables influencing channel character, consideration of all three spans of time is necessary.

Table 4-1 attempts to illustrate this problem by listing, in a hierarchy of increasing degrees of dependence, variables influencing river morphology for the three different spans of time. The absolute length of these time spans is not important. Rather the significant concept is that a drainage system, its components, and the variables influencing the system may be considered in relation to time spans of different duration.

Geologic time refers to a time span encompassing an erosion cycle (perhaps 200 million years). Geologic time, therefore, extends back from the present to the beginning of an erosion cycle. A fluvial system, when viewed from this perspective, is an open system undergoing continued change, and there are no constant relations between the dependent and independent variables as they change with time. During this time span only time, initial relief, geology, and paleoclimate are independent variables.

Time itself is perhaps the most important independent variable of geologic time. It is simply the passage of time since the beginning of the cycle; that is, time zero is when initial relief is established by uplift of Earth's crust. Nevertheless, it determines the accomplishments of the erosional agents and the progressive changes in the morphology of the system under past climatic conditions. For example, if at the beginning of the erosion cycle relief was very great, the orographic effect produced a very different climate than that pertaining at present. During this time, of course, paleohydrology reflected the different climate and landform influences and is considered to be a dependent variable. The relief of the landscape and the depth, width, and slope of major river valleys still reflect the influence of the paleohydrology of geologic time. Thus, at any time during the geologic time span, the details of the landscape are unknown, but relief and valley dimensions of today are dependent on the variables listed above them in Table 4-1. The remaining variables are indeterminate, for average annual climatic and hydrologic conditions changed through geologic time, as did channel morphology (although some paleochannels are preserved for study).

The graded time span refers to a shorter span of time during which a graded condition or dynamic equilibrium exists. When viewed from this perspective one sees a continual   4-10

375

Table 4-1. River Variables During Time Spans

Variables	Status of variables during designated time spans		
	Geologic	Graded	Steady
1) Time (stage)	I	N.R.	N.R.
2) Initial relief	I	N.R.	N.R.
3) Geology (lithology, structure)	I	I	I
4) Paleoclimate	I	I	I
5) Paleohydrology	D	I	I
6) Relief or volume of system above baselevel	D	I	I
7) Valley dimensions (width, depth, slope)	D	I	I
8) Climate (mean ppt, temp., seasonality)	X	I	I
9) Vegetation (type and density)	X	I	I
10) Hydrology (mean discharge of water and sediment)	X	I	I
11) Channel morphology	X	D	I
12) Observed Qw Qs (reflecting meteorological events)	X	X	D
13) Hydraulics of flow	X	X	D

I = independent
D = dependent
N.R.= not relevant
X = indeterminate

adjustment between elements of the system, for events occur in which negative feedback dominates (self-regulation). In other words, the progressive changes of geologic time appear during graded time as a series of fluctuations or approaches to a steady state (Fig. 4-4).

During a graded time span, arbitrarily defined as the last few 100 years, the classification of some of the variables listed in Table 4-1 changes. For example, time has been eliminated as an independent variable, for although the drainage system as a whole may be undergoing a progressive change of very small magnitude, a graded stream will show no progressive change (Fig. 4-4). Initial relief also has no significance because it is the present relief or remaining mass of the landscape that is significant. However, geology is still an independent variable because it determines to a large extent the quantity and type of sediment fed into the stream. Paleoclimate and paleohydrology could be considered to be not relevant to modern channel morphology, but if they have determined the dimensions and slope of the valley in which the river flows then they should be retained as independent variables. (For example,

4-11

376

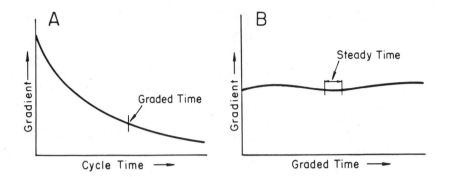

Fig. 4-4. Diagrams illustrating time spans of Table 4-1.
Channel gradient is used as the dependent variable
in these examples (from Schumm and Lichty, 1965).
A. Progressive reduction of gradient during geologic
time.
B. Fluctuations of gradient above and below a mean
during graded time. Gradient is constant during
the brief span of steady time.

see Malde's (1968) discussion of the effects of a prehistoric
flood on the Snake River.) Relief, climate, and vegetation
determine the average hydrologic regimen of a river system.
Hydrology exerts the major influence on channel morphology, the
only dependent variable during graded time.

     Some of the variables that were dependent during the geo-
logic time span become independent during the shorter span of
graded time. The newly independent hydrologic variables, runoff and sediment yield, are especially important because during
graded time they take on a statistical significance and define
the specific character of the drainage channels; however,
momentary sediment and water discharge and the hydraulics of
flow are indeterminate.

     During a steady time span (defined as one week or less) a
true steady state may exist in contrast to the dynamic equilibria of graded time (Fig. 4-4). These brief periods of time are
referred to as steady time, because in hydraulics steady flow
occurs when none of the variables involved at a section change
with time. During this brief time span, channel morphology
assumes an independent status because it has been inherited from
graded time. The present or observed discharge of water and
sediment and flow characteristics can be measured at any moment
during present time, and these variables are no longer indeterminate, but are the only dependent variables.

     It is during the brief span of steady time that the possi-
bility of an apparent reversal of cause and effect may occur
due to feedback from the dependent to the independent variables.
For example, a major flood during this brief span of time might   4-12

377

so alter the flow characteristics that a modification of channel
dimensions and shape could occur. Just as water depth and velocity can be adjusted in a flume to modify sediment transport,
so there is a feedback from flow velocity to sediment discharge
and channel morphology. That is, as discharge momentarily increases, sediment that was previously stationary on the channel
floor may be set in motion. The resulting scour, albeit minor,
will influence channel depth, gradient, and shape. Thus, short
term changes in velocity can cause modification of some of the
independent variables.

These modifications are usually brief and temporary, and
the mean values of channel dimensions and sediment discharge
are not permanently affected. Nevertheless, a temporary reversal of cause and effect can occur which, when documented quantitatively, may be a source of confusion in the interpretation
of geomorphic processes. This is best demonstrated by comparing
the conflicting conclusions that could result from studying
fluvial processes in the hydraulic laboratory and in a natural
stream. The measured quantity of sediment transported in a
flume is dependent on the velocity and depth of the flowing
water and on flume shape and slope. An increase in sediment
transport will result from an increase in the slope of the flume
or an increase in discharge. In a natural stream, however, over
longer periods of time it is apparent that mean water and sediment discharge are independent variables which determine the
morphologic characteristics of the stream and, therefore, the
flow characteristics. Furthermore, over geologic time the
independent variables of geology, relief, and climate determine
the discharge of water and sediment with all other morphologic
and hydraulic variables dependent. Kennedy and Brooks (1963)
used this identical example to illustrate the need to consider
how time spans are relevant to the explanation of fluvial phenomena.

Kennedy and Brooks (1965) state (Q and Q_s are water and
sediment discharge):

"Streams are seldom if ever in a steady state (because of
finite time required to change bed forms and depth) and
transitory adjustments are accomplished by storage of water
and sediment. Water storage is relatively short (hours and
days) and occurs simply by the increasing of river stage or
overbank flooding; sediment storage (+ or -) occurs by deposition or scour. Thus for the short term, Q_s may be considered a dependent variable, with departures of the sediment inflow from the equilibrium transport rate being absorbed in temporary storage (for months or years). But in
the long term the river must assume a profile and other characteristics for which on the average the inflow of water and
sediment equals the outflow; consequently for this case
(called a "graded" stream by geologists), Q and Q_s are
...independent variables."

Table 4-1 can be of immediate use in considering problems
of fluvial morphology. For example, if flow characteristics

4-13

378

are dependent variables during steady time, then currents or the helicoidal flow measured at river bends should not be the cause of meanders; rather the helicoidal flow reflects the presence of the bends. In other words, sinuosity of the river (the ratio of valley slope to channel gradient) influences the flow character and not the converse.

During graded and steady time, channel morphology reflects a complex series of independent variables, but the discharge of water and sediment integrates most of the other independent variables; and it is the nature and quantity of sediment and water moving through a channel that largely determines the morphology of stable alluvial channels.

4.4 INFLUENCE OF WATER AND SEDIMENT DISCHARGE ON CHANNEL MORPHOLOGY

If the sediment and water moving through a stream channel are the primary independent variables influencing modern channel morphology, then it should be possible to show quantitative relations between water discharge, the nature and quantity of sediment, and all aspects of channel morphology such as channel dimensions, shape, gradient, and pattern. Lane (1955) summarized these relations by presenting a qualitative relation between bed-material load, Q_s , water discharge Q , sediment size d_{50} , and gradient S , as follows:

$$Q_s \; d_{50} \simeq Q \; S \; . \tag{4-1}$$

He concluded that a channel could be maintained in dynamic equilibrium by balancing changes in sediment load and sediment size by compensating changes in water discharge and river gradient.

Numerous empirical relations among these variables have been developed by geologists and engineers, and some of these will now be reviewed.

Channel Dimensions and Shape. The greater the quantity of water that moves through a channel, the larger the cross-section of that channel will be. Preceded by numerous studies of canal morphology and stability (Leliavsky, 1954), Leopold and Maddock's (1953) paper demonstrated that for most rivers the width (b, in feet) and depth (d, in feet) increase with mean annual discharge (Qm in cfs) as follows:

$$b = k \; Qm^{.5} \; , \tag{4-2}$$

$$d = k \; Qm^{.4} \; . \tag{4-3}$$

The coefficient varies for each river, however, and in some cases with a downstream increase in discharge, width or depth decreases. It is probable, therefore, that another factor is

4-14

379

influencing channel dimensions, and this must be sediment load. For example, along the Smoky Hill-Kansas River system in Kansas, discharge increases in a downstream direction, but channel width decreases from about 300 feet to less than 100 feet in central Kansas. Farther east at the junction of the Smoky Hill River with the Republican River there is a marked increase in width. These and other changes are attributed to changes in the type of sediment load introduced by major tributary streams. Tributaries introduce large suspended-sediment loads where the width decreases and large sand loads where the width increases. Data are not available for total sediment loads, but bed and bank samples were collected. Although there were no systematic changes in the size of the bed and bank materials, it was determined that the shape of these channels is closely related to the percentage of silt and clay in the sediments forming the perimeter of the channel (Schumm, 1960). Silt-clay was measured as the sediment smaller than 0.074 mm. The width-depth ratio (F) of this channel and of many other stable channels was found to be related to the percentage of silt-clay in the channel (M), as follows:

$$F = 255 \ M^{-1.08} \ . \tag{4-4}$$

Correlation coefficient (r) is 0.91 and the standard error (Se) is 0.20 log units. The relation is such that relatively wide and shallow channels contain only small percentages of silt and clay, and narrow and deep channels contain large percentages of silt and clay. Initially it appeared that M reflects only bank stability, but as the bed and banks are composed of sediment transported through the channel, it was concluded that M is an index of the type of sediment being transported through the channel. For only five locations, where both total sediment load data are available and where M has been calculated, M is found to be inversely related to that part of the total load that is bed-material load (Ob , percentage of total sediment load that is bed-material load) at a given discharge, as follows:

$$M = \frac{55}{Qb} \ . \tag{4-5}$$

The collection of data on channel dimensions, bed and bank sediments, and water discharge permit the development of empirical equations for channel width and depth. The equations are based on data collected at 36 stable alluvial river reaches. All of the channels are located in the semiarid to subhumid regions of the Great Plains of the United States and the Riverine Plains of New South Wales, Australia. Each is formed of sediments transported by the river itself, and none of the channels contain more than about 10% gravel. Thus, bed material in most cases is sand (Schumm, 1968, pp. 40, 45).

4-15   The channels are defined as stable because they have shown no progressive channel adjustment during the last 10 years of record, and they are described as alluvial channels because the their bed and banks are composed of sediment that is being transported by the river.

Analysis of these data produced the following relations:

$$b = 2.3 \frac{Qm^{0.38}}{M^{0.39}}$$

$$r = 0.93 \quad ; \quad Se = 0.14 \text{ log unit} \quad , \tag{4-6}$$

$$d = 0.6 \; M^{0.34} \; Qm^{0.29}$$

$$r = 0.89 \quad ; \quad Se = 0.13 \text{ log unit} \quad . \tag{4-7}$$

The equation for channel width indicates that 88% of the variability of width can be accounted for by mean annual discharge (Qm) and type of sediment load; both being about equally important. The relationship for channel depth is not quite as good with about 81% of the variability of channel depth accounted for. Nevertheless, only about 40% of the variability of channel dimensions is accounted for by discharge alone. Similar equations with equivalent correlation coefficients were obtained using mean annual flood discharge instead of mean annual discharge (Schumm, 1969).

To summarize, for the river channels for which data are available no relation between size of sediment and channel dimensions was obtained, but when an index of the type of sediment load (M) was combined with discharge, excellent correlations with width and depth were obtained. However, when discharge is used with M to develop a multiple regression equation for width-depth ratio, only a slight improvement over Eq. 4-4 is obtained.

$$F = 56 \frac{Qm^{0.10}}{M^{0.74}}$$

$$r = 0.93 \quad ; \quad Se = 0.15 \text{ log unit} \quad . \tag{4-8}$$

Hence, one may conclude that variations in channel dimensions with constant discharge are probably attributable to changes in the type of sediment load. Local variations may, of course, be strongly affected by local variations in bank resistance (Fisk, 1947; Simons and Albertson, 1960; Ackers, 1964), but the width-depth ratio of alluvial channels appears to be primarily determined by the nature of the sediment transported through the channel. This conclusion is supported by the observation of Leopold and Maddock (1953) that "decreasing width at a constant velocity...results in increased capacity for suspended load at constant discharge," and "at constant velocity and

4-16

discharge, an increase in width is associated with a decrease
of suspended load and an increase in bed load transport."
Therefore, a high width-depth ratio is associated with large
bed-material load.
  Channel Gradient. The gradient of a stream if not influenced
by uplift or variations in bedrock will usually show a downstream decrease in gradient that is associated with an increase
of discharge and a decrease in size of sediment (Shulits, 1941;
Lane, 1955). In fact, Lane's relation (Eq. 4-1) indicates that
gradient is directly related to both bed-material load and
grain size and inversely related to water discharge. Unfortunately, only sediment size can be readily obtained at any cross-
section, but when samples are obtained near gaging stations,
both sediment size and discharge can be related to gradient.
Hack (1957) found for streams in Virginia and Maryland that
drainage area was closely related to mean annual discharge. He
used drainage area as an index of discharge and found that a
ratio of median grain size (d_{50}, in mm) to drainage basin area
(A in square miles) was related to gradient (S in feet per
mile) as follows:

$$S = 18\left(\frac{d_{50}}{A}\right)^{0.6}$$
(4-9)

Hack (1957) and Brush (1961) found that the downstream decrease
in stream gradient depended on the resistance of the rocks being
eroded and supplied to the channels. For example, Brush found
that for a given distance downstream or length of channel (L
in miles) the gradient decreased most rapidly for shale, then
limestone, and least for sandstone, as follows:

$$S \text{ shale} = 0.034L^{-.81} \quad ,$$
(4-10)

$$S \text{ limestone} = 0.019 \, L^{-0.71} \quad ,$$
(4-11)

$$S \text{ sandstone} = 0.46 \, L^{-.67} \quad .$$
(4-12)

When data on type of sediment load (M) was used with
discharge, the following multiple regression equation resulted:

$$S = 60 \, M^{-0.38} \, Qm^{-0.32}$$

$$r = 86 \, Se = 0.15 \text{ log unit} \quad .$$
(4-13)

The range of grain size of the bed material was too small to
permit an evaluation of the effect of grain size on the gradient of these rivers, but for each the slope of the alluvial
valley surface on which the channel flowed was closely related
to the gradient of the stream. This seems trivial, for slope

4-17

382

is correlated with slope; but if, in fact, the valley slope reflects past discharges and sediment loads, then it is an independent variable influencing modern channel gradient. What is interesting, however, is the fact that for some channels gradient and valley slope are almost identical, and for others the valley slope is three times that of the channel. This suggests that although the valley slope exerts an influence on the modern channel, the present discharge and sediment load characteristics explain the variation between valley and channel slope (Schumm, 1969, p.51). This matter will be considered again with regard to the variation of channel pattern.

In summary, the gradient of a stream is strongly influenced by the hydrology and geology of the drainage basin. The latter provides sediment of various sizes and resistance, and the former provides the transporting medium; which together determine the longitudinal profile and gradient of an alluvial river.

Channel Patterns. The basic patterns formed by drainage networks are illustrated in Fig. 4-2, but the channels that comprise a drainage network also form diverse patterns. The most easily recognized are the braided and meandering patterns. These are single-channel patterns, but multiple-channel patterns also exist. Although at low water braided streams have islands of sediment or relatively permanent vegetated islands exposed in the channels, this should not obscure the fact that the islands are in a single large channel. However, any type of single-channel can be part of a multiple-channel system. Multiple-channel rivers are those that are flowing on an alluvial surface and are distributary systems such as alluvial-fan distributaries, alluvial-plain distributaries, and delta distributaries.

Clarification is needed regarding multiple-channel systems that branch and rejoin in contrast to the permanently separated distributary systems of alluvial fans and plains and deltas. The terms "braiding" and "anastomosing" have been used synonymously for braided river channels in this country, but elsewhere, particularly in Australia, "anastomosing" is a common term applied to multiple-channel systems on alluvial plains (Hills, 1960, p. 61; Whitehouse, 1944). The channels branch and rejoin, but each is a distinct channel bounded by the surface of the alluvial plain, and each channel is very stable in contrast to the channel of a braided river.

All previous work on meandering has demonstrated that meander wavelength is related to the discharge of water through the channel (Leopold and Wolman, 1957; Dury, 1965; Speight, 1965, 1967).

Dury (1965) found that meander wavelength (λ in feet) is related to mean annual flood (Qma in cfs) as follows:

$$\lambda = 30 \ Qma^{0.5} \qquad (4-14)$$

4-18

383

Carlston (1965) found the following relation between meander wavelength and mean annual discharge, Q_m :

$$\lambda = 106 \; Q_m^{0.46} \;\; . \tag{4-15}$$

However, for these relations there is a ten-fold variation of meander wavelength at a given discharge. When information on type of sediment load (M) is included, a vastly improved relation is obtained for both mean annual discharge and mean annual flood as follows:

$$\lambda = 1890 \; \frac{Q_m^{0.34}}{M^{0.74}}$$

$$r = 0.96 \;\; ; \;\; Se = 0.16 \text{ log unit } , \tag{4-16}$$

$$\lambda = 234 \; \frac{Q_{ma}^{0.48}}{M^{0.74}}$$

$$r = 0.93 \;\; ; \;\; Se = 0.19 \text{ log unit } . \tag{4-17}$$

Additional relations between channel width, discharge, and width of the meander belt have been reviewed by Leliavsky (1955, p. 133-135). For stable alluvial rivers of the Great Plains, the degree of meandering or the sinuosity $(P$, ratio of channel length to valley length) is related to M as follows:

$$P = 0.94 \; M^{0.25}$$

$$r = .91 \;\; ; \;\; Se = 0.06 \text{ log unit } . \tag{4-18}$$

Hence, streams transporting little bed-material load are relatively narrow, deep, and sinuous. One may assume that rivers that transport small quantities of sand are always sinuous and that the tendency to meander depends entirely on the type of sediment load moved through the channel. However, some rivers that appear to be transporting only very fine sediment are very straight (low sinuosity). A partial explanation may reside in the relation shown in Fig. 4-5. Here we see that low sinuosity streams have a gradient very near that of the valley slope and these streams have a low percentage of silt and clay in their channels. In some cases, valley gradient is almost three times as great as stream gradient.

If tectonic factors have not modified the slope of a valley the gradient of the alluvial surface should be at just that slope required for the movement of the water sediment mixture through the valley. The fact that the surface of the alluvium

4-19

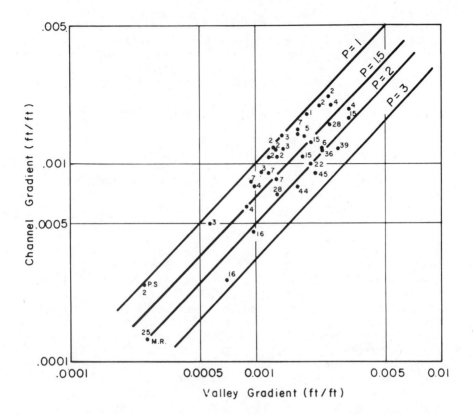

Fig. 4-5. Relation between alluvial valley slope and channel
gradient. Numbers beside points indicate percentage
of silt-clay in channels (M). Four lines of equal
sinuosity (P) are shown (from Schumm, 1968).

is too steep in most cases requires an explanation which depends
on an understanding of the changes in stream regimen during the
past 20,000 years. Most of the rivers from which the data
shown on Fig. 4-5 were obtained are located on the Great Plains
of western United States. All of these rivers flow on the upper
surface of alluvium which fills valleys cut into bedrock. The
deep valleys and the alluvium are the result of changes in base
level, climate, and hydrologic conditions during and following
the Pleistocene epoch. The alluvium filling these valleys
decreases in size from gravel and coarse sand at the base of the
deposit to either fine sand or silt, clay, and fine sand at the
present valley surface. Great variability of sediment type
occurs in these alluvial deposits, but all available information
shows a decrease in size of the alluvium toward the surface of
the fill.

Depending on the type of rocks exposed within a drainage
basin, the load of a river might change from gravel and sand to

4-20

385

sand alone or from silt, clay, sand, and gravel to predominantly silt and clay during deposition in the valley (see Fig. 5-4D). For example, in a stream draining areas underlain by sandstone, the size of the load decreased, but the proportion of bed-material load to total load probably changed little. A stream draining areas of sandstone and shale underwent not only a decrease in the size of sediment load but also a reduction in the ratio of bed-material load to total load. As a result, the stream draining areas of mixed sediments, after deposition of the coarser fraction of the sediment load, was flowing on alluvium with a gradient in excess of that required for transport of the predominantly wash load. A reduction of gradient by degradation could be only partly effective, for with incision the stream encountered the coarser sediments transported during a previous regime, and the development of an armor of coarse sediment would prevent further degradation. The formation of a sinuous course appears to have been the only alternative. Rivers draining areas of relatively coarse or sandy sediments were less affected by the change in size of sediment load and continued to flow on a gradient which is today essentially that of the valley itself, because they have been transporting relatively large amounts of bed-material load throughout their history. An increase in sinuosity and the accompanying decrease in stream gradient reflect the need to dissipate the energy, in excess of that expended in friction and sediment transport, that became available as the proportions of bed-material load and wash or suspended load changed. Thus, in Fig. 4-5 the rivers with sandy channels (low M) plot high (low sinuosity), and the rivers with high silt-clay channels plot low.

Apparent exceptions to this conclusion occur. For example, streams draining the mountain meadows of South Park, Colorado, are meandering, yet their beds are composed of cobbles. A possible explanation is that the coarse sediment acts as an armor over which the stream meanders. Under the present regimen these coarse sediments are not moved; therefore, the predominant sediment load is transported in suspension. In addition, it appears probable that, although a stream is transporting fine sediments, the valley gradient may be so gentle as to inhibit meandering. Examples of this may be the Mississippi River below New Orleans (Fisk, 1947) and the Illinois River (Rubey, 1952). Both rivers flow on surfaces which slope very gently downstream, and both rivers are essentially straight although they transport fine sediments.

It appears then, as suggested in Table 4-1, that valley gradient may be an independent variable influencing the present pattern of an alluvial river. This is an appealing explanation for the development of a sinuous river course. It is not an original one, but it can be supported by field evidence. For example, the points labeled M.R. and P.S. on Fig. 4-5 represent two channels on the Riverine Plain of New South Wales, Australia. One is a paleochannel (P.S.) that was functioning at least 10,000 years ago. It contains, and therefore must have

4-21

386

transported, large quantities of sand (low M) across an alluvial plain at the slope of the plain (sinuosity about 1.0).
Since the time that this channel was functioning, the climate
has changed, the vegetational cover in the headwaters has improved, and the quantity of sand to be moved has decreased
markedly. The modern river, Murrumbidgee River (M.R.), which
drains the same sediment source area now meanders across the
alluvial plain with a sinuosity of about 2 (Fig. 5-5). In
order to reduce its gradient, the paleochannel could have
either incised into the plain or developed a sinuous course.
Incision would require the movement of tremendous quantities of
sediment, and in order to reduce the gradient by half, incision
in the headwaters would need to be very great. A much simpler
means of reducing gradient was to develop a sinuous course, and
it was in this way that gradient reduction was accomplished and
the pattern of the Murrumbidgee River established.

4.5 RIVER CHANNEL CLASSIFICATION

In order to focus attention on the most important factors
that determine river morphology and to summarize the previous
material, a classification of alluvial river channels will be
presented.

All rivers may be separated into two major groups depending
on their freedom to adjust their shape and gradient. Bedrock-
controlled channels are those so confined between outcrops of
rock that the material forming their bed and banks determines
the morphology of the channel. Alluvial channels are free to
adjust their dimensions, shape, pattern, and gradient in response to hydraulic changes, and they flow through a channel
with bed and banks composed of the material transported by the
river under present flow conditions.

Rivers have been classified according to their stage of
development in the erosion cycle as youthful, mature, and old
(Davis, 1899), and also, according to their pattern of development on a land surface, as antecedent, superposed, consequent,
and subsequent (Thornbury, 1969, p.113). However, none of the
previous classifications consider the two independent variables,
discharge and type of sediment load, upon which the morphology
of alluvial channels depends.

A classification may be applicable only to segments of a
river system, for the characteristics of a stream channel can
change significantly within a short distance if it becomes unstable or receives sediment of a different type from a tributary. Therefore, this is a classification of channels rather
than river systems.

Discharge is an independent variable that largely determines the size of stream channels and the amplitude and wave
length of meanders. Discharge, however, is not a valid basis
for a classification of stream channels unless size is considered most important, although a qualitative distinction among
stream channels can be made on the basis of discharge

4-22

387

characteristics (i.e., ephemeral and perennial streams). The other independent variable is sediment load. We frequently refer to channels as muddy, sandy, or as a cobble or boulder channel. This implies that size of material in and transported through the channel may be a prime consideration. It is true that as one moves downstream along a river many river characteristics appear to change as grain size changes (Nevins, 1965), but there can be great changes in the morphology of a stream when the median grain size of bed material is essentially constant. For this reason, a tentative classification is based on the nature of the sediment load or the predominant mode of sediment transport. Type of load and mode of transport is simplified here to mean the transportation of sediment as either suspended load or bedload.

The term bedload as used is synonomous with the term bed-material load, which is defined as that part of the sediment load of a stream which consists of particle sizes represented significantly in the bed of the stream. The emphasis on significant representation excludes the small percentage of silt and clay usually found in most bed material (Einstein, 1950, pp. 6, 7).

The term suspended load as used is synonomous with wash load, that part of the sediment load not significantly represented in the bed of the stream (Einstein, 1950, p. 7). As discharge increases in a stream channel, the amount of bed material transported by suspension increases. Nevertheless, bed-material load differs from wash load because at low flows bed-material load is stationary or moves on the bed; wash load is always in suspension as it is washed through the channel. In the channels of the Great Plains rivers bed-material load is usually composed of sand, whereas wash load is composed of silt and clay.

Although a single grain size, which would form the boundary between suspended load and bedload, cannot be selected from available sediment transport data, it is suggested that, in general, silt and clay are transported in suspension and that sand and coarser sediment are transported on or near the streambed.

A further major division of alluvial channels can be made on the basis of stream stability or lack of it. These differences can be thought of with respect to the total sediment load delivered to the channel. An excess of total load causes deposition, a deficiency causes erosion, and between the extremes lies the stable channel. Although a given river channel often cannot be clearly identified in the field as stable, eroding, or depositing, it is possible to think of all rivers as falling into one of these three classes.

The stable channel is one that shows no progressive change in gradient, dimensions, or shape. Temporary changes occur during floods, but the stable channel, if the classification was not restricted to short segments of the river, would be identical to the graded stream as defined by Mackin (1948) in

4-23

388

which "over a period of years, slope is delicately adjusted to provide, with available discharge and with prevailing channel characteristics, just the velocity required for the transportation of the load supplied from the drainage basin."

The eroding channel is one that is being progressively degraded and/or widened by bank erosion. Conversely, the depositing channel is one that is being aggraded and/or having sediment deposited on its banks. Classification of river channels on the basis of stability as eroding, stable, or depositing emphasizes the diversity among rivers and stream channels; each of the three classes can be considered as distinct from the others.

The classification of alluvial channels is summarized in Table 4-2. Nine subclasses of channels are shown, based on channel stability and the predominant mode of sediment transport. Although variations in the proportions of bed and suspended load are transitional, it is possible to think in terms of a suspended-load channel transporting perhaps 0 to 3 percent bedload, a bedload channel transporting greater than 11 percent bedload, and a mixed-load channel transporting from 3 to 11 percent bedload. The boundaries between these groups are based on the relation between M and percentage of bedload and on the known characteristics of streams having varying amounts of silt and clay in their channels. The range of channel shape and sinuosity are established for each subclass, but gradient is expressed qualitatively, for gradient depends to a large extent on discharge which can vary greatly for a given value of M. Although sinuosity, as has been shown, depends on valley slope, ranges of sinuosity can be established for each type of stream.

The manner by which channels are modified by erosion and deposition has been fairly well established for ephemeral streams in the West (Schumm, 1960) and for perennial streams elsewhere. Information for six classes of unstable channels is given in Table 4-2.

In summary, alluvial-stream channels have been classified on the basis of one of the two independent variables influencing stream morphology. Discharge is not used as a basis for the classification because it controls mainly the size of the channels. The dimensionless properties of the channels depend mainly on the type of sediment load moved into the channel. The type of material transported or the mode of its transport as bedload or suspended load appears to be a major factor determining the character of a stream channel, and the classification of channels is based on this relation. Absolute size of the sediment load may be less important than the manner in which it moves through the channel. Channel stability depends on the balance or lack of balance between sediment load and transportability, and three classes of channels result: stable, eroding, and depositing.

This classification of stream channels is tentative, but will afford a basis for discussion until more data become available on total sediment load and the influence of sediment size on channel shape and pattern.

4-24

389

Table 4-2. Classification of Alluvial Channels

Mode of Sediment Transport and Type of Channel	Channel Sediment (M) Percent	Bedload (Percentage of Total Load)	Channel Stability		
			Stable (Graded Stream)	Depositing (Excess Load)	Eroding (Deficiency of Load)
Suspended Load	20	3	Stable suspended-load channel. Width-depth ratio less than 10; sinuosity usually greater than 2.0; gradient relatively gentle.	Depositing suspended load channel. Major deposition on banks cause narrowing of channel; initial streambed deposition minor.	Eroding suspended-load channel. Streambed erosion predominant; initial channel widening minor.
Mixed Load	5-20	3-11	Stable mixed-load channel. Width-depth ratio greater than 10 less than 40; sinuosity usually less than 2.0 greater than 1.3; gradient moderate.	Depositing mixed-load channel. Initial major deposition on banks followed by streambed deposition.	Eroding mixed-load channel. Initial streambed erosion followed by channel widening.
Bedload	5	11	Stable bedload channel. Width-depth ratio greater than 40; sinuosity, usually less than 1.3; gradient relatively steep.	Depositing bedload channel. Streambed deposition and island formation.	Eroding bedload channel. Little streambed erosion; channel widening predominant.

4.6 NOTATION

A   drainage area in square miles
b   channel bankfull width in feet
d   channel bankfull depth in feet
d_{50} median grain size in mm

F   width-depth ratio
L   length of channel in miles
λ meander wavelength in feet
M   percentage of silt and clay in channel perimeter
P   sinuosity, ratio of channel length to valley length or of valley slope to channel slope
Q   water discharge in cfs (Lane's equation)
Q_m mean annual discharge in cfs
Q_{ma} mean annual flood in cfs
Q_s bed-material load (Lane's equation)

Q_b bed-material load as percentage of total sediment load

r   correlation coefficient
S   channel gradient in ft/mile
S_e standard error

REFERENCES

Ackers, P., 1964, Experiments on small streams in alluvium: Jour. Hyd. Div., Am. Soc. Civil Eng. Proc. HY4, pp. 1-37.

Adams, R.M., 1965, Land behind Baghdad: Chicago, Univ. of Chicago Press, 187 p.

Beckinsale, R.P., 1969, River regimes: in Water, Earth and Man, R.J. Chorley, editor: London, Methuen and Co., pp. 455-472.

Brock, B.B. and Pretorius, D.A., 1964, Rand basin sedimentation and tectonics: in Some Ore Deposits of Southern Africa, S.H. Haughton, editor: Geol. Soc. South Africa, v. 1, pp. 25-62.

Brush, L.M. Jr., 1961, Drainage basins, channels, and flow characteristics of selected streams in central Pennsylvania: U.S. Geol. Survey Prof. Paper 282-F.

Carlston, C.W., 1965, The relation of free meander geometry to stream discharge and its geomorphic implication: American Jour. Sci., v. 263, pp. 864-885.

Coleman, J.M., 1969, Brahmaputra River: Channel processes and sedimentation: Sedimentary Geology, v. 3, pp. 129-239.

Craig, L.C., and others, 1955, Stratigraphy of the Morrison and related formations, Colorado Plateau region: U.S. Geol. Survey Bull., 1009-E, pp. 125-166.

Davis, W.M., 1899, The geographical cycle: Geographical Jour., v. 14, pp. 481-504.

Davis, W.M., 1954, Geographical Essays, D.W. Johnson, editor: New York, Dover Publication, 777 p.

Dury, G.H., 1965, Theoretical implications of underfit streams: U.S. Geol. Survey Prof. Paper 452-C, 43 p.

Einstein, H.A., 1950, The bed-load function for sediment transportation in open channel flows: U.S. Dept. Agriculture Tech. Bull. 1026, 71 p.

Embleton, C. and King, C.A.M., 1968, Glacial and periglacial geomorphology: London, Edward Arnold, 608 p.

Farrand, W.R., 1962, Postglacial uplift in North America: American Jour. Sci., v. 260, pp. 181-199.

Fairbridge, R.W. (editor), The Encyclopedia of Geomorphology: New York, Reinhold Book Co., 1295 p.

Fisk, H.N., 1947, Fine-grained alluvial deposits and their effects on Mississippi River activity: Mississippi River Comm. Waterways Experiment Station, Vicksburg, 82 p.

Gilbert, G.K., 1917, Hydraulic mining debris in the Sierra Nevada: U.S. Geol. Survey Prof. Paper 86, 363 p.

4-27

Gilbert, G.K., 1914, The transportation of debris by running water: U.S. Geol. Survey Prof. Paper 86, 363 p.

Hack, J.T., 1957, Studies of longitudinal stream profiles in Virginia and Maryland: U.S. Geol. Survey Prof. Paper 294-B, pp. 45-97.

Haughton, S.H., 1969, Geological History of Southern Africa: Geol. Soc. South Africa, Cape Town. 535 p.

Hills, E.S., 1960, The physiography of Victoria; Melbourne, Whitcombe and Tombs, 292 p.

Holmes, A., 1965, Principles of Physical Geology: London, T. Nelson and Sons, 1288 p.

Howard, A.D., 1967, Drainage analysis in geologic interpretation: A summation: American Assoc. Petroleum Geol. Bull., v. 51, pp. 2246-2259.

Hunt, C.B., 1969, Geological history of the Colorado River: U.S. Geol. Survey Prof. Paper 669, pp. 59-130.

Kennedy, J.F. and Brooks, N.H., 1965, Laboratory study of an alluvial stream at constant discharge: U.S. Dept Agriculture Misc. Pub. 970, pp. 320-330.

Lane, E.W., 1955, The importance of fluvial morphology in hydraulic engineering: Am. Soc. Civil Engineers Proc., v. 81, no. 745, 17 p.

_____1957, A study of the shape of channels formed by natural streams flowing in erodible material: U.S. Army Corps of Engineers, Missouri River Div., Omaha, Neb., Sediment Ser. 9, 106 p.

Leliavsky, S., 1955, An introduction to fluvial hydraulics: London, Constable & Co., 257 p.

Leopold, L.B. and Maddock, T. Jr., 1953, The hydraulic geometry of stream channels and some physiographic implications: U.S. Geol. Survey Prof. Paper 252, 57 p.

Leopold, L.B. and Wolman, M.G., 1957, River channel patterns: Braided, meandering and straight: U.S. Geol. Survey Prof. Paper 282-B, 85 p.

Leopold, L.B., Wolman, M.G., and Miller, J.P., 1964, Fluvial Processes in Geomorphology: San Francisco, W.H. Freeman and Co., 522 p.

Mackin, J.H., 1948, Concept of the graded river: Geol. Soc. America Bull., v. 59, pp. 463-512.

Malde, H.E., 1968, The catastrophic late Pleistocene Bonneville Flood in the Snake River Plain, Idaho: U.S. Geol. Survery Prof. Paper 596, 52 p.

Martin, R., 1966, Paleogeomorphology and its application to exploration for oil and gas (with examples from western Canada): American Assoc. Petroleum Geol. Bull., v. 50, pp. 2277-2311.

Milliman, J.D. and Emery, K.O., 1968, Sea levels during the past 35,000 years: Science, v. 162, pp. 1121-1123.

Morisawa, M. 1968, Streams, their dynamics and morphology: New York, McGraw-Hill, Inc., 175 p.

Nevins, T.H.F., 1965, River classification with particular reference to New Zealand: Fourth New Zealand Geography Conf., Proc., v. 4, pp. 83-90.

Parde, M. 1964, Fleuves et rivieres: Paris, Librairie Armand Colin, 223 p.

Rubey, W.W., 1952, Geology and mineral resources of the Hardin and Brussels quadrangles (Illinois): U.S. Geol. Survey Prof. Paper 218, 179 p.

Schumm, S.A., 1960, The shape of alluvial channels in relation to sediment type: U.S. Geol. Survey Prof. Paper 352-B, pp. 17-30.

_____1963, The disparity between present rates of denudation and orogeny: U.S. Geol. Survey Prof. Paper 454-H, 13 p.

_____1965, Quaternary paleohydrology: in Quaternary of the United States (eds. Wright, H.E., Jr., and Frey, D.G.): Princeton Univ. Press, pp. 783-794.

Schumm, S.A., 1968, River adjustment to altered hydrologic regimen - Murrumbidgee River and paleochannels, Australia: U.S. Geol. Survey Prof. Paper 598, 65 p.

Schumm, S.A. and Lichty, R.W., 1965, Time, space and causality in geomorphology: American Jour. Sci., v. 263, pp. 110-119.

Shulits, S., 1941, Rational equation of river-bed profile: Am. Geophys. Union Trans., v. 22, pp. 622-631.

Simons, D.B. and Albertson, M.L., 1960, Uniform water conveyance channels in alluvial materials: Jour. Hyd. Div., Am. Soc. Civil Eng. Proc. HY5, pp. 33-71.

Speight, J.G., 1967, Spectral analysis of meanders of some Australian Rivers: in Landform Studies from Australia and New Guinea: Australian Nat'l Univ. Press, pp. 48-63.

_____1965, Meander spectra of the Anabunga River: Jour. Hydrology, v. 3, pp. 1-15.

Stoddart, D.R., 1969, Climatic geomorphology: Review and Assessment: Progress in Geography, London, Edward Arnold, v. 1, pp. 160-222.

4-29

Thornbury, W.D., 1969, Principles of Geomorphology: New York,
    Wiley & Sons, 594 p.

Von Bertalanffy, L., 1952, Problems of life: London, Watts
    and Co., 216 p.

Whitehouse, F.W., 1947, The natural drainage of some very flat
    monsoonal lands: Australian Geographer, v. 4, pp.183-196.

Wilhelmy, H., 1969, Das Urstromtal am Ostrand der Indusbene
    und das Sarasvati-Problem: Seit. Geomorphologie, Supple-
    mentband 8, pp. 76-93.

Chapter 5

FLUVIAL GEOMORPHOLOGY:
CHANNEL ADJUSTMENT AND RIVER METAMORPHOSIS

By

S. A. Schumm, Professor of Geology,
            Colorado State University, Fort Collins, Colorado

Chapter 5

FLUVIAL GEOMORPHOLOGY:

CHANNEL ADJUSTMENT AND RIVER METAMORPHOSIS

5.1 INTRODUCTION

The engineer is well aware of the type of channel response
that results from his efforts to control river behavior, and
engineering literature is replete with descriptions of local
but rapid channel-response to man's influence. The geologist,
on the other hand, recognizes in alluvial deposits and river
terraces evidence of long-term adjustment of entire river
systems to the effects of climate change, mountain building
processes, and sea level fluctuations.

According to the empirical relations and the classification
of rivers presented in Chapter 4, it appears likely that with
time a channel may undergo a complete change of morphology
(river metamorphosis) if changes in discharge and sediment load
are of sufficient magnitude. That is, a suspended-load channel
could be converted to a mixed-load or bedload channel. The
equations demonstrate that for most changes of hydrologic regimen, which involve both a change in discharge and type of sediment load, many aspects of channel morphology will adjust. In
addition, the reaction of a channel to altered discharge and
type of load may result in changes of channel dimensions contrary to those indicated by the standard regime equations.
That is, it is conceivable that under certain circumstances
with a decrease of discharge, depth will decrease and width
will increase.

Equations 4-4, 4-6, 4-7, 4-13, 4-16, 4-17, and 4-18 provide a basis for the discussion of natural and man-induced
changes of river morphology, and an attempt will be made to
discuss river metamorphosis within the framework of these equations. First, however, it should be re-emphasized that they
result from an analysis of stable alluvial rivers that transport only small quantities of gravel and that are, for the most
part, located in subhumid and semiarid regions. Even if the
equations are shown to have a wider application, the parameters
will be expected to change as more data from a wider range of
geologic and hydrologic conditions are accumulated. Therefore,
the following treatment will stress directions of change rather
than magnitudes.

Equations 4-6, 4-7, 4-16, and 4-17 indicate that channel
width (b) , depth (d) , and meander wavelength (λ) are
directly related to discharge (Q) whereas Eq. 4-13 demonstrates
that gradient (S) is inversely related to discharge. From
these equations the following generalized relation is obtained:

$$Q \simeq \frac{b, d, \lambda}{S} \qquad\qquad (5-1)$$

Either mean annual discharge (Qm) or mean annual flood (Qma) can be substituted in this and subsequent equations. Considerable independent information is available to demonstrate that the relations expressed by Eq. 5-1 are valid.

Equations 4-6, 4-13, 4-16, and 4-17 demonstrate that channel width, meander wavelength, and gradient are inversely related to the type of sediment load (M) , whereas Eqs. 4-7 and 4-18 indicate a direct relationship between channel depth, sinuosity (P) , and type of sediment load (M) . The percentage of silt-clay in the perimeter of a channel reflects the nature of the sediment load moving through that channel, expressed as the percentage of total load that is bed-material load (Q_b) , but for one channel or for channels of similar average discharge, M probably will vary inversely with the quantity of bed-material load that moves through the channel. Therefore $1/Q_s$ can be substituted for M in these equations if discharge is constant. From these equations the following generalized relation is developed:

$$Q_s \simeq \frac{b, \lambda, S}{d, P} \qquad (5\text{-}2)$$

Width-depth ratio, F , is not included in Eq. 5-2 although it is highly dependent on M , because both width and depth appear separately in the equation. Nevertheless, the relation between width-depth ratio and M (Eq. 4-4) will prove useful for interpreting changes of channel width and depth in subsequent relations.

To discuss in more detail the effects of changing discharge and sediment load on channel morphology, a plus or minus exponent will be used to indicate how, with an increase or decrease of discharge or bed-material load, the various aspects of channel morphology will change. For the relatively straightforward cases of an increase or decrease in discharge or bed-material load alone, Eqs. 5-3 through 5-6 are obtained.

$$Q^+ \simeq b^+, d^+, \lambda^+, S^- , \qquad (5\text{-}3)$$

$$Q^- \simeq b^-, d^-, \lambda^-, S^+ , \qquad (5\text{-}4)$$

$$Q_s{}^+ \simeq b^+, d^-, \lambda^+, S^+, P^- , \qquad (5\text{-}5)$$

$$Q_s{}^- \simeq b^-, d^+, \lambda^-, S^-, P^+ . \qquad (5\text{-}6)$$

An increase or decrease in discharge alone could be caused by diversion of water into or out of a river system. An increase of Q_s will result from increased erosion in the catchment area, which can be induced by deforestation or by an increase in the area under cultivation. A decrease of Q_s will result from improved land use or a program of soil conservation.

An increase or decrease in discharge changes the dimensions of the channel and its gradient, but an increase or decrease in bed-material load at constant mean annual discharge changes not

5-2

397

only channel dimensions but also the shape of the channel (width-depth ratio) and its sinuosity.

In nature, however, rarely will a change in discharge or sediment load occur alone. Generally, any change in discharge will be accompanied by a change in the type of sediment load and vice versa. Under these circumstances, we should no longer assume that M, which can have the same value for both very large and very small streams, is related to the reciprocal of Q_S, because discharge is changing. However, changes of average discharge (Q) in a river will always be considerably less than the order of magnitude differences of discharge between large and small rivers. Hence, it is probable that M can be an index of both type of sediment load (Q_b) and quantity of bed-material load (Q_S) in a river subject to moderate changes of average discharge.

Using the plus or minus exponents to indicate an increase or decrease in a variable, four combinations of changing discharge and sediment load can be considered. For example, if both discharge and bed-material load increase, perhaps as a result of diversion of water from a bedload channel into a suspended-load channel, Eq. 5-7 suggests the nature of the resulting channel changes.

$$Q^+ \, Q_S^{\,+} \simeq b^+, \, d^{\pm}, \, \lambda^+, \, S^{\pm}, \, P^-, \, F^+ \, . \qquad (5\text{-}7)$$

Equation 5-7 indicates that, with an increase of both discharge and bed-material load, width, meander wavelength, and width-depth ratio should increase and sinuosity decrease. The influences of increasing discharge and of bed-material load on channel depth and gradient are in opposite directions, and it is not clear in what manner gradient and depth should change. However, by including width-depth ratio in Eq. 5-7, an estimate of the direction of change of depth can be obtained. Width-depth ratio is predominantly influenced by type of load (Eq. 4-4) and, therefore, it increases in Eq. 5-7. This suggests that depth will remain constant or decrease because both width and width-depth ratio increase. Channel gradient will probably increase because sinuosity decreases, thereby straightening the channel and increasing its slope.

When both Q_S and Q decrease, a result of dam construction, the reverse of Eq. 5-7 pertains, as follows:

$$Q^- \, Q_S^{\,-} \simeq b^-, \, d^{\pm}, \, \lambda^-, \, S^{\pm}, \, P^+, \, F^- \, . \qquad (5\text{-}8)$$

When, as common in nature, the changes in Q and Q_S are in opposite directions, the following relations are obtained:

$$Q^+ \, Q_S^{\,-} \simeq b^{\pm}, \, d^+, \, \lambda^{\pm}, \, S^-, \, P^+, \, F^- \, , \qquad (5\text{-}9)$$

$$Q^- \, Q_S^{\,+} \simeq b^{\pm}, \, d^-, \, \lambda^{\pm}, \, S^+, \, P^-, \, F^+ \, . \qquad (5\text{-}10)$$

The situation expressed in Eq. 5-9 could result from a combination of controls, for example, dam construction with impoundment of sediment and diversion of water into the channel from another source. The situation expressed by Eq. 5-10 could result from increased water and land use, thereby decreasing discharge but increasing bed-material load.

Equation 5-9 shows that with an increase in discharge but with a decrease in bed-material load the channel depth and sinuosity will increase while gradient and width-depth ratio decrease. With an increase in depth and a decrease in width-depth ratio, channel width will probably decrease. Meander wavelength will remain unchanged or will either increase or decrease, depending on the magnitude of the changes of discharge and load. However, as sinuosity increases, it seems likely that meander wavelength would decrease. The situation described by Eq. 5-10 is the opposite of that of Eq. 5-9.

The above relations demonstrate qualitatively how channel metamorphosis occurs with changes of discharge and sediment load. The magnitude of the changes of channel characteristics can be estimated through the use of the Eqs. 4-4, 4-6, 4-7, 4-8, 4-13, 4-16, 4-17, and 4-18 if the magnitudes of the changes of discharge and the percentage of bed-material load are known.

The significantly different channel dimensions, shapes, and patterns that are associated with different quantities of discharge and bed-material load indicate that, as these independent variables change, major adjustments of channel morphology can be anticipated. When changes of channel width and depth as well as of sinuosity and meander wavelength are required to compensate for a hydrologic change, then a long period of channel instability can be envisioned with considerable bank erosion and lateral shifting of the channel occurring before stability is restored.

5.2 EXAMPLES OF RIVER METAMORPHOSIS

It should be possible to substantiate the conclusions concerning the effect of changed discharge and sediment load on river channels, and some information, although incomplete in many cases, is available for major river changes both during historic time and during the recent geologic past.

Historic Examples of River Metamorphosis. First, a few examples of the conversion of what appear to be suspended-load or mixed load channels to bedload channels will be cited. These changes occurred on rivers that were not subject to significant regulation of flow, and the formerly meandering rivers were converted to straight channels by a combination of high peak discharges and an influx of coarser sediment. For example, the highly sinuous, relatively narrow and deep Cimarron River channel of southwestern Kansas was destroyed by the major flood of 1914. Between 1914 and 1939 the river widened from an average of 50 feet to 1200 feet, and the entire flood plain was destroyed. Large floods moved considerable sand and caused this

5-4

399

transformation despite the fact that annual discharge was probably less during the drought of the 1930's. The hydrologic record is short, but an abrupt increase in annual discharge after 1940 was recorded at the Wyanoka, Oklahoma gaging station.

Precipitation data indicate that the years 1916-41 were generally a period of below-average precipitation. Thus, during years of low runoff and high floodpeaks, the Cimarron River was converted from a narrow sinuous channel characterized by low sediment transport to a very wide, straight bedload river. These changes were apparently the result of climatic fluctuations, although agricultural activities within the basin may have increased the flood peaks and the sediment loads by destruction of the natural vegetation (Schumm and Lichty, 1963).

It appears that large floods override the effect of decreased mean annual discharge and that the change in Cimarron River morphology can be considered analogous to that caused by increased Q and Q_S (Eq. 5-7). An increase in bed-material load must have occurred as the channel was widened, and the gradient increased by straightening of the channel (decreased sinuosity), but there are no data to support this suggestion.

A startling example of change along one of the major American rivers is reported by Towl (1935). He states that the length of the Missouri River from the mouth of the Big Sioux River (near Sioux City, Iowa) to the mouth of the Platte River was about 250 miles in 1804 at the time of the Lewis and Clark Expedition. In 1935 the distance between these two tributaries was about 150 miles, which is 40 percent shorter (Fig. 5-1). Towl attributes this change to the cutting of timber on the floodplain and the great flood of 1881. Apparently this and subsequent floods straightened and widened the river. This transition was accompanied by a 40 percent increase of gradient, but over this shortened course the decrease in altitude remained constant. According to more recent information (R. H. Livesey, Corps of Engineers, Omaha District, written communication, 1970), the river distance between Sioux City and the mouth of the Platte River was about 167 miles in 1890, 146 miles in 1941, and 135 miles in 1960. This represents a 32-mile shortening of the river between 1890 and 1960. However, much of the channel shortening since about 1930 is man induced.

Smith (1940) indicated that channel changes of several rivers in western Kansas were Cimarron-type changes. The Smoky Hill River originally "had alternating sandy stretches and grassy stretches with series of pools. Later the former were widened, and the latter were sanded up***." Smith further stated that the Republican River was greatly affected by the flood of 1935. "Formerly a narrow stream with a practically perennial flow of clear water and with well-wooded banks, the Republican now has a broad, shallow sandy channel with intermittent flow. The trees were practically all washed out and destroyed, much valuable farmland*** was sanded over, and the channel has been filled up by several feet." Since then, however, regulation of flow at the Harlan County Dam has

5-5

400

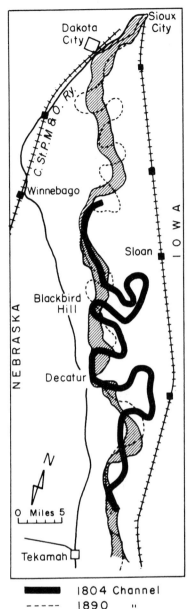

▬▬▬▬	1804 Channel
-----	1890 "
▨▨▨	1930 "

Fig. 5-1. Channel patterns of Missouri River in 1804, 1890, and 1930 between Sioux City, Iowa and Tekamah, Nebraska (from Towl, 1935).

reduced both the magnitude of peak discharge and mean annual discharge, as measured at Bloomington, Nebraska. This has caused a reduction in channel capacity between 1952 and 1957 owing to the growth of willows in the channel and the formation of islands and a new floodplain (Northrop, 1965).

The Republican River example indicates that a decrease in the magnitude of peak discharges and a decrease in the movement of bedload will result in channel narrowing. After the great widening of the Cimarron River between 1914 and 1942, a period of well-above-average rainfall ensued, and although annual runoff increased, no major floods moved through the channel between 1942 and 1951. According to measurements made on aerial photographs taken in 1939 and 1954, the average width of the river decreased from 1200 to 500 feet, so that, in effect, the width-depth ratio was reduced by half (Schumm and Lichty, 1963).

Equally great changes along some major rivers east of the Rocky Mountains can be documented. Especially impressive is the conversion of the broad North and South Platte Rivers and the Arkansas River to relatively insignificant streams owing to flood-control works and diversions for irrigation. The width of these rivers, as shown on topographic maps published during the latter part of the 19th century, can be compared with the width shown on new maps of the same areas. For example, the North Platte River near the Wyoming-Nebraska boundary has narrowed from about 1/2-3/4 mile wide to about 200 feet wide (Fig. 5-2). In eastern Nebraska just upstream from the junction of the

5-6

401

Fig. 5-2. Channel changes of North Platte River at Scotts
Bluff, Nebraska.
A. U. S. Geological Survey photograph taken by
N. H. Darton in 1895.
B. North Platte River in 1967.

5-7

Loup River at Columbus, the river has narrowed from 3/4 mile wide to 2000 feet wide (Schumm, 1968).

The South Platte River has always been cited as a classic example of a braided stream. About 55 miles above its junction with the North Platte River, the South Platte River was about a half mile wide in 1897, but it had narrowed to about 200 feet wide by 1959 (Fig. 5-3).

The tendency of both rivers is to form one narrow well-defined channel in place of the previously wide braided-channels. In addition, the new channel is generally somewhat more sinuous than the old.

The narrowing of the North Platte can be attributed to a decrease in the mean annual flood from 13,000 to 3,000 cfs and to a decrease in the mean annual discharge from 2300 to 560 cfs as a result of river regulation and the diversion of flow for irrigation. The major decrease in annual runoff occurred about 1930. A similar change occurred on the South Platte during the drought of the 1930's. However, the annual discharge of the South Platte increased after 1940, partly as a result of trans-mountain diversions, whereas, because of upstream regulation, the discharge of the North Platte did not. A decrease in the magnitude of the annual momentary maximum discharge occurred for both rivers, and this decrease was undoubtedly the major factor determining the present channel size. Data on changes of sediment load are lacking, but it is probable that much less sand is being transported through these channels at present.

Similar changes have occurred along the Arkansas River. In eastern Colorado and western and central Kansas, the Arkansas River was about 1000 feet wide in 1890, but in 1950 it was about 200 feet wide at the same locations. The width of the river has changed significantly, apparently in response to man-induced changes of hydrologic regimen. A long record of discharge of the Arkansas River at Holly, Colorado, just west of the Colorado-Kansas boundary, shows no significant change in annual discharge between 1910 and 1950, although flood peaks did decrease. It may be that the significant hydrologic changes were initiated even before the gage was established. In fact, Mead (1896) recognized that as early as 1880 the hydrologic regimen of the Arkansas River had changed significantly owing to man's activities in the basin.

The records of relatively recent channel changes on the Great Plains of the United States reveal that where man's activities have altered the hydrologic regimen, the wide sandy channels have changed, and, with time, they may assume the character of a mixed-load or suspended-load channel. It is doubtful that the adjustments will be complete, because the channel changes are not in response to a climate change, which would alter the hydrologic regimen of the entire drainage basin. The tributary streams below the point of main-channel regulation still introduce their burdens of water and sediment into the main channel, and until the water and sediment yields from the tributary basins are controlled, transformation of the main channels to a

5-8

403

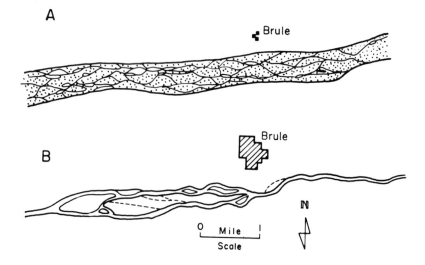

Fig. 5-3. South Platte River at Brule, Nebraska.
        A. Sketch of channel based on surveys made in 1897.
        B. Sketch of channel based on aerial photographs
            taken in 1959.

suspended-load type of channel cannot be complete. Nevertheless, the tendency toward this type of change has been demonstrated locally along these rivers.
    Significantly, these major changes of river character have
accurred without significant change in altitude of the channel.
Adjustments to altered runoff and sediment load were accomplished primarily by changes in channel shape and pattern. Of
course, where a major increase in the quantity and size of sediment load occurs, aggradation will occur and may be very significant. For example, destruction of natural forest vegetation on steep slopes in the humid regions of New Zealand and
replacement of this vegetation with exotic grasses has caused
erosion problems of major proportions. Stable, narrow, sinuous
rivers have changed to wide straight channels, as a result of
an influx of coarse sediment into the channels from the steep
slopes, and aggradation and an increase in flood peaks has occurred (Grant, 1950; Campbell, 1945). A somewhat similar problem arose in California when hydraulic mining debris was fed in
great quantities into the rivers draining from the gold fields
of the Sierra Nevada (Gilbert, 1917).
    Although data on changes of sediment load are not available
for the historic examples of channel metamorphosis, it may be
assumed that, as rivers are widened and steepened by destruction of their original channels, larger quantities of bed-
material load are moved through the channels by the recorded

5-9

404

high flood peaks. If this condition persisted the channels
would have remained wide and straight. However, with decreased
flood peaks, deposition of sediment in the wide channel and
the encroachment of vegetation into the channel caused narrowing
of the channel, and a tendency toward development of meanders
is evident.

Although sediment-load data for the rapidly changing channels of the past 70 years is not available, changes similar to
those described may also occur along one channel when tributaries introduce vastly different types of sediment load. The
differences in channel characteristics along the Smoky Hill-
Kansas River system, as described in Chapter 4, demonstrate
clearly that for stable alluvial channels water discharge and
type of sediment load determine channel morphology, as described
by the empirical equations.

Geologic Examples of River Metamorphosis. The historic examples of river metamorphosis, although interesting, do not provide a complete picture of river response to changes of hydrologic regimen. That is, the changes were in some cases local
and temporary. However, the changes of climate and sea level
during relatively recent geologic time produced examples of complete channel metamorphosis. Again, information concerning water and sediment discharge will be indirect, but for two examples (Mississippi and Murrumbidgee Rivers) river metamorphosis
can be documented in considerable detail.

One of the most intensively studied rivers of the world is
the Mississippi River. The pioneering work of Fisk and his
colleagues provides insight into the effect of climate and sea
level changes on river morphology. The two factors which determined the behavior of the Mississippi River between the maximum
extent of the Wisconsin or last glaciation and the present,
were the presence of the ice sheet itself, which supplied
tremendous quantities of melt water and sediment to the Mississippi Valley, and the lowering of sea level to a maximum depth
of about 130 meters about 15,000 years ago (Milliman and Emery,
1968). The fall of sea level lowered the base level of the
Mississippi River system, permitting removal of earlier alluvial
deposits and scour of the floor of the valley. The details of
the history are summarized from Fisk's (1947) report as follows:

During the time of maximum lowering of sea level the
Mississippi River was entrenched between 400 and 450 feet (Fig.
5-4A). In addition, the tributaries incised their channels to
produce an irregular valley floor with an average slope of 0.83
ft/mile. The slope increased in steepness seaward, suggesting
that the erosion of the channel to grade had not been complete.

When the continental ice sheet began to waste away, the
introduction of water and sediment into the Mississippi Valley
was greatly increased at the same time that sea level began to
rise rapidly between 14,000 and about 4000 years ago. Deposition in the valley accompanied the rise of sea level, and deposits grading upward from coarse sands and gravels through
clean sands were formed. The upward decrease in particle size

5-10

405

resulted from the progressive decrease in slope and the northward retreat of the margins of the ice, which supplied the
greater part of this material. In effect, a wave of alluviation
moved slowly upstream and into the tributary valleys so that
the entire drainage system was affected. However, the tributary
streams still transported coarse sediments, and huge alluvial
fans were built into the valley.

The lack of fine sediment (silts and clays) in this part
of the alluvium indicates that these fine sediments were transported to the sea. According to the evidence of these deposits,
the Mississippi River at this time was a braided stream shifting across the alluvial valley on a slope of about 0.75 foot
per mile (Fig. 5-4B).

With continued but slower rise of sea level and a decrease
in the size of the sediments moving from the north and from the
tributary valleys, the sediment load was eventually reduced to
fine sands, silts, and clays. However, the quantity of material
carried into the valley was sufficient to cause deposition of
fine sediment on the reduced valley slope. According to Fisk
(1947, p. 22) "The braided streams, during this stage, wandered
widely on the plain and built low alluvial ridges of sands and
silts ..." The basins which were created between alluvial
ridges received a filling of silts and clays contributed by
floodwaters (Fig. 5-4C). As valley alluviation continued, the
gradient of the valley was reduced to about 0.60 foot per mile
and "the size and amount of sediment contributed to the river
decreased." At this stage the river was flowing on a slope
only 0.15 foot per mile less than that when it was braided.
With essentially constant sea level and reduced sediment load,
the river began to meander. According to Fisk (1947, p. 23)
"The change from a braided stream to a meandering one brought
about the confinement of the Mississippi flows through a single
deep channel..." No longer did the river wander "freely in
shallow channels across the alluvial surface as did the braided
stream" (Fig. 5-4D).

This outline of Mississippi River history is similar to
that suggested for the rivers of the Great Plains to the extent
that they too transported larger quantities of coarser sediment
and apparently reduced their gradient by developing a sinuous
course (Schumm, 1963). The history of the Mississippi River
strongly supports the idea that meandering is largely the result of a river's attempt to reduce its gradient in response
to changed hydrologic regimen.

Nevertheless, one may question whether the Pleistocene
rivers were truly different from those of the present and if so,
were the changes in discharge and sediment load responsible for
the assumed metamorphosis? When rivers are confined to valleys,
any evidence related to the dimensions of the ancient channel is
destroyed by the channel adjustment. However, when the rivers
flow across an alluvial plain and the position of the river
shifts with time, the possibility of preservation of the paleochannel is improved. Fortunately, at least one example exists

5-11

406

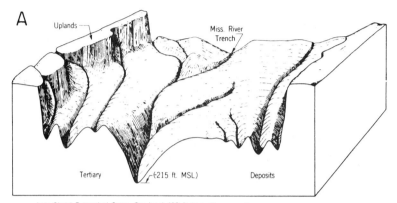

A

Uplands

Miss. River
Trench

Tertiary   (-215 ft. MSL)   Deposits

Late Glacial Entrenched Stage - Sea Level 400 ft. lower than present.
Valley slope 0.83 ft. per mile.
Master stream overloaded, braided, carrying gravels to Gulf of Mexico.

Fig. 5-4.   Block diagrams illustrating late Pleistocene and
            recent history of Mississippi River (from Fisk,
            1947).
            A. Late Pleistocene entrenched stage.
            B. Valley aggradation stage 1; tributaries building
                alluvial fans.
            C. Valley aggradation stage 2; tributaries building
                alluvial fans.
            D. Valley aggradation stage 3.

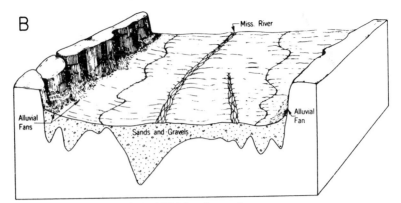

Valley Aggradation Stage 1 - Sea Level 100 ft. lower than present.
Valley slope approx. 0.75 ft. per mile.
Master stream overloaded, braided, carrying sands and fine gravels as far downstream as present Gulf
    shoreline.

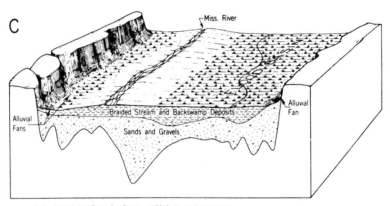

Valley Aggradation Stage 2 - Sea Level 20 ft. lower than present.
Valley slope 0.68 ft. per mile.
Final period of overloaded braided stream. Mississippi River carrying silts and sands. Thick deposits of
    backswamp silts and clays building up in marginal lowlands.

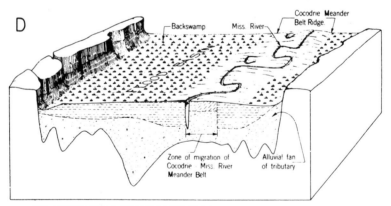

Valley Aggradation Stage 3 - Sea Level at present elevation.
Valley slope approx. 0.60 ft. per mile. Construction of Cocodrie Meander Belt.
Meandering deep-channel stream with great stage variation gradually replaced braided shallow-channel
    constantly flooding stream.

5-13

408

where the channels have not been destroyed by the change, and they can be studied in the field on the Riverine Plain of New South Wales, Australia (Schumm, 1968).

The sinuous Murrumbidgee River (Fig. 5-5) drains from the highlands of southeastern New South Wales toward the west. It crosses the Riverine Plain, an alluvial plain that slopes at about 1.5 feet per mile to join the Murray River at the New South Wales-Victoria border. The channel is about 200 feet wide, and it is confined to an irregular flood-plain on which are preserved large oxbow lakes which are evidence of a past time of high discharge (paleochannel 1, middle arrow, Fig. 5-5) The trace of an older low-sinuosity stream channel (paleochannel 2) crosses the lower quarter of the photograph (lower arrow, Fig. 5-5). In the upper half of its drainage basin the Murrumbidgee River is confined within a valley, and no evidence pertaining to its past condition exists because the old channels have been destroyed. On the alluvial plain, however, the position of the channel has shifted and three different types of channels are visible. The morphology of these channels reflects the hydrologic regimen of the time when each channel was functioning. In Table 5-1 the dimensions and other form characteristics of these three channels are presented with data on sediment characteristics and hydrology. Pedologic and geomorphic evidence from the Riverine Plain indicate that the oldest of the paleochannels was functioning during a climate drier than that of the present and that the youngest paleochannel was functioning during a climate more humid than that of the present.

The channel changes occurred not only because the water discharge increased or decreased, but also because climatic changes significantly altered the type of sediment load moved from the headwaters across the alluvial plain. At present, erosion is not a problem in the Murrumbidgee drainage basin. A good cover of vegetation protects the source area, and the river transports small quantities of sand, silt, and clay. An increase in precipitation will further improve the vegetation, and although runoff will increase, the sediment yield will decrease. On the other hand, a decrease in precipitation will decrease the amount of runoff, but will also greatly increase the yield of sediment from the drainage basin (Schumm, 1965, 1968). Calculations of the quantity of sand that could have been moved through the channels at bankfull discharge show that paleochannel 2 was competent to move large quantities of sand (Table 5-1). The abandoned channel of paleochannel 2 is filled with sand, whereas the abandoned channel of paleochannel 1 is filled largely with silts and clays. This suggests that, although paleochannel 1 could have transported relatively large quantities of sand, this type of sediment was available in large quantities only during the existence of paleochannel 2.

As fascinating as the paleochannels of the Riverine Plain may be, they are of concern here only as an illustration of the types of river changes that can occur naturally. If, for simplicity, it is considered that the paleochannels represent

5-14

409

Table 5-1. Morphology of Riverine Plains Channels

Location	Channel width, in feet	Channel depth, d, in feet	Width-depth ratio, F	Sinuosity, S	Gradient, S, in feet per mile	Meander wavelength λ, in feet	Median grain size in millimeters	Channel silt-clay, M, in percent	Bed-load, Q_s, in percent	Bankfull discharge, in cu. ft. per second	Sand discharge at bankfull in tons per day[b]
(1)	(2)	(3)	(4)	(5)	(6)	(7)	(8)	(9)	(10)	(11)	(12)
Murrumbidgee River (Upper arrow, Fig. 5-5)	220	21	10	2.0	0.7	2,800	0.57	25	2.2	11,000	2,000
Paleochannel 1. (middle arrow, Fig. 5-5)	460	35	13	1.7	0.8	7,000	--	16	3.4	51,000[a]	21,000
Paleochannel 2. (lower arrow, Fig. 5-5)	600	9	67	1.1	2.0	18,000	0.55	1.6	34	23,000[a]	54,000

[a]Calculated by use of Manning equation and channel area.

[b]Calculated by Colby's technique.

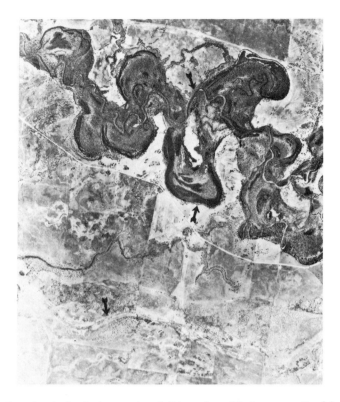

Fig. 5-5. Aerial photograph of Riverine Plain near Darlington
Point, New South Wales, Australia. Murrumbidgee
River (upper arrow) is 200 feet wide and follows
meandering course on flood plain that shows evidence
of large meander scours and oxbow lake of young
paleochannel 1 (middle arrow). On surface of alluvial plain trace of old paleochannel 2 (lower arrow) is
visible (Photograph courtesy of New South Wales Lands
Dept.).

changes from a channel which initially was like that of the
modern Murrumbidgee River (Fig. 5-5), we can discuss the channel
changes which will occur if the present climate of southeastern
Australia becomes wetter (paleochannel 1) or drier (Paleochannel
2). An increase in precipitation in the Murrumbidgee River
headwaters will result in increased annual discharge and increased mean annual flood, but only a small change in sediment
concentration and in the type of sediment load moved through
the channel. In response to this hydrologic change, which is
similar in effect to that described by Eq. 5-3, the shape of
the channel will not change, but it will become wider, deeper,
and meander wavelength and amplitude will increase. The initial response will undoubtedly be severe channel erosion until
the new dimensions are established. The result will be a relatively stable channel, but one larger than the modern river.

5-16

411

On the Riverine Plain it is significant that although deepening of the channel did occur, the increased discharge did not cause major incision. Gradient remained essentially constant.

On the other hand, a decrease in precipitation in the headwaters of the Murrumbidgee River will not only cause a decrease in annual discharge, but through reduction of vegetation density, it will increase peak discharges and greatly increase the amount of sand moved through the channels. The result will be a complete transformation of the river system. To transport the increased sand load with less water, the channel will become wider and shallower. The greater slope required to transport this load will not be developed by deposition and steepening of the Riverine Plain, which would require movement of immense quantities of sediment. Rather, the channel pattern will be changed. The gradient of the channel will be doubled without significant deposition by a reduction of the sinuosity from about 2 to about 1. These changes are in complete accord with Eq. 5-10.

As noted above, the events that occurred on the surface of the Riverine Plain were the reverse of the above sequence with the wide, straight, steep channel changing under the influence of altered hydrologic conditions to a relatively deep and sinuous channel (Fig. 4-5, points M. R. and P. S., Fig. 5-5). In fact, the documented changes are in accord with those suggested by Eq. 5-9.

The Riverine Plain paleochannels provide an example of adjustment of gradient by a major change of channel pattern. This supports the suggestion made earlier that, if unconfined, rivers may decrease their gradient by meandering rather than by major degradation. Therefore, modern bank erosion problems may be only the initial stage of river metamorphosis if a reduction of river gradient is required by man-induced changes of river regimen.

5.3 EFFECT OF GEOLOGIC HISTORY ON RIVER STABILITY

The metamorphosis of the Mississippi and Murrumbidgee River channels supports the assumption that paleohydrology and valley morphology do influence channel morphology, especially the pattern of modern rivers (Table 4-2). Rarely, however, does an entire river system pose an engineering problem. Rather the "unstable reaches" are of prime concern. These reaches may be naturally unstable or unstable as a result of manipulation of runoff or man's activity in the drainage basin. Nevertheless, based on what we now know about the adjustment of river systems to changed climate, etc., it should be possible to explain downstream variations in river pattern and behavior. For example, a river may be relatively straight except for locally sinuous reaches, or vice versa. The engineer is tempted to straighten the reaches of high sinuosity to develop a more "efficient" channel. If the variation in pattern reflects changes of valley slope to which the river has adjusted by developing a locally

5-17

412

more sinuous pattern in order to maintain a relatively constant
gradient, then realignment will cause channel instability.

It is surprisingly difficult to locate data on variations
in gradient, valley slope, and sinuosity that is presented in
sufficient detail to be meaningful. However, Brice's (1964)
study of the Loup River in Nebraska provides such information
for the Calamus River, a tributary to the North Loup River.
The longitudinal profile of Calamus River is relatively straight
and the gradient, with minor variations, is about 6 feet per
mile over the last 25 miles of its course (Brice, 1964, p. 33).
However, an abrupt steepening of the valley slope occurs about
12 miles above the junction with North Loup River. This increase in valley slope is probably the result of the movement
of large quantities of sediment from a large tributary (Gracie
Cr.) into the valley at this point during the higher discharges
of the Pleistocene. The fact that the modern river shows only
a slight increase in gradient over this steeper reach of the
valley indicates that the tributary at present is not transporting large quantities of sediment to Calamus River. The
sinuosity of Calamus River is 1.4 above the steeper reach of
the valley; it is 2.1 over two-thirds of the steeper reach, but
decreases to 1.3 on the part of this reach where the modern channel steepens slightly. Farther downstream the sinuosity decreases to 1.1. Just as the larger Mississippi and Murrumbidgee
Rivers adjusted to a steep slope by developing a sinuous course,
so this smaller river adjusted to a local steepening of its
valley by developing high sinuosity over about 2 miles of its
course.

Another example of past influences on valley slope is the
Jordan River between Lake Tiberias and the Dead Sea (Schattner,
1962). Over much of this course, tributary sediments are deposited along the flanks of the structural trough occupied by
the Jordan River and do not reach the river. Nevertheless, the
influence of these tributaries on the pattern of the modern
river can be noted. Where during the past, alluvial fan type
deposits have been built into the valley, changes of the modern
valley slope occur. The valley slope decreases as the Jordan
approaches a tributary junction and increases as the river
passes the junction and flows down the steeper down-valley part
of the alluvial deposit. The Jordan is a very sinuous river
over much of the southern part of its course, but as the Jordan
approaches a major tributary junction, sinuosity decreases.
In general, the river remains relatively straight for some distance beyond the junction and sinuosity then increases. The
variations in sinuosity are attributed to changes in valley
slope due to tributary influence.

A convincing example of these influences on channel pattern
is provided by the Mississippi River. It was concluded that
this river meanders because it is flowing on a valley slope
established when it was a straight braided river transporting
a large load of sand and gravel. However, the sinuosity of the
Mississippi River is variable, and the greatest sinuosity occurs   5-18

413

below the junction of the Arkansas and Red Rivers. Above the junction of the Arkansas River (Helena, Ark. to junction), sinuosity is about 1.7; below the junction to Lake Providence, La. the sinuosity is 2.5, and for that reach of the river between the junction and Greenville, Miss., sinuosity is 3.3. Sinuosity was measured following the state and county boundaries that were established before the river was straightened during the second and third decade of this century and before some natural cutoffs occurred during the latter part of the 19th century. Thus, sinuosity as measured is the essentially natural sinuosity of the river of the 19th century.

Between Natchez and Angola, La. near the junction of the Red River, sinuosity is about 2.1, but below the junction it is about 2.6. Below Donaldsonville, La. to the Head of Passes sinuosity reflecting the very flat valley slope is only 1.3.

Fisk (1947, plate 1) shows a steepening of the Mississippi valley slope at the junctions of the Arkansas and Red Rivers. The increased valley slope probably reflects a time of major sediment contribution from these tributaries during and at the close of the period of valley aggradation (Fig. 5-4C). Therefore, the most sinuous reaches of the modern Mississippi River were formed in response to the steeper valley slope established at the close of Pleistocene time. At present, as a result of artificial cutoffs between the Arkansas River and Greenville, sinuosity has been decreased to about 1.4. This means that the gradient of the river has been more than doubled through this reach, which is the steepest part of the valley.

Without knowing a great deal about the problems of this river one could speculate that the straightening of this section of the Mississippi has created severe problems of channel stability. In effect, the river will attempt to reduce its newly steepened gradient by the development of a sinuous course with a sinuosity approaching 3.0.

The artificial straightening of a meandering channel may do more than cause upstream scour as a result of steepening of river gradient. It may, in fact, begin a period of unstability as the river attempts to reduce its gradient by generating a sinuous course on the steeper portions of the valley floor. Perhaps it will be necessary to consider means of realigning the course of a sinuous river that will be a compromise between an efficient but unstable straight course and a less efficient but perhaps relatively stable course of intermediate sinuosity.

5.4 CONCLUSIONS

Emphasis has been placed on long-term response of rivers to natural changes. In many cases the magnitude of environmental manipulation by man approaches the natural changes of the past. As a result, significant response of river systems have occurred and more may be anticipated.

The examples cited show long-term metamorphosis of entire rivers; hence, the observed short-term adjustment of a channel

5-19

414

to changed sediment load and runoff may be only the initial response, which precedes a complete change of river morphology. For example, river regulation for irrigation generally reduces peak discharge and prolongs the flow, in effect transforming an ephemeral or intermittent channel to a perennial one of low discharge. The result is a reduction in the size of the channel. The accompanying reduction of bedload will cause a decrease in channel width-depth ratio and an increase in sinuosity. The eventual result should be a very stable channel. Therefore, many of the wide, sandy, "unstable" rivers of the world could be transformed to stable channels by reducing flood peaks and bedload transport. This can be done either by controlling the main stream or the tributaries. However, where major tributaries exert a significant influence on the main channel by introducing large quantities of coarse sediment, upstream control along the main channel may permit the tributary to dominate the system with deleterious results. For example, where high discharges are required to clear a channel of sediment contributed from tributaries, serious aggradation with accompanying flood problems may arise if periodic flushing of the sediment from the channel does not occur. The alternative is regulation of the bedload tributaries, those draining areas that are sources of sand and gravel. Selective tributary control seems mandatory if river metamorphosis is desired. Thus, a basin-wide evaluation of tributary sediment loads and discharge is required before the effects of main stream regulation can be determined.

As sediment loads from tributary streams are reduced by upstream control, the effect on relatively stable main streams may be similar to that which has already occurred naturally in the Mississippi valley and on the Riverine Plain. For example, the contribution of sediment from the Missouri River and other major tributaries to the Mississippi River probably has been significantly reduced by dam construction. Geologic evidence suggests that reduction of gradient and a change of channel dimensions and shape should occur under these circumstances. That is, if by upstream regulation the present gradient of the river becomes too steep, the river will adjust to reduced peak discharge and sediment load in the manner suggested by Eq. 5-8. The changes of meander wavelength and sinuosity should introduce a period of channel instability that will persist for a long time.

Great changes along the courses of rivers can be anticipated if the activities of man continue undiminished. In addition, these changes may occur over long distances downstream. Much depends on the climate and geology of each system, but a major change in hydrologic regimen should trigger a response that will completely transform channel morphology. Further, it is not safe to assume that adjustment of channel slope by degradation will be the only response of a river. The equations have shown that, in fact, all aspects of river morphology may respond depending on the magnitude of the change of discharge and sediment load.

5-20

415

5.5 NOTATION

b   channel bankfull width in feet
d   channel bankfull depth in feet
F   width-depth ratio
λ meander wavelength in feet
M   percentage of silt and clay in channel perimeter
P   sinuosity, ratio of channel length to valley length or of valley slope to channel slope
Q   water discharge in cfs (Lane's equation)
Q_m mean annual discharge in cfs
Q_{ma} mean annual flood discharge in cfs
Q_s bed-material load (Lane's equation)
Q_b bed-material load as percentage of total sediment load
S   channel gradient in ft/mile

REFERENCES

Brice, J. C., 1964, Channel patterns and terraces of the Loup Rivers in Nebraska: U. S. Geol. Survey Prof. Paper 422-D, 41 p.

Campbell, D. A., 1945, Soil conservation studies applied to farming in Hawke's Bay, Part 2: New Zealand Jour. Sci. Tech. (sec. A), v. 27, p. 147-172.

Fisk, H. N., 1947, Fine-grained alluvial deposits and their effects on Mississippi River activity: Mississippi River Comm. Waterways Experiment Station, Vicksburg, 82 p.

Grant, H. P., 1950, Soil conservation in New Zealand: New Zealand Inst. Eng., Proc., v. 36, p. 269-301.

Gilbert, G. K., 1917, Hydraulic mining debris in the Sierra Nevada: U. S. Geol. Survey Prof. Paper 105, 154 p.

Mead, J. R., 1896, A dying river: Kansas Acad. Sci., Trans., v. 14, p. 111-112.

Milliman, J. D. and Emery, K. O., 1968, Sea levels during the past 35,000 years: Science, v. 162, p. 1121-1123.

Northrup, W. L., 1965, Republican River channel deterioration: U. S. Dept. Agriculture Misc. Pub. 970, p. 409-424.

Schattner, I., 1962, The lower Jordan valley: Pub. Hebrew Univ., Jerusalem, v. 11, 123 p.

Schumm, S. A., 1963, Sinuosity of alluvial rivers on the Great Plains: Geol. Soc. America, Bull., v. 74, p. 1089-1100.

Schumm, S. A., 1965, Quaternary paleohydrology: in Quaternary of the United States (eds. Wright, H. E., Jr., and Frey, D. G.): Princeton Univ. Press, p. 783-794.

Schumm, S. A., 1968, River adjustment to altered hydrologic regimen - Murrumbidgee River and paleochannels, Australia: U. S. Geol. Survey Prof. Paper 598, 65 p.

Schumm, S. A., and Lichty, R. W., 1963, Channel widening and flood-plain construction along Cimarron River in southwestern Kansas: U. S. Geol. Survey Prof. Paper 352-D, p. 71-88.

Smith, H. T. U., 1940, Notes on historic changes in stream courses of western Kansas, with a plea for additional data: Kansas Acad. Sci., Trans., v. 43, p. 299-300.

Towl, R. N., 1935, The behavior history of the "Big Muddy": Eng. News-Record, v. 115, p. 262-264.

References

Ackers, Peter, 1964, Experiments on small streams in alluvium: *J. Hyd. Div. Am. Soc. Civil Eng.,* V. 90, pp. 1–37.

Birot, Pierre, 1961, Reflections sur le profile d'equilibrium des cours d'eau: *Zeit. Geomorph.,* V. 5, pp. 1–23, 89–105, 226–249.

Brush, L. M., Jr., 1961, Drainage basins, channels, and flow characteristics of selected streams in central Pennsylvania: U.S. Geol. Survey Prof. Paper 282-F, pp. 145–180.

Carlston, C. W., 1969, Downstream variations in the hydraulic geometry of streams: *Am. J. Sci.,* V. 267, pp. 499–509.

Chitale, S. V., 1970, River channel patterns: *J. Hydraulics Div., Am. Soc. Civil. Eng.,* V. 96, pp. 201–221.

Chorley, R. J., Dunn, A. J., and Beckinsale, R. P., 1964, *The history of the study of landforms:* Methuem and Co., London, 678 p.

Chow, Ven Te, 1959, *Open-channel hydraulics:* McGraw-Hill Book Co., New York, 680 p.

Colby, B. R., 1964, Scour and fill in sand-bed streams: U.S. Geol. Survey Prof. Paper 462-D, 32 p.

Daly, R. A., 1945, Biographical Memoir of William Morris Davis 1850–1934: *Nat. Acad. Sci. Biog. Mem.,* V. 23, p. 263–303.

Dana, J. D., 1850, On the degradation of the rocks of New South Wales and formation of valleys: *Am. J. Sci.,* (series 2), V. 9, pp. 289–294.

Davis, W. M., 1926, Biographical Memoir of Grove Karl Gilbert 1843–1918: *Nat. Acad. Sci. Biog. Mem.,* V. 21, 5th mem., 303 p.

Dury, 1964, The principles of underfit streams: U.S. Geol. Survey Prof. Paper 452-A, 67 p.

Dury, G. H., 1966, The concept of grade *in Essays in Geomorphology:* American Elsevier, New York, pp. 211–233.

De La Noe, G., and De Margerie, Emm., 1888. Les formes du terrain: Service Geographique de l'armee, Paris, 205 p.

Einstein, Albert, 1926, Ober die ursacher de Maanderbildung der Flusse and des Baer'schen Gestres: *Naturwiss.,* V. 14, pp. 223–225.

Fisk, H. N., 1947, Fine-grained alluvial deposits and their effects on Mississippi River activity. Mississippi River Commission Waterways Experiment Station, 82 p.

Gilbert, G. K., 1914, The transportation of debris by running water: U.S. Geol. Survey Prof. Paper 86, 263 p.

419

Gilman, D. C., 1899, *The life of James Dwight Dana:* Harper and Bros., New York, 409 p.

Gregory, H. E., 1938, The San Juan Country, A geographic and geologic reconnaissance of southeastern Utah: U.S. Geol. Survey Prof. Paper 188, 123 p.

Gregory, H. E., 1950, Geology and geography of the Zion Park Region, Utah and Arizona: U.S. Geol. Survey Prof. Paper 220, 200 p.

Gregory, H. E., 1951, The Geology and geography of the Paunsagunt Region Utah: U.S. Geol. Survey Prof. Paper 226, 116 p.

Horton, R. E., 1945, Erosional development of streams and their drainage basins; hydro physical approach to quantitative morphology: *Geol. Soc. Amer. Bull.,* V. 56, pp. 275–370.

Howard, A. D., 1967, Drainage analysis in geologic interpretation: A summation: *Amer. Assoc. Petrol. Geol., Bull.,* V. 51, pp. 2246–2259.

Inglis, C. C., 1949, The behavior and control of rivers and canals: Central Waterpower Irrigation and Navigation Res. St., Poona, *Res. Pub.* 13, 2 vols., 487 p.

Johnson, D. W., (Ed.) 1954, Geographical Essays: Dover Publications Inc., New York (Reprint of 1909 edition), 775 p.

Kennedy, R. G., 1895, The prevention of silting in irrigation canals: *Inst. Civil Engrs.,* V. 119, pp. 281–290.

Lacey, Gerald, 1929, Stable channels in alluvium: *Proc. Inst. Civil Engrs.,* V. 229, pp. 259–285.

Leliavsky, Serge, 1955, *An introduction to fluvial hydraulics:* Constable and Co., London, 257 p.

Leopold, L. B., and Miller, J. P., 1956, Ephemeral streams—Hydraulic factors and their relation to the drainage net: U.S. Geol. Survey Prof. Paper 282-A, p. 1–36.

Leopold, L. B., and Wolman, M. G., 1960, River meanders, *Bull. Geol. Soc. Amer.,* V. 71, pp. 769–794.

Leopold, L. B., Wolman, M. G., and Miller, J. P., 1964, *Fluvial processes in geomorphology:* Wilt Freeman and Co., San Francisco, 522 p.

Livesey, R. H., 1965, Channel armoring below Fort Randall Dam: U.S. Dept. Agriculture, Misc. Pub. 970, pp. 461–469.

Mackin, J. H., 1963, Rational and empirical methods of investigation in geology: In *The Fabric of Geology* (C. C. Albritton Jr., ed.), Addison-Wesley Pub. Co., Reading, Mass., pp. 135–174.

Merrill, G. P., 1906, Contributions to the history of American geology: *Ann. Rep. Smithsonian Inst. 1904,* pp. 189–733.

Miller, J. P., 1958, High mountain streams: Effects of geology on channel characteristics and bed material: State Bur. of Mines and Min. Res., New Mexico Inst. Mining and Tech., Memoir 4, 53 p.

Morisawa, Marie, 1968, *Streams their dynamics and morphology:* McGraw-Hill Book Co., New York, 169 p.

Moss, J. H., 1961, Seismic evidence supporting a new interpretation of the Cody Terrace near Cody, Wyoming, *Bull. Geol. Soc. Am.* V. 72, pp. 547–556.

Nixon, Marshall, 1959, A study of the bank-full discharges of rivers in England and Wales: *Proc. Inst. Civil Eng.,* V. 12, pp. 157–174.

Raudkivi, A. J., 1967, *Loose boundary hydraulics:* Pergamon Press, London, 331 p.

Rubey, W. W., 1933, Equilibrium conditions in debris-laden streams. *Trans. Am. Geophys. Un.,* 1933, pp. 497–505.

Rubey, W. W., 1952, Geology and mineral resources of the Hardin and Brussels quadrangles (Illinois), U.S. Geol. Survey Prof. Paper 218, 179 p.

Schaffernak, F., 1950, *Fluss morphologie und Flussbau:* Springer-Verlag, Vienna, 115 p.

Scheidegger, A. E., 1970, *Theoretical geomorphology:* Springer-Verlag, Berlin, 427 p.

Schumm, S. A. and Lichty, 1965, Time, space and causality in geomorphology: *Am. J. Sci.,* V. 263, pp. 110–119.

Shen, H. W., 1971, (Ed.), River mechanics: Water Resources Publications, Fort Collins, Colo., 1322 p.

Simons, D. B., and Richardson, E. V., 1963, Forms of bed roughness in alluvial channels: *Trans. Am. Soc. Civil Eng.,* V. 128, pp. 284–302.

Speight, J. G., 1967, Spectral analysis of meaders of some Australian rivers in *Landform Studies from Australia and New Guinea*: Australian Nat'l Univ. Press, Canberra, pp. 48–63.

Sundborg, Ake, 1967, The River Klaralven, A study of fluvial processes: *Geografiska Annaler*, V. 38, pp. 125–316.

Tricart, J., 1960, Mise au point: Les types de lits fluviaux: *L'Information Geographique*, N. 5, pp. 210–214.

Wolman, M. G, 1955, The natural channel of Brandywine Creek, Pennsylvania, U.S. Geol. Survey Prof. Paper 271, 56 p.

Woodford, A. O., 1951, Stream gradients and Monterey sea valley: *Bull. Geol. Soc. Am.,* V. 62, pp. 799–852.

Zernitz, E. R., 1932, Drainage patterns and their significance: *J. Geol.,* V. 40, pp. 498–521.

Author Index

Abbot, H. L., 177
Ackers, P., 392
Adams, R. M., 392
Aki, K., 218
Albertson, M. L., 394
All, K. A.-S., 334

Bagnold, R. A., 334
Bailey, R. W., 177
Bancroft, W. D., 177
Barton, D. C., 177
Bates, R. E., 177, 192, 281
Baulig, M. H., 177, 218
Beckinsale, R. P., 392
Bondurant, D. C., 307
Bottomley, W. T., 115
Brice, J. C., 417
Brock, B. B., 392
Brooks, N. H., 300, 334, 335, 393
Brown, C. B., 177, 218
Brush, L. M., Jr., 392
Bryan, K., 177
Buckland, W., 22
Buckley, A. B., 116
Buckley, R. B., 116

Campbell, D. A., 417
Carey, W. C., 334
Carlston, C. W., 392

Chatley, H., 281
Christensen, R. P., 334
Colby, B. C., 334
Colby, B. R., 127, 334
Coleman, J. M., 392
Conrad, T. A., 22
Conybeare, 23
Corbett, D. M., 127
Corey, N. T., 192
Cornelius, E., 23
Craig, L. C., 392

Dana, J. D., 22
Darandandana, N., 334
Darwin, C., 22
Davis, J. R., 127
Davis, W. M., 22, 177, 192, 219, 233, 392
Dittbrenner, E. F., 300
Dobby, E. H. G., 193
Dobson, G. C., 177
Dobson, P., 23
Dowd, M. J., 192
Dury, G. H., 392

Eakin, H. M., 177, 281, 346
Einstein, H. A., 392
Elata, C., 334
Eliassen, S., 192

423

424

Subject Index

429